The Path Forward

Likrawkra Publishing

KAWTHOOLEI

THE
PATH
FORWARD

TOWARD LIBERTY, VIRTUE, AND
PROGRESS OF THE NATION

SAW LAHKBAW

A Reflective Guide to Rebuilding Kawthoolei

Published by *Likrawkra Publishing*.

https://likrawkra.info

ISBN: 979-8-9986199-0-8 (Paperback – color content)
ISBN: 979-8-9986199-1-5 (Hardcover – black and white content)
ISBN: 979-8-9986199-2-2 (Hardcover – color content)
ISBN: 979-8-9986199-3-9 (eBook)
ISBN: 979-8-9986199-4-6 (Hardcover – color content, international distribution)

Cover Design: *SawLah@design*

This book is dedicated to the memory of

Saw Poe Kyar,

my late grandfather, who gifted my sibling a bicycle

—the wheels to education.

TABLE OF CONTENTS

INTRODUCTION

This book is a letter to my people—the sons and daughters of Kawthoolei.

It was born of quiet reflection and heartfelt conversations with those who carry both the burden and the dream of Kawthoolei. Writing it was a journey of perseverance, tested by interruptions both anticipated and unexpected—challenges that mirrored the broader struggles of our people. Like our community, the work pressed on. Though many forces tried to bring it to a grinding halt, it moved—steadily—forward.

All around, I see many, except those who content with the status quo, growing restless with the state of our political and social stagnation. Voices of unease rise—on the ground and in the air— lamenting our disoriented course, yet a clear path forward has not been charted—one that is visible, viable, and grounded in the will of the people and the survival of the nation.

In the stillness of sleepless nights—within a solitary refuge, far removed from the daily trials of survival—these thoughts gradually took shape, forming a message meant for my people. Not all the ideas within are the product of deliberate search, but of thoughts and visions that arrived unbidden, illuminating what Kawthoolei can become. I am grateful to share this book, shaped by that sense of purpose, on my own terms.

To be clear, this book is not a history of the Karen people, nor a study of traditional culture. Rather, it calls for the making of history, the refinement of culture, and the elevation of political thought. Nevertheless, throughout its pages, I allude to the history and way of life of our people as they connect to the themes discussed.

This book is written to inform, inspire, and invite those seeking answers about rebuilding Kawthoolei. Its purpose is not to persuade skeptics of Kawthoolei's cause or appease critics of the issues discussed. Also, readers expecting a specific political view to be endorsed may not find what they seek—some may discover something far greater than they anticipated.

This book does not exist to validate any political ideology. Its aim is to provide clarity and direction for those in pursuit of understanding and meaningful action. Covering a range of topics, it is like *Dar-Pwort-Hae*, a spicy veggie jumble mountain dish with bold flavors—those unprepared for its intensity may find it challenging to take in.

This book stands as a humble offering to the people of Kawthoolei. I have aimed to make it accessible for both those for whom English is a second language and those who speak it daily. Given our linguistic landscape, English is the most common denominator and the best choice for forward-looking content. It is a deliberate choice—one made for transparency and accessibility.

Some of the messages may come across as too direct, uncomfortable, or revealing, but certain issues require nothing less than direct sunlight—shining truth to expose and drive away the prolonged shadows of deceit and decay. For those interested in political philosophy, the chapters in the *Political Thoughts Concerning Kawthoolei* section explore the ideological challenges Kawthoolei faces.

This project is a collaboration between human creativity and machine intelligence. Modern tools assisted in streamlining the writing process—enhancing efficiency, refining grammar, and improving sentence flow. Yet, the ideas, content, literary style, voice, and tone are entirely my own and any shortcomings remain my sole responsibility.

This project grew from the goodwill and voluntary contributions of the community—those who gave their time to review draft chapters, driven by their belief in the importance of this work. Some needed gentle nudges, while most found joy in the process, discovering meaning as the raw edges of an early draft came to life. Yet, there were some who showed little interest in Kawthoolei—a reminder that this mission must be accomplished, for if Kawthoolei were already a prevailing wind, this book would not need to be written.

This project was undertaken without external funding. While I deeply appreciate the goodwill of those who offered their support, I chose not to seek financial assistance. The journey of writing and publishing this book has been monumental, yet I believed it best to take full responsibility— both creatively and financially. This choice allowed me to preserve the independence needed to shape these pages with sincerity and integrity.

This book was born from ideas that demanded a more expansive format than my usual online platforms could offer. Its chapters unfold in a deliberate progression—from Kawthoolei's ideals and political philosophy to the pursuit of a national identity rooted in dignity and progress, to the role of STEM education, cutting-edge technology, and the emerging economy, and finally, to the practical aspirations and actions needed to bring those visions to life. Each chapter builds upon the previous one and is intended to be read sequentially. However, each chapter is also self-contained, allowing readers to begin with any topic that resonates with them.

Together, these chapters explore the challenges we face and offer a blueprint for rebuilding a nation that leaves a lasting legacy—a better world for future generations—while acknowledging our fleeting time in this complex world.

PART I

THE KAWTHOOLEI VISION

Kawthoolei is divine.

Kawthoolei is ineffable.

She is beyond description

who can never be fully compared,

nor wholly comprehended.

SawLah@Photography 2022

Chapter 1

Kawthoolei Ideal

S ome say Kawthoolei means *the Land Without Darkness*. Others see a land of flowers, drawn from syllabus *lei*, a garland worn with grace. To some, it is a name to fear; to others, a home to hold dear. Many do not care. Yet beyond names and perceptions awaits something greater—a vision, a calling, an ideal waiting to be realized.

Preconceived notions have long distorted the understanding of Kawthoolei. While it may be convenient to dissect a name in search of meaning, Kawthoolei must be understood in its entirety—not as broken pieces. For, Kawthoolei must be complete—that is, recognized, understood, and thus rebuilt with a holistic vision.

More than a name or a territorial claim, Kawthoolei holds something the Karen people have long cherished—virtuous living as the essence of life. Its deeper meaning can be traced in the rhythm of the Karen people's way of life, in the historical events that shaped this name, and in the hopes and dreams carried forward through generations with timeless aspiration.

When broken down syllable by syllable—*Kaw, thoo,* and *lei*—the elements translate respectively to "country land," "blackness," and "clear of," meaning free from thorny vines and dense undergrowth in a tropical forest. While this literal breakdown may be alluring, it fails to capture broader insight.

There are many interpretations of Kawthoolei. Some, drawn by its phonetics, liken it to the tropical bulb-tuber *Thoolei-boe* (crêpe ginger), suggesting it refers to any land where such plants grow. Playful and amusing though this interpretation may be, it rests on false cognates. Others, influenced by religious perspectives, have translated Kawthoolei as "Land Without Evils." Earthly and earthy as Kawthoolei is, it cannot demand such extremity but rather welcomes human beings as they are.

A narrow pursuit though some may see Kawthoolei, its spirit is expansive. Open and generous as they are, the Karen people have never claimed their land exclusively for themselves—unlike other nationalities that name their lands after their own identity, such as Deutschland, Scotland, or Chinland. It is not Karenland, but Kawthoolei—idea rather than identity.

To those unfamiliar with Kawthoolei—and even to sons and daughters schooled in a formal yet foreign education—it may appear as little more than a mythical construct. But perhaps this signals something deeper: when understanding is detached from the spirit and rationale of a people, knowledge is misplaced.

Kawthoolei remains a tangible homeland—a living homeland—where one can touch the soil, breathe the earthy scents in the air, rest beneath the trees under the tropical sun, savor their fruits, and hear the laughter of schoolchildren at recess.

It is a land of ever-becoming, a realm of moral enlightenment, where liberty and virtue flourish, and all prosper together. It is to be a place where freedom and goodness abound, where no one is deprived of basic human needs where society thrives free from aggression, theft, and strife.

To see Kawthoolei as a utopia is a grave misconception—a misunderstanding that invites disrespect. Misunderstanding has abused her—physically and verbally—stripping her clothes of dignity. She has suffered long in the darkness of misunderstanding, wounded and scarred by theft and deceit, scam and greed, suspicion and conspiracy, attack and betrayal, neglect and disdain—but above all, by misunderstanding. The scars have not yet healed. And the wounds still bleed.

Real as much as ideal, Kawthoolei is transcendental—a place that cannot be fully grasped through knowledge or experience alone. In the Kantian sense, *transcendental* refers to what lies beyond empirical reality, existing in the realm of concepts, morals, and ideals rather than what can be seen or measured. Kawthoolei is not merely a physical space but a higher ideal—a moral and spiritual homeland, both a place of dwelling and a place held in the heart.

Creatures and biodiversity abound. Who counts the chirps of a house gecko on a midsummer afternoon? To the casual onlooker, the chirping of a house gecko may seem like mere noise; the alarm call of a woodpecker flying over a village at night may appear to be nothing more than erratic animal behavior. But for those bound to the land, these are not random sounds—they are higher messengers, whispers of a deeper harmony between life and place.

Yet Kawthoolei was meant for more—the current political struggle remains incongruent with the yet-unrealized dream. When viewed solely through the lens of war and current affairs, Kawthoolei may appear to be nothing more than a political aspiration. But Kawthoolei is not merely a political vision—it carries a moral commission, one that seeks to shape the fabric of society rather than simply define a polity or territorial claim. Its citizens are called to uphold civic virtues—honesty, simplicity, tranquility, orderliness, faithfulness, cleanliness, cooperation, and service—as the foundational principles of a nation.

For one, Kawthoolei is envisioned to prosper through the hard work of its citizens. The Karen people also value hard work and eating well. The customary greeting, "Marr-Nay-Or-Kae' (မၤန့်အီၣ်ကဲ), conveys the message: "Work hard and enjoy the fruit of your labor!" The compound word expresses a wish for *good health and prosperity*. This greeting is still widely exchanged during Karen New Year celebrations.

For others, sacredness and virtue feel increasingly foreign in the modern world. Yet, the West owes its roots to an intellectual tradition shaped by Socrates and his successors—thinkers who championed ethics, virtue, and truth. Socrates laid the foundation of Western thought, placing truth, self-examination, and moral excellence at its core. Yet today, these ideals seem eclipsed by liberalism's focus on individualism and material progress, even as it traces its lineage to a tradition once grounded in virtue.

Though fragmented, the virtues of Kawthoolei still endure within the diverse Karen communities. From urban centers, where many have embraced foreign religions, to in the foothills and hill districts where native animism remains faithful, moral values such as honesty, simplicity, hospitality, steadiness, and straightforwardness quietly permeate the rhythms of daily Karen life.

Honesty, a defining trait of the Karen people and enshrined in their National Anthem, is translated from *"taw"*. It embodies uprightness, straightforwardness, faithfulness, and purity [တၢ်ထံတၢ်တီ, တၢ်တီတၢ်လိၤ, တၢ်စီတၢ်ဆှံ]. Simplicity, another hallmark of Karen people's character, living a life unburdened by cunning, hidden agendas, or deceit—a virtue that endures among many of the people to this day. Yet, some may mistake this simplicity for gullibility or lack of sophistication, failing to see the quiet strength it holds.

Language, however, is imperfect for perfect translation; its true meaning is embedded into culture, with translations offering only approximations. In the national anthem, the phrase *"You cherish honesty"* (နအဲၣ်တၢ်တီတၢ်လိၤ) is more than words—it embodies a cultural ethos. Cherishing honesty is a universal value, however; even the cunning, deceitful, and unfaithful recognize its worth. For generations, the Karen people have carried a deep self-awareness in their interactions with others.

Among the Karen people, theft is not just an immoral act—it is a source of irredeemable shame, suppressed before it even enters the mind. In many regions where Karen and non-Karen communities coexist, to find a Karen villager caught stealing is unthinkable. During the harvest season, farmland owners patrol their fields to deter theft, a problem exacerbated by the country's economic hardship and weaker moral nature in neighboring communities. Thieves are often apprehended through community efforts in those places. The Karen people's ingrained values make stealing a moral impossibility. Though not every place upholds such high moral standards anymore, the Karen people's commitment to this virtue remains a defining strength of their culture. Even Karen families who moved to cities still carry this moral caliber within them. A few may adopt new traits, but most remain true to its roots.

HOSPITALITY MANIFESTS THE KAREN PEOPLE'S COMPASSION.

Karen people's hospitality is more than a social custom—it is a moral virtue embedded in their way of life. When a guest arrives, they are always offered a full meal—rice and its accompaniments—ensuring they leave neither hungry nor unwelcomed. Everyone who comes to a Karen home is expected to share a meal—a protocol still observed in both cities and rural areas to this day, even amid challenging economic and social realities. This act of generosity extends beyond individual households, manifesting a community-wide ethos of care and inclusivity. Into Kawthoolei's limited liberation zone, urban dwellers come for refuge after running from military persecution in the cities. In the far east of the mountainous frontiers, Karen villages and armed organizations accepted the influx of guests unquestioned. In the same token, in regions away from conflict where communities gather for sports, the participants who bring food, drink, and snacks to friendly football matches are consistently the Karen ones.

As the earliest settlers in the fertile valleys of the Irrawaddy and Sit-Taung rivers (ပျ၄ာလ၈ာ်ကျိ, ပရ၈ာ်ကျိ), two major waterways of present-day central Burma the Karen embraced newcomers without resistance. Whereas, these newcomers, with their vibrant cultures, disturbed the tranquility, encroached lands, and eroded the moral foundations that the Karen people cherished. Over time, seeking peace and freedom from the theft and disorder of the lower lands, the Karen retreated into isolation, preserving their values and way of life in the hills.

ADMIRING THE INVISIBLE COUSINS

Mythical yet mysterious, the Karen ancestors' belief in invisible virtuous beings has persisted into the modern era, occurring in isolation yet across many regions (ပုသ္ဂပုဂိုၤ). Though endowed with supernatural qualities, these invisibles are still earthly beings—they work, eat, fall in love, and multiply. Most enchanting is their selective revelation; they appear only to those whose virtue and worthiness merit their presence. Walking pass near their habitats, a passerby might hear the laughter of children playing, the hum of a bustling community, or the chanting of evening poems in the air. For others, they remain hidden, a whispered secret of the world.

Kawthoolei embodies this transcendental element, reflecting their ancestors' belief in a dwelling place for virtuous beings. Purity of thought, purity of consumption, and purity of action were timeless virtues they esteemed—and yet are universal. Karen people seem to hold admiration and still be inspired by these invisible cousins.

In some hill districts, as dawn approaches and fires crackle in the living room hearth, elders speak of the seven layers of worlds, where beings intertwine with the human realm. Each layer must remain in harmony—healthy and balanced—for the well-being of all. When certain spirits are disturbed, illness may creep in, or disunity may unsettle the peace of the community. Scholars might call this *Relational Ontology* or *More-than-Human Agency*. Scientists may speak of microbes, abiotic factors, and biological agents. But to the Karen, it is simply life—a world where everything is interconnected.

Boys and girls move with care, observing the delicate rules of courtship and relationships, while birds and spirits lend their voices, murmuring discontent at nightfall when boundaries are crossed. Here, life is lived with reverence, not only for what is visible but also for the invisible forces that quietly shape their world.

KAWTHOOLEI RESONATES UNIVERSALLY.

Notwithstanding its captivating allure, the moral values of Kawthoolei resonate universally, for every society aspires to a land free from theft, aggression, and quarrels. Societies seek to resolve conflicts and tensions through elaborate legal systems, civic culture, and political structures. To create a livable world, societies keep humanity's darker impulses in check, wielding state power with judicial and law enforcement—sometimes with lethal forces—and appeals to human goodness, balancing intimidation with moral persuasion.

In developed regions like North America, families often move to suburban communities with lower crime rates, a slower pace of life, and quieter streets with more smiles, common courtesies, and everyday pleasantries. Cities and towns are designed to minimize social vices, addressing the root causes of crime through social policies and economic opportunities, thereby creating environments that echo the essence of a "land without evils."

To achieve such a society, the developed world fosters sound civic and legal cultures through both schools and community-based initiatives. This civic foundation enables them to cultivate a society that, while imperfect, has made significant strides toward collective well-being.

Regrettably, the land of Burma has long been plagued by the vices of stealing and lying at many degrees, and all levels of society. A society rife with thieves will eventually destroy itself—this is an axiom established both theoretically and empirically—parasites rampantly exploiting a host organism, or likewise thieves within a society eroding and ultimately destroying the country.

In a sense, it is a reactionary measure that the Karen forebears envisioned Kawthoolei out of necessity. Long after when the Karen people first settled in the Green Land, it was uneventful, but over time, newcomers with a flamboyant nature brought noise, theft, and aggression. Even today, Karen villagers living near the plain valleys know the difficulties of coexisting with those whose moral nature is incompatible with their own. Farm produce, cultivated through months of hard work, can be stolen; fruits and plants were picked without permission; and fragile shoots and seedlings trampled underfoot. These relentless burdens took an economic and psychological toll on the wellbeing of the ancestors so much so that they long for a world free from thieves, quarrels, and erosion of their peace.

KAWTHOOLEI IS A PREAMBLE TO DIVERSITY.

Kawthoolei embodies the essence of diversity. It demands only the absence of darkness so that every other color may shine.

Diversity makes business sense, not only moral sense. It fosters creativity, openness to new ideas, innovation, and resilience. Advanced nations progress by harnessing the strength of diversity. Various expertise converges to make greatness. A variety of perspectives and talents drives innovation, which, in turn, creates economic dynamism and robust human resources.

World superpowers like the United States owe their strength to diversity. The U.S. remains a global leader because it attracts and retains a wide range of talents from across the world. Its advancements in research, development, and innovation are the result of its ability to integrate and celebrate diverse contributions.

In contrast, nations reliant on a single resource—like oil-rich countries—or a single talent remain vulnerable to disruptions from technological breakthroughs or scientific discoveries. As old skills become obsolete, traditional crafts are replaced by new technologies and shifting public tastes.

Modern Karen people are native to diversity. Though they see themselves as a single people of Sino-Mongoloid descent, outsiders often perceive the Karen people as a mosaic of cultures, distinguished by their diverse dialects, religious beliefs, and geographical dispersion. These differences have contributed to a broad range of physical appearances among Karen people. Moreover, Karen traditional attire showcases a remarkable variety of any possible colors, diversity unmatched by any other ethnic group in the region.

At a pivotal moment in history, an antithesis to diversity occurred within the Karen nationalist movement. In the aftermath of World War II, as the weakened British prepared to relinquish their Burma colony, Karen nationalist leaders sought to create a homeland where their people could live free from domination. Some envisioned an ethnic nation-state called 'Karenistan,' but the idea was quickly abandoned. Though the name lingers in occasional writings, it remains an archaic reference that appears sporadically in records and scholarly discussions.

The Karen people, loving and welcoming as they are, found jingoism distasteful. They recognized that the proposed Kawthoolei state was already home to a diverse population, including Karenic-speaking groups such as the Pa'O, Bwe, Paku, Mornaybwa, Geko, Geba, Pwo, and Breh, as well as non-Karenic groups such as Mon-Khmer and Shan-Tai descendants, Daweithaa, Indians, Chinese and Burmese speakers. Accordingly, the name *Kawthoolei* was revived to reflect the ancestral vision and social values of the people—a name symbolizing the clearing away of darkness and deliberately not based on any specific linguistic or ethnic identity.

In writing, it is believed that Thara Wira-Kyaw coined the term, and later formally adopted when Saw Ba Oo Gyi declared the establishment of Kawthoolei Governing Body in June 1949. However, the term *Kawthoolei* and its essence had existed long before that historic moment.

Kawthoolei does not merely embrace diversity—it *is* diversity. Its name aligns seamlessly with the reality of the land, manifesting the essence of its people and their enduring values.

KAWTHOOLEI SPEAKS A PRELUDE TO HUMAN EQUALITY.

Kawthoolei rejects the disastrous path of Burman ultra-nationalists, who sought to forge *a nation with one race, one voice, one command*—a vision that led to inevitable self-destruction. Today, Burma is known to the world as a living hell, a land of breathtaking mountains and tropical beauty now marred by the daily sight of scattered dead bodies. To heal this land, human equality must flourish, for Kawthoolei is for the people, not for a race.

The name Kawthoolei stands as a testament to the Karen people's rejection of narrow nationalism. It promotes the ideals of shared sacrifice, hard work, and collective effort devoted to the progress and prosperity of the whole nation. It is a sanctuary where pride, patriotism, and public service flourish. Where public spirit thrives, citizens rise above self-interest and idleness.

The Kawthoolei dream may appear to be a conservative ideal if narrowly viewed as the Karen people's desire to preserve their traditional values. Yet, at its core, it embodies a fundamental liberal principle—the right of every nation to envision and pursue its own national dream. By living and acting as a nation rather than as an ethnic tribal minority, the Karen people affirm their right to national self-determination, a right rooted in the universal ideals of equality and sovereignty.

Kawthoolei stands for the preservation of national virtue; thus, engaging in unethical business practices under its name fundamentally defeats its purpose. A nation cannot be reclaimed by destroying the very principles that define it. Gambling, prostitution, human trafficking, and other degrading enterprises have no place in Kawthoolei, for they are the antithesis of its values. Those who profit from such international crimes betray Kawthoolei. Equally culpable are collaborators who give comfort to the enemy, damaging the cause from within. They are public enemies and enemies of the State, and in due course, must be held accountable and tried for treason.

Even in a nation as open, advanced, and individualistic as the United States, prostitution remain broadly prohibited, recognizing that violations of human dignity erodes the moral fabric of communities. Such acts ultimately corrupt the foundation of a nation, leading not to progress but to decay—moral, social, and political.

KAWTHOOLEI IDEALS TRANSCEND POLITICAL IDEOLOGY.

Whether in the United States, China, or Iran, nations, regardless of their stated state's political ideologies, share a common concern for public morals and national spirit, recognizing their importance to societal stability and progress.

Kawthoolei does not explicitly define family values, yet they are inherently understood. The Karen people are rooted in family cohesion, from the fidelity of husband and wife to the supportive networks of extended relatives to community. Kawthoolei rejects individualistic appetites that threaten to erode family bonds, knowing that the strength of families underpins the strength of the nation. Families are the smallest building blocks of a nation, and for the structural integrity of the whole, every family unit must be healthy. Healthy families form the foundation of thriving communities, and thriving communities create a healthy society. A healthy society, in turn, builds a strong nation.

Humanity is restless in search of a better society. The rise and fall of civilizations reflect humanity's this continuous search. Feudalism, liberalism, individualism, communism, socialism, capitalism, nationalism, and internationalism are but chapters in humanity's ongoing search. Kawthoolei may offer spaces to many of the questions humanity has long pondered.

KAWTHOOLEI EMBODIES THE ESSENCE OF THE NATURAL WORLD.

The term *"Kaw"* in its name reflects a connection to the harmony of earthly environments and the natural order, extending far beyond political structures. It is a living homeland. It is where spirit and soil, water and people, animals and ecology form an inseparable whole—the sacred land of *Kaw*, a web of interconnected life.

Understanding Kawthoolei may elevate the understanding of political, social, and environmental-ecological dynamics, the globalized world order, common-sense decency, and human-nature harmony, emphasizing the need for compatibility between artificial and natural orders on this tiny blue dot in the vast expanse of the universe.

KAWTHOOLEI BEARS A DIVINE RESPONSIBILITY—A LIGHT AMONG NATIONS.

The Green Land Burma is sinking, and no nation will be spared.

When Ywa-Doh created the first nation (Poe-Wal-Koe), it was called Pwar-Ka-Nyaw—the human. The eldest sibling was entrusted with the solemn duty of caring for the younger. Ywa-Doh saw that the eldest was slow, simple, and gentle, yet blessed them with strength, entrusting them to watch over their kin.

This is not a tale of a distant past. The Karen people have long carried this burden in quiet resolve. A generation or two ago, the Karen Revolution gathered all tribes and nations in a series of agreements to fight against evil forces that had seized the land for so long. The gentle eldest sibling was betrayed and exploited, yet this did not strip them of their divine responsibility. Even now, nations in Burma look up to the Karen people to lead. Kawthoolei must walk ahead, bearing the weight of wisdom and strength.

KAWTHOOLEI IS SACRIFICIAL.

Born from the sacrifice of countless lives, blood, tears, and sweat, Kawthoolei stands as a sacred homeland reclaimed through enduring struggle. Yet, Heaven and Earth have not forsaken. Endowed with striking topography, Kawthoolei has been a fortress through the ages. During this multi-generational war for liberation, the land has been protector. Beneath its rugged mountains, within hidden valleys, and under the dense canopy of rainforests, freedom fighters and villagers have found sanctuary, nurtured and shielded by the land they hold dear.

Kawthoolei and the Karen people are inseparable. When Kawthoolei weeps and wails, Karen hearts across the world are shattered and weary. When Kawthoolei burns and fades, Karen souls everywhere long for the darkest nights to clear away. All this generational long national tragedy, hope remains steadfast. Like a self-fulfilling prophecy, Kawthoolei will come true when its people believe in it. The prophecy of the promised land is realized when people come back together to reclaim what is rightfully theirs. Without Kawthoolei, however, the survival of the Karen people is at risk, for Kawthoolei is not merely their land—it is their life, their identity, and their future.

For the Karen people, Kawthoolei is:

- ☐ National Liberation
- ☐ The Ancestral Homeland
- ☐ The Spiritual Homeland
- ☐ The Cultural Homeland
- ☐ A Land of Fertility and Livelihood
- ☐ Indigenous Territories
- ☐ A Model Society

Kawthoolei is not merely a physical space; it is an ideal—a vision encompassing freedom, heritage, spirituality, knowledge, and progress. It aspires to be a sanctuary of culture and intellect, a foundation for an advanced society, and a model for nations seeking virtue and prosperity.

Though the virtues of Kawthoolei stem from the Karen people's traditions, they hold a universal essence that any society can embrace. Kawthoolei is neither a descriptive framework nor a prescriptive formula for a nation-state; rather, it stands as a sacred proposal—one that preserves the Karen people's timeless values while offering principles from which all humanity, including the Karen people themselves, may draw wisdom and strength.

A Land Without Darkness

In the land without darkness
Where the light always shines

The motherland Kawthoolei
Where my heart aches with longing, that grows with time

Clothed with garlands of grace
Surrounded in a world of hardships and strife

Lies a land with visions of peace
Virtuous is the people's essence of life

Not just a land but an ideal that is our identity
Where even the nature of the land breathes messages of harmony

Where honesty and hospitality are not just values, but a lifestyle
Living along with nature, the interconnected reverence for this legacy

Multicolored threads of humanity and diversity are woven into the
fabric of this land
Where family connection and love constantly stay rooted

Like the care of a gentle elder sibling always watching
A history of light dwells in this land, long constituted

@Teresa.L

Chapter 2

Rebuild Kawthoolei

Constitutional Blueprint: Principles and Vision

Before an elegant structure rises, the architect must first draw a thoughtful blueprint. Before the journey to a promised homeland begins, a clear path must be charted. So is it with the making of a nation: on the road toward liberty, virtue, and lasting progress, a solid foundation must be laid—political, moral, and cultural. The constitution of a nation serves as its compass, offering direction and clarity, so the country does not drift into disorder or chaos. Nation-building is not driven by passion alone—it is the work of vision, steady discipline, and careful design.

WITHOUT ITS SOUL, KAWTHOOLEI CANNOT LIVE ON

Kawthoolei cannot exist without Kawthoolei values. When the most beautiful people among us turn to deceit, Kawthoolei will cease to exist. When a land once bound by trust and social cohesion is torn apart by bitterness, barriers, and betrayal, its spirit breaks down. Have jealousy and fragile pride already consumed hearts once known for honesty? Can a people of high integrity and gentle smiles find themselves entangled in gossip and ruinous slander?

When self-serving authorities govern without principle, and public life loses its moral anchor, what follows is not progress—but cronyism and chaos. Beneath our feet lie gold and silver, veins of wealth hidden in the earth—but without virtue, they are perishable, no more lasting than the precious hardwoods already stripped from our hills. Greed and aggression have turned green forests into barren hills, while the people remain dusty poor on the own land.

Kawthoolei is a land of abundance, rich in fertile soil and wide, open terrain. But if its people stand incapable and careless, they will become strangers on their own ancestral land—landless farmers serving distant corporate powers reign.

Only if the people of Kawthoolei uphold its values will it endure—by choice, not endowment.

THE DUTY AND THE MOMENT

We may be the last generation with a chance to rebuild Kawthoolei. A time for generational responsibility may also well be a once-in-a-generation opportunity. The Green Land, Burma, has ruined in lies. The Union still dances colorfully, but the stage of lies is collapsing under its own weight. Death stalks every corner. Even in the cities, violence is constant—a sudden bomb blast, a nighttime arrest, family members vanishing without a trace. Terror reigns.

Airports are locked down, sealing off any escape for the youth. High-tech fighter jets thunder across the skies, raining destruction with chilling precision—schools and hospitals are no longer collateral damage but deliberate targets. The country is broken—politically, economically, socially, morally, spiritually, and intellectually. Myanmar ranks among the most corrupt countries. Evil and darkness prevail. Distrust and suspicion are prevalent.

Spiritually, the land is crowded with symbols of faith, yet virtue is elusive. The corrupt have crowned themselves guardians of the nation. Meanwhile among our own, waiting for the military clique to reform itself for a just and fair union is like wishing a curly dog's tail to grow straight. Some still defend the status quo—the status quo equates suffering, shame, hopelessness, and endless chaos.

And yet, in these darkest hours, light persists. Every day, new territory is liberated—fields and forests returned to those who have tilled them for generations. The faithful and the loyal hold fast. Villagers cling to their roots, refusing to be uprooted—even in the face of ruin. Our brave soldiers stand at the edge of death, reclaiming the land with unshaken resolve. Step by step, courageous and unfazed, they press forward. Hope flickers in their eyes—the hope of a new era, a life free from fear, and a chance to rebuild what was stolen.

Piece by piece, the land is reborn. Our commanders, leading their troops, look to the future and call upon talents to return—to rebuild, to begin anew. Creative minds and skilled engineers are needed. Landmines must be cleared, bridges built. With every reclaimed field, every rebuilt home, the dream of Kawthoolei grows stronger.

Our language and customs, once vibrant in the rhythm of daily life but now encroached upon by foreign tongues, must be reclaimed. The future awaits—ready to be shaped by the talents we have forged through struggle and grace.

THE REPUBLIC OF KAWTHOOLEI TO BE

To call it the *Republic of Kawthoolei* means the country is not ruled by a king, a dynasty, or unelected leaders. Power does not come from bloodline or tradition—it comes from the people. This idea is called *popular sovereignty*, where the people are the source of authority. Leaders are chosen by the people, and they must serve the people. If they fail, they can be replaced.

A republic also means *rule by law*, not by the will of a few. Everyone, including leaders, must follow the law. It is a system where power must be used with responsibility and trust.

Most of all, a republic is built on *shared ideals*—not family ties. You do not need to be born into a tribe or clan to belong. What matters is your commitment to the values of the nation: honesty, justice, freedom, and unity.

By calling it the Republic of Kawthoolei, we are saying this is not just a region, a rebel group, or a linguistic community. It is a nation—one that belongs to its people, guided by principle, and built for a better future.

REBUILD KAWTHOOLEI NATIONAL GOVERNMENT

Kawthoolei needs a true national government—not fragmented entities doing leases and agreements, nor scattered organizations claiming to represent fragmented territories. It does not merely need the title of a "Government of Kawthoolei"; it requires a competent and accountable government that can govern with integrity and prioritizes the well-being of its citizens.

Without a government for the people, Karen people have no guarantee of safety, even abroad. A Karen man was murdered at abroad, yet there is no legal recourse. A promising political leader was assassinated, yet no investigation was conducted. A well-known Karen celebrity was killed, and no one could challenge the case. Karen migrant workers and refugees remain vulnerable and unprotected without the people's government.

Non-governmental organizations (NGOs) play a role in voicing concerns, but they are not state actors; they cannot guarantee security or deliver justice. Humanitarian aid provides only temporary relief—it cannot liberate a people, nor is it meant to. Prolonged dependency only cripples a nation. Only a functioning government can organize essential public services and establish the laws, policies, and structures necessary for order, security, and national progress.

THREE TIERS OF REBUILDING THE NATION

Firstly, rebuilding Kawthoolei begins with rebuilding our *national character*—our ways of doing things, political and organizational culture, moral values, ethical standards, work ethics, our daily habits, and sense of duty. It is about strengthening our discipline and rekindling our national self-esteem. A nation can rise only if it does believe in itself.

Secondly, equally vital is rebuilding our *institutions and system of governance*—schools and colleges, government departments, tax and revenue systems, audit and inspection mechanisms, banking and accounting sectors, public and private organizations, hospitals and schools, education and defense institutions, and military and civic training grounds. These institutions operate within the framework of a national constitution, which provides the structure for law, order, and national stability. They promote innovation, project our diplomatic identity, and shape the character of our youth, civil servants, military officers, and political leaders who will lead the nation forward.

Thirdly, rebuilding Kawthoolei also means adopting *the right technology*—best practices, automation tools, and digital networks to advance the nation's infrastructure and competitiveness. The right technology is a force multiplier.

The success of rebuilding Kawthoolei depends on getting the fundamentals right. Technology and infrastructure can accelerate progress only when built on solid foundations of people, culture, rules, and constitutional order. Therefore, the rebuilding process must be multi-domain, holistic, and comprehensive.

Only through a complete rebuilding of Kawthoolei—across these three layers of character, institutions, and technology—can we advance liberty, virtue, and progress for the nation.

> The first and most urgent task in rebuilding Kawthoolei is to mend moral deterioration. In parallel, our social stagnation cries for a radical change; our retrograde traditions and culture are long overdue for a revolution.
>
> Without a foundation with integrity, everything else we attempt to build will crumble, easily tumbled by the force of nature or the weight of routine. Suspicion, distrust, and betrayal have taken root and demoralized the people, while the land itself is stolen or sold away. This toxic land and polluted air must be cleansed before renewal can begin. A moral foundation must be unshakable, the bedrock upon which spiritual, intellectual, economic, social, and environmental growth can thrive.

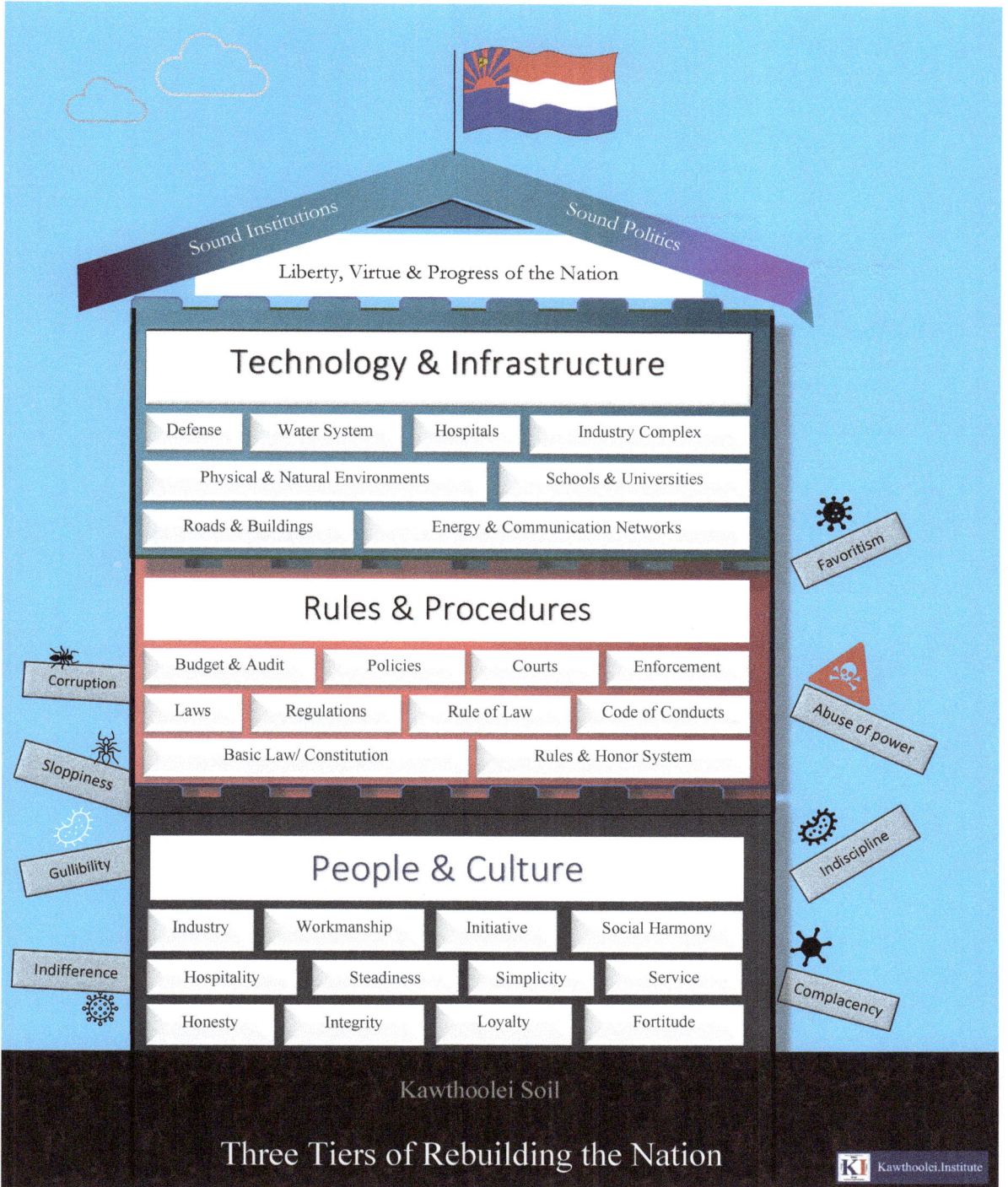

Figure 1. Three-Tier Rebuilding the Nation

THE DUTY OF GOVERNMENT

The duty of government is to govern, not to control or restrict. Good governance formulates policies that promote national progress and safety of its people. A confident government attracts and nurture talent that contributes to the nation's growth. A corrupt government shuts out talents while allowing bad actors to thrive.

Just as a well-built house has a strong fence, a nation must secure its borders—through sound trade policy, monetary strategy, regulatory frameworks, and clear procedures commerce. These safeguards keep bad actors out while ensuring lawful access and economic flow.

A forward-looking government anticipates future challenges and fosters innovation by creating environments that promote economic development. Strategic initiatives such as economic zones, industrial hubs, innovation parks, and research centers lay the foundation for national economic and social progress. Such a government does not waste its citizens' time and energy on trivial pursuits like singing ceremony or endless tribal festivities.

What sets innovation and invention apart from traditional schooling is that they cannot be forced or confined within fixed curricula. The role of government is to create opportunities, attract talent, and build an environment where creativity can thrive. Its responsibility is to provide support and clear direction—not unnecessary bureaucratic red tape.

THE CURRENT PROBLEMS

The problem today extends beyond ineffective governance. Agreements are made, leases signed, and permits issued that enable harmful actors to establish themselves, while those with goodwill and talent face suspicion, excessive scrutiny, arbitrary policies, and bureaucratic hurdles.

As the world advances rapidly, Kawthoolei's leadership must remain informed and open to new ideas. Too often, our energy is poured into humanitarian aid—portraying us in the image of a hopeless needy ethnic minority, rather than a capable and resilient people. Progress is not a passive inheritance—it must be actively pursued. Ignorance cannot shield incompetence. In an era of growing complexity, structured education alone is not enough—leaders must stay informed, think critically, and adapt constantly to navigate an ever-changing world, instead of chasing charity.

Now, the world perceives scattered armed organizations as mafia warlords in a collapsing state. Kawthoolei must rise beyond this fragmented condition. It needs a government that enforces justice and protects its people with fairness and foresight. Above all, it is the shared duty of every Karen—at home and abroad—to contribute to rebuilding the true Kawthoolei National Government.

BORDER FUNCTIONALISM

Table 9.1 Border functionalism following the Kireev typology [Ali]

Function of the border	Objects of regulation	Examples of regulation
Political regulation	Relations of political powers, their influence on their participants, means and resources	Fighting international terrorism or conducting intelligence activities
Economic regulation	Movements of material goods, factors of production, objects of exchange and consumption, actors, means and resources	Customs taxation of goods, quotas for the import of foreign labor, national sanitary and technical standards
Social regulation	Transborder processes of production and reproduction of social capital, their participants, means and resources	Rules for obtaining residence, marriage to foreigners, measures to encourage educational migration
Cultural regulation	Ethnic consciousness, information, knowledge, values, behavioral patterns, their actors, means and resources	Censorship of imported foreign literature, registration of foreign media, cultural exchange and assimilation programs
Ecological regulation	Flow of natural resources in the form of water, wildlife, and biotic resources

Examples of biotic resources are forests, animals, birds, fish, and marine organisms. | Water impoundments/ dams; fencing/walls, quarantine mechanisms |
| **Health Regulation** | Mitigating the spread of pandemic and promoting public health | Ebola, Covid 19 |

Figure 2. Border Functionalism (Ali, *Earthly Order*, 2022)

REBUILD CHARACTER INFRASTRUCTURE

Physical infrastructure endures only when supported by a national character. Without cultivating such discipline, roads, bridges, and buildings will crumble—not from time alone, but from neglect, poor workmanship, and lack of skill. The earth may tremble, but sound engineering has shown how to withstand disaster. What must be built alongside the concrete and steel is the character to preserve it.

Once, a Japanese engineer overseeing a bridge project in the 1990s in Kayin (Karen) State Myanmar expressed deep frustration over the widespread theft of building materials, corner-cutting practices, and sloppy workmanship. In his dismay, he remarked that an entire generation of Myanmar people might need to pass before real progress could be made in building enduring infrastructure—so ingrained had poor character taken root in the society.

Poor workmanship and unskilled labor often end up costing far more. When structures crumble, they waste time, resources, and materials. For instance, a brick fence at a high school in Kayin State collapsed within a month of its construction, even while work was still in progress. The effort, time, and materials spent clearing the rubble and rebuilding cost far more than if skilled laborers had built it properly the first time, with careful attention, calibrated tools, and quality materials.

The physical landscape mirrors the character of a nation—the quality of its roads, the aesthetics of its architecture, and the practicality and elegance of its design all serve as a reflection of the work ethic, discipline, and talent of its people. It is in the attention to detail, the commitment to precision, and the rejection of mediocrity that a nation's true character is revealed.

If mediocrity is a habit, then old habits must die for the Nation to live.

After character infrastructure, Kawthoolei needs institutional infrastructure where everyone can work collectively for the common good. Under civil institutions, Buddhist Karens, Christian Karens, Native Believer Karens, Liberal Karens, and Conservative Karens, White Karen, Black Karens, Gray Karens, rainbow Karen, non-Karen, and all Kawthoolei citizens can come together to build schools, civic centers, colleges, and universities—institutions that will, in turn, create more institutions, fostering education, civic engagement, and national progress, built on solid foundation of national character.

CONSTITUTIONAL THINKING: PEOPLE NEED STRUCTURE

To rebuild Kawthoolei, the nation needs a formal written constitution—a structured document that outlines its system of governance and guiding principles, serving as both the legal foundation of the country and an expression of the nation's spirit. Equally importantly, this constitution must reflect the true essence of the people, free from imposed ideologies that are incongruent to Kawthoolei's values.

Nearly every country on earth has a written constitution, with a few notable exceptions: the United Kingdom, New Zealand, Israel, and Saudi Arabia. These nations rely on established conventions, common law, and formal legal procedures. Israel has Basic Laws that function as its constitutional framework, while Saudi Arabia is governed by the Quran and the Sunnah, which serve as its de facto constitution, supplemented by royal decrees and statutes.

The United States has the oldest written constitution, ratified in 1787. It became a model for many countries, especially in the distribution of power among the *executive*, *legislative*, and *judicial* branches. Despite being over 200 years old, the U.S. Constitution has proven remarkably durable, with only 27 amendments, including the first 10—the Bill of Rights—introduced by the First Congress.

In contrast, some countries frequently rewrite their constitutions. Thailand, for example, has had 20 constitutions and charters since 1932, averaging a new one every four to five years. In many nations, constitutional authority is often overridden by those in power or by entrenched political conventions. Some constitutions are reshaped to serve political objectives rather than remain a permanent, guiding document. China's constitution, first adopted in 1982, has been amended multiple times to reflect the evolving priorities of the Chinese Communist Party (CCP). In 2018, the most recent amendment removed the two-term limit for the presidency, allowing President Xi Jinping to remain in power indefinitely.

Taiwan has its own evolving constitution with five branches of government—executive, legislative, judicial, and two unique branches: the Examination Yuan and the Control Yuan, which handle civil service examinations and government oversight, respectively. The time-tested system of government with three branches is foundational. The executive branch enforces laws and administers authority, the legislative branch drafts laws, formulates bills, and oversees executive actions, while the judicial branch interprets laws, holds hearings, and ensures accountability. These branches are designed not only to check and balance one another but also to support each other in governing the nation.

A Vision for Kawthoolei's Government Power Balance

In addition to the essential three-branch government structure—executive, legislative, and judicial—a *State Controller*, responsible for financial oversight, auditing, and ensuring accountability, would help build public trust and improve national governance. The State Controller could serve as an independent auditor general, providing advice and monitoring government spending to ensure transparency and the responsible use of public resources.

In its early years of rebuilding, Kawthoolei will need strong executive leadership to guide the nation forward. While some fear authoritarianism and seek to limit leadership power, this often results in weak, fragmented governance where no one takes decisive action. Worse, weak leadership fosters division, with leaders competing rather than uniting the people, leaving power unchecked and vulnerable to corruption and incompetence.

A strong executive must be accompanied by a robust legislative branch to monitor and oversee executive power. The legislative branch must be foresighted by the power of assembly to create laws, approve executive appointments, and provide the necessary oversight to ensure national security and prosperity. The legislative branch must be powerful in unity to work with the executive to make a strong government. A weak government, on the other hand, breeds chaos and discord, leaving the nation vulnerable to external attacks and internal disunity. The leaders of all branches must build public trust and garner support through integrity and effective governance.

The judicial branch must enforce the rule of law, guaranteeing fairness and justice in society. It should serve as an independent body with enough power to guide the national government on legal matters, protecting citizens and ensuring a just society. In Kawthoolei's national governance, the executive must collaborate with the National Assembly to define the nation's direction for economic development, social growth, and security. Only by working together can these branches create a fair and just society, where every citizen's rights are respected, and national prosperity is within reach.

"We shape our buildings and afterwards our buildings shape us."

— Winston Churchill (Referring to the shape of the legislative assembly responsible for two-party British parliamentary democracy.)

Structure of the Government of Republic of Kawthoolei

Legal Advisory Council (LAC)

Kawthoolei Court

Three Justices
- Interpret Constitution and Law
- Ensure equal justice under law
- Resolving Disputes

Supported by:
- Marshals Service
- Kawthoolei Bureau of Investigation (KBI)

Kawthoolei Congress

Supported by Committees and Congress Consultative Council (CCC)

Vice President chairs the Congress, vote only when tie.
Bicameral - Senate (District Representatives) -House (County Representatives)
Makes Laws - Meet annually
Power to remove President from office
Power to remove Justices from office

House of Representatives
- Draft bills, propose laws
- Impeachment Presidents/Justices by 51%
- Elect Speaker of the House

Senate
Amend/Approve bills
Approve President's Nomination
Try impeachment
Remove President/Justices by 2/3

Current: 7 provinces + 1 HQ => 16 Senators + 24 Representatives = 40

Auditing Committee

State Comptroller

Oversee all fiscal activities of the Government
- Nominated by The President and elected by Senate
- Report to Congress
- implement state audit, hear public complain

reports to

elect

can impeach

can impeach

nominates

approve

appoints

The President of the Republic of Kawthoolei

- Commander in Chief of Kawthoolei Armed Forces
- Sign bills into laws & Veto bills
- Appoint Judges (with confirmed of Congress)
- Appoint Cabinet members (confirmed by Congress)
- Appoint Ambassadors and officials
- Meet Foreign Dignitaries

appoints

Supported by Presidential Advisory Council (PAC)

The Cabinet

General Secretary
- Secretary of State
- Secretary of Defense
- Secretary of Interior
- Secretary of Education
- Secretary of Public Health
- Secretary of Culture and Arts
- Secretary of Finance and Commerce
- Secretary of Agriculture and Forestry
- Secretary of Natural Resources
- Secretary of Industry
- Secretary of Transport and Communication
- Secretary of Energy
- Attorney General
- Director of National Intelligence

Duties of the cabinet
- Advise the President
- Execute Government policies
- Implement projects, laws
- GS is Chief of Cabinet Members
- GS and Department Secretaries are nominated and appointed by President on Senate approval

The People of Kawthoolei (or Kawthoolei National Congress) elect the President, Vice President, and Representatives. Senators are appointed by Provincial Administration

Kawthoolei.Institute

Figure 3. Proposed Structure of the Government of Kawthoolei

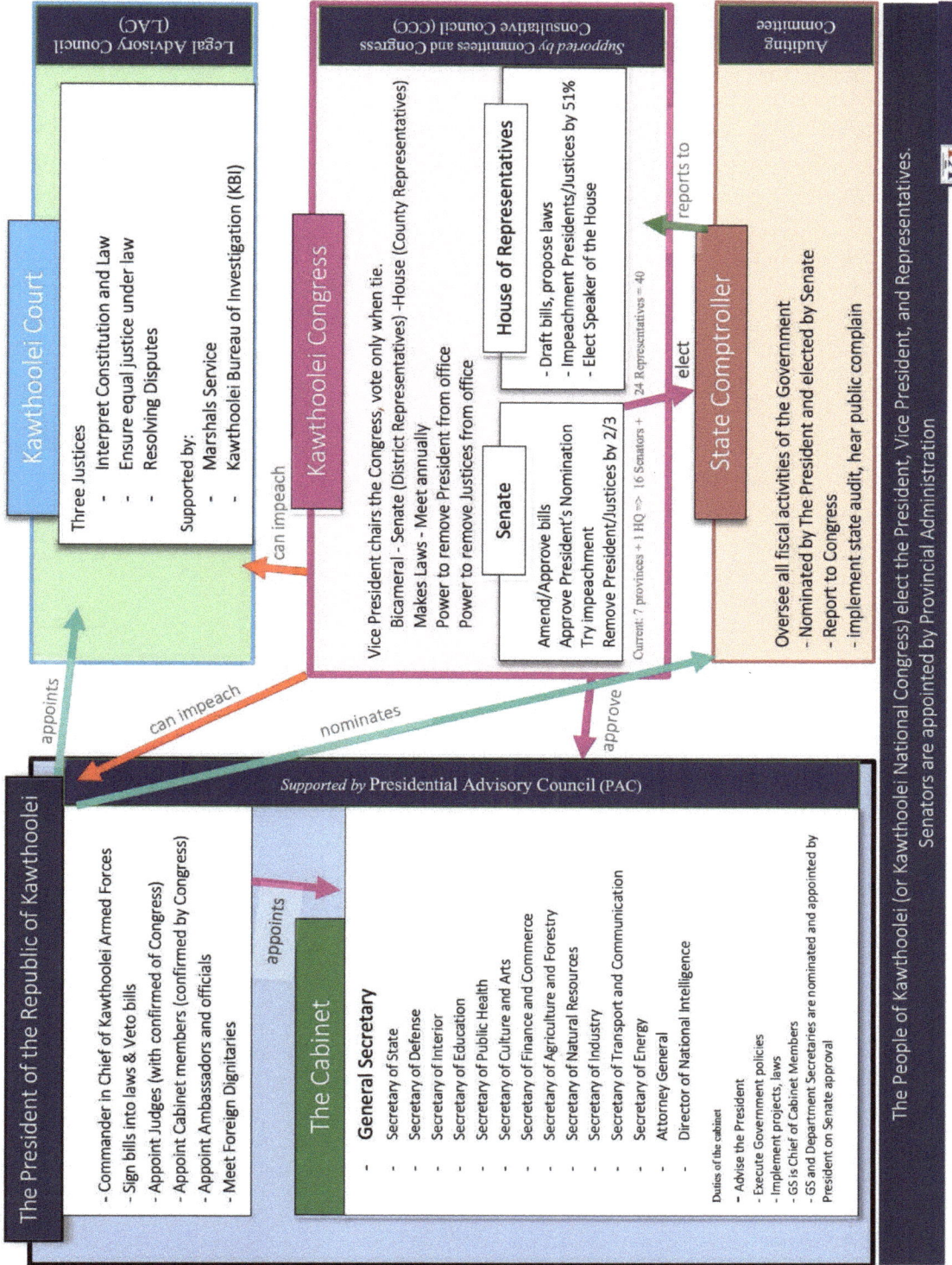

INCLUSION AND CONSIDERATIONS

1. ADVISORY AND CONSULTATIVE COUNCILS AT ALL BRANCHES

To strengthen the governance of this emerging republic, each of the three primary branches of government will be respectively supported by a formal Advisory or Consultative Council. These councils will consist of experts and intellectuals from both within Kawthoolei and the global Karen diaspora, ensuring that diverse perspectives inform national policy and decision-making.

The President and senior officials will invite distinguished figures and specialists to serve on these councils, with membership subject to congressional approval. Members will hold advisory roles without voting power, ensuring that their influence remains consultative rather than political.

2. EXECUTIVE STRUCTURE

The Executive Branch will designate a General Secretary as the chief aide to the President and Cabinet. In contrast to the parliamentary model's ministries, the Executive Branch will appoint Secretaries to lead government departments, following a structure similar to the U.S. system. Given the Karen people's familiarity with the General Secretary role, this approach will foster understanding and acceptance of the new power structure.

3. LAND OWNERSHIP AND CONSERVATION

Restoring land ownership in KNU-administered areas—long impacted by conflict—will be a national priority. While Kawthoolei holds vast land resources, ownership must not become concentrated or unchecked. Land and water conservation will be central to protecting the cultural and environmental heritage of the Karen people. No individual shall hold exclusive ownership over any waterway.

Non-citizens will be prohibited from owning land, following models such as Thailand's land ownership laws. Long-term land leases will be limited to 10 years and must comply with Kawthoolei's regulations and oversight. All leases involving foreign entities will require both district and congressional approval.

To prevent abuse, institutions such as a Bureau of Land Management, an Inspection Agency, and an Audit Authority must be established to ensure accountability and safeguard against bad actors on the sovereign soil.

4. CONSTITUTIONAL ADAPTABILITY AND ELECTION SCENARIOS

The constitution must remain flexible to accommodate various stages of national stability, including eventual recognition as a sovereign nation-state with peace and security, enabling universal elections.

Initially, official positions in the three branches may follow the KNU model, where delegates at a National Congress elect the President and other key officials. As stability is achieved in Kawthoolei, universal, direct, and secret ballot elections will be conducted under the supervision of an independent Election Commission, allowing full participation by the people.

5. BICAMERAL LEGISLATURE

A bicameral legislature will ensure equitable representation and promote an efficient division of labor within the legislative process.

- The Senate will focus on adjudicating legislative matters, including confirmations and approvals.
- The House of Representatives will collaborate with committees to draft legislation, investigate matters of national importance, and hold public officials accountable through hearings and questioning.

6. SPECIAL PROVISION ON SECURITY INTEGRATION

> "No relinquishment of control over the Police Force or the Kawthoolei Armed Forces except by referendum."

A special provision will safeguard Kawthoolei's sovereignty by preventing security integration without the consent of its citizens. This is essential in light of pressures that small nations often face to join military alliances or undergo forced integration. The recent experience of the Karen National Liberation Army (KNLA), which faced potential integration into the Myanmar Tatmadaw following the signing of the Nationwide Ceasefire Agreement (NCA) of 2015, underscores the importance of such safeguards.

7. STRONG EXECUTIVE WITH CONGRESSIONAL OVERSIGHT

The Executive Branch must be robust to provide effective leadership in Kawthoolei's formative years. However, it must remain accountable to Congress, ensuring transparency and preventing authoritarian tendencies.

Appointments of judges, cabinet members, advisors, and senior officials will require congressional approval, maintaining checks and balances while fostering public trust in government operations.

OMISSION AND EXCLUSION

1. MARKET ECONOMY AND RESOURCE PROTECTION

A market economy is not a foundational principle of Kawthoolei. The nation should refrain from opening its economy to market-driven resource extraction until comprehensive policies and regulations are in place. Premature liberalization risks crony capitalism and long-term environmental degradation, as evidenced by recent history.

In the early stages, the government will manage key sectors, gradually allowing private sector growth under careful oversight and regulatory frameworks.

2. SOCIAL SERVICES: WEIGHT ON THE STATE

Education, social welfare, and healthcare are essential government responsibilities. However, in order to prevent overburdening the government during its formative years, these services should not be detailed in the constitution. Instead, they can be established and expanded through legislation as the state's capacity grows.

3. TERRITORY BOUNDARY: LEAVE IT TO THE NATIONAL ASSEMBLY

The duty of defining territory and boundary of Kawthoolei should be entrusted to the National Assembly, which can make decisions based on methodical surveys and well-reasoned assessments of military, political, and economic realities.

Simply adhering to the 1947 boundary specifications may lead to unintended problems. Those boundaries were not drawn through thorough surveys or mutual political agreements but were hurriedly determined by Karen elders from various regions with differing levels of understanding of Burma's geography and political landscape of the time.

Today, Karen people live across Burma and around the world, making rigid attachment to outdated boundaries impractical. A prosperous nation does not require vast territory—it depends on competent governance, organization, and the strength of its people. Singapore, with its small landmass, serves as an example. It holds the world's most powerful passport and has the largest military spending per capita in the region, demonstrating that strategic planning, competent human resources, and capable leadership are the true foundations of national strength.

4. LOCAL AUTONOMY AND DIVERSITY

Kawthoolei's population is highly diverse, comprising Karenic-speaking peoples, Burmans, Mons, Shans, Tayov, Indians, Chinese, and others. Local autonomy should be governed by democratic principles under a local constitutional framework, with administrative structures determined by the national legislature. All-inclusive National Assembly must formulate legislation that promotes national unity.

Effective decentralization will respect cultural diversity while maintaining national unity, ensuring that all communities have a voice in Kawthoolei's future.

A Proposed Constitution **Preamble**

Defining the Nation's Founding Spirit

"We, the people of Kawthoolei,

inspired by our forebears, whose wish was to restore
peace, harmony, and moral virtues in this land—
Kawthoolei, our ancestral home since time immemorial—
to be free of vice, villains, and external threats,

to embark on a new era that brings the cessation of hostilities,
alleviate the suffering endured by generations,
and reverse the destruction in the land, thereby
reclaiming, defending, and preserving our ancestral land for posterity,

to govern our own affairs in accordance with the will of the people,
pursuing progress of the nation and happiness in our traditional way of life,

to establish justice and order, safeguard the security of citizens,
to ensure liberty and respect for human dignity,

to promote stability in the region,
and to strengthen democracy, independence, and peace among nations
in the spirit of solidarity and openness to the world,

do hereby ordain and establish this Constitution for the Republic of Kawthoolei."

Nationhood Built on Structure

Kawthoolei Needs Structural Clarity on Factions

The fragmented condition Kawthoolei faces today is not unique in the history of nation-building. Many nations have walked this difficult path. What distinguishes Kawthoolei, however, is the sheer scale and complexity of its internal divisions. It harbors nearly every imaginable faction under the sun—divisions in political and social ideology, religious belief and practice, geography and linguistic dialect, educational attainment, and worldview.

One encounters a devout strain of Baptist conservatism, an insular form of Seventh-day Adventism, various other denominations, devoted Buddhists, and faithful animists. Across these branches of faith—whether native or foreign—run the undercurrents of linguistic kinship and traditional social customs. Kawthoolei yet as a nation-in-the-making is pulled in many directions. The greater danger lies not in the diversity of factions, but in their encroachment into the political sphere. In such a setup, no coherent state can emerge. No country can endure this level of strain.

Compounding this fragility is the rise of Karen armed groups—once liberation forces—now entrenched as localized power blocs with private economic realities. They all bear the name of the people, but in practice, they function as warlords. Under such circumstances, no national progress can take root. Without a unified state and a legitimate national government, the people will remain unable to experience economic prosperity or social progress.

A nation needs structure—an overarching framework where all social domains, however diverse, may converge for the common good. Social, political, and ideological diversity should enrich the system of governance, not pull it apart. Without a defined shared vision, fragmentation becomes the norm, and collective purpose dissolves into rivalry and regression. For this reason, Kawthoolei needs structure where factions must remain social—not political.

As Roger Scruton once noted of America's founding:

> "The Constitution of the United States succeeded largely because those who devised it sought to found a republic in which the obligation to strangers would find concrete embodiment in the institutions of the Union: a *republic* in which factions would have only *social*, rather than *political*, power." (Scruton, 2019, p68)

1. A Rule-Based Nation From Small Details

Kawthoolei can thrive only on a governance structure grounded in written rules, standard procedures, and clear norms that emphasize the importance of detail. A culture of treating small matters seriously will prevent minor issues from escalating into national disasters. Organized and proactive culture must become second nature—in writing and in action—valuing prevention over reaction.

2. Setting Rules before Starting Business

No ground should be broken for mineral extraction until a comprehensive regulatory framework is established. Kawthoolei's natural resources are abundant, but without regulation, they risk becoming a curse rather than a blessing. The unregulated gold mining creates reckless exploitation that can destroy paddy fields, contaminate water sources, and leave toxic scars on both the environment and public health. Most Districts in Kawthoolei have suffered in the last decades.

Strong environmental policies will safeguard Kawthoolei's land, water, and public health. Regulation is not an obstacle to progress; it is the foundation for sustainable development. As demonstrated in state like California, an extensive regulatory framework fosters innovation while protecting shared resources. However, people will have the duty to watch for regulation becoming overreached and regulation that stifles progress.

3. The Land Belongs to the People: Safeguarding Local Rights

In Kawthoolei, land is sacred—a place where the spirits of ancestors still roam. Breaking the ground without respect and proper ceremonies invites curses. The local natives must be acknowledged as the rightful stewards of the land. Comprehensive regulatory frameworks will prevent abuses of power and ensure fair resolution of conflicts.

4. The Danger of a Market Economy

Kawthoolei must avoid premature economic liberalization. A market economy requires expertise and sound policies to function effectively. Without clear regulations, free-market practices can breed crony capitalism and severe inequality.

In the early stages, state management of key economic sectors is essential to ensure growth that benefits all citizens, not just an elite few. Private sector growth should be gradually allowed under careful oversight, with policies designed to protect public interests.

5. Leadership with Qualities

Great leadership rests on three pillars: integrity, management, and vision—with integrity always coming first. Without it, the other qualities lose their meaning. Without management with strategy and skill to allocate and mobilize resources, a leader's vision remains unrealized. Without vision, even the most intelligent and principled leaders risk short-sightedness. Skillful leadership without integrity may seek power for its own sake, while leadership without vision merely circles in place. Kawthoolei's future leaders must embody the highest standards of character, competence, and vision.

Leadership must be bound by rules and regulations, not personal ambition or unchecked power. A strong judicial system, operating within a transparent legal framework, is essential to safeguarding human rights, upholding the law, and ensuring order.

6. Institutional Culture: Building Impersonal Organizations

Kawthoolei's success hinges on professional, rule-based civic organizations. Personal connections must give way to institutional trust. The aviation industry offers a lesson: global coordination does not rely on personal relationships but on predefined rules and specialized roles all around the world, from ground crew, cabin crew, ticketing system, airport security, cyber connection, and many services collaborate.

Kawthoolei's wealth must serve the people, not a privileged few. The feudal mindset that grants unearned advantages based on family ties to authority must be eradicated. Every child of a public official must be held to scrutiny when granted privileges—reward must be based on merit. Building professional, impartial institutions governed by predefined rules—rather than personal relationships—is to foster fairness and equality.

In Kawthoolei, strong institutions—from the judicial system to the education sector and government bodies—must uphold common standards of conduct, ensuring fairness and accountability at every level.

7. Cultural Norms and the Role of Schools and Universities

A nation is shaped as much by its culture as by its laws. Schools and universities must play a leading role in fostering civic values, national identity, and practical skills. Patriotism and sound politics should be taught alongside diligence, integrity, and initiative to build a disciplined, united society.

> "Not all cultural practices are good nor always good. Only good practices are reinforced and codified, and the laws intervene when there are signs of problems. A good institutional culture is no accident – it requires intentional daily maintenance from every member of the people in the society"
> — *University of California Ethical Training*

8. Learning from the Success of Others

The technical how-to aspects can be learned from others. History offers many lessons. California's water infrastructure, built a century ago, ensured that no one went thirsty despite a decade-long drought in 21st Century. Health issues like malaria could be eradicated within five years, following the successful example already set east of the Salween River. Israel eradicated malaria in 40 years through careful planning and relentless execution. These examples demonstrate that forward-thinking policies and infrastructure can overcome even the most daunting engineering challenges.

Kawthoolei can achieve similar success by learning from others' experiences. Scientific solutions, best practices in business and infrastructure, sound governance, and respect for tradition and culture can transform the nation within a generation.

Rebuilding the Nation: One Generation, One Vision

With a sound structure and clear direction, we can rebuild our people within one generation, instilling shared norms and values that unify them in loyalty, organization, and collective purpose—essentials for nation-building and progress.

Culture dictates norms and expectations, even when laws and enforcement mechanisms are in place. If we want Kawthoolei to be a land without theft, deceit, or aggression, we cannot rely solely on laws and law enforcement. Only a high ethical culture can create a society that is truly free from such vices.

Where harmful cultural practices and bad habits exist, the rule of law must intervene as a safeguard. Meanwhile, schools and universities must play a proactive role in promoting civic values, patriotism, and sound politics. Among these values are honesty, equality, industry, initiative, integrity, service, and duty to the nation's common cause, along with a commitment to maintaining order and cleanliness in public and private life.

The judicial system ensures fairness and justice by following a predefined set of rules, while sound policies cultivate a healthy institutional culture. These pillars—culture, law, and education—work together to lay the foundation for a fair and well-functioning society.

Through sound economic policies, we achieve a stable and healthy economy that reduces hardship for citizens. Good education strengthens social progress, builds national unity, and fosters the national spirit necessary to transform Kawthoolei into a thriving nation.

The progress we envision is wholesome and holistic—moving the nation forward in social, economic, political, intellectual, and spiritual progress.

Tree of Kawthoolei Ideal

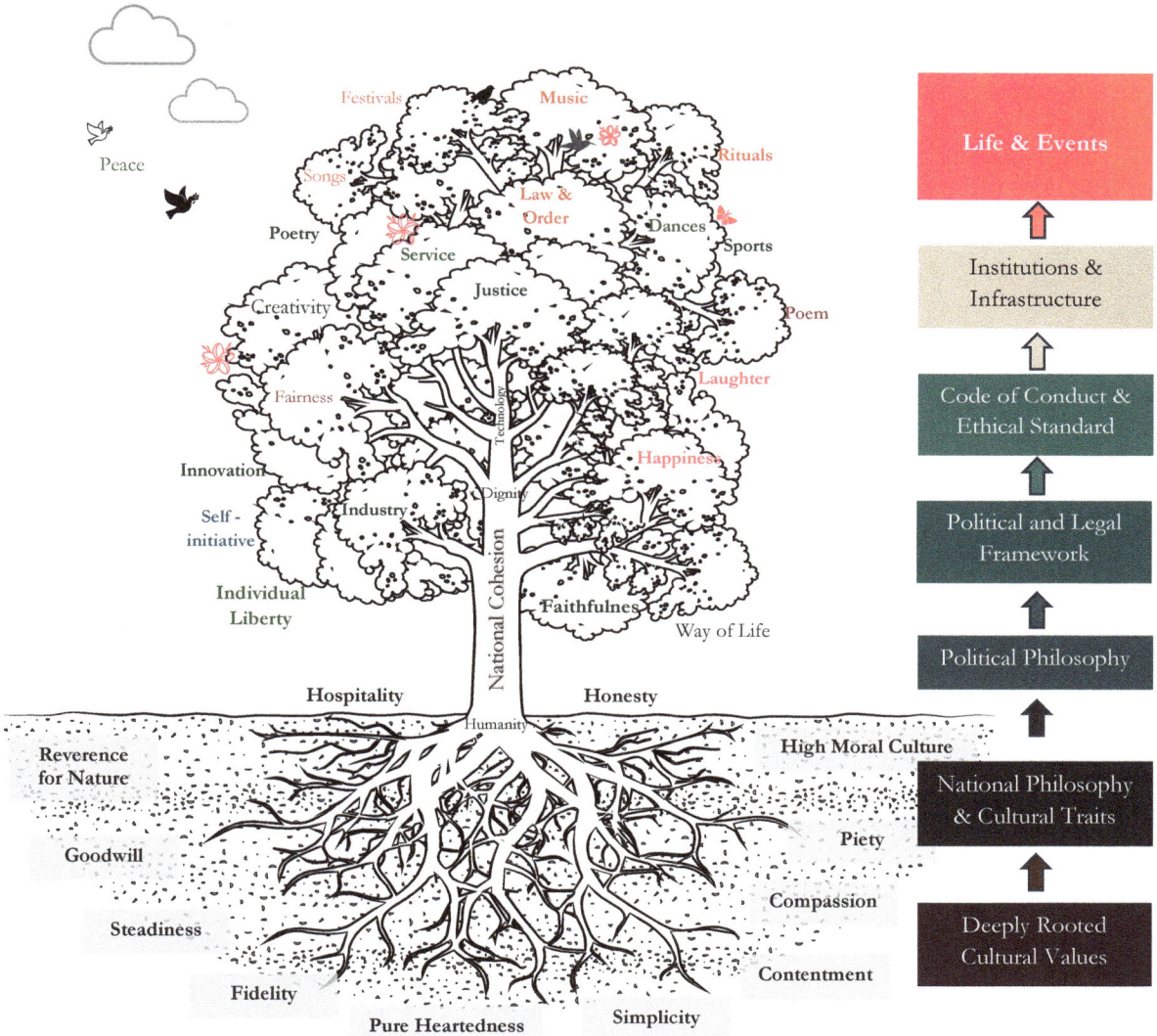

Figure 4. Tree of Kawthoolei Ideal

Tree of Kawthoolei Ideal

FROM CULTURAL ROOTS TO CONSTITUTIONAL REALITY

A review of a dozen constitutions from both Western and Eastern societies—including those in Southeast Asia, East Asia, and the Middle East—reveals more than legal frameworks; it reveals the soul of a people. From the sacred preamble to the final clause, every line reflects underlying moral values, cultural traditions, and political histories that shape a nation's identity. These constitutions do not emerge in isolation—they are written expressions of its society's beliefs about justice, liberty, order, and unity. To understand a nation's constitution is to grasp the invisible foundations beneath it: the worldview, the collective memory, and the cultural roots that give it meaning.

Kawthoolei's passage toward becoming a prosperous nation begins with its foundation—its values and constitution—unwritten and written. Just as a tree cannot grow strong without deep, nourishing roots, a nation cannot flourish without a strong moral and cultural core. These roots anchor the nation, providing clarity, stability, and the strength needed to build functioning institutions and ensure lasting prosperity.

A tree cannot thrive in barren soil, nor can it grow strong under the shadow of another. Freely, it must embrace both the sun and the storm to be strong. Likewise, of its own sovereignty, Kawthoolei's tree will grow tall and verdant only when it stands in the open, weathering fierce winds and basking in the light. The trunk gains strength by enduring tempests, while seasons of drought force its roots to reach deeper, drawing sustenance that ensures abundance when the rains return. There is a time for dry summer, a time for shower, and a season of blossoming and a season of ripening fruit. A tree must endure all of those times to be strong, and a strong tree embrace all of those.

The soil must be rich, free from toxic elements. Healthy roots drawing nourishment from the soil fortify the national spirit. Kawthoolei's roots are enriched by its enduring values: honesty, simplicity, respect for human dignity, and harmony with nature. These principles form the ethical bedrock that sustains the nation.

With deep roots, a tree can withstand storms. With a strong cultural foundation, a nation can build a sustainable and cohesive identity, forming resilience against external pressures and internal discord. However, when its roots are corrupted, the entire shelter risks collapse.

The trunk of the nation is its constitutional framework, emerges from the nation's political philosophy, which, in turn, arises from national character. A constitution is not merely a legal document; it reflects how a people understand themselves, how they wish to organize their society, and what principles they seek to uphold. This foundational document displays the spirit of its people.

The institutions and physical infrastructure form the tree's branches, providing the vital energy needed for growth. These include border security, customs control, trade policies, education, health, and systems of law and order. Well-designed institutions, shaped by nation's philosophy and rooted in cultural values, nourish societal progress and create an environment where citizens can flourish.

As the tree matures, its branches bear leaves, flowers, and fruit—the visible expressions of a flourishing nation. In Kawthoolei, this corresponds to the vitality of its people, the vibrancy of its culture, and the richness of its music, arts, festivals, sports, poetry, and celebrations. These manifestations of national spirit can only thrive when sustained by deep-rooted values, a strong constitutional framework, and well-functioning institutions.

Above all, the canopy represents the visible expressions of national life—daily activities, creativity, and public discourse. Just as a tree's leaves absorb sunlight and transform it into energy, these expressions translate the nation's values into shared experiences. Each fiber of the family must be strong for young leaves to sprout, making the health of the entire society. The canopy draws admiration from the outside world while sustaining the inner life of the nation.

Like a tree thrive in a forest, Kawthoolei will flourish among the community of nations by engaging in both international cooperation and competition. It is through this interplay—like the mycorrhizal network connecting roots and sharing nutrients and information—that Kawthoolei will grow from its roots to its trunk and branches, maturing into a nation that not only survives, but thrives. With deep roots, a strong constitution, and flourishing institutions, it will stand as a symbol of resilience, independence, and unity—a tree that withstands storms, both great and small, and stands tall within the forest of nations.

COME BACK AND PROSPER

"Come back and sacrifice" is a dangerous narrative—one that paves the way for exploitation on the goodwill. Those with talent and intellect will not serve the ambitions of the corrupt or the incompetent in the office.

Instead, the call must be: *Come back and prosper.* Return not to be consumed, but to build. Reclaim what is yours, not through suffering alone, but through strength. Rebuild the nation that belongs to you. Fulfill the dreams of your ancestors, not as martyrs, but as visionaries and missionaries. Kawthoolei is broken, but it can rise. Earn, learn, and lend a hand—not in servitude, but in creation.

Public service may demand sacrifice, but talent must not be repaid with insult. A nation that diminishes its best minds is a nation that betrays itself. That is not the world we seek to build. Every individual carries a unique gift, but true strength lies in unity. When talents converge with purpose, the whole becomes greater than the sum of its parts.

You may hold the passports of some nations, or you may have none at all—stateless, without a country to claim. Yet, this is your ancestral land, your people's home, your nation's heart. Return and serve. You will gain more than you give.

How privileged are those who shape a nation with their own hands, who see the fruits of their labor endure for generations to come? When they depart this world, they leave not only memories, but a lasting legacy.

Come back help liberate, come back help rebuild.

PART II

POLITICAL THOUGHTS CONCERNING KAWTHOOLEI

Chapter 3

On Liberalism

In the borderlands of Kawthoolei, the rhetoric of rights has grown commonplace—a currency casually spent to justify nearly every act. Such casual invocation risks not only inflating the concept of individual rights but also emptying them of substance and dulling their moral clarity. Likewise, the superficial application of other liberal ideals warrants scrutiny.

Ideologies rise and fall, borne on the shifting winds of time and circumstance. The moral fervor that surrounds them is rarely enduring. A posture of superiority built on ideological trends seldom leads into lasting virtue. In the countries where such ideas first emerged, enthusiasm has long since waned. Ironically, from afar, we receive them as novelties—echoing their rhetoric as emblems of refinement and progress. In doing so, we begin to regard our own social values not as enduring wisdom, but as outdated relics—quaint, unsophisticated, and in need of replacement.

The Karen people have always shown openness to ideas that align with their moral values. Just as Christianity found a natural home among them—its sacred stories and virtues mirroring their own traditions—the language of *human rights* has also been warmly embraced. This acceptance is not accidental; it comes from a deep-rooted compassion, a moral clarity, and an instinctive respect for human dignity. Despite being scattered, Karen society sustained itself for ages with high principles of humanity, without needing indoctrination from the outside world.

Liberalism, as a political ideal, has evolved into a multifaceted concept, requiring adjectives—classical, modern, or neo-liberalism—to specify which variant is under discussion. Each version has spawned numerous offshoots, adapted to different contexts. As a result, any discussion of liberalism demands a precise definition, encompassing the ideology, the liberals who advocate it, and the actions that align with its principles. The fact that the discussion has to now label the original idea as "classical liberalism" shows how much it has been corroded or altered by newer versions.

At its core, liberalism advocates individual liberty and equality of opportunity. In the context of Kawthoolei, it is crucial to distinguish the liberalism subtly consumed in the Kawthoolei-Thailand border region from a deeper, more comprehensive vision—one that integrates individual rights, collective liberty, and shared responsibility.

CLASSICAL LIBERALISM

Once upon a time in 17th-century Europe, kings ruled by divine right, controlling religion, land, and the lives of humans as their subjects. Against this rigid backdrop, thinkers like Thomas Hobbes and John Locke ignited a transformation in governance. They argued that laws should not restrain freedom but instead preserve and expand it. They argued people surrendered certain natural rights to the state for the sake of security, but respecting the rights of others remained essential to a just society.

Thomas Hobbes argued that to escape the chaos, individuals must surrender certain rights to a sovereign authority to secure social order, peace, and the collective good. John Locke, a principal architect of liberal thought, defined liberty not as unrestrained freedom, but as freedom from arbitrary authority. In his *Two Treatises of Government* (1690), Locke argued that individuals should be free to pursue their interests, so long as they respect the rights of others. For Locke, true liberty meant living under laws that protect natural rights—life, liberty, and property—safeguarding individuals from the capricious will of rulers. Laws, in this view, are not instruments of restriction but guarantors of freedom. This foundational concept laid the groundwork for modern liberalism and continues to shape debates about the balance between individual rights and state authority, a balance widely achieved in stable democracies with mature state institutions.

Today, some proponents of a progressive liberal agenda increasingly seek to impose certain rights, sometimes disregarding community norms and cultural nuances. This shift has disrupted the delicate balance between individual freedom and collective responsibility—a hallmark of classical liberalism. Demanding that developing nations adopt the same expansive liberal agenda as wealthier countries can be akin to expecting families struggling to provide basic necessities to prioritize the same luxuries enjoyed by the affluent. In Kawthoolei, some individuals, perhaps consumed by these progressive liberal values, may echo such demands without fully considering the local context or uttering out of habit.

Locke's vision of liberty as protection from arbitrary authority remains vital, but the scope of liberalism has expanded significantly. What once aimed to *constrain* state power now calls on governments to ensure health, education, and even *promote* well-being. Yet, without cultural context and a sense of shared responsibility, individual rights risk morphing into a self-serving individualism, becoming a source of division, undermining social cohesion and the well-being of communities. This emphasis on individualism weakens intrinsic communal bonds—such as filial piety, reciprocity, service, sacrifice, and devotion—once abundant, now *increasingly scarce*. Fortunately, for many, these ties remain sacred.

GLOBAL LIBERALISM IN DECLINE

Liberalism—free trade, open competition, freedom of expression—has been the reigning ideology in global institutions like the UN and WTO for decades. But its reign is being challenged. Nationalist movements, from Brexit to the Orbán phenomenon, reject liberalism's globalism outright. Authoritarian states like Russia and China offer a compelling narrative. The once-cherished idea that economic development inevitably leads to liberal democracy has been exposed as a fallacy: Russia's authoritarian resurgence and China's economic miracle without political reform provide compelling evidence—unless until ultimately flawed. The populist surge in the US and Brazil further fractures societies, undermining the basis of liberal democracy. And, as a final twist of 2024, Trump is back. The oldest democracy can die off, warmed by many scholars, including by Prof. Steven Levitsky and Prof. Daniel Ziblatt in the book *How Democracies Die*.

CHALLENGES TO MEDIA FREEDOM OF SPEECH

Freedom of speech and a free press are core tenets of liberalism. However, many mainstream media outlets—particularly in the United States—have become ideologically polarized, leaning heavily to either the left or the right. As audiences are continually exposed to one-sided narratives, the risk of entrenched ideological bias grows. What were once celebrated as pillars of an informed and critically engaged society—freedom of the press and open discourse—have increasingly been politicized and weaponized, straying from their original purpose.

In search of more balanced reporting, some Americans turn to international outlets such as the BBC or to media focused on markets and economic analysis. While the U.S. upholds freedom of speech as an inviolable right—even extending protections to hate speech—the power of the state remains far-reaching. The Federal Communications Commission (FCC), for instance, regulates communications across radio, television, internet, Wi-Fi, and cable. Social media and messaging apps make a permanent digital fingerprint. The state authority has multiple investigative and enforcement mechanisms (federal levels: FBI, DOJ, HSI, DEA, ATF, Secret Service, EPA, IRS, Inspectors General, GOA, SEC, many more in state-level and local agencies) that have ability to track its citizens when needed. This dual reality reveals a tension between the ideal of unbounded expression and the enduring reach of state authority.

THE PARADOX OF MODERN FREEDOM

Western societies often prize individual freedom, valuing personal autonomy above traditional obligations like filial piety. No longer legally bound by parental authority, an 18-year-old is free to chart their own course. Yet, even as this independence is celebrated, individuals remain enmeshed in a web of laws and customs shaped by generations past, a social contract they never explicitly signed. They must abide by a host of rules and regulations to which they never directly consented, yet constantly and directly impacting their lives.

Consider a man in USA. As he stepping outside his American home, he enters a world governed by layers of authority, each more abstract than the last. First, the hyper-local homeowners' association (HOA) dictates everything from house color to lawn height. Beyond the HOA lies layers of governance: from township regulations, then county ordinances, followed by state laws—all crafted by representatives he may never have met. Federal laws, enacted in the distant halls of the nation's capital and interpreted by life-appointed judges, represent the highest level of governance. Even his car, a symbol of personal mobility, is subject to strict regulations: safety standards, mandatory insurance (a reflection of collective responsibility), and roads designed by engineers and administrators who never considered his individual preferences. Policies affecting his daily life are often implemented by unelected bureaucrats. These laws, largely pre-existing, shape his existence with little room for dissent.

A woman in the US, for example, may choose her career, vote, and determine her lifestyle, but her freedom is inextricably linked to the responsibilities that underpin social order. She must obey laws, pay taxes, serve on juries, and adhere to workplace policies. Even personal choices related to her body are influenced by state and federal laws, as she participates in public healthcare systems and infrastructure. These responsibilities, though often implicit, are crucial for a just society. Her freedom, therefore, is not isolated but embedded within her civic duties, reinforcing Locke's belief that liberty thrives within a framework of laws that protect the rights of all. Freedom, then, is not the absence of rules, but the presence of just laws that balance individual autonomy with the collective good.

This system reveals the paradox of modern freedom: individuals may feel autonomous, yet their actions are shaped by decisions of predecessors in a system they barely control. Locke reminds us that true liberty lies within laws that protect freedom, not in unbounded autonomy. Freedom under law carries responsibilities. Beyond legal compliance, society expects acts of decency—kindness and politeness—essential for human interaction, though not legally required.

CIVILIZATIONS OF SUNRISE AND SUNSET

The U.S. and Burma share a couple of commonalities although they may seem as distant from the blue sky to the dark soil. One is the legacy of British colonial rule; the other is their continued use of the imperial measurement system—one of only three countries in the world to do so (the third one is Liberia). But their similarities largely end there. In Myanmar's political circles, many admire the U.S. for its constitutionalism, federalism, and multiculturalism—liberal ideals often seen as aspirational. Yet, Myanmar's distinct ethnic composition, social tradition and ethical values, and entirely different historical path make such comparisons difficult.

The American political Founding Fathers were shaped by the European Enlightenment and Greco-Roman political thought—such intellectual traditions largely unknown in Burma. By 1824, when the British East India Company waged its first war against superstitious feudal Burma, the U.S. had already elected its seventh president. A decade later, when Burmese peasants led by Saya San, claiming his royal descent, revolted against British rule in the 1930s using sickles, shovels and homemade tools, the U.S. was building modern engineering marvels like the Golden Gate Bridge (1933) at the western coast of California.

Beyond their shared colonial past, the two countries could not be more different. The U.S., shaped by Enlightenment ideals, centers on individual liberty, democracy, and rule of law. Burma, by contrast, is grounded in feudal monarchies, cultural continuity, diverse people with their own national psyche. Any admirers of American liberalism in Burma may need to account for these stark differences.

ENLIGHTENMENT AND THE GREATEST IRONY

One of the greatest ironies of the Enlightenment lies in its contradiction between ideals and realities. Between the 17th and 19th centuries, while its thinkers extolled human equality and the triumph of reason. Their revolutionary ideas flourished in societies that stood at the height of colonialism. Western nations, proclaiming liberty and progress, evolved into highly organized political entities, through scientific progress, armed with advanced technologies and superior weaponry—tools they wielded to conquer, plunder, and exploit distant lands.

The same civilizations that championed universal rights, rational thought, and human dignity amassed their wealth and global dominance through systematic subjugation and dehumanization. This paradox reveals the darker undercurrent of the so-called Age of Reason—a time when ideals of equality and reason coexisted with imperial ambition and ruthless exploitation. A more fitting name for this era would be the Age of Plunder.

Now, those nations, resting on the wealth amassed by their forefathers through centuries of conquest and exploitation, occupy a position of privilege. From this vantage point, they champion ideals such as human equality, human rights, multiculturalism, diversity, and global climate responsibility as the superior values of our time. Yet, these noble pursuits often come with an air of moral authority, the wild wind blowing toward our shores. The irony deepens as these nations promote progress. A more dramatic irony is when our people buy into it with high appraisal.

LIBERALISM'S BALANCE

Imposing Western liberal ideals on societies rooted in Eastern values—where family and community prioritize collective well-being over individual desires—can be unsettling. Sudden exposure to unfamiliar freedoms brings its own challenges. Like forcing a square peg into a fragile hole, it risks braking. Social media amplifies uncivil discourse, degrading public debate and weakening communal bonds. Freedom of expression requires balance and constrain; unchecked, it becomes toxic. Individualism, without shared purpose, corrodes the social fabric.

Liberalism and democracy, though often linked, are not inherently intertwined. History shows they can diverge—democracies can turn illiberal, while unelected authority sometimes upholds liberal values. Nazi Germany, where Hitler rose to power through elections, is a stark reminder of democracy's risks. In the U.S., individual liberties rely on the unelected Supreme Court and judiciary, not popular vote.

Today, populist leaders in the West gain support by promoting closed borders and protectionism. Excessive permissiveness often triggers a backlash. This paradox reveals how democracy, meant to protect liberty, can slide toward the tyranny it seeks to prevent—driven by populism fueled by fears of social change.

Liberal Party leader and legendary Canadian Prime Minister Pierre Trudeau (the 15th PM, father of Justin Trudeau, Canada's 23rd PM, 2015-2025) was renowned for his staunch advocacy of individual rights and his articulation of liberalism in intellectual terms. However, during the October Crisis of 1970, he took extraordinary measures, invoking the War Measures Act, which led to the detention of hundreds without charge to counter a perceived national security threat. His firm stance was controversial, yet he justified it as necessary to prevent Canada from falling into chaos.

The challenge is balancing individual rights with collective responsibility. Unbridled individualism, detached from shared purpose and civic duty, fragments society. Liberalism, without wisdom and cultural context, risks unraveling itself.

NEOLIBERALISM'S EXPLOITATION

Neoliberalism champions unregulated markets and minimal government intervention, with advocates claiming free trade leads to prosperity. In reality, unregulated capitalism worsens inequality, stripping safety nets from the vulnerable. Inequality surges as free trade rewards those with capital and technology, leaving others behind. Yet even this rampant surge of inequality looks pale compared to authoritarian crony capitalism of Burma, where poor Burmese have nothing, but misery is plenty while military-linked billionaires Burmese are plenty.

In Burma, political and economic liberalization during the 2010s abetted rampant crony capitalism. Without regulations—or the ethical tradition to tame their greed—corruption thrives. Without a need for troops and military operations, neoliberalism could ravage Kawthoolei just as easily, exploitation without regard for indigenous rights.

About five years ago, in southern Kawthoolei, workers at a gold mining site dumped mercury into the water out of convenience. When warned to dump chemicals properly on land, they shrugged. "When you're in the water and need to pee, you don't get out," one said. In northern Kawthoolei, a villager reported wastewater from nearby mines flooding the river, turning downstream paddy fields into swamps of yellow-streaked water. "The water no longer feeds the rice; it drowns it. You dare no longer drink the water," he lamented. These incidents are stark reminders of the dangers of unchecked liberalization. Left unregulated, progress turns into exploitation, leaving behind poisoned waters and ruined lands.

The lesson taught us that no ground in Kawthoolei should be broken without a full-fledged regulatory framework that includes inspection mechanisms, enforcement, legal recourse and environmental mitigation procedures, and protections for indigenous communities. Development that benefits corporations while destroying the land is no development—it is a betrayal. Liberalization that disregards the people is unsustainable. Development that damages the environment is not progress; it is a path down toward ruin. The ruins usually come with baggage—economic, social and moral.

And when it comes to freedom of expression, it cannot be introduced recklessly to the children of Kawthoolei without instilling civic responsibility, preserving Karen cultural decorum, and promoting respect for the dignity of others. Any foreign teaching of "freedom of expression" must be mindful of the social context: while the Karen people are known for their gentleness, unrestrained freedom, like in any community, can lead to emotional volatility and disrespect, potentially tearing the social fabric apart. Fostering social cohesion is essential for maintaining harmony and building a just society. For liberalization to truly bring prosperity and freedom, it requires more than just laws; it demands a mature culture of rule of law and a strong regulatory framework supported by enforceable mechanisms.

THE KAREN PEOPLE AND HUMAN RIGHTS IDEALS

Among Burma's many ethnic nationalities, few have adopted the language of human rights as fully as the movement in the Karen community. It echoes in their liberation movements, activism, organizations, and conversations across generations. From seasoned leaders to young activists, the ideals of human rights are spoken not as foreign theories, but as if they were part of the Karen people's own cultural inheritance.

But this openness carries a risk. Human rights, though noble in principle, do not arrive at our shore free of ideological baggage. They come wrapped in assumptions, political agendas, and foreign values of civilization mission. The Karen people, in their sincerity and simplicity, have often embraced these ideals without questioning their origins or hidden motives. Those who introduce foreign ideas with superiority often vilify native beliefs, showing no regard for how they have sustained communities and provided solace for millennia. This openness has made the Karen people vulnerable to exploitation by external forces—organizations, and opportunists—who recognize Karen people's sincerity yet manipulate it for their own ends.

What began as a heartfelt embrace of universal values has sometimes become a tool for external agendas—agendas that neither align with the Karen people's long-term freedom nor their short-term well-being, much less their dignity.

The path forward requires the Karen people to safeguard their moral clarity with critical awareness. Human rights can be a guiding principle, but not as blind slogans or borrowed tools. These ideals must be reshaped to align with the Kawthoolei's vision—integrated into our moral standard to elevate our cultural foundations. Only then can this higher claim truly serve the cause of dignity, freedom, and self-determination.

A YOKE ON THE STATE

In the border community, nearly every organizational goal, objective, and mission is adorned with the label of 'human rights,' as if invoking the phrase alone grants credibility or moral high ground. Rights to education, healthcare, and livelihoods are meaningful only when the state has the capacity to uphold them; otherwise, they remain idealistic aspirations. This heavy burden falls on a nascent state—more a spirit than a structured entity—lacking stable revenue and reliant on the fragile scaffolding of revolutionary armed organizations struggling to maintain order.

Placing such a yoke on this precarious framework does little more than strain an already burdened entity—expecting too much from a weary parent, impoverished yet striving to provide with whatever meager means remain is only hurtful. Even in wealthy nations, where both material and human resources are abundant, though not unlimited, such sweeping demands on the state would be met with scrutiny and caution.

LIBERALISM THRIVES WHEN GROUNDED IN CONTEXT

Gender rights, children's rights, and environmental rights can hardly be secured in a climate of political instability. When the state fails to guarantee law and order, our young girls remain vulnerable to abuse—along with children, women, and men alike. Basic human rights require a functioning judicial system, sound politics, and well-crafted policies to safeguard human dignity—

not the unchecked proliferation of NGOs at the expense of state institutions. Prolonged dependency of humanitarian politics is not only a temporary opioid for political problems; it also stifles the human spirit.

Liberalism, by its very nature, seeks to *constrain* the state. Its purpose is to limit state power, ensuring that individual freedoms act as a counterbalance to authority. These principles flourish in nations with robust institutions, clear separation of powers, and a respect to the rule of law—contexts predominantly found in Western nations, where liberalism coexists with strong state structures capable of maintaining order and justice.

Many of our educated Karen individuals have been shaped by liberal education in these settings, absorbing ideals tailored to societies with centuries of institutional stability. However, upon returning, a small but vocal segment often attempts to *transplant* these ideals directly into our fragmented context—a setting where no coherent state exists, only a patchwork of de facto authorities competing for power. In such an environment, liberalism cannot function as a moderating force. Instead, it risks becoming a destabilizing agent, amplifying division rather than fostering cohesion.

State-building involves building state institutions—it is a pragmatic and context-sensitive process of constructing authority, governance, institutions, and order where little or none exists. It demands patience, resilience, and an acute understanding of local realities.

Nation-building, on the other hand, bringing people together to build a nation, transcends political theories altogether. It is not about systems or slogans; it is about unifying a people under shared values, collective identity, and a sense of purpose. It is an instinctive, moral duty—a deeply human responsibility to protect, uplift, and empower one's own people before engaging with others with dignity and decency. When a nation is strong and state institutions are well-functioning, liberalism may flourish.

When treated as an *ideology* rather than a set of *adaptable principles*, liberalism becomes as dangerous and absurd as any other rigid doctrine. It harms community yet not benefits individual liberty. National liberation and state-building must come *first* to have a stable society before that society improves. Above all else, building a cohesive nation takes priority to achieve social cohesion, strong communities, and unity among citizens. Only when there is a foundation—a functioning state with clear authority and robust institutions—can liberalism play its role as a moderating and balancing force. Otherwise, neither of national liberation nor individual liberty may ever come.

Promoting liberalism in Kawthoolei should reflect local values and must contribute to national liberty, virtue, and progress.

SawLah@Photography 2022

SawLah@Photography 2023

Chapter 4

On Democracy

If the virtue of democracy lies in the power of the numerical majority, it becomes ill-suited for Burma, where noisy, aggressive factions dominate the discourse, drowning out more numerous but quiet voices.

The tantalizing promise of democracy flickered briefly during the short-lived period of semi-democracy under military dominant the 2008 Constitution in the second decade of the 21st century. In this brief window, the country experienced the good, the bad, and the ugly of democratic governance. Unprecedented economic development unfolded within a decade, fueled by international aid and diplomatic support. Yet, this progress came at a cost: it legitimized the central government's oppression of ethnic armed resistance. The international community downgraded these groups to mere rebels, treating them as enemies of the state and obstacles to national progress. Democracy demanded they ceasefire—or cease to exist.

Tocqueville and John Stuart Mill warned of the tyranny of the majority, a persistent threat even in well-meaning democracies. Sir Roger Scruton echoed this caution succinctly: "Majority opinion may be wrong; majority desires may be wicked; majority strength may be dangerous" (Scruton, 2019). Democracy, hailed as the pinnacle of fairness, equality, and collective decision-making, reveals its flaws when put into practice.

Democracy is only as strong and virtuous as the people who uphold it. In the second decade of the 21st century, Burma briefly flirted with democracy. It was during this so-called democratic dawn that one of its darkest chapters unfolded. The genocide against the Rohingya began under civilian rule—initially described by the United States in 2017 as a "textbook example of ethnic cleansing" and later, on March 21, 2022, formally recognized as genocide. The once-revered democracy icon also fell from international grace. When she was later detained in 2021 by the military she had propped up, few voices abroad rose in her defense.

In a land where Buddhism is venerated, Burmese Buddhist nationalists intensified the suffering of over three-quarters of a million displaced people, wielding social media as a weapon to spread hatred. In the digital age, what happens online is both public and permanent—racism, once confined to whispers, is now immortalized.

Burma's long-awaited democracy, once a beacon of hope, now stands tarnished—stained not only by its failure to protect the vulnerable but by its complicity in their suffering.

Democracy flourishes on a sound constitution, institutions, an engaged citizenry, and a commitment to democratic norms among the elite. In the U.S.A., these pillars form a formidable barrier against the prospect of a coup. Even if a fanatic president were to reject electoral results and attempt such an act, the discipline of the U.S. military and the steadfast adherence to democratic principles by military leaders and the broader establishment would prevent it. The deeply ingrained respect for democratic norms serves as a safeguard, ensuring that even in times of crisis, the democratic order endures.

In both principle and practice, the U.S. is not a pure or a direct democracy. The U.S. president is not directly elected by the people. The framers of the Constitution, wary of the volatility of direct democracy, created the Electoral College—a system where citizens vote for electors who then select the president. This structure is less an expression of pure democracy and more an embodiment of a republic, designed so that cooler heads, as the framers intended, might prevail.

Further distancing itself from direct democracy, the U.S. Supreme Court, one of the government's three branches, is composed of justices who are neither elected by the public nor accountable to them. Nominated by the president and confirmed by the Senate, these justices serve for life, wielding power that can shape the nation for generations. Their rulings influence every facet of American life—economy, social norms, political policies. In many respects, these unelected officials act as de facto rulers, their decisions capable of overruling even the president. This lifetime tenure, designed to ensure impartiality and continuity, also concentrates immense authority in the hands of a few, far removed from democratic oversight.

Yet, it may be this concentration of unelected power that keeps the U.S. stable. The Supreme Court, despite its detachment from democratic processes, retains the public's trust. When the Court speaks, the nation listens, even when the rulings are contentious. This deference to the Court's authority is particularly striking, given its occasional forays into the political arena, including elections.

The 2000 U.S. presidential election serves as a stark example. Democrat Al Gore won the popular vote, but a contested count in a single state led the Supreme Court to intervene, ultimately awarding the presidency to George W. Bush, despite Gore's majority. This episode echoes Thailand's 2023 election, where Pita Limjaroenrat and the Move Forward Party secured the popular vote, yet governance was decided not by the people, but by a select elite and a monarchy-aligned conservative establishment, overriding the democratic mandate.

History offers a grim reminder: many authoritarian leaders ascend not through violence but through the democratic processes they later undermine. The extreme case of Nazi Germany, where Adolf Hitler rose to power through the ballot box, is often cited as a warning. Yet closer to home, we find equally telling examples. With tight media control, political suppression, and legal measures to weaken opposition, Malaysia's Mahathir Mohamad and Singapore's Lee Kuan Yew, both regarded as authoritarian in their governance, were elected through democratic means. Indian Prime Minister Indira Gandhi rose to power through democratic means, but when her leadership was threatened by political and legal challenges, she declared a state of emergency, unleashing a wave of repression against the opposition to consolidate her authority.

These leaders, though different in their methods and legacies, underscore a paradox at the heart of democracy: the electorate's power to choose leaders who, once in office, may dismantle the freedoms that brought them to power. It is a reminder that while democracy is a safeguard against tyranny, it is not invulnerable to being used as a gateway to it. Or a country needs to be ruled by a stable few than the popular masses.

The U.S. democracy presents itself as a vibrant system, with election campaigns stretching over months, turning the political process into a spectacle of engagement and participation. Yet beneath this facade, American politics is increasingly divisive, angry, and steeped in a pervasive sense of disillusionment. Every issue, no matter how mundane, is politicized, and the atmosphere becomes charged with sensitivity. In professional settings—whether in workplaces or service offices—politics is often treated with the same caution as religion, a private matter best left unspoken to avoid conflict. This reflects a deeper undercurrent in American society, where the topics meant to unite and advance public discourse are now sources of tension and division.

In Burma, those seeking political solutions lean toward a diluted power structure, where no single strong leader exists, hoping that by dispersing authority, they can stave off the rise of authoritarianism. The vision of a federal democracy—a democratic federal Burma—has become a beacon for many. Yet, in the pursuit of weakening centralized power, there is a danger of creating a leadership so fragmented and feeble that it cannot function effectively. What Burma may truly need is not a dilution of power, but a strong, charismatic, capable leadership—one that is firm enough to guide the nation with conviction yet wise enough to listen, bridging divides rather than deepening them with weak leadership. A strong leader could provide the coherence necessary to unite diverse voices in a federal structure, balancing strength with inclusivity.

Democracy may still be a distant hope for Burma, even if the current military dictatorship toppled. The deep-seated divisions and widespread distrust in democratic institutions will not simply vanish with the fall of a single regime. The journey to true democracy demands far more than the absence of dictatorship; it requires a radical transformation of the political culture—a process that may take far longer than a generation.

Burma's future might necessitate an interim period of strong, principled leadership, rather than ideological or chasing the West or the Red, someone capable of uniting the country and laying the groundwork for a more inclusive and resilient democracy where each group participates with its own autonomy. Perhaps what Burma needs is another leader like Aung San, but one who is both genuinely committed to bringing together the diverse peoples of Burma and who has the longevity to see this vision through. This leader must not only inspire but also earn the trust needed to navigate the complexities of building a democratic future from the fractured present. First of all, that leader has yet to be born if there is a peaceful and prosperous union to exist.

Burma Could Have Been Indonesia

Burma and Indonesia, despite their strikingly similar political trajectories in the later part of the 20th century, have diverged sharply in their modern outcomes. Both nations experienced prolonged authoritarian rule—Burma under authoritarian Generals Nay Win and Than Shwe, and Indonesia under Sukarno and Suharto. Burma, particularly under Than Shwe, modeled its infamous 2008 Constitution after Indonesia's military-guided *disciplined democracy*, seeking to maintain military control while appearing democratic. Democratic Republic of Singapore's Lee Kwan Yew had a pragmatic authoritarian taste himself and advised Gen. Nay Win to create a military-controlled system like Indonesia's, which at the time enjoyed sustained economic growth and political stability under Suharto's rule (1967-98). The 2008 Constitution, crafted during Than Shwe's reign, was a strategic move to legitimize the military's role as the "sole guardian of the nation," absolving its leaders of accountability.

After 1989, Than Shwe consolidated military rule in Burma with minimal opposition, reinforcing his grip through the narrative of "135 official ethnic groups." This classic divide-and-rule politically crafted myth was designed to project an illusion of military controlled unity within Burma's highly diverse population, mimicking Indonesia's perceived success in maintaining stability despite its vast diversity. Indonesia, with over 18,000 islands and more than 700 languages, achieved national cohesion and political stability under military rule.

In contrast, Burma's "135-ethnic" claim lacks credible surveys or census data, yet academics and researchers—including some Karen scholars who dedicated years to advanced studies—have uncritically adopted this narrative. By accepting this framework, they unwittingly perpetuate a politically constructed myth that bolsters military control. This adoption often stems from convenience, as Burma remains under-studied globally, with most university classrooms barely acknowledging its details. Burma/Myanmar is obscurely unknown to the world.

Today, Indonesia enjoys a relatively free democracy, boasting a trillion-dollar GDP (as of 2024) and surpassing regional neighbors in political freedom. According to Freedom House, Indonesia's freedom index (57) is higher than both Malaysia (53) and Thailand (36). Meanwhile, Thailand, despite its constitutional monarchy since 1932 and its frequent military coups, has seen its political freedom lag behind Indonesia. Once neck-and-neck in GDP growth with Thailand, Indonesia's economy surged following the 1998 Asian Financial Crisis and now stands nearly three times larger than Thailand's: Indonesia with $1.319 trillion USD in 2022 compared to Thailand's $495 billion USD, tripled its measurable growth at top five in Asia.

Burma, on the other hand, has been trapped in a cycle of dictatorship, civil wars, and democratic resistance now at the bottom in the regional neighbors with among the highest fragility index. While the military has remained highly organized, drawing on a feudal mindset of Burmese supremacy, democratic movements in Burma have often been fragmented and overly ideological hence lacking pragmatism. The military has often shown tactical flexibility, striking deals with ethnic armed groups, while democratic forces, though brave, have been less organized and more idealistic, often projecting a Western-style freedom narrative to gain support from Western powers. However, these movements have mostly attracted non-state actors and NGOs, whose sympathy has not translated into meaningful political or economic support, whereas the reality of the international system works on state-to-state relations based on sovereignty, not sympathy, determines the fate of nations.

NATION BUILDING BEFORE DEMOCRACY

Democracy thrives only when the foundation of nation-building is firmly laid. A cohesive national identity, robust institutions, and a shared sense of purpose are not mere prerequisites but the very scaffolding upon which democracy stands. Where political, social, and economic frameworks are unaligned, democratic processes falter, unable to bridge the divides of a fragmented society. Representation, accountability, and the rule of law cannot flourish in the absence of unity, trust, and collective responsibility.

American democracy may appear boisterous and fragile, yet its underlying structure is remarkably resilient. The United States spans diverse geographies and climates, from the Atlantic to the Pacific, from the Arctic landscapes of Alaska to the tropical shores of Florida. Despite these variations, its cities and towns share a striking uniformity in culture and organization, with franchise-like landscapes—McDonald's and similar brands serving as a kind of national identity. Most products and services are universally available with modern supply management, unified under a market-driven system and organized within institutions, with only slight variations across states. English functions as an unofficial yet national language, further unifying this vast and diverse country under a common linguistic thread.

American democracy, coupled with federalism, is often held as an ideal. This system thrives on a shared respect for the Constitution, which serves as the bedrock of governance with a check and balance system. Interestingly, however, the U.S.'s Constitution makes no mention of the word "democracy," a remarkable omission for a system so deeply associated with the concept.

Democracy, in its purest form, is not merely a system of governance but a reflection of a nation's soul—a collective expression of its character. Without a shared national ethos, democracy becomes a hollow shell, vulnerable to the winds of division and strife. It is the binding force of common values, a sense of belonging to something greater than the sum of individual parts, that allows democratic institutions to thrive. In the absence of this unifying spirit, the democratic process can unravel, giving way to factionalism, where the cacophony of competing interests drowns out the voices of reason and compromise. A nation without a cohesive identity lacks the moral compass necessary to navigate the complexities of self-governance, leaving democracy to flounder in the mire of discord. Thus, the endurance of democracy depends not only on laws and institutions but on the strength of the national character that underpins them, for it is this character that breathes life into the ideals of liberty, justice, and collective responsibility.

The rhetoric of federal democracy in Burma has garnered distrust, both in principle and practice, due to its lack of sincerity and effectiveness. The vision of a future Burmese federalism is built on the outdated assumption that unity must be forged through associations with immediate neighbors. Yet, the world has changed so profoundly and rapidly that this assumption now seems obsolete. Consider the computer that composed these words—a device conceived in California, assembled in China, with a microchip made in Taiwan using lithography tools crafted in the Netherlands—all made possible by a global supply chain that spans countless nations across the vast Pacific Ocean. This modern reality illustrates that collaboration and interdependence are no longer confined by geography. So why persist in the notion of unity with neighbors who share more history of conflict than cooperation? In an era where global networks and alliances extend across continents, the insistence on a federal structure bound by proximity appears less like progress and more like an attachment to a past that no longer serves the future.

The two-party system in the United States has deepened a divide that increasingly resembles a racial-religious schism, with political beliefs becoming almost tribal in nature. Each side paints the other as villains, both claiming to hold the moral high ground, embodying practicality, and championing humanity. This polarization has turned democracy into a battleground. The essence of democratic discourse—dialogue, debate, and mutual respect—has been eroded, as each side becomes more entrenched in its own righteousness, leaving little room for the collaborative spirit that democracy requires to thrive. What thrives in the United States may not survive in Burma—and it did not—given the vastly different underlying foundations.

THE KAREN CAUSE AND THE FAILURE OF DEMOCRATIC ENGAGEMENT

Democratic practice, though imperfect, remains the best model for being responsive to the public will. However, the Karen armed struggle and political leadership face a more critical challenge: a lack of genuine democratic engagement. The future of the Karen liberation movement depends not on outdated slogans but on whether organizational leaders can give political leadership, realigning with the broader aspirations of the Karen community.

The KNU's current "Big-Five" model, a relic of China's early Politburo, relies on internal elections within the party, creating a widening gap between those in power and the people they claim to represent. As a result, popular interest has waned, support has eroded, and criticism has mounted, compounded by questions of integrity. Doubt and distrust are spreading, with many viewing the leadership as lacking the diplomatic skill, charisma, and political acumen needed to advance the movement—both among the Karens in Burma and the millions of Karen in the diaspora, spread across Thailand, Malaysia, Singapore, and countries in East Asian and in the West.

There is a disconnect in the model. Even in authoritarian China, where the Communist Party maintains strict control, local citizens have elected village leaders since the 1980s. The adoption of the Organic Law of Village Committees in 1998 gave rural communities the right to elect leaders every three years. These local officials, though tightly overseen by the Party, are held accountable to the people they serve, fostering a degree of responsiveness and trust, a political structure rarely recognized by outside of China. This approach has helped the CCP maintain legitimacy by prioritizing economic stability and prosperity.

The Karen political leadership's failure to evolve from the outdated "big-five" model is more than a structural issue—it risks alienating the population it is meant to lead. Leadership that disconnects from public sentiment operates on borrowed time. Without adaptation, the movement drifts towards isolation and collapse. The leadership must embrace a more inclusive, responsive approach, or it will soon find itself without the popular support it needs to survive. To remain relevant, they must evolve—or face irrelevance and eventual demise. Considering their place of residence and attachment to the people, this urgency may hold little significance for them.

Successful leadership in a bloody revolution requires a balance of both fear, and trust. Without either, questions abound, and doubts linger. While intellectuals and commentators, distasteful to strong leadership, may endlessly debate the correct path, the ultimate course of action can only be validated once the goal is achieved. And without support of the public, no path can lead to victory. Unconditional loyalty and unwavering support can create unity that leads to victories, as seen with the Arakan Army and the global solidarity of the Arakan people. When the public trusts a leadership's vision, they are willing to sacrifice immediate comforts for the promise of long-term liberation. This places a heavy burden on leaders, who must navigate public sentiment carefully, even in the absence of elections or direct feedback. Leadership incapable of commanding both fear and trust may find temporary solace but risks stagnation, indecision, and eventual irrelevance.

Focusing exclusively on alliances and coalitions, while neglecting the immediate support of its people—the Karen people, one of the most populous people of Burma—has not proven a winning strategy for the movement. Relying on coalitions and expecting others to fight for your freedom is both dishonest and shortsighted. Ignoring your immediate base weakens the movement at its core. Armed movements in the Kachin, Shan, and Arakan regions underscore the importance of securing local support as the foundation for any successful liberation effort.

Historically, the Karen people have played a pivotal role in Burma's political landscape, providing leadership and military training to various ethnic armed movements. However, the current political leadership faces widespread distrust, accused of compromised moral integrity and an inability to lead effectively. What was once a unifying force is now seen as fragmented and lacking the vision needed to guide the Karen people in their ongoing struggle for autonomy and recognition.

DEMOCRATIC PEACE THEORY

In international relations, the Democratic Peace Theory posits that democratic nations are less likely to go to war with one another. This idea is not rooted solely in the inherent value of democracy but in the principles and values that democratic systems tend to uphold. Democracies are open societies where war is seen as a last resort, pursued only after all peaceful avenues have been explored. Conflicts between nations often stem from infringements on dignity and a lack of mutual respect—values that democratic systems are more likely to nurture.

Democratic nations foster mutual respect and refrain from undermining the dignity of others. They encourage values like mutual cooperation and open competition, where differing ideas are freely debated, appealing to intrinsic human morality even when populist sentiments dominate.

The Democratic Peace Theory is grounded in three fundamental points:

1. *Shared Norms and Values*: Democracies share norms of conflict resolution, respect for human rights, and political transparency, naturally discouraging aggression between them.
2. *Public Accountability*: In democratic systems, leaders are accountable to the public, making war an unattractive option due to its unpredictability and high cost, which could alienate voters.

3. *Institutional Constraints:* Democratic governments operate within systems of checks and balances, which serve as safeguards against unilateral decisions to engage in war. These institutional constraints require a rigorous process before conflict can be initiated, reducing the likelihood of war.

This framework suggests that democratic governance promotes peaceful interactions and creates an environment where war is less likely, particularly between democracies.

These principles are crucial to first flourish among the nations in Burma if they aspire to American federal democracy. In the United States, every state operates under a republic democratic government. Having an equal political system makes coming together possible.

POLITICAL ECONOMY IN AUTHORITARIAN RULE

In political economy, the rise of East Asian economies has challenged the traditional belief that democracy is essential for economic success. Japan, South Korea, Taiwan, Singapore, and China demonstrate that economic growth can flourish under non-democratic or authoritarian systems.

South Korea and Taiwan, once governed by authoritarian rule, laid their economic foundations under strong state control before transitioning into full-fledged multiparty democracies. Today, they arguably have more stable political frameworks than democracies like the U.S., where the two-party system often breeds volatility and polarization.

However, one-party or authoritarian systems can become unresponsive to market demands and public needs if leaders fail to remain attentive. Conversely, a strong authoritarian state—when led by responsive and strategic leadership—can be highly agile, swiftly adapting policies to shifting economic and geopolitical conditions.

Democratic nations can falter economically because the constant fighting on ideas leads to fragmentation and slower decision-making on critical and time-sensitive policies. In democracies like India and Brazil, vibrant political debate often delays decisive action, complicating efforts to sustain rapid economic growth. This political fragmentation weakens social cohesion, a key element for economic vitality. When public opinion is divided, trust in institutions erodes, making it difficult to implement collective decisions. In contrast, authoritarian regimes can swiftly enforce unified policies, sidestepping the delays and compromises that democratic processes often require. This top-down control fosters stability and predictability, creating conditions for economic activities to flourish.

While democracy thrives on open debate and competition, it struggles to balance these freedoms with the need for swift, cohesive economic strategy. Centralized authoritarian governments, free from the gridlock of democratic processes, often achieve this balance more efficiently.

China's electric vehicle (EV) infrastructure exemplifies this advantage. With the world's largest EV charging network, China has rapidly expanded coverage to meet soaring demand, supported by robust infrastructure development. Its one-party system enables swift, top-down decisions, such as nationwide charging station rollouts—demonstrating the speed and decisiveness of centralized governance.

By contrast, the U.S. lags behind, with China boasting 4 million EV charging stations compared to just 160,000 in the U.S. as of 2023—a stark contrast despite America's efforts and rhetoric.

LEADERSHIP OVER SYSTEM: THE KEY TO KAWTHOOLEI'S FUTURE

Most political science studies focus on systems and structures. But good leaders often outperform even the best-designed systems. The character and spirit of the people matter more than institutional design—or the absence of it.

At the beginning, Kawthoolei may not need a full-fledged direct democracy to thrive, but rather a representative stabilizer. The democratic practice of elections is not only costly but also depends on an established political and institutional culture—factors that may struggle to take root without first securing stability. Instead, Kawthoolei could benefit from a responsive republic, Kawthoolei Republic, with a form of representative democracy, provided its leaders possess the vision, dignity, and political acumen to guide the nation with strength and purpose.

The election process itself is highly resource-intensive, demanding careful planning, skilled personnel, and significant investments in census on citizenship, voter registration, polling stations, security, and post-election analysis, and dignity of the election mechanism and public trust in the process. Given these challenges, a full democracy with frequent elections may not be essential. Effective governance can be achieved through a more streamlined system that emphasizes responsive leadership without the constant burden of electoral cycles.

Ultimately, Kawthoolei's future will rest more on the quality of its leadership than on the particular system it adopts. While structures matter, it is the integrity, vision, and competence of those in power that truly shape a nation's destiny. Leaders who are wise, responsive, and able to unite the people will move the nation forward, regardless of the framework in place. Rather than rigid ideology, Kawthoolei's long-term success will depend on the quality of its leadership—and, of course, the quality of Kawthoolei people.

TOWARD A NEW SOCIETY

If Burma is to embrace democracy—a genuine democracy—with a flourishing multicultural society with a vibrant multi-party electoral system that accommodates every individual with mutual respect, two fundamental conditions must be met:

First, the complete dismantling of the Myanmar Tatmadaw (the Burmese military) is essential. This entity must be officially declared and recognized globally as a criminal organization, much like the Nazi Army (Wehrmacht) and the paramilitary SS (Schutzstaffel) were after World War II, or how Japan's Imperial Army was disbanded and demobilized. The Burma Tatmadaw, after all, was born under the shadow of the Japanese fascist army during WWII and is now widely referred to by democratic movements as "Pat-sit sit tat," meaning the fascist army. Until it is abolished and held accountable for its crimes, any true democratic progress will be obstructed.

Second, the symbolism—the stamps, the seals, the statues, the anthem—that props up domination and embodies the Burmese psyche and old regime must all be obliterated. This includes the three towering statues claimed as Burmese kings—A-Naw-Ra-hta, Ba-Yint-Naung, and A-Long-Payaa—who supposedly founded the three major dynasties. These statues, much like Saddam Hussein's statue in 2004, must be pulled to the ground and crumbled into pieces, as they represent an oppressive past. Recently, Bangladesh dismantled statues of its founding father Sheikh Mujibur Rahman, symbolically ending his legacy's hold on the nation. The three stupas stand as projection of lies, insults, and intimidation toward the country's diverse population. The country's name itself, "Burma" or "Myanmar," which symbolizes Burmese domination, must be changed—a proposal non-Burman ethnic leaders have alluded to on multiple occasions. The state seals with two lion serjeants (mythical Manuthiha), emblems that represent only Burmese (Barmans), and flags rectified by Tatmadaw, national anthem that represent the old regime must be replaced with new symbols that reflect a fresh spirit of unity and respect for human dignity.

Before WWII, the German national anthem included the lines "*Germany, Germany above all, above all in the world, when it always, for protection and defense, brotherly stands together*" in the first stanza, and "*Unity and justice and freedom for the German Fatherland! After these let us all strive, brotherly with heart and hand!*" in the third stanza. However, after the war, only the third stanza was legally retained as the national anthem, symbolizing a deliberate shift away from nationalist sentiment toward the ideals of unity, justice, and freedom. Even in a culturally homogenous country like Germany, with its shared language, history, intellectual tradition, and ethical values, this change was made to embrace a new identity and set of values for the future.

Unless these two minimal conditions are met, hold on democracy, Burma will remain a land of curses, bound in perpetual conflict, a country at war with itself, marked by an inherent disrespect for human life and dignity. One ethnic elite's desire to dominate the whole country will continue to plague the land. Unless the Burmese democratic forces have the courage to take these bold steps toward creating a truly new country, staying together is accepting old abuse. Democracy built on the crumbling foundations of the old regime, upheld by the same broken system, outdated institutions, feudal psyche, flawed constitution, and hollow symbolism, is destined to fail—just as February 1, 2021, so brutally proved. The past cannot birth a future of freedom; it only drags the nation back into the same cycle of repression and betrayal.

Chapter 5

On Nationalism

In the quiet resolve of Kawthoolei's districts, in the steadfast march of those who defend its land, and in the whispered prayers of elders longing for justice, the spirit of Kawthoolei endures. It lives in the hands that rebuild, the voices that teach, and the hearts that refuse to forget.

Often mischaracterized as mere nationalism, Kawthoolei is perceived as a political pursuit. Let truth find the light. It was born from a deeper struggle for liberation—a noble quest to restore the virtues of its people and the dignity of their ancestral homeland, a land that has endured beyond the weight of history.

In the history of the Karen armed struggle for liberation, prevailing political ideologies such as socialism and communism briefly influenced the revolution. Yet, while parallel movements like the once-mighty Burma Communist Party (BCP) crumbled with the shifting tides of global geopolitics and the withdrawal of external support the late 80s, the Karen struggle endured. This resilience was rooted in nationalism—a bond uniting all Karen people, from farmers to elites. For that, at its 9th Congress in September 1974, the KNU reaffirmed this foundation, declaring *the revolution to be supported by farmers, workers, elite educated, and every stratum of Karen society*. Without this national unity, the struggle would have long since faded into obscured history.

Nationalism: "The desire by a group of people who share the same ethnic group, culture, language, etc. to form an independent country." [Oxford Learner Dictionary, 2025]

NATIONALISM VS. PROVINCIALISM

Nationalism is the pursuit of a collective destiny—an assertion of sovereignty that unites a people through shared purpose and vision. It is expansive, forward-looking, and rooted in the belief that a nation can shape its own fate.

Provincialism or parochialism, by contrast, is insular and self-limiting. It reduces identity to tribal loyalties, regional factions, and narrow self-interest. It prioritizes immediate, familiar circles over the broader national good, fragmenting a people who might otherwise rise together.

At its core, nationalism weaves together two inseparable threads: sentiment and identity. Sentiment is the emotional bond one shares with the nation—a connection so profound that it inspires dedication and sacrifice, even for those one may never meet but considers kin. It means that though I reside in the Taw-Oo mountains of Northern Kawthoolei, I see myself reflected in the lives of those in Bleat-Dawai's southern edge. We speak the same mother tongue, sing the same songs, and share the same values, folklore, and traditions—a unity that transcends geography. A Karen man in the Irrawaddy Delta may feel the same sentiment as a Karen in Taw-Oo, willing to sacrifice for the cause of national liberation, because both are bound by a common identity.

Identity, on the other hand, defines how one perceives themselves in the global arena. At an international airport, it is not wealth or family ties that determine one's place, but the passport they carry—the pride of declaring themselves a citizen of a nation. It is this shared national identity, rather than individual achievements, that binds people together. Nationalism, therefore, is both potent and contentious—it urges individuals to look beyond themselves and envision a future that honors a collective past.

Yet nationalism is not an automatic inheritance; it must be nurtured. For some Karen, identity is still tied to locality—*"I am from Thu-Kay-Therr," "I am from Taw-Oo," "I am from Bleat-Dawai."* This mindset, while natural, can breed parochialism when it limits one's concern to their immediate region, rather than the nation as a whole. The sentiment of *"I will help only those from Duu-Tha-Htu"* illustrates this limitation. True nationalism transcends these narrow affiliations, fostering a greater sense of belonging. It calls for individuals to devote themselves to a collective cause. *"I never knew you, my love, but I will die for you and your future generations—for, you are my nation."*

A HISTORICAL REFLECTION FROM THE WEST

Modern nationalism traces its roots to the Enlightenment, a movement that championed logic, reason, and the idea of a common humanity beyond class privilege. This intellectual fervor helped ignite the French Revolution, where revolutionaries sought to forge a new national identity that celebrated individual dignity. Before this awakening, identity was tied to locality and class—one would say, *"I am the son of Duke Satan"* or *"I hail from Yonder."* Nationalism shattered these parochial ties, urging individuals to see themselves as part of a greater whole.

Compared to the English and the French, the Germans were latecomers to national consciousness. Their disunity persisted for centuries, resembling the fragmentation among Karen armed groups today. In 1766, Imperial Privy Councillor Friedrich Carl von Moser posed a critical question: *"What are the Germans?"* His response was striking:

> "For centuries, we have been a puzzle of political constitution, a prey of our neighbors, an object of their scorn. Disunited among ourselves, we are weak from division, strong enough only to harm ourselves, powerless to save ourselves. We are insensitive to the honor of our name, indifferent to the glory of our laws, envious of our rulers, distrusting one another, inconsistent about principles, coercive in enforcing them—a great but despised people; a potentially happy but lamentably unfortunate one." *(The Course of German Nationalism, Hagen Schulze)*

This lamentation echoes a reality that feels all too familiar.

Like the Germans of Moser's time, the Karen people remain fragmented, weakened by internal strife, and vulnerable to external forces. We are often indifferent to the honor of our heritage, inconsistent in our principles, and quick to distrust one another. Weak enough to harm ourselves, yet too divided to secure our own future—we are a people rich in potential but burdened by misfortune.

The challenge is real, the hope is near, too. Our history is not just a record of struggle but a testament to resilience. If we are willing, we can mend the nation.

IDEOLOGY WITH NO MASTER TEACHER

While many thinkers have theorized about nationalism, it did not originate from an ideology crafted through deliberate intellectual design, like socialism or liberalism, but rather from an instinctive drive. With no specific ideological founder, it emerged naturally, driven by the forces of history and the human need for belonging.

Two principal schools of thought have emerged: one views nationalism as a social construct, while the other considers it to be rooted in primordial nature.

CONSTRUCTIVISM VS. PRIMORDIALISM

Humanity did not live in caves forever but came out to the open world and built structures artificially and organized communities with shared commonality. Nationalism, often described as an *imagined community*, and the process of nation-building are indeed social constructs, a deliberate effort. Yet, a nation cannot simply materialize from thin air, nor can it lie dormant in some primordial state, waiting to be awakened. It demands tangible foundations—linguistic affinities that connect hearts through a common tongue, moral traditions that bind people through shared values, and territorial roots that ground them in a specific place. A nation is built through shared struggles, where challenges strengthen a common sense of purpose. Out of ancient connections, people find belonging; from existing communities, they form a larger one. Rooted in ancestral ties and socially constructed bonds, nations are forged.

But these alone are not enough. A nation must also be woven together by the threads of everyday life—by the food that nurtures, the music that moves the soul, and the clothing that adores its people. These symbols, seemingly mundane, are powerful markers of identity. They transform an abstract idea into something real and lived. It is in these concrete elements that the imagined community becomes more than just an idea—it becomes a living, breathing reality, capable of uniting diverse peoples under a common banner.

KAREN NATIONALISM AND WAR IN MODERN BURMA

In the beginning, Karen national leaders under British rule believed they could forge a common destiny with all of Burma, envisioning an imagined community that included everyone. In the first official Karen New Year message, the leaders addressed the Karen people, diplomatically saying:
> "Progressive in thinking, constructive in planning, and courageous in living, we can share responsibility with other communities for the making of Burma a united people. Our conviction is that our two million Karen have a significant part to play in Burma's destiny" (1938, the First Official Karen New Year Message).

Together, the creation of the official Karen New Year, National Flag, and National Anthem marked the tangible awakening of Karen nationalism, yet a shared destiny.

Even after Burma gained independence in 1948, The Karen Rifles, Karen professional armed groups, brave and professional as they were, under Karen leadership fought alongside Burma's central government suppressing communist insurgencies and other formidable rebellions. However, U Nu and Burmese nationalist elites—under fear and distrust and jealousy—made a grave mistake in 1949 when they turned their guns on the Karens, igniting a full-scale Karen liberation movement calling for a separate state. Our ancestors had struggled to build a shared destiny and a shared belonging, but that vision was ultimately shattered. Some people, many Karens, are dreaming of rebuilding that shattered dream and yet downplay the national unity of the Karen people in the liberation movement.

A Glimpse into the Historical Context

Historian Ryan Chapman notes that Nationalism is often overlooked, yet it remains one of the most powerful forces shaping the modern world. Over the past century, its influence has become so deeply embedded in society that it is rarely questioned—taken for granted as an inevitable part of human organization. John Mearsheimer, a prominent American political scientist and theorist of international relations, has voiced similar observations.

In the 20th and 21st centuries, nationalism achieved unprecedented political success. The aftermath of World War II and the collapse of the Soviet Union marked its rise as the dominant global ideology. This ascent was neither sudden nor accidental but the culmination of long historical processes that reshaped the world.

In *Nations and Nationalism*, Ernest Gellner defines nationalism as a political principle that insists on the alignment between political and national units. He argues that nationalism is not the awakening of nations to self-consciousness; rather, it *creates* nations where they did not previously exist. By fostering a shared identity and common culture—often imposed from above through state institutions—nationalism constructs and perpetuates the very idea of a nation.

The concept of the nation, with its symbols—the flag, the people, the territory, the anthem—has defined modern political structures. The United Nations stands as a testament to this evolution, embodying the nation-state as the foundation of international relations. Yet, at the vast expense of world political history, the idea of nation is a recent phenomenon. The world was not always divided into neatly defined nation-states; this political form only gained momentum in the 18th, 19th, and 20th centuries.

Before the advent of nations, political societies were often tied to rulers rather than land or people. Borders were fluid, and sovereignty was linked to dynasties, not national identity. Take China, a country now synonymous with nationalism. Two millennia ago, it was not a nation-state but a vast civilizational sphere of influence, with loosely governed frontier regions maintaining their own systems. The idea of China as a single, centralized entity with fixed borders did not exist. Instead, its political legitimacy rested on dynastic rule, where the people were subjects, not citizens. When a dynasty fell, it left a political void, but the cultural and civilizational continuity of China remained intact, eventually giving rise to the modern nation-state.

This pattern was not unique to China. Ancient Greece followed a similar trajectory. While the Greeks recognized a shared identity, they did not form a unified nation until the 1820s, when they united against the Ottoman Empire, leading to the establishment of modern Greece in 1830. For much of antiquity, Greece remained fragmented into city-states, often in conflict, uniting only when facing external threats. The idea of nationality developed gradually, often in opposition to the 'other'—outsiders labeled as barbarians. Similarly, the Chinese viewed those beyond their borders as barbarians, seeing themselves as the Middle Kingdom—the center of civilization in a world of chaos.

CONFLICT AND THE FORGING OF NATIONS

National identity is often forged in the fires of conflict. The Hundred Years' War between England and France played a pivotal role in shaping both nations. As historian Robert Tombs notes in *The English and Their History*, France's national identity was still in its infancy when the war began. However, the prolonged struggle against England solidified the sense of French nationhood we recognize today.

Yet, while nationalism has shaped the past, its future remains uncertain. Military alliances like the North Atlantic Treaty Organization (NATO), cultural reintegration through the European Union (EU), and regional integration efforts such as the African Union (AU) and the Association of Southeast Asian Nations (ASEAN) signal a shift toward military, economic, and cultural cooperation that transcends national borders. The rise of global interconnectedness, the blending of cultures through digital platforms, and the expansion of international governance through institutions and laws increasingly challenge the permanence of the nation-state.

This carries profound implications for Kawthoolei. While Kawthoolei as a nation-state may not endure into the 22nd century, in the generation of our great-grandchildren, the *Kawthoolei ideal* must live on—carried forward, preserved, and shared with the world—to the end of time.

BURMANIZATION AS NATION BUILDING

It is cunning, it is effective, yet it is ultimately a failed project.

From at the peak of the British Empire to a crumbling low after WWII, Burma's history illustrates the legacy of a province within a British colony, abruptly left to stand as a nation in 1948. After that for three-quarters of a century, attempts to forcibly weave diverse peoples into a single nation have proven unnatural, especially in a land where the mountains shelter distinct nations, each with its own deep-rooted loyalties. Such efforts defy the very principles of human nature, with attachment to stories embedded in linguistic essence, beliefs, and ways of life. Nationalism, at its core, taps into a primal sense of belonging—a collective identity shaped over centuries by shared history, culture, and struggle.

After taking power in 1962, General Ne Win systematically dismantled all missionary and private schools, enforcing Burmese as the sole language of instruction. Before that, generations of Karen people were able to study in their language until post-ten. But now non-Burmese languages were suppressed, and from the 1960s onward, generations of children were educated primarily in

Burmese, even as they clung to their mother tongues at home. Ne Win's vision of nation-building, with Burmese at its core, proved remarkably effective. Many Karens in the plains and cities underwent a profound cultural transformation—losing their ancestral languages and adopting Burmese identities. A few resist fiercely, as evident in the youth in cities who still speak their mother tongue.

Ne Win's project was so successful that today, many Karens in urban centers are indistinguishable from the Burman majority. They speak like Burmese, act like Burmese, smell like Burmese and, in time, have come to *see* themselves as Burmans. In this transformation, something fundamental has been lost—the humility, simplicity, and moral integrity that once defined Karen identity. Some resisted, sheltering their culture within religious institutions, but many simply faded into assimilation. Burmanization has quietly seeped into the nation's identity, with entertainment in Burmese language serving as its most subtle yet blaring vehicle. In villages where the Karen language once flowed through daily life, the youth now find themselves drawn to the allure of Burmese songs, their melodies drifting through the air like a siren's call, capturing the hearts of the young. Burmese films flicker on screens in modest homes, casting shadows of the city's promiscuous life, another language, another identity, another social values, onto the walls and the mind.

Literature, once written in the familiar script of Karen, is increasingly replaced by the formal strokes of Burmese from schools, as young people begin to read and write in a language that is not their own. This adoption of Burmese culture is not merely a pastime—it is seen as a gateway to a higher status, a sophisticated identity that promises to elevate them above their humble origins. In this quiet revolution, the unique rhythms of Karen's life stories are slowly being overwritten by the dominant narrative. The youth, drawn to what they see as a more refined and cultured existence, begin to turn away from their heritage—implicitly viewing their own indigenous culture as wild and uncivilized.

In the remote heights of Mutraw, where the mountains cradle the ancient ways of the Karen people, the mornings are now filled with the sound of Burmese love songs blasting from speakers. The youth, once rooted in their own language and traditions, are now falling in love in Burmese—captivated not just by the melodies, but by the romantic psyche that these songs carry.

Burmanization destroys the innate spirit that values our mother tongue, our ways of life, our identity, hence our existence. However, it is not an effort to erase the Karen people—it is to be used as a stool to elevate the so-called superior race. Ethnic attire and traditional dances, such as Done Dance or Bamboo Dance, are reduced to spectacles, meant to amuse, to decorate, and to complete the image of Burman supremacy.

THE CAUSE OF ASSIMILATION

Around eighth grade, one of my cousins—who had left our village to study in the city—returned with a language and demeanor that felt unfamiliar. The transformation was striking. A childhood friend, with whom I had shared playground laughter and Sunday school lessons, had become nearly unrecognizable. There was a new, unsettling cunning in their behavior, a willingness to deceive for personal gain. Once tried to trick me into lending money. It felt as if the city had stripped them of their essence, replacing it with something foreign—a painful reminder of how far they had drifted from what we once held in common.

Burma's military-driven nation-building through education is not an isolated phenomenon; it mirrors the tactics of authoritarian regimes worldwide. Under General Ne Win, the government systematically reshaped the country's linguistic landscape, enforcing Burmese as the sole language of instruction. This policy was never just about language—it was about control. By erasing the cultural and linguistic heritage of ethnic minorities, the regime sought to create a uniform, obedient citizenry.

As Noam Chomsky astutely observed, *"The education system is the indoctrination of the young."* In Burma, this indoctrination was carried out with ruthless precision. History was rewritten—every city-state, every dynasty, every landmark was presented as Burmese, belonging to Burmese kings and queens. The contributions of non-Burmese peoples were erased, reducing them to peripheral, insignificant minorities. This narrative remained unchallenged, offering many Burmese a comforting illusion of historical supremacy.

Such policies are not unique to Burma. Many nations have used language standardization as a tool of cultural assimilation. From Italy's unification under a common tongue to the forced suppression of indigenous languages in American schools, history is filled with examples of education wielded as an instrument of control.

In Burma, the impact was profound. The Karen people, once rich in linguistic and cultural traditions, found themselves increasingly absorbed into the dominant Burmese culture. In the cities and plains, they spoke, read, wrote, ate, and behaved like Burmese, their distinct heritage fading under state-sponsored assimilation. Education, rather than fostering intellectual growth, became a tool for erasure—a means to replace Burma's diverse identities with a singular, state-sanctioned narrative.

While our grandparent generation were forced into Burmanization, later generations embraced it. Many Karens became unwitting architects of their own assimilation, taking pride in speaking and learning Burmese, even championing it as their own. As their new identity took root and flourished within them, their true heritage withered. With it, the virtues once embedded in their souls—non-lying, non-bragging, non-stealing, non-aggression—died off into silence, buried beneath a new identity.

SWALLOW ME IF YOU CAN

Assimilation into Burmanization has not gone unchallenged. Many Karen youths in the cities stand firm, actively preserving their language in churches, monasteries, homes, and community spaces, recognizing it as a vital link to their heritage. Their commitment is an act of defiance—a declaration that their cultural identity will not be erased.

My secondary and post-secondary education took place in central government schools, where Burmese was the primary language of instruction. My years at Yangon University and Dagon University deepened my immersion in Burmese literature and urban culture. In the city's dormitories and classrooms, I forged friendships with Burmese students from across the country, sharing rides, meals, travels, studies, laughter—and the inevitable romance, the slow walks, the quiet talks along the campus Main Street. Youthful years shaped experiences, leaving indelible memories. Yet, this immersion did not sever my connection to my heritage; it sharpened my awareness of Burmanization and the relentless pull of assimilation that Karen urban dwellers face. That awareness has only deepened my resolve to safeguard my cultural roots.

I find value in the fact that Burmese is among my native languages. Like many in Myanmar, Burmese once overtook my mother tongue and became my primary language. But I had the privilege of reclaiming my native tongue, ensuring it remains the language I speak with my people. Even when surrounded by those fluent in Burmese, I choose my own language—a quiet and firm stand against assimilation.

Far from diminishing my identity, my Burmese education fortified it, believing that preserving heritage requires conscious and deliberate effort. Resistance to Burmanization—or any form of temptation—is a lifelong endeavor.

As a strategy for both nation-building and state-building of Burma/Myanmar, Burmanization has been effective in many respects, yet too coarse to swallow, sparking bloody resistances. In the end, this approach failed to achieve its intended goals. In the process, Burma itself has failed—irreversibly.

INTERNATIONAL SPORT COMPETITIONS AND NATIONAL CONSCIOUSNESS

Sports competitions play a vital role in shaping national consciousness, particularly in countries with diverse ethnic groups. They provide a unifying platform where people from different backgrounds rally under one flag, setting aside divisions in the spirit of competition. In international events like the Olympics or the World Cup, national pride transcends ethnic divides as victories become collective triumphs. Athletes serve as symbols of unity, their success celebrated by all, reinforcing a shared sense of belonging.

Beyond competition, sports wield soft power in defining national identity. The Myanmar Olympic Committee, founded in 1946 by U Zaw Weik, a Western Pwo Karen, during Burma's time under British rule, was part of a broader effort to assert a common Burmese identity. Events like the Olympics and SEA Games cultivate national unity, where athletes compete under a single flag, overriding ethnic distinctions. Whether Myanmar or Thailand, spectators identify with their national team, not as Kachin from northern Burma or Karen from northern Thailand, but as members of a larger whole. These moments of pride fuel the pursuit of national cohesion— something that forceful policies like Burmanization have struggled to achieve.

In Southeast Asia, the biennial SEA Games serve as a regional stage for friendly competition, stirring unique national sentiments. As Myanmar's athletes compete, people from various ethnic groups—including the Karens—unite under the Burmese flag to cheer them on. At the same time, Karen communities in Thailand stand behind Thailand's athletes, aligning their support with the nation they now call home.

For Myanmar's millions of migrant workers and stateless refugees, this duality runs deep. Abandoned by their homeland yet unrecognized in their adopted country, they watch as Myanmar and Thailand face off in the arena, confronted by the complexity of their own national consciousness. In those moments, allegiances are not automatic—they are chosen. Between the country they left behind and the one that shelters them, their cheers reveal where their hearts truly reside.

Nurturing National Loyalty

How the US and China Cultivate National Allegiance

A successful nation constantly nurtures national loyalty. Throughout the 19th and 20th centuries, nations strengthened themselves by crafting national programs that instilled loyalty, pride, and solidarity among their citizens. The United States, for instance, introduced the Pledge of Allegiance to schools at the turn of these centuries as a means of constructing national unity from a young age.

The United States' Pledge of Allegiance resonates with the ideals of freedom and unity:

> "I pledge allegiance to the flag of the United States of America and to the Republic for which it stands, one nation under God, indivisible, with liberty and justice for all."

This pledge not only celebrates the American spirit of individual liberty but also builds a sense of loyalty to the nation. Yet, it honors the right of those who choose to abstain, reflecting the country's deep respect for personal freedom. Today, forty-seven states require the Pledge of Allegiance to be recited in public schools, though students and staff may opt out.

In a similar vein, China's educational system, deeply rooted in Confucian values, instills a sense of duty, respect, and national pride. These principles shape school life, urging students to honor their school, parents, and country. This spirit is encapsulated in the pledge recited by students:

"为了祖国，为了荣誉，为了我们的父母，我们要努力学习!"

Translated: *"For the country, for honor, for our parents, we will study hard!"*

Infused with Confucian ideals, this pledge embeds loyalty to the nation within the hearts of students from an early age.

Both nations, through their respective pledges, cultivate a deep allegiance to something greater than the self—whether through the lens of individual freedom or the preservation of cultural heritage.

Meanwhile, the United States grapples with the challenge of maintaining national cohesion while embracing diversity. This delicate balance fuels constant friction in the political arena, where opposing sides often talk past each other, unwilling to engage. The sensitivity of America's two-party system has made political discussions a taboo in workplaces, while social media debates frequently spiral into hostility. The discourse is dynamic yet often divisive, as nearly every issue becomes politicized—underscoring the nation's ongoing struggle to reconcile its ideals with its realities.

NATIONALISM AS NATION-BUILDING IN THAILAND

Western political thought, shaped by Europe's historical experience, often fails to illuminate the realities of Southeast Asia, where climate, culture, and social structures differ profoundly. Distant models may not offer better insights than what is closer to home.

King Vajiravudh (Rama VI) (r. 1910–1925) envisioned Thailand as a corporate body, united by a common identity and a shared purpose, where public interests took precedence over private ones. His efforts successfully forged both a Siamese nation and a modern nation-state, a crucial factor in preserving Thailand's independence amid rising colonial pressures.

Thailand remains the only nation in Southeast Asia to have resisted colonial rule, emerging from a fragmented past of city-states and contested kingdoms. Yet nation-building is an ongoing process, with education as a central pillar, integrating diverse ethnicities, including millions of Burmese migrants. Indigenous Karen communities are gradually assimilating, shaped by Thailand's schools and economic realities. Unlike their ancestors, content with subsistence and tradition, many younger Karen have embraced materialistic values, adapting to the dominant Thai culture. Thailand's success in state-building ensured that Bangkok remained uncolonized, yet today, it thrives as a globalized metropolis, a thriving expatriate enclave, where farangs roam freely everywhere, enjoying a city never claimed by Western empires.

Despite its economic achievements, much of Thailand's working class remains poor, unable to afford the very world-class services that cater to foreign visitors. This inequality diverges from King Rama VI's vision of national prosperity. Thailand's monarchical nationalism, once a shield against external domination, has at times hindered its adaptation to a rapidly changing world. While it attained peace and stability earlier than most, its inward focus has sometimes left it trailing behind global economic and political shifts.

This tension between tradition and modernity is stark in Thailand's political landscape. Move Forward Party leader Pita Limjaroenrat captured the hearts—and votes—of the people yet remains unable to claim power.

MULTICULTURAL SINGAPORE

The most successful example of nation-building in a multicultural, multilingual, and multi-religious society close to Kawthoolei is Singapore. In Singapore, the Chinese population identifies themselves as Singaporean first. During 2023 U.S. Congressional hearing when a Chinese ethnic TikTok's CEO confidently asserted his Singaporean identity in response to a senator's question, leaving a media sensation of the senator perplexed for not distinguishing between being Singaporean and Chinese. The Singapore nation had started with ethnic division and racial riots almost unredeemable. This success was not solely due to the people's openness to a new society, but also to the discipline of Singapore's founding leaders. They rejected corruption and had the courage to confront the challenges of nation-building, uniting Chinese, Malays, and Indians—each with strong cultural heritages—into a single nation.

INTELLECTUAL BIAS AND NATIONAL LOYALTY

Progressive intellectuals champion internationalism, presenting themselves as advocates of shared humanity. Yet beneath this ideal lies a attachment to national loyalties and identities.

Take the discourse on China's rise, particularly regarding human rights in Xinjiang. American intellectuals are quick to condemn China's actions, yet their analyses often reflect national biases, framing the issue to reinforce Western moral superiority rather than exploring the complexities of Chinese governance or the historical roots of ethnic tensions.

The reaction to China's Belt and Road Initiative (BRI) exposes similar biases. U.S. scholars portray it as economic imperialism, a tool for expanding Chinese influence while sidelining the West. Yet across Asia and Africa, roads, bridges, and ports are reshaping economies under China's design. To Beijing, the BRI is more than infrastructure—it is a modern Monroe Doctrine of China, an assertion that its rise will not be obstructed. Critics see unchecked ambition, yet much of the analysis remains trapped in a Western-centric lens, more concerned with containment than understanding the shifting balance of power.

The U.S.-China trade war follows the same pattern. Western intellectuals often frame it as a necessary defense against Chinese economic aggression, rarely acknowledging China's historical experiences of foreign exploitation or its pursuit of economic security. Fear and distrust—reflexive responses to perceived threats—shape the discourse, reinforcing national narratives over genuine engagement with a multipolar world.

As an Asian and an outsider, I recognize these subtle biases, though I hold no personal attachment to China. This awareness reveals a fundamental truth: no matter how much people claim to embrace a borderless intellectual world, national loyalties and cultural biases continue to shape—and often distort—perceptions.

People naturally seek comfort in belonging, even in multicultural spaces like California, where diversity is celebrated. Yet the reality remains: Black people gravitate toward Black communities, whites toward whites, Asians toward Asians, Latinos toward Latinos. Shared experiences and unspoken understandings bridge differences, reinforcing a deeper truth about human nature—no matter how inclusive the environment, the pull of identity remains strong, quietly shaping the communities we form.

In America's tech industry, where many professionals of Indian descent and immigrants from India work, racism and microaggressions persist as daily realities. These tensions often stem from cultural differences and divergent social norms between groups. Even in elite institutions, bias remains entrenched. When comfort in belonging outweighs mutual respect, the instinct to seek familiarity can turn into exclusion and prejudice, transforming a natural desire for connection into a source of division and discrimination.

WHAT THINKERS SAY

Nationalism as human expression and organization culture has undergone a transformation across times and spaces, through different eras and regions, evolving through a myriad of expressions. From the early German romantic nationalism to the resistant spirit of Jewish persecuted nationalism, and ultimately to the extreme form of Nazism, nationalism has manifested in both noble and nefarious forms. The pendulum swings between these extremes. Despite its varied uses and abuses, surviving reinterpretation and misinterpretation, it has endured as one of the most effective means of forging a cohesive society. Criticism against it is strong, but it is the enduring force of the modern world.

The Abbe Sieyes, in his inflammatory pamphlet, *What is the Third Estate?* Of 1789, expressed the point succinctly. "The nation is prior to everything. It is the source of everything. Its will is always legal … the manner in which a nation exercises its will does not matter; the point is that it does exercise it; any procedure is adequate, and its will is always the supreme law."

Roger Scruton, a prominent British philosopher and public intellectual, encapsulates nationalism succinctly: "Nationalism, as an ideology, is dangerous in just the way that ideologies are dangerous."

He further elaborates: "Sentiments of national identity may be inflamed by war, civil agitation, and ideology, and this inflammation admits of many degrees. But in their normal form, these sentiments are not only peaceful but also a form of peace between neighbors." (Scruton, 2019).

New World Ethnicity and the Rise of Networked Identity

In the traditional sense, nationalism is rooted in a shared sentiment and identity tied to ethnicity and geography. But in today's hyper-connected world, people increasingly find their tribes through professions—bonding over common expertise, specialized knowledge, and daily interactions in a shared professional language. I am comfortable with the Karen traditional diet and social values, yet I find my strongest sense of belonging among technologists—those with whom I share tribal knowledge, passion, and a historical backdrop of STEM. With them, I can engage in philosophical discussions about the state of our field and its global implications. I am fortunate enough to have a few folks with STEM. and I usually find that many technical people seeing the political human affair with more objective philosophical lens.

I have found kinship with computer programmers in Argentina—whether of Mestizo, European, or Japanese descent—because we share the same profession and intellectual pursuits. I have engaged in technical and philosophical conversations with people of Indian descent—whether from southern India, northern India, or the Sikh community. I have also spent hours talking with a Chinese graduate student from Berkeley during a flight from San Francisco, discussing the state of computer science and how state authorities leverage technology in governance. We spoke a common language—the shared tribal knowledge of U.S. and Chinese technological landscapes and their political terrains, reflecting the contrasting approaches of Washington and Beijing to policy and implementation.

Ethnicity is like a soulmate—an unspoken bond of trust where conversation flows naturally, without pretense. Paradoxically, I struggle to sustain a deep conversation with many of my fellow Karen while finding professional, intellectual, or emotional ground. The book *The Network State* also propose to create a nation-state that based on global network. The world has evolved; knowledge has specialized, and ethnic affiliations have shifted from physical geography to professional and intellectual connections.

IF NATIONS CEASED TO EXIST

The ideals of common humanity, global community, and internationalism— bolstered by the connectivity of information technology, global trade and supply chain interdependency—have undoubtedly influenced the collective psyche. Yet, despite this sentiment, not one of the 193 recognized states in the United Nations is prepared to embrace John Lennon's vision of a world without countries, religions, or borders. Lennon's utopia, while inspiring, remains a distant dream in a world still anchored by national sovereignty, cultural identity, and geopolitical boundaries.

If every nation were to truly embrace this internationalist vision, Kawthoolei, with its open-hearted people, would be among the first to welcome such a new world. Until then, the people of Kawthoolei have a divine duty to continue building their nation to stand shoulder-to-shoulder with others with dignity, mutual-respect, and goodwill.

THE SPIRIT OF KAWTHOOLEI NATIONALISM

Kawthoolei nationalism is a pledge to virtue, unity, and the well-being of its people—above all differences—ethnicity and region, language and dialect, religious beliefs and preferences, educational attainment, or economic status.

One may declare with pride: "I am KNyaw, I am Monaybwar, I am Plone, I am Pa'O, I am Shan, I am Bamar, I am Mon, I am Dawai-Tharr, I am Kalarr, I am Nagarr, I am A-ler-garr." One may express their faith as Baptist Christian, believer in native deities, Hindu, Catholic, Seventh-day Adventist, or Theravada Buddhist.

One may define themselves by their home and craft—city-dweller or mountaineer, farmer or engineer, scientist or entrepreneur. Yet above all, we, Kawthoolei must come first.

This truth must be the foundation of our pledge:

To Kawthoolei I pledge my allegiance. With all my strength and all the talents, with all my wealth and all that I am, I shall serve to honor this land.

For liberty, for virtue, for the Nation's progress—shall I stand firm to Kawthoolei.

The Sun sees your burning eyes.

A billion stars hear your murmuring heart.

The monsoon rain one day will wash away your tears.

Kawthoolei, come. You are mine.

SawLah@Poetry

SawLah@Photography 2023

BRING ME MEN TO MATCH MY MOUNTAINS
SAM WALTER FOSS

Chapter 6

On Self-Determination

True self-determination for the Karen people arises only when our community shapes political institutions according to our own philosophical foundations, ensuring they embody our collective will and core values. We own both the foundational principles and the process of their creation. Expert input may offer insights, but the path forward must remain free from external imposition—whether from the Burmese state, Western academics, or foreign political brokers.

When others dictate our political course, it ceases to be self-determination and becomes *other-determination*. Both the design of our autonomy and the execution of that design must remain uncompromised by those who presume to understand our needs better than we do. Self-determination means we design our systems of governance, and we carry out the day-to-day responsibilities of governing ourselves.

The future political arrangement of Burma—whether as a bottom-up association, a top-down union, an upside-down unitary, or a sideway federation—must be designed by members of the community and shaped according to the will of the people to gain genuine support. Genuine support springs from designs born within the community, not from distant shores. In the Thailand border, some voices have recently championed "bottom-up federalism," a concept carried on the winds from faraway academics after the 2021 coup. Meanwhile, other ethnic nationalities in Burma remain silent on federalism, showing no enthusiasm for the idealistic notion of multi-cultural, multi-ethnic, multi-religious unity. Disconnected from grounded realities that inspire human's action, these external ideas are attractive yet misguided and unlikely to garner lasting or widespread support. The time, money, and energy offered may come with good intentions, but they cannot betray the essence of self-determination or undermine the integrity of its legacy.

What various schools of thought teach us is that schools of thought do not matter. Ideology does not matter. Chart your own course and walk it. Stick to one path to reach the destination.

CLEAR SELF-DETERMINED PATH

Self-determination is not allowing others to design your constitution, dictate your government framework, and compel you to govern according to their will. It is not self-determination when you are granted so-called "self-administration" within a prescribed zone but remain constrained by the rules and frameworks set by others. It is like a machine executing instructions programmed by someone else—predictable, dependent, and devoid of true agency. Such "self-administration" is neither self-determination nor a path to meaningful progress for the people.

In Burma, the self-administered zones exemplify this illusion. These regions do not operate under constitutions of their own making, nor does their day-to-day governance signify genuine freedom. Instead, they function as extensions of military rule, repackaged in a different format. The semblance of autonomy is a façade, concealing the continued subjugation of the people.

Federalism, properly understood, does not mean waiting passively for others to design a governing system for you, nor does it mean governing only when permission is granted. True self-determination requires writing your own political destiny and crafting your own political framework. Also, without a foundation of ownership and independence, alliances cannot be effectively formed or sustained; association cannot be meaningful.

Consider California as an example. It operates under its own constitution and has a clearly defined process for amending it—a more important aspect of governance. California's citizens vote directly to amend their constitution, and with every election cycle, provisions are adjusted to reflect the majority's will. This direct democracy that covers initiative, referendum, and recall is different from a larger U.S. system. This system demonstrates how self-determination is rooted in active participation and ownership, ensuring that governance evolves in alignment with the people's collective aspirations.

California may appear erratic to outsiders, with its frequent shifts on contentious policies like petty theft laws or housing affordability. However, this process embodies the principle of self-determination. The people themselves decide the rules they live by, swinging back and forth as public opinion evolves. This system ensures that governance is rooted in the will of the majority, even when that will changes over time.

In contrast, some of us have a tendency to wait for others to act on our behalf. When we advocate for federalism, we often do so as though pursuit of full self-determination would somehow conflict with federal principles. This misconception arises from our habit of forming opinions without critical thinking. We tend to like or dislike, love or hate, without investing the effort to learn or act decisively.

Prioritizing alliances against the entrenched Burmese military state may hold moral virtue. However, inspiring ethnic pride and fostering a sense of ownership among your people is of practical necessity—and it must take precedence. A higher virtue that fails to generate practical results ultimately undermines the ends it seeks to achieve.

Self-determination is not a gift to be granted; it is a responsibility to be claimed. It demands the courage and intellect to design and govern according to our own principles, without deferring to others to define our political future. To chart a clear self-determined path forward, we must claim our agency, design our frameworks, and govern with integrity and vision.

AGENCY, VOLITION, AND AUTONOMY

Agency is the capacity to act independently and make choices that influence one's life and surroundings. Volition refers to the act of using one's will to make conscious choices. It is the inner drive or determination to act intentionally. Autonomy is the state of self-governance and freedom from external control. It reflects the ability to act in alignment with one's values, free from coercion or dependency.

Self-determination is built upon the pillars of agency, volition, and autonomy. At the *individual level*, it represents the power to make decisions and the freedom to define one's own identity. Within *communities*, it manifests as the strength to take action toward common goals. On a *national scale*, it transforms into the ability to govern independently, chart a course for the future, and uphold the values that define a people.

Without self-determination, the Karen generation becomes drifting aimlessly, singing, dancing, and loitering in festivity as many do today, with some idling their time away in hammocks, disconnected from the energy and ambition needed to shape a better future. Psychologists describe self-determination as an innate human need—a driving force behind motivation. Without agency, volition, and autonomy, this motivation falters. Without motivation, there is no drive; without drive, the energy and talents remain untapped to achieve greatness.

The Karen people, like any other, cannot flourish under the rule of others. Even under benevolent rule, progress cannot be sustained without self-determination. During the British colonial era, the Karen people experienced limited advancement, but it was the result of controlled, extrinsic motivation. True progress demands intrinsic motivation—where full agency, volition, and autonomy converge to inspire genuine growth and achievement.

SELF-DETERMINATION SHOULDERS SELF-RESPONSIBILITY

Self-determination stands opposed to the comfort of milk-drinking dependency. It comes with responsibility to be self-initiative. It calls for the courage to take control of our future. In many aspects of our national lives, the habit of relying on others to make decisions for us has taken root over time. The appetite to rely on the Burmese state to provide, decide, or manage stands against the principles of self-determination. The Myanmar government is neither a benevolent caretaker nor a steward of our interests.

In the economic realm, dependence on the central state to develop our land has led only to exploitation rather than progress. If we allow them to manage, they will plunder our resources, leaving behind barren, toxic lands inhabited by people with dusty faces. True self-determination demands the creation of our own economic development board, drawing our own economic planning to focus on both immediate needs and long-term plans for sustainable growth to ensure our resources are managed to serve the well-being of our people, not external interests.

For over a decade, administrators have prioritized integrating education with Myanmar's system—a decision made out of convenience, not vision. But aligning with a framework that lags behind global standards is not just shortsighted; it is a disservice to our future. If we truly want to uplift Burma, we should do so by elevating our own education system, setting a standard for them to follow—not lowering ourselves to theirs. Dependence allows others to dictate what we learn and what language we speak, eroding both our identity and independence. A self-determined education system must be distinctly our own—rooted in our values, striving for global excellence, and preparing our people to lead, not follow, in an increasingly competitive world.

Health challenges remain a pressing issue, with infectious diseases like malaria continuing to claim lives and weaken our communities. While wealthy nations have eradicated malaria within their borders, they show little interest in addressing it elsewhere. We must take control, invest in our own research, and find solutions ourselves—whether through indigenous medicine, scientific discovery, or a combination of both. With advancing technology, we have the tools to achieve breakthroughs. By relying on our own expertise and determination, we can eliminate preventable diseases, secure a healthier future, and set an example for others facing similar struggles.

Self-determination is about building our own systems across all domains of life, carrying immense responsibilities and challenges.

A GLIMPSE ON THE BACKGROUND

The concept of self-determination, though globally recognized today, was most prominently articulated by U.S. President Woodrow Wilson in the early 20th century. After World War I, Wilson championed this idea in his 1918 Fourteen Points speech, advocating for the right of all peoples to determine their political status and shape their futures. His vision aimed to dismantle empires and pave the way for new nation-states in Europe, offering a model for colonial territories.

However, Wilson was not the first to articulate self-determination. Its philosophical roots trace back to earlier thinkers like Jean-Jacques Rousseau, who emphasized popular sovereignty and the general will. National liberation movements around the world carried this principle forward. Wilson saw self-determination as both a moral imperative and a practical solution to the ethnic and nationalist tensions that plagued Europe. He believed that global peace and stability were best secured when peoples and nations were free from external domination, governing themselves according to their own identities and values. His vision extended to the dissolution of empires like the Austro-Hungarian and Ottoman, and although his application of the principle was uneven, his advocacy laid the groundwork for future movements toward independence.

Wilson's vision for international cooperation found its expression in the creation of the League of Nations, the world's first international organization and a precursor to the United Nations. He envisioned a global arena where nations would come together to resolve disputes, avert wars, and promote lasting stability. The League was designed to be a forum where countries could uphold their sovereignty while ensuring that the principle of self-determination was respected. Through dialogue and peaceful conflict resolution, Wilson hoped to protect newly independent states and minority groups from external coercion.

However, at the close of World War I, which left 40 million dead, the League's grand ambition quickly faced reality. In 1920, it was officially established, yet its foundation was weakened from the start. The United States, driven by a shift in public sentiment that rejected entanglement in Europe's endless imperial conflicts, refused to join. This absence of American leadership critically undermined the League's authority. Instead of ushering in a new era of peace, the League failed to prevent the descent into another world conflict. With over 80 million fatalities—more than double the previous war—World War II shattered the fragile international order, revealing the tragic limitations of Wilson's once-hopeful vision.

Wilson's vision remains a powerful reminder that true cooperation among nations is built on the foundation of freedom and respect for each nation's right to self-governance. Without self-determination, genuine international cooperation cannot exist. A nation must first have the freedom to govern its own affairs; only then can it engage in meaningful and equitable cooperation with other nations.

Two immediate factors shaped Burma's path to independence, casting a long shadow that lingers to this day. First, the Atlantic Charter, signed during the height of World War II when Britain was cornered by Germany's military might, forced the British to confront the inevitable collapse of their empire. Under pressure from Roosevelt, Churchill reluctantly pledged to decolonization. After the war, the electoral defeat of Churchill brought Attlee's Labour Party to power, with a clear anti-colonial agenda that accelerated Burma's independence. Yet Burma's journey to self-determination was flawed from the outset. The assassination of Aung San, the most capable leader who had brokered vital ethnic agreements, left the country adrift, bereft of unity and direction. Financially exhausted and morally diminished, Britain hastened its exit, leaving Burma without the stability and preparation necessary for true independence. The result was a fragile state, born out of hurried decisions, fractured by unresolved internal conflicts, and unprepared for the challenges of self-governance. Burma could have waited, perhaps following the more measured transitions seen in Malaysia (1957) or Singapore (1959), that took a decade of transition after the Burma Independence (1948).

Had Churchill remained in power, the Karen delegation, led by Saw Ba U Gyi, might have negotiated a different path to autonomy. Churchill, with his wartime leadership and deep ties to his military commanders who had fought alongside the Karen during World War II, may have been more receptive to their aspirations. The Karens, recognized as loyal allies by many British generals, might have leveraged their wartime contributions to strike a more favorable deal under Churchill's leadership—one that acknowledged their distinct identity and need for self-determination within Burma. The hurried, fragmented transition that occurred after this departure deprived the Karen people of a more deliberate and equitable outcome.

Under Wilson's banner of self-determination, Britain relinquished Burma from its crumbling empire—but not without a sinister twist, a curse that would haunt the nation for generations. Burma, a country molded by deception and coercion, soon spiraled into authoritarianism. Wilson's vision, while noble in its pursuit of a more just world, faltered in execution. His principles were applied selectively, complex realities were reduced to oversimplified solutions. Not just for Burma, the unintended consequences continue to fuel debates about his true legacy. The abrupt end to colonial rule in Burma left a power vacuum, plunging the country into economic, political, and social chaos. Most devastating, however, has been the erosion of moral decay, the deepest wound of all.

SAW BA OO GYI'S FOUR PRINCIPLES

"The recognition of the Karen State must be complete."

To be complete, the recognition must be both internal and external. Internally, it begins with the Karen people affirming their identity and sovereignty. Externally, it must extend to acknowledgment by the Burmese people, other ethnic nationalities, neighboring countries, and the international community.

The recognition should encompass the full and proper geographical and territorial boundaries of the Karen State. It is not merely symbolic but must be endorsed by global powers and the broader international community.

To achieve international recognition of Kawthoolei as a sovereign state, it is essential to first secure internal recognition through the establishment of robust institutions. Kawthoolei must build institutions on par with those of other sovereign states, enabling it to engage on an equal footing in a world where no nation thrives alone but in mutual interdependence.

To participate in international commerce and global trade, Kawthoolei needs world-class economic institutions, including rules and regulations for business and banking systems. It also requires a comprehensive legal framework, including a constitution and laws accepted by its people. Establishing courts, law enforcement agencies, and oversight bodies remains essential for earning the trust and recognition of the international community.

Diplomatic recognition will depend on skilled diplomats and clearly defined territorial boundaries. Additionally, Kawthoolei must have a stable government capable of effectively governing its people, providing security, stability, and essential services, while facilitating trade and commerce for the welfare of its citizens. Kawthoolei must also establish a respectable defense force, capable of forming alliances with other nations.

We must recognize ourselves before others can recognize us.

The recognition of the Karen State must be complete in every aspect—in essence and substance, in spirit and practice. It must be a recognition that is firm, both in principle and in action. The sovereignty of Kawthoolei and the autonomy of the state must be whole and undivided. Hence, "The recognition of the Karen State must be complete."

Often confused with a territory within a country, the term "State" in this context refers to the legal concept of a sovereign country, standing as an equal partner on the world stage. Saw Ba Oo Gyi, with his legal training, chose each word with deliberate care. The word "state" in English has numerous meanings across various domains, but in political science, it closely aligns with the idea of a nation's authority and governance.

People often mistakenly use "complete**d**" when they mean "complete," misled by their similar meanings. In this context, the distinction is crucial.

"Complete," as an adjective, refers to something that is whole, finished, and fully realized. It denotes a state where nothing is lacking, and all necessary components are present. In the phrase "Recognition of Karen State must be complete," "complete" conveys the need for thorough and unambiguous recognition, encompassing every aspect.

And, proclamations or political statements cannot make the recognition to be complete.

Conversely, the word "completed" in the phrase "Recognition of Karen State must be completed" sounds awkward and inadequate in this context. It is not just about reaching a conclusion but about achieving a comprehensive and fully established acknowledgment—one that carries both legitimacy and permanence.

Therefore, "Recognition of Karen State must be complete" is the more precise choice, underscoring the need for a recognition that is both holistic and fully realized, beyond mere formalities.

THE PEACE OF WESTPHALIA

The nation-state, as a political structure, is a relatively recent development in world history. The rise of new nation-states is largely rooted in the principle of self-determination, which emerged primarily in the 17th century and gained momentum in the 19th and 20th centuries.

The Treaty of Westphalia, signed in 1648 in the Westphalian cities of Osnabrück and Münster, Germany, marked a foundational moment in the development of international law. After three decades of conflict fueled by religious domination in Europe, with no side emerging victorious, the nations involved were utterly exhausted. The treaty that finally brought an end to the Thirty Years' War, known as the Peace of Westphalia, was signed by 109 delegates representing the Holy Roman Emperor, the kings of France, Spain, and Sweden, the leaders of the Dutch Republic, and numerous German princes. The negotiations, which lasted four years, culminated in this historic agreement.

Professor Pierre d'Agent, in his teachings, emphasized the simplicity and significance of the model it introduced to Europe. "The basic social model that was used to bring peace to Europe was a simple one," he noted.

> **"In order to live together in peace, states would live separately, each being sovereign over its own territory and equal to one another."**

This concept of equal sovereignty was revolutionary at the time, forming the cornerstone of what we now recognize as the liberal legal order. In this framework, each state is autonomous, free to establish its own laws and governance, yet bound by the mutual respect for the sovereignty of others. This arrangement allowed states to coexist, interacting as equals on the international stage, and creating obligations through treaties and agreements that respected the independence of each polity.

The war had drained the resources and morale of nations, leading to widespread recognition that a new approach was needed. The Peace of Westphalia thus marked a turning point: the recognition that peace could be maintained not through dominance or conquest, but through mutual respect and the establishment of a balanced, sovereign order. This peace agreement not only brought an end to a devastating war but also laid the groundwork for the modern system of nation-states, where sovereignty and equality among states became guiding principles in international relations.

The legacy of Westphalia is still evident today, as the principles of sovereignty and equal standing among states continue to underpin international law and diplomatic relations.

After World War II, many nation-states emerged based on the principle of self-determination. However, the paths they took and the outcomes they achieved varied significantly. Some cases offer valuable insights into how these nations have fared over time.

THE SINGAPORE CASE

Singapore, a small island nation led by the uncompromising Lee Kuan Yew, recognized the necessity of building a strong foundation before seeking recognition and partnership on the global stage. After the British departure in 1963, Singapore initially joined the Malaysian Confederation, hoping to share destiny with its former colonial sibling. However, deep-seated racial tensions stifled progress, prompting Singapore to break away and chart its own course.

Defenseless in a region surrounded by less-than-friendly neighbors, Singapore understood that true sovereignty required not only economic strength but also a robust defense. Today, Singapore stands shoulder to shoulder with global powers, forging alliances and negotiating on equal terms with the United States. Before engaging in these high-stakes relations, Singapore focused on developing its economy and creating a strong defense force, the Singapore Armed Forces (SAF).

Remarkably, Singapore did not even have its own army when its first parliamentary session convened in December 1965 to govern the country as an independent state. Yet, despite its modest size—comparable to just a fraction of Kawthoolei—Singapore emerged as an equal partner with both economic and military strength.

Singapore's commitment to excellence is most evident in its defense strategy. The SAF maintains one of the largest foreign military training presences in the United States, reflecting Singapore's forces are not only capable but respected on the international stage. In 2020, Singapore was even able to procure 12 F-35 jets worth $2.75 billion, the latest and most advanced aircraft from the United States, navigating the stringent Congressional Notification process—one of the most cumbersome yet powerful mechanisms of the U.S. government.

Through strategic investments in both economic infrastructure and defense capabilities, Singapore has positioned itself as a formidable and respected player, proving that even a tiny island can stand as an equal partner among the world's great powers.

THE TAIWAN CASE

Taiwan has built its nation's sovereignty not merely with guns and powers, but with silicon chips edged by advanced lithography. Their talents and technological superiority are not just their greatest asset, but also their best defense shield. The world's advanced nations depend on Taiwan's microchips for both economic and security needs. To hurt Taiwan is to hurt one's lifeline for the technology supply chain. The People's Republic of China (Mainland China) cannot simply bomb the Republic of China (Taiwan) in the name of unification; doing so would be self-defeating, as it would destroy the microchip industry and destabilize the geopolitical landscape, with unknown consequences of war. This is known as the "silicon shield" that protects Taiwan from a Chinese invasion.

DW News describes microchips as "they are tiny, they are mighty, they power the modern world; computer chips run everything from smart phones to our dishwasher." They are everywhere from cars on the road to planes in the sky, from machineries in factories to screens in schools.

Taiwan has been excluded from UN membership, but it operates with full sovereignty, maintaining its own passport, immigration control, individual liberty, and healthy political culture with a vibrant multi-party democracy better than that of the U.S. The people of Taiwan, with their high morale and moral values, are working hard at preserving their traditional values while marching forward as a leading nation among the world's most developed countries. The streets of Taipei are clean and designed with environmental consciousness in mind. In this safe and orderly city, motorbikes in street parking are left unattended helmets on them overnight—a testament to both the high level of public safety and the integrity of its people. At Taiwan's airports, immigration control is so advanced that no human personnel check travelers at the exit— your face is your identity. This level of technological confidence is found in only a handful of countries worldwide at the moment. Taiwan does not try to reclaim UN membership or declare its secession. They have decided their own political destiny in alignment with geopolitical realities.

Kawthoolei must remember that full sovereignty and prosperity do not depend on UN membership but on the talents and morale of its people. Neither does UN membership guarantee liberty, progress, or prosperity.

THE SOMALILAND CASE

Somaliland declared independence from Somalia in 1991, yet no country has recognized its sovereignty in the decades since. Despite this lack of international legitimacy, Somaliland has built a relatively stable democracy and attracted significant foreign investment. However, as it continues to pursue its own investment deals and assert its sovereignty, tensions with Somalia have escalated. The region's push for autonomy and development, even without formal recognition, increasingly puts it at odds with the central government in Mogadishu.

In contrast to South Sudan, which has been a UN member since 2011 as the 193rd member but suffers from severe humanitarian crises, Somaliland has proven to be more livable. Despite lacking international recognition, Somaliland, known as the breakaway state in the Horn of Africa, has managed to attract foreign investors and maintain a stable democracy. The people of Somaliland take pride in having rebuilt their country from the ground up, holding elections observed by Western European countries. Meanwhile, South Sudan, a recognized state, faces ongoing turmoil, with millions displaced and widespread hunger.

THE KOSOVO CASE

In 2008, Kosovo declared independence from Serbia, driven by the desire of its majority ethnic Albanian population to govern themselves after enduring years of conflict, including the brutal Kosovo War in the late 1990s. This declaration followed a period of UN administration and was intended to solidify Kosovo's autonomy.

However, Kosovo's path to full sovereignty has been fraught with challenges. While over 100 countries, including major powers like the United States, Germany, and the United Kingdom, recognize Kosovo's independence, key global players like Serbia, Russia, and China do not. This split in recognition has left Kosovo in a precarious position—functioning as an independent state with its own government, military, and foreign relations, but without the full legitimacy that comes with universal recognition.

This partial recognition has real-world consequences. For example, Kosovo's inability to join the United Nations due to opposition from countries like Russia has limited its influence on the global stage. Additionally, Kosovo's athletes compete under the Olympic flag rather than their national one, reflecting the ongoing debate over its status.

Kosovo's struggle highlights the tension between the right to self-determination and the principle of territorial integrity, especially when powerful nations have a vested interest in the status quo. Despite its efforts to assert its sovereignty, Kosovo's journey shows that achieving self-determination is often only the first step in a broader, more complex battle for international legitimacy.

THE BANGLADESH CASE

Some Karen enthusiasts, without fully understanding Burma's political realities and international relation, have advocated for a Unilateral Declaration of Independence (UDI) or unilateral secession. However, history shows that no country has successfully achieved independence through a UDI and gained UN membership—except Bangladesh.

Bangladesh's success was not a matter of luck or merely the strong spirit of a people determined to form a nation-state. It required specific historical and geopolitical conditions. The Indian Army intervened decisively, and Bangladesh's geographical advantage—being physically separated from West Pakistan—made independence more achievable. Yet, this path was marked by immense destruction, loss, and suffering.

Even sovereignty does not guarantee liberty, virtue, or progress. Despite its independence, Bangladesh remains a nation grappling with internal struggles, and it has not become a universally sought-after destination for those seeking liberty or prosperity. No Karen, nor people from Burma, are longing to migrate there in search of freedom or opportunity.

The UN may provide guidelines and frameworks for self-determination, but in reality, the UN General Assembly holds limited power without the consensus and backing of superpowers in the Security Council. In the 2024 annual UN General Assembly, nations passionately expressed the urgent need for reform amidst ongoing wars in Ukraine and Russia, the Israel-Gaza conflict, and escalating Middle Eastern tensions. Yet, after the live-streamed speeches and impassioned declarations, representatives returned home, and their words became nothing more than archived records—with little meaningful change achieved.

Self-determination is one of the most misunderstood political concepts. For nations in Burma, achieving self-determination is not as simple as declaring independence. It requires careful consideration of political dynamics, demographic composition, and geographical realities. The principle exists, but it demands grinding-teeth determination to shape a nation capable of self-determination, liberty, and enduring progress.

Learning from cases around the world, we understand that self-determination is our sole responsibility to chart our own path. Global support and universal recognition will come naturally.

If Kawthoolei fails to assert its self-determination, it risks being dismissed by the international community—not as a sovereign entity, but as a war-torn burden, unworthy of standing as an equal on the global stage. We must see clearly the agenda of aids and the mission of liberation. Seeking sympathy without a clear political vision undermines the spirit of self-determination. The lure of humanitarian aids as a bait will only distract the people from the mission of liberation. International allies will support only those who hold belief that they can rise. The survival of the Karen people hangs in the balance, and this generation could be the last remembered before they fade from the world's consciousness. Future generations may find themselves subject to the will of a larger, dominant nation, forced to adopt customs, moral standards, and attitudes not their own, laboring under burdens that enrich another master.

UNITED NATIONS ON SELF-DETERMINATION OF PEOPLES

The United Nations remains ambiguous and calculated ambivalence when addressing self-determination for stateless nations like the Karen people. The following excerpts from how the UN has officially framed the concept of self-determination within its foundational documents:

1. United Nations Charter (1945):
   "To develop friendly relations among nations based on respect for the principle of equal rights and self-determination of peoples." — Article 1(2)

2. International Covenant on Civil and Political Rights (1966):
   "All peoples have the right of self-determination. By virtue of that right they freely determine their political status and freely pursue their economic, social and cultural development." — Article 1

3. Declaration on the Granting of Independence to Colonial Countries and Peoples (1960):
   "The subjection of peoples to alien subjugation, domination, and exploitation constitutes a denial of fundamental human rights, is contrary to the Charter of the United Nations, and is an impediment to the promotion of world peace and cooperation."

   "All peoples have the right to self-determination; by virtue of that right they freely determine their political status and freely pursue their economic, social, and cultural development." — Resolution 1514

4. Declaration on Principles of International Law concerning Friendly Relations and Cooperation among States (1970):
   "Every State has the duty to promote, through joint and separate action, the realization of the principle of equal rights and self-determination of peoples."

5. UN General Assembly Resolutions and Practices:
   "Alien domination and subjugation" are incompatible with fundamental human rights and the principles of the UN Charter.

The United Nations, a body forged by nation-states fiercely protective of their own sovereignty, champions the idea of self-determination in theory, yet balks at extending that right to groups within their own borders. The UN is an institution that claims to stand for independence and autonomy. In truth, the UN is largely a coalition of governments, many complicit in institutionalized oppression, prioritizing the preservation of territorial integrity above the freedoms of stateless peoples. As long as these parent states cling to their control, self-determination remains an abstract ideal rather than a concrete right.

This inherent contradiction—asserting sovereignty for itself while refusing to grant it to groups within one's own territory—is woven into the UN's 1960 resolution. While affirming the right to self-determination in many articles, the 1960's Resolution 1514 Article 6 asserts that *"any attempt aimed at the partial or total disruption of the national unity and the territorial integrity of a country is incompatible with the purposes and principles of the Charter."* In this careful balancing act, the UN promotes self-determination on one hand while safeguarding the *geopolitical status quo* on the other. It means entire communities, such as the Kurds, Sikhs, and Karen people, are left without the right to govern themselves in a sovereign state. The principle of sovereignty, in essence, permits nations, like Myanmar with an absurd military, to do as they please within their borders, as long as their internal conflicts do not spill over to threaten the wider regional safety or global order.

THE SILENT MAJORITY IN UN MEMBER STATES

United Nations member states are often perceived as large nations with populations in the tens or hundreds of millions. However, among the 193 recognized member states, 69 countries have populations under 5 million, and 37 nations have fewer than 1 million citizens. Tiny states are not exceptions—they form the majority.

Number of Countries vs. Population Range in the UN

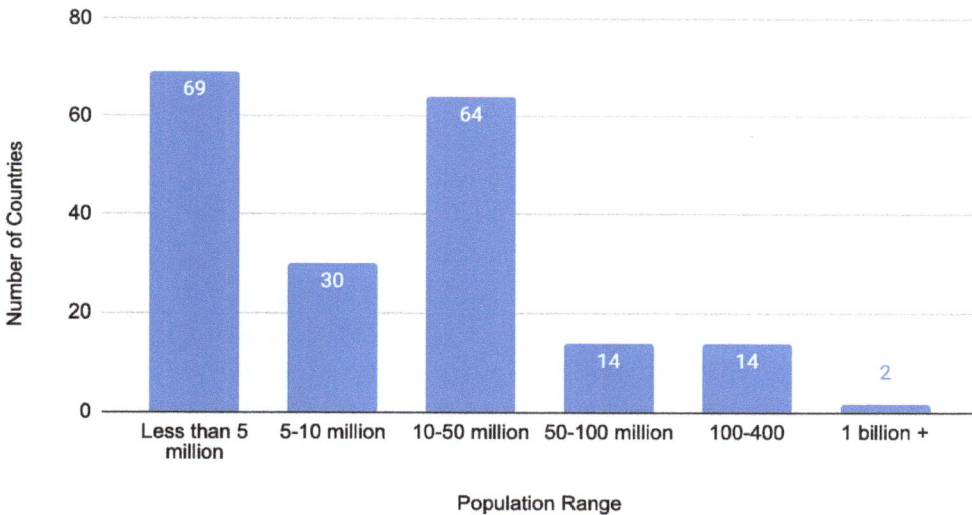

Data Source: worlddata.info (2025)

Most member states are not monocultural but instead consist of diverse and intricate tapestries of languages, traditions, and identities. The populations of smaller nations are often smaller than a single district in a megacity elsewhere. In shaping national identity, many UN member states are influenced by a dominant ethnic group or political elite, often sidelining the voices of other communities within their territories.

Also, in the UN General Assembly, the principle of "one nation, one vote" is often at odds with the ambitions of larger powers. The UN Security Council, meant to safeguard global peace, frequently becomes a stage for superpowers to veto and maneuver policies, sidelining smaller nations caught in their rivalry. They are comfortable sacrificing people like the Karen people to keep their global peace.

TEND YOUR OWN GARDEN

The modern international system rests on two core principles: sovereignty and territorial integrity. Ever country wants to claim keeping the entrenched territory boundary as territorial integrity. Yet, redrawing borders is not always a violation of territorial integrity; sometimes, it is a restoration of a rightful homeland. Surrendering land to invaders cannot be territorial integrity—it means preserving what is justly one's own. In such cases, territorial integrity must align with higher moral and humanitarian principles, affirming the right of peoples to self-determination.

In a world where no single entity holds absolute moral authority, humanity tends to act in its own interest, a sentiment echoed by Voltaire in *Candide* with his famous advice to "tend your own garden." This suggests that when larger powers fail to uphold justice, individuals or groups must take charge of their own fate, focusing on what they can control and improve. No philosophy or ideological -ism hold an absolute a higher moral ground. It does create boisterous philosophical debates, but noise does not help to determine who is right or wrong. The right or the left is not always right.

As with many UN declarations, without political will, they remain mere documents. Those are usually crafted by a combination of legal experts, diplomats, academics, and representatives with no direct connection to the will of the people, rendering them ineffective in practice unless legally binding resolutions. True change does not stem from words on paper, but from the collective will and action of the people. When that will is strong enough, nations are born, self-governing entities are carved out, regardless of external recognition. Kosovo is a testament to this reality—the UN and international law, neither fully endorsed nor outright rejected its independence, yet it exists, governed by its own people. In the mythical land of Burma, look out for what the will of Arakan people can do.

Burma is often subjected to fear-mongering narratives about the country fracturing into "Balkanization" due to its diverse ethnic groups and fragmented de facto governments. However, the people in Burma are not the Balkans; they come from different climates, cultures, and social norms. Another fear arises from comparisons to failed states in Africa. The fear of Burma descending into a failed state, perpetually embroiled in conflict, overlooks a critical truth: the real source of conflict lies with the military, which actively fuels conflicts and ruins the country. Most of Burma's non-Burman ethnic groups, along with the Burmese public, are inherently peace-loving and seek stability, not conflict. The fears of Balkanization ignore European history, where different empires attempted to control everything, leading to endless wars—until self-determination among nations was respected.

SELF-DETERMINATION, A LIFESTYLE OF FOCUS

Self-determination is a lifestyle—a lifestyle of focus. A transient being has limited time and energy as a nation has finite resources. Yet, many of our people invest their energy in the shifting tides of Burmese politics and literature at the expense of our own progress. If a businessman spends more time watching ticker signs than building his enterprise, his business is unlikely to thrive. If a sailor spends more time watching the wind than steering the ship, the journey is unlikely to move forward.

Burmese politics can shift direction unpredictably, like a fickle wind—one moment leaning toward negotiation, the next toward annihilation, and every moment toward assimilation. Being well-versed in Burmese politics does not necessarily make one wiser; history shows that Karen leaders who immersed themselves in it did not emerge any stronger, from, Saw San Po Thin and Saw Ba U Gyi to Saw Mutu Say Poe. Engaging too deeply in it becomes a distraction, diverting us from the steady course we must set for our nation.

Likewise, Burmese journalism, while often captivating, frequently falls short of its primary purpose—to inform. Much of it leans toward sensationalism, with some outlets constantly displaying a tendency to demean the Karen cause. They show that appetite regularly. Analysts too often rush to criticize Karen internal affairs without undertaking thorough investigations or understanding the complexities at hand. Overconsumption of such shallow reporting is a poor investment of our limited time, much like the uncritical consumption of news in general.

Our focus ought to be the pursuit of self-determination. Burmese political landscapes may shift from red to green, but that does not mean we must follow their every turn. For decades, and in the last decade, we have pursued illusions—shuttling between peace agreements, security workshops, and constitution drafting—only to find ourselves stalled in building our own foundation. This pattern has cost us valuable time—time that ought to have been spent strengthening our people, institutions, and vision. The rainy season is long, and the dry season should be devoted to preparing for those inevitable challenges. Yet the fair season is already over, leaving us with little choice but to press on with what we have and do the best we can under changing skies.

A nation must first focus inward to build its foundation. Its leaders must inspire, guide, and mobilize their people, rather than relying on fleeting alliances or external forces to achieve self-determination. Self-determination is not something granted by others; it is forged through our own collective effort, discipline, and clarity of vision. Alliance comes and goes. If our foundation is strong, a true alliance will come, even if our political values are not aligned.

Self-determination is not mere political aspiration, it is a way of life.

We Shall Decide

Self-determination is not merely a principle; it is a nation's lifeline. Those who advocate for minorities in Myanmar to live in peace and harmony under multiculturalism, while allowing the ethnic majority to dictate their political fate, should first demonstrate this model on a global scale. Let small nations in Europe become ethnic minorities among a billion-strong Chinese population and embrace multiculturalism there first.

This scenario is not hypothetical. China is rising, and historically powerful European nations—the former colonial powers—are now scrambling to *decouple* themselves economically and politically from China. This has become official and public in the year 2024. Despite their efforts, they are realizing the limits of such actions. It is a realization coming too late, with too little effect.

At its core, self-determination reflects a nation's desire to live freely, to take ownership of its destiny, and to make decisions that ensure its survival and progress. Preaching multiculturalism in Burma without first establishing mutual respect, strong foundations, and functional institutions is hollow and counterproductive. For too long, others have decided our fate, and we have endured not progress, but misery. Now, we must decide—whether to stay together or part ways. Forced association serves no one, neither the oppressed nor the oppressors. One day, we may return as a willful association, just as European nations came together to form the European Union, having learned from centuries of failed empires. A closer example lies in ASEAN, where sovereign nations stand shoulder to shoulder, bound not by coercion, but by shared aspirations.

Self-determination is about agency, responsibility, and ownership. It is the act of making choices for the well-being of a people. Deciding our own political destiny is not just a right—it is a national obligation and a moral imperative.

Kawthoolei must recognize itself *first* and recognize the fact *that* self-determination has taken different forms around the world, as shown by Singapore, Taiwan, Bangladesh, and Somaliland. Singapore transformed from a small island into a thriving nation through strategic economic and defense planning. Taiwan, standing firm amid global power struggles, asserted its sovereignty not just through military might but through technological prowess, becoming indispensable to the world's economy. Somaliland, despite lacking international recognition, built a stable democracy from the ashes of conflict, challenging the notion that legitimacy is granted solely by recognition. The paths to self-determination are as varied as the histories of these lands, yet the principles of autonomy and self-reliance remain unshakable. In a world where the contours of power are ever-shifting, self-determination remains a constant struggle that can challenge even the most sovereign nations.

The paths to self-determination may differ, the pursuit of true autonomy is a common thread. Kawthoolei must also define what self-determination means for its people on its own. This journey is not merely about achieving political independence; it is about laying the groundwork for a comprehensive and enduring autonomy that encompasses every facet of national life within the context of prevailing world order.

Political self-determination is not an end in itself, but the foundation upon which a broader and more comprehensive autonomy is built. It is the bedrock from which we shake hands with other heads of state, shape our economic future, design and govern our educational systems, preserve and elevate our language and culture, command our national finances, control borders and customs, oversee immigration, forge military and security alliances, conduct diplomacy on our own terms, safeguard our health and food standards, and instill civic values that align with our climate and cultural heritage.

Salween River, the Super Highway

Lives Disturbed Undisturbed

A fighter jet cuts the midnight sky
drops its bombs
then away swiftly flies.
Crickets and frogs
resume their chirping spree.
Above the trees, stars still shine
      —clear and steady;
the River Salween, roaring mighty, still flows
      —wild and free.

SawLah@Poetry

Chapter 7

The Benevolent Trap

DONATION IDEOLOGY BAGGAGE

Dependency is a poison—an insidious addiction, seeping into the veins of a nation, rotting its spirit, and dulling its will to stand. It corrodes, not with the violence of a blow, but with the slow, quiet death of forgotten strength. If not rooted in dignity and purpose, proliferation of unchecked charity can breed a culture of dependency.

The Kawthoolei-Thai border is teeming with organizations eager to aid the people of Burma, from humanitarian groups of all sizes to brokers of health and education donations, policy lobbyists, experts and intellectuals from a distant tower, political intermediaries, and peace-brokers. Each pursues its own vision of salvation, safely ensconced on the other side of the border while the war against one of the world's most savage armies rages on. These organizations, however well-meaning, are rarely neutral, carrying with them cultural and ideological baggage. Even those that appear least political, such as education donation brokers, often come with strings attached, pushing their ideological knives into the throats of vulnerable recipients.

A nation in trouble needs a hand that lifts, but too often, outstretched hands hold both money and an agenda.

This phenomenon, known as *The Benevolent Trap*, illustrates how well-intentioned charity can inadvertently promote dependency rather than resolve underlying problems. Aid that seems beneficial on the surface may, over time, entrench reliance, stifling independence and self-sufficiency.

African nations have faced exploitation under the banner of humanitarianism, stifling entrepreneurship and meddling in their political affairs, fueling constant instability. Burma, despite its proximity to the rapidly developing Asian Tigers and Dragons—nations like South Korea, Taiwan, Singapore, Thailand, Malaysia, Indonesia, and Vietnam—bears a closer resemblance to fragmented and impoverished African nations. These nations are often caught in a dependency trap, relying on foreign aid and suffering from the mismanagement of abundant natural resources. This leads to the so-called "resource curse," where wealth in resources hinders rather than drives sustainable development. Despite its rich reserves of natural treasures—precious metals, gemstones, and valuable hardwoods—Burma remains entrenched in poverty. These resources have brought more harm than good to its indigenous populations.

During the decade of 2010s, international donors poured hundreds of millions of dollars into peace efforts in Burma, but there is little to show for it. As the 2021 began, Burma did not move toward peace—instead, it descended into a full-scale war engulfing the entire country.

For the Karen people, multigenerational-long suffering has created fertile ground for humanitarian and rights organizations. While aid may ease immediate pain, it risks becoming a distraction, creating dependency rather than empowering the Karen to take control of their own destiny. Instead of bolstering the liberation movement, these organizations often treat the symptoms of suffering while inadvertently eroding the spirit of struggle. Their efforts, though maybe well-intentioned, fail to confront the core issue: the absence of true sovereignty. Without self-government to manage their well-being and systematically address crises, the Karen are left to depend on external support.

Reliance on donation brokers further entrenches power imbalances, making local organizations dependent on foreign donors and stifling the development of their own capacities and autonomy. Goodwill donors may unintentionally suppress the people they aim to uplift.

Orphanage schools are another one where individuals invest their thought and creativity in how to solicit donations by creating them as a business. Instead of focusing on preventing the occurrence of orphanages through the liberation movement, the culture of donations—tempering with the lowest melting points of human sympathy on children and hardship—encourages the expansion of orphanage schools in Kawthoolei. Any attempt to establish orphanage schools as a business should face scrutiny akin to a congressional hearing.

When misdirected, donations become a default solution—mistaken for easy money—stifling critical thinking and weakening self-reliance. Over time, this fosters not creativity but manipulation. A grown man from the mountains befriends a foreign visitor only to ask for a motorbike. A housemother welcomes her returning friend from abroad, only to request gold earrings. A traveler aid asks visitors for a headlamp and donation. Dignity is sacrificed. Among borderland communities, such dependency can be more damaging than a bullet—it damages the brains and corrodes the soul. The habit of solicitation must be examined before it spreads too far.

The more a people made depend on charity, the further a nation sinks—eroding the spirit of initiative, the drive for entrepreneurship, and the dignity of self-reliance. Donations to be meaningful, it ought to focus on the business of the liberation movement rather than the business of solicitation handouts.

HUMANITARIAN AIDS TO NON-ACTIVE CONFLICT DISTRICTS

In March 2024, Thailand delivered 4,000 aid packages, valued at approximately $138,000, to Kayin (Karen) State under the auspices of ASEAN, as part of a broader peace initiative aimed at facilitating talks between warring factions amidst a near-nationwide conflict. This effort to establish a "humanitarian corridor" comes as the United Nations estimates that 2.8 million people are displaced, and 18 million are in urgent need of assistance (Reuters.com). The aid convoy, organized by the Thai Red Cross and delivered to its counterpart in Myanmar, was directed to areas in Kayin State under Myanmar military control—districts where there is no active conflict or immediate humanitarian need. In these regions at the time, life continues largely undisturbed by the violence that devastates other parts of the country. The aid, however, has been co-opted by the Myanmar military—the entity responsible for much of the humanitarian crisis—and is now being used for propaganda purposes. They stage photo ops of aid distribution for the media while summoning the local population in need and sermonizing at them.

Thailand's Vice Foreign Minister, Sihasak Phuangketkeow, remarked in a Reuters report, "This is a display of good intentions from Thailand to the people of Myanmar," expressing hope for peace, stability, and unity in the region. The initiative rests on the assumption that small-scale aid directed to non-conflict zones could spark dialogue between the Myanmar military (State Administrative Council - SAC) and the alliance of Ethnic Revolutionary Organizations and urban fighters (People's Defense Force). The idea that $138,000 could coax warring factions to the negotiating table sounds fascinating and fantastical (APnews.com). If the three-quarters of a century long Burma crisis could be solved so simply, peace would have come long before most of today's generation was born.

Meanwhile, aid organizations, including those under the UN, operate under military control in Myanmar, adhering to a memorandum signed with the Myanmar military. In contrast, several Karen civil society organizations (CSOs), which have long served their people with professionalism and a profound understanding of the local context, have far better access to areas where the need is most acute. Nevertheless, aid organizations working within Myanmar military-controlled zones insist on their role as the official and professional global entities, advocating those donations be channeled through them—often sidelining the more effective, locally-rooted efforts of Karen groups.

AIDs AND AFRICAN STORIES

On the path forward, we do not need to repeat the costly mistakes that have plagued many nations. Extensive studies and wealth of literature have already exposed the consequences of aid in Africa. Kawthoolei can learn from these lessons rather than reliving history of failures.

Once upon a time, the world viewed foreign aid as a beacon of hope for Africa—a noble gesture from the wealthiest nations, intended to lift the continent out of poverty and despair. Trillions of dollars flowed into African countries over the decades, with the promise of progress and prosperity. But as the years passed, the reality on the ground began to tell a different story—one that was far less hopeful and far more troubling.

Dambisa Moyo, in her groundbreaking work *Dead Aid* (2009), unmasked this harsh reality. She argued that the endless stream of aid had become more of a curse than a blessing. Consider Zambia, her homeland. Since independence, the country has received billions in aid, yet it remains one of the poorest nations in the world, with over 60% of its population living below the poverty line. Moyo did not just critique aid in theory; she laid bare the data: countries heavily reliant on aid saw their economies stagnate, with average growth rates lagging far behind the global average. Aid had created a dependency that crippled the entrepreneurial spirit and allowed corrupt regimes to flourish, unchecked and unaccountable.

William Easterly, in *The White Man's Burden* (2006), delved deeper into the failures of the aid industry, which he described as an empire of top-down solutions imposed by Western nations. Take the example of the Millennium Villages Project, a well-intentioned initiative to eradicate poverty by providing targeted aid to specific African communities. The project, backed by billions of dollars and touted as a model for future aid programs, eventually fell short of its ambitious goals. Easterly pointed out that these villages, rather than becoming self-sustaining, often slid back into poverty once the aid dried up, proving that imposed solutions, no matter how grand in design, rarely take root in foreign soil.

Yash Tandon's critique in *Ending Aid Dependence* (2008) cuts to the heart of a more insidious reality: aid as a tool of neo-colonial control. He argued that donor nations, under the guise of altruism, use aid to exert influence and maintain a strategic foothold in Africa. For instance, the structural adjustment programs of the 1980s, mandated by the IMF and World Bank as conditions for aid, forced African countries to adopt policies that benefited Western economies while devastating local industries and services. Tandon's words are a stark reminder that aid often serves the interests of the giver far more than those of the recipient.

Peter Bauer had sounded the alarm long before these critiques gained traction. He observed that aid distorts local economies by displacing local businesses and fostering a culture of reliance rather than innovation. For example, in Ghana, local textile industries once thrived, employing thousands. But with the influx of free or subsidized clothing from abroad, these local industries collapsed, unable to compete with the flood of cheap imports (Bauer, 1981). Bauer's insights show how aid, rather than building economies, often undermines them, creating a vicious cycle of dependency and decline.

Michael Maren, drawing from his personal experiences in Somalia, provided a vivid account of aid's unintended consequences in *The Road to Hell* (1997). He described how aid, instead of alleviating suffering, often exacerbated it. In Somalia, food aid intended to save lives ended up fueling conflict, as warlords seized control of the supplies, using them as weapons in their power struggles. Maren's story is not just a critique—it is a chilling reminder of how good intentions can go disastrously wrong when the complexities of local politics are ignored.

David Sogge, in *Give and Take: What's the Matter with Foreign Aid?* (2002), pulls no punches in exposing the ulterior motives behind aid. He points to cases like Ethiopia, where in the 1980s, billions in aid flowed into a country ruled by a brutal dictatorship. Much of that aid was siphoned off to fund military campaigns and prop up a regime responsible for mass atrocities. Sogge's analysis reveals the dark side of aid: it often props up the very forces that keep nations in poverty, all while serving the geopolitical interests of donor countries.

These critiques, drawn from decades of data, case studies, and firsthand accounts, converge on a single, stark conclusion: the promise of foreign aid to Africa is largely a mirage. Instead of fostering development, aid has often stunted it, creating a dependency that drains Africa's potential. The story of aid is not one of salvation but of missed opportunities and misplaced trust.

Aid is often compromised because it tends to be driven not by the needs of poor countries, but by the interests of wealthy nations seeking to bolster their own economies. Much of what is labeled as foreign aid never actually leaves the donor country; instead, it is used to purchase domestically-produced goods or to hire local consultants, benefiting the giver more than the recipient. (The Associated Press, 2007)

In much of Africa, the reliance on foreign aid continues to shape development priorities while harming perceptions of possibility. Aid can carry unintended consequences—dampening local initiative, distorting incentives, and reinforcing cycles of dependency. Across the continent, there are growing signs of a quiet shift: communities choosing enterprise over entitlement, trade over charity, and self-determination over imposed direction.

The future seems most promising where agency is reclaimed—where those who know the land, the culture, and the challenges are taking the lead.

EDUCATION THAT PROMOTES THE WRONG LANGUAGE

The influence of education donation brokers is equally unsettling, as they often carry with them ideological baggage that fractures the community bonds rooted in language and culture. Around the border, the education system is frequently forced to conform to languages and curricula dictated by donors, relegating native languages to secondary status. This shift is often facilitated by supposedly educated Karen persons who have lost attachment, proficiency, and respect for their mother tongue.

Promoting the Burmese language in Karen-speaking schools accelerates the Burmanization agenda that has persisted since the era of dictator General Ne Win, aiming to unify the country by erasing linguistic diversity since 1962. Decisions about maintaining native languages or adopting specific political values are often made by donation brokers rather than by local communities, who are better positioned to reflect their own values and needs. While these donations are intended to help, they come at the expense of the community's autonomy, dignity, and cultural heritage.

MULTICULTURALISM EXPERIMENT

Outsiders often introduce their version of multiculturalism, applying a standardized ideology—a concept that remains unfulfilled even in their own societies. Liberal democratic countries in the West, once tempted by the allure of multiculturalism, now find themselves trapped in a quagmire of fractured, quarreling societies. What was once celebrated as diversity has devolved into a battleground of conflicting identities and competing grievances. What was meant to be a harmonious mosaic of cultures has often become a battleground of competing priority, leaving many feelings disconnected and lost.

In their pursuit of idealistic inclusion, some outsiders bring in the idea they wrestle at home, attempting to graft ideals onto unfamiliar soil, searching for solutions abroad that have failed at home. Too often, the Karen people became a testing ground for social experiments.

BANNERS TO SAVE

Some of these outsiders arrive at Kawthoolei under a heroic banner, intent on saving the poor-looking people of Kawthoolei. They hand out soaps and buckets, suggesting the people to cleanse themselves. Instead of fostering dignity, they promote pity, filthy with internet selfies, perpetuating a savior-victim profile. They find these words irresistible, rolling them off their tongues with ease, as if savoring their taste. "Refugees," "ethnic minority," "hill tribes," "stateless"—terms that comfortably fit their narrative of marginalization. They speak those without hesitation, unaware or indifferent to the weight they carry, repeating them without reserve, rarely questioning how these labels reduce human lives.

CIVIL SOCIETY BEFORE THE STATE

Some helping hands carry political baggage waving the banner of democracy, eager to implement it in regions where nation-building struggles to take root. They overlook the fact that in the West, democracy emerged only after a long and complex history of state-building. Nations like France, Germany, and the United Kingdom spent centuries in feudal fragmented states, later establishing stable governance before evolving into democratic states. Expecting fragile states to leap directly into democracy without a foundation of stable institutions is like expecting a tree to bear fruit before its roots have taken hold.

Supported by entrenched elites, successive dictators have attempted to build a unified state through coercion—a method both ineffective and counterproductive in Burma. Since its inception, the country has remained fractured, with various state actors scattered across the land unable to be controlled by the central government, despite central Burma maintaining a disproportionately large military relative to its population and economy to suppress these competing regional actors.

Outsiders often assume that Burma's future rests in embracing a multicultural, pluralistic liberal democracy. Yet, generations of distrust and trauma, deeply wounded by the successive generation of dictatorships. Coercive and corrupt power grip on the nation have shattered the well-being of its people. Wounds yet unhealed, scars run deep, making it far from certain that Western models of governance can take root in such fractured soil.

The Karen people's armed revolution, though unsuccessful in its broader aims, managed to carve out a stable base in the mountainous frontier from 1975 to 1994. During this period, they established Mar-Ner-Plaw (recently re-captured), a de facto nation-state providing governance and services to their community. This semi-self-governing pattern is seen elsewhere in Burma. Goodwill entities could have played a crucial role in strengthening the institutions and governance of such self-governing states rather than piecemeal donation.

Dr. Henry Kissinger, the late U.S. The Secretary of State noted in one of his writings: "The institutions of the West developed gradually while those of most new states were put into place in elaborated form immediately. In the West, a civil society evolved side-by-side with the maturation of the modern state" (Yew, 2000).

Institutions and civil society can nurture self-governing autonomy when rooted in respect for local governance, rather than imposed through donor agendas that disregard the local political framework.

Human Rights vs. Human Liberation

In a region still fighting for self-governance, democratic ideals cannot take root without a stable state and successful nation-building. The path to establishing a self-governing state that guarantees human security demands personal sacrifices—often at odds with the principles championed by human rights organizations. Without the authority to safeguard these rights, the doctrines of individual freedom risk undermining the struggle for liberation they seek to support.

When human rights are universally interpreted without considering cultural context or applied without regard for situational realities, the approach can erode the camaraderie essential for unity and mutual support among those fighting for collective rights. Human rights, rooted in Western values of individualism and liberal democracy, carry an implicit assumption of superiority over indigenous communal values, sidelining them in favor of what is deemed "modern" or "progressive." These individualistic ideals dilute the Karen ethos of collective sacrifice for the greater good.

In the Karen community, mutual respect and collective welfare are the bedrock of social cohesion. Among the service members in Kawthoolei, this sense of community is so strong that, on one occasion, when a group of four had only three candies, none ate to demonstrate unity and shared sacrifice. Some community members lament that insensitive imposition of individual rights threatens this cohesion, leading to social fragmentation and the erosion of communal bonds.

Human rights claims, at times, undermine order and discipline, particularly when misused to resist order and rightful authority. In Kawthoolei's armed resistance, where discipline and command are crucial, this misuse of rights becomes problematic. An unmotivated service member can randomly appeal to individual rights. A superficial understanding of human rights has eroded discipline and adherence to order, both of which are essential to the resistance. For some, human rights have come to represent an easy life, threatening the principles of struggle and sacrifice.

The Singapore's Case for Human Rights and Discipline

Human rights are often assumed to be universal, but in practice, nations act according to their sovereignty and rule of law. Disciplinary action and punishment cannot be easily dismissed under the blanket claim of human rights. In 1994, a U.S. teenager convicted of vandalism in Singapore was sentenced to prison, fined, and given six strokes of caning—a punishment that involves a strong man striking the naked buttocks with a cane, often resulting in severe injury. The case sparked public controversy, with President Clinton and the U.S. Congress appealing for leniency. After diplomatic negotiations, the caning was reduced to four strokes. While Singapore's punishment may seem excessive and even barbaric, public opinion in the U.S. was nearly split, with 49 percent approving and 48 percent disapproving of the sentence, according to a Los Angeles Times poll. Despite the controversy, neither branch of the U.S. government could intervene effectively. In April, during a local television program, then Senior Minister Lee Kuan

Yew said that the US was neither safe nor peaceful because it did not dare to restrain or punish those who did wrong, adding, "If you like it this way, that is your problem. But, that is not the path we choose".

The incident momentarily strained the U.S.-Singapore relations, but Singapore gained respect for standing its ground, even as the punishment appeared brutal to many. This firm stance extends to its treatment of drug traffickers, where the death penalty is enforced without exception, with 16 executions carried out in 2023 alone. In Singapore, the right to life is forfeited when one's actions threaten to destroy hundreds of families through addiction. In a world increasingly shifting toward leniency and a reluctance to condemn human errors with harsh punishment, Singapore's approach may seem severe. Yet, its success as a nation is undeniable—stranger than fiction, a testament to the power of sovereignty and the respect a tiny island commands.

If Kawthoolei does not firm on disciplinary action but pleasing every imported ideology, it risks becoming a perpetual object of ridicule from both the left and the right, and even the rights groups. Letting loose sloppy behaviors lead to weak character. Small misdemeanors unchecked will encourage criminal offenses, and petty theft will breed widespread corruption, further eroding the moral and social structure of the land. Corruption breeds distrust in leadership, fracturing unity within organizations and undermining social cohesion.

UDHR in Its Birthplace

Anyone who wishes to advocate for human rights in the war-torn land of Kawthoolei should first read the Universal Declaration of Human Rights (UDHR) with an understanding of the spirit from the practicality. The UDHR, adopted at the founding of the United Nations, stands as the cornerstone of international human rights law.

In the wake of the Myanmar military coup in 2021, thousands connected to Burma gathered one Saturday at the United Nations office in San Francisco—the birthplace of the Universal Declaration of Human Rights—to voice their rejection of the military's authoritarian seizure of power. Yet it was the weekend, and their chants and speeches fell on no ears. The demonstration went largely unnoticed, blending into the typical weekend bustle of San Francisco, where the noise likely annoyed more passersby than it inspired. One wonders what Eleanor Roosevelt, the architect of the UDHR, would say if she saw how its birthplace has lost its sense of taste—and perhaps, of hearing while a distant comer in far east find it fractionable to speak of human rights.

In Kawthoolei—as anywhere in the world—every person deserves to live in dignity, free from fear, exploitation, and injustice, whether imposed by governments or external agencies. No one should be subjected to the kind of suffering witnessed in Myanmar or in parts of Kayin State now gripped by gambling, trafficking, and scams, and above all forced labor. Yet freedom imposed as ideology often loses its meaning. Rights without responsibility, and liberty without discipline, lead to imbalance. Nation-building demands both liberty and order.

THE CASE OF JOURNALISM

Journalism, when funded by institutional donations, often carries the weight of political values that are anything but neutral. This reality is where the struggle for control and influence is as much about narratives as it is about territory.

Take the Kawthoolei-Thailand border, where journalism is as crowded as the refugee camps that dot the landscape. Here, the press—backed by donors with specific political agendas—operates under the banner of transparency and support for democracy. The recent Burma Act of 2023 [James M. Inhofe National Defense Authorization Act for Fiscal Year 2023 (NDAA 2023)] even includes provisions to bolster journalism, framing it as a tool to support the struggle for democratic reform. But this journalism does not just report; it shapes the conflict by selectively highlighting certain activities or leaking sensitive information. In doing so, it disrupts the delicate balance of the liberation movement, pushing some political values to the forefront while obscuring others. Whereas policy in Washington D.C. can shift with new presidents or Congress.

Contrast this with the situation in northern and western Burma. In the north, the Kachin people operate without the persistent gaze of what some might call "petty journalism." Their struggles and strategies remain under the radar, free from the scrutiny that often accompanies institutional backing. Similarly, in the western fronts, the Arakan and Chin people navigate their own complex realities without the interference of journalists who might inadvertently—or intentionally—tip the scales of conflict through their reporting.

In these regions, the absence of such media presence allows the local movements to progress without the pressure of external narratives. But on the Kawthoolei-Thailand border, the story is different. Here, journalism funded by institutional donations becomes a double-edged sword—meant to inform and support, but often leading to the exposure of vulnerabilities and the amplification of specific agendas. In conflicts as complex as these, journalism is rarely a neutral observer. It is a player, and its presence can alter the course of events, that serve interests far removed from those on the ground.

In the early 2000s, as tensions simmered between Karen armed splinter groups and the main Karen military forces, a chilling remark made by a Karen reporter captured the stark reality of the situation. "Let them fight against each other, it creates jobs for us." His words, uttered without hesitation, revealed a deep-seated cynicism and a complex, often troubling, relationship between journalism and conflict.

This reporter's comment was not just a slip of the tongue; it was a reflection of the intersection between media and war, where the conflict that tore communities apart simultaneously provided fodder for news stories and, by extension, a livelihood for those who reported on it. His casual acknowledgment of the role conflict played in sustaining his work also unveiled his true allegiance—not to the cause of Karen liberation, but to the perpetuation of a struggle that kept him employed.

Such moments expose the motivations and ethics of those who report from the frontlines. While many journalists may claim to stand with the people they cover, the reality can be far more complex, with personal and professional interests sometimes taking precedence over the larger struggle for freedom and justice. In the fog of war, the lines between ally and opportunist can blur, revealing the harsh reality that for some, conflict is not just a tragedy, but a business.

A SOUTH KOREAN STORY

Foreign aid, while often critiqued for its potential to foster dependency and corruption, is not always the villain in the story of development. In fact, it can be an essential tool for nations struggling to stand on their own feet, especially in the aftermath of conflict or crisis. The story of South Korea offers a compelling counterpoint to the harsh critiques of aid.

Sixty years ago, South Korea was emerging from the devastation of war, its economy in shambles, its infrastructure in ruins. The country faced immense challenges—widespread poverty, political instability, and the daunting task of rebuilding a nation from the ground up. South Korea was poorer than poor African countries. In this critical period, U.S. aid played a crucial role. Billions of dollars in financial assistance, coupled with technical expertise, flowed into South Korea, helping to stabilize the economy, rebuild infrastructure, and lay the groundwork for future growth.

But South Korea's success was not merely a product of external support. What made the difference was the country's strong leadership and disciplined national character. Leaders like Park Chung-Hee recognized that aid was a temporary lifeline, not a permanent solution. They used the aid strategically, investing in education, industrialization, and infrastructure. As the flow of aid began to diminish, South Korea did not falter; instead, it accelerated its efforts to become self-reliant. The government implemented rigorous economic reforms, fostered a culture of hard work and innovation, and gradually shifted from an aid-dependent economy to one driven by exports and industrial growth.

By the 1980s, South Korea had transformed itself into a burgeoning industrial power. The country's rapid economic ascent—often referred to as the "Miracle on the Han River"—was a testament to what can be achieved when aid is combined with visionary leadership and a strong, disciplined populace. South Korea's experience illustrates that foreign aid, when used effectively, can provide the necessary foundation for a nation to rebuild and eventually thrive on its own.

South Korea's narrative does not negate the valid criticism of aid, particularly in cases where it has perpetuated dependency or supported corrupt regimes. However, it highlights the complexity of the issue—aid is neither inherently good nor inherently bad. Its effectiveness depends largely on how it is used and the context in which it is deployed. South Korea's story shows that with the right leadership and a commitment to self-reliance, aid can be a powerful catalyst for long-term development and independence.

SINGAPORE STORY

When Lee Kuan Yew visited Japan in the early years of Singapore's independence, he observed a line of Asian leaders seeking compensation for wartime atrocities committed during the Japanese occupation of World War II. At the time, Japan was still emerging from the ruins of war, struggling to rebuild its economy and establish a manufacturing base. The Japanese expected Lee to join the queue—another statesman with a grievance. But he earned their respect by refusing to join the line with a begging bowl.

STABLE STATE, GOODWILL, AND REALITY

Ideals such as equity, diversity, and inclusion are important. Developed countries have managed to achieve stable and powerful state authority through elaborate bureaucratic mechanisms and various institutions, within which individuals can challenge authority. However, with the advancement of technology, state authorities, if permitted, can tap into vast databases to track nearly every aspect of their citizens' life—income, credit history, purchasing habits, and residential records are meticulously logged, creating a digital footprint accessible at any time by agencies like the FBI. This pervasive surveillance gives the state power to act decisively while citizens appear to enjoy their individual liberty.

The insistence on imposing a distant democratic model—one that balances state authority with individual freedoms or dilutes leadership through excessive checks on power rooted in deep-seated distrust—presupposes the existence of a stable state. Only after achieving this foundation can the balance between state power and individual freedoms be effectively developed. Otherwise, goodwill donors, despite their generous resources, will struggle to make a meaningful impact. Even when goodwill messengers spread teachings with sincere efforts, locals often misinterpret them due to differing frames of reference.

Promoting human rights without the necessary resources or enforcement mechanisms is not only ineffective but can also be counterproductive. While the rhetoric of rights echoes across the Kawthoolei border, in developed nations, human rights are rarely a topic of daily discourse. Instead, individuals are bound by institutions and systems that prioritize responsibilities over mere assertions of rights. To elevate rights above social cohesion and community discipline without the structures to sustain them suggests a superficial understanding.

People in underdeveloped countries might perceive those in wealthy nations as having both big pockets and generous hearts. While wealthy liberal democracies often champion humanitarian values, they are not without their own struggles at home. A simple telling example: a small college town in California—the wealthiest and most liberal state in America—where government office restrooms are locked with passcodes to prevent shelterless Californians from using them for basic hygiene or relief. Perception and reality often diverge: a big bank account and a big heart and a big idea do not always translate into big respect to human dignity.

Human dignity matters more than abstract rights within the family and community. A homeless man by the street may possess human rights, but he may still struggle to support a family. By contrast, a factory worker—giving up his days to put food on the table and keep loved ones sheltered—upholds dignity through service and sacrifice. In nation-building, human rights alone—without service, sacrifice, and responsibility—will not build anything that lasts. By extension, building a nation demands that citizens shoulder significant responsibilities.

DONATION BAGGAGE

In the context of Kawthoolei, this "baggage" manifests in several ways:

1. Power Imbalance: Donors often wield significant influence over local decision-making processes, sidelining grassroots leadership and traditional structures.
2. Cultural Displacement: Donations tied to specific ideological values (e.g., individualism, liberalism, or Western democratic ideals) can be incongruent with Kawthoolei's communal traditions and cultural norms.
3. Dependency Cycle: Continuous reliance on donations risks creating a cycle of dependency, weakening local self-sufficiency and resilience.
4. Moral Superiority: Donor organizations sometimes project a sense of moral or intellectual superiority, disregarding local wisdom, lived experiences, and context-specific solutions.
5. Agenda Setting: Donors may prioritize certain causes (e.g., human rights campaigns or education reforms) that align with their own global narratives, rather than addressing the most pressing local needs.

To address this baggage, Kawthoolei must assess the implications of external aid, assert local priorities, and negotiate partnerships that respect their sovereignty and cultural values. Every donation to be distributed must pass through governmental approval and oversight. A truly beneficial partnership must be anchored in mutual respect, transparency, and alignment with Kawthoolei's long-term vision of nation-building and self-determination.

FREEBIE CAN POISON

Organizations of various forms often portray people in Karen clothing as needy, using their images to solicit donations. Social media is flooded with photos of children and women, often families clutching plastic bags filled with a few snacks and toiletries—symbols of charity that strip away dignity. The faces of recipients speak unspoken shame in the transaction that reinforces helplessness in their photos.

Repeated handouts create an expectation that aid will always come from somewhere, habituating a mindset that weakens self-reliance. For children raised in such an environment, this conditioning can be damaging, stunting their sense of initiative and resilience in formative years. At the same time, one rarely sees images of the donation collectors and organizers looking anything but well-fed and well-dressed, while those they claim to help remain visibly impoverished—an imbalanced victim-savior complex contour.

Charity creates expectation. Creating the wrong expectation to younger children with handouts of a bag of snack and a pack of juice with a photo taken cannot nurture their dignity. Unearned gifts can erode character. Growing up as a student in a frontline district of Kawthoolei, I witnessed and lived through how war and economic hardship intertwined, pressing families—regardless of race, gender, or origin—under the same unforgiving weight. In those classrooms, scarcity was not just an economic reality; it was a constant presence etched into every worn-out textbook, every pencil sharpened down to its last fragile inch, every notebook with pages rationed like precious metal. School supplies were not merely objects; they were symbols of sacrifice, purchased with hard-earned money, yet poor in quality, and treated with reverence.

A refugee camp along the border shared a troubling story. In classrooms with freely distributed pens and pencils from aid organizations, students casually threw them at one another to tease each other. That would be unthinkable in the schools of inner Kawthoolei regions where I grew up—the careless wasting of tools meant for learning. These objects had lost their meaning when no effort was required to earn them. What is lost is not only a sense of earned value, but a sense of respect and reverence and character.

But it was not just the school supplies; it was the food. Stories of food aid managers hoarding sacks of beans, reselling them back into the donation system, painted a grim picture. Meals that should have nourished children were instead traded like commodities in a cruel cycle of corruption. Families often endured hunger—not because food was entirely absent, but because what little reached them had been diminished by greed. Yet they did not die, nor could they escape. They were trapped in a system that allowed them to survive but denied them dignity.

Thailand, though not bound by international refugee agreements, accepted Karen refugees out of a sense of humanity and business practicality. Yet, over time, this arrangement evolved into a transactional system—aid became an industry, and refugees, commodities. Camps meant as temporary shelters turned into stagnant settlements, trapping generations in limbo. A refugee camp should never become a permanent home that supports the aid industrial complex. Five years should be the threshold before real political solutions are pursued with urgency. Beyond that, the camp becomes more than a physical confinement—it becomes a prison of the spirit, eroding ambition, dulling resilience, and stifling the regeneration of a people.

The effects of prolonged dependency did not remain confined to the camps. Even among those who resettled in wealthier industrious nations, traces of the freebie mindset lingered in some families. Habits formed in prolonged dependence—waiting for handouts, thinking government assistance as if exhaustible heavenly wealth, treating free provisions with carelessness—did not fade easily. Even in lands overflowing with opportunity, these remnants acted as chains holding back potential. The poison goes generational.

Some within the community linger in an echo chamber of perpetual sympathy-seeking and donation appeals; over time, they come to see the idea of new money system and making money—whether through trading, creative investment venture, or innovative entrepreneurship—as "funny, stupid, and impossible."

However, this is not where the hopeless story ends. The Karen people are resilient. Out of war, scarcity, and decades of confinement, many emerged with determination engraved into their spirit. Men and women who once lived on survival donated rations grew into hard-working citizens, building lives of meaning and purpose in foreign lands. They are learning and exploring a world that beyond comfort zone and pursuing cutting-edge idea. Their success stands as a testament to a truth that cannot be denied: the character of the Karen people cannot be easily broken.

> Humanitarian relief is meant as temporary relief for severe pain—like an opioid medicine, it can ease suffering in the short term. But when relied on long-term, it becomes harmful and can ultimately destroy the life it was meant to save.

No nation makes real progress through charity. We are here to build our nation with dignity—not dependency—for dependency stands the direct antithesis to nation-building. Ours must be a nation where every individual possesses both the drive and the opportunity to earn a living for their family while uplifting their community and contributing to the progress of the country.

Goodwill Ambassador, Meaningful Impact

A goodwill ambassador will focus on helping the people getting out of dependency, not entrapped in it. For this, Kawthoolei will have to learn to stand on its own, harnessing its resources and organizing its human capital so that external support can make a meaningful impact.

If donors seek to make a lasting impact, they should focus on investing in physical and institutional infrastructure, the essential foundations for lifting people up. Reliable institutions, effective governance, and a commitment to service are essential local foundations for foreign aid to create meaningful change. These qualities also attract long term foreign investment, as they signal integrity and reliability to the world.

Far and wide, many helping hands from different parts of the world have extended their hands to Kawthoolei in its darkest times. Not all helping hands carry an agenda, many are living angels walking on earth, here in Kawthoolei. Amid the jungles, mountains, and valleys of Kawthoolei, countless brave souls stand as quiet heroes, risking their lives in the face of bombs falling from the sky, bullets cutting through the air, and mines buried beneath the soil. They have left behind the comfort and safety of wealthy nations, dedicating themselves selflessly to the people of Kawthoolei.

These helpers are goodwill ambassadors, providing more than medical care—they offer confidence, comfort, and hope to those who suffer, becoming beacons in the darkest of times—living angels roaming on earth. Even many Karen natives find it too daunting, given the high risks and the absence of basic human needs—no showers, no privacy, no comforts of bed—only disease-bearing mosquitoes, and venomous creatures—scorpions, centipedes, hornets, leeches, and snakes of every kind lurk in every shadow. These individuals and organizations should be forever etched into the history of our struggle for freedom and human dignity, for they have given more than their time; they have given hope and their only selves.

PART III

GROWING NATION

Are We Deserving of a Nation?

My identity runs deeper
than language, culture, and tradition.
It lives in the way I carry myself.

Polite, wholesome, and assertive,
a rare blend for than our ancestry.
Has long marked by
soft, timid, and meek spirits.
Yet I am learning to hold both
meekness woven with strength,
humility rooted in respect.

Sophisticated, yet sharp-witted.
Softy, yet confident.
Shy, yet a great listener.
Gentle, yet firm.

Does these qualities reflect the dream
That so many of us hold
to build Kawthoolei as a nation?

@kgpotree

Chapter 8

Aspiring Nation, Growing Identity

Kawthoolei is the rightful destiny of national progress, but only if we grow toward that destiny.

The social challenges we face are so far-reaching that they have swelled into national crises: our character has weakened, our youth struggle with discipline; we have become a subject of ridicule among our neighbors; our education system focuses more on making students impress on other nations than nurturing integrity; our educated are trapped in an outdated world outlook, unable to anticipate a course that could advance beyond recognition; adults indulge themselves in beer and soccer while our youth are absorbed into sports and loitering in number; our girls in the border drawn to materialistic appearances and superficial makeup busying themselves with beauty pageants; our boys spending their days running under the sun, building their body but little of their intellects; community leaders organize national days with trivial sports tournaments instead of public recognition of talents; our parents are captivated by the empty glamour of entertainment, and our communities are lost in the whirl of festivities, leaving little time and energy for learning and growth; gladiator-style boxing and mixed martial arts match our grown men's appetite; we dress to reinforce a tribal stereotype; we disparage our traditional cuisine with poor table manners, and even streaming it online, lacking respect to our time-tested traditional diet; we belittle ourselves with the label of 'ethnic minority,' degrading our worth and perspective; some of our beliefs hold us back, and uncanny teachings in weekend assemblies failing to illuminate the path to progress grounded in reason; our online discussions erode decency and civility, echoing each other in a small chamber; our armed forces wearing many badges of K-Alphabet are strong enough to resist unity under one command, yet weak enough to suck our own blood; our leaders inspire little trust; our Politicians often echo old ideas, stumbling through a new world, serving neither our interests nor destiny; diplomatic strategy is more pleading than partnership in a world that demands strength and vision.

If we are to grow as a nation fully realize our potential, these challenges must not go unaddressed.

So shall we grow and rise above these challenges, confronting them head-on to cultivate the strength and foresight needed to transform Kawthoolei into the nation it is meant to be. For us to become a nation worthy of the global stage, we must grow in character, mature in emotion, and elevate in intellect.

CLEANLINESS AND CIVIC DUTY

Many Karen people frequently chew betel nuts in public, a trend on the rise with chewing and spitting becoming commonplace. The use of betel quid produces red-colored saliva, which, when spat out indiscriminately, causes unsightly stains and contributes to biological waste pollution in public spaces.

Betel nut chewing should be regarded similarly to smoking—a private activity kept out of public view. There is no "human right" when personal actions harm the public image. Beyond creating an unsightly mess, the act of spitting after chewing falls short of basic standards of civility. Also, there is a health concern for the spread of tuberculosis, hepatitis B and other contagious diseases from public spitting.

In public speaking, officials chew betelnut mumbling during official meetings in the tone of casual village interactions rather than formal discourse. This habit not only disrupts clear communication but also undermines the professionalism expected in official settings.

In the 2023 *Karen Socio-Economic Household Survey*, betel nut was identified as the second largest cultivated crop after rice—one a staple food of the people, the other an addictive leisure commodity. I grew up in a region sustained by the betel nut economy, where orchards were beautiful and serene, and farming them was less labor-intensive than rice cultivation. Even today, betel nut farming remains the backbone of many communities in Kawthoolei. For the nation to grow, our farms must transform into a new economy. To cut old habits, we must cut clear off our betel nut trees.

Notwithstanding the thought of transitioning to a new economy can be daunting, people once moved from candles to electricity, leaving the candle-making industry confined to decoration. Economic shifts, as well as character shifts, are inevitable if we are for the new light of electricity.

In solitude, alone in the jungle, one has no compulsion for the finer moral virtues—cleanliness, quietude, or respect for community well-being. There is no need to observe boundaries of public decorum or to cover one's private affairs or body parts for modesty and decency. But in society, where many live together, our actions ripple outward, affecting those who share our space, land, water, and air—the resources and environment that sustain us all. Civic duty, then, becomes a guiding principle, enabling us to live harmoniously together.

When people live side by side, every small choice we make—what we eat, how we eat, where we source our food, and how we cultivate the land—impacts the community. Clean water, pure food, and healthy surroundings are not merely personal privileges; they are shared rights, preserved only through responsible stewardship.

Civic duty encompasses how we present ourselves and interact. In public space, our table manners, daily attire, and even the places we choose for personal relief reflect our respect for those around us. These social norms are more than formalities; they are safeguards of dignity and markers of mutual respect, preserving social order and character within the community. To live in society is to practice restraint and consideration—not as burdens, but as expressions of our shared humanity, recognizing that our personal choices are inseparable from the well-being of others.

A GLIMPSE INTO HOW OTHERS DID IT

In 1940, Plaek Phibunsongkhram, a former Prime Minister of Thailand, initiated a transformative campaign aimed at encouraging citizens to abandon the habit of chewing betel quid. In a bold move to modernize the nation, he ordered the systematic cutting down of maak trees across the country and banned betel chewing in government buildings. This marked the beginning of an anti-betel chewing movement, where those who continued the practice in government spaces found themselves denied services. The campaign was driven to foster a modern society and cleansing the cities of the red-stained residue that marred streets and roads, a mark of filth and unhygienic living that no longer had a place in a nation striving for progress.

In a series of Thai cultural mandates, Phibul (as known in the West for being nationalistic) aimed to align dress codes, work habits, and daily routines with the vision of a productive nation. He discouraged idleness and urged citizens to seek stable careers to serve the nation, honor the flag, and prioritize national interests in commerce and consumption. He banned references to regional identities like Southern or Northern Thai to foster national unity, emphasized duty without shirking, prescribed appropriate dress (banning undergarments-only attire in public), promoted polite international or traditional clothing, encouraged set mealtimes, and advocated for 6-8 hours of sleep.

As a result, modern Thais are known for their neat appearance and are considered cultured by Mandate 12. Nowadays, Thai cuisine is globally recognized for its presentation and taste, with restaurants present across U.S. cities. Thai craftsmanship also enjoys a good reputation. In 2014, the government introduced the "12 Core Values of Thailand" as a moral guide for the youth, ensuring that Thai students are disciplined, both physically and in character. A Karen official once remarked that Thai school children showed more discipline than our soldiers. While some may view Thailand schools as overly rigid, its disciplined environment is appealing to creative youth worldwide, making the country a top destination for exploring life.

The betel nut, once chewed for recreation like drinking tea and coffee, now serves as a poor image for the choices we face. Just as Thailand chose to let go of this practice to embrace a new era, so too must we discern the elements of our culture that propel us forward from those that hold us back.

AND THUS SINGAPORE RISES

In the 1960s, Singapore began as a poor nation where people commonly spat and littered in public. It has embraced the "Green and Clean Singapore" initiative, campaigning vigorously against spitting and littering in public spaces, which has helped cultivate a public culture of cleanliness and innovation. Now, Singapore is known for its cleanliness and safety, a reputation built with strict regulations. For instance, bringing chewing gum in packs into Singapore is illegal—a commitment to maintaining order and cleanliness by forbidding trivial leisure.

The way they treat their municipal waste is also innovative. Since Singapore lacks land resources for waste disposal, it has developed a highly efficient system where waste is incinerated, with the heat used to generate electricity and the ash repurposed to create new land. For a nation to rise to world-class standards of civility, difficult-to-break habits, such as spitting, must be left behind.

Lee Kuan Yew once declared with resolute conviction,

> "I am often accused of interfering in the private lives of citizens. Yes, if I had not done so, we wouldn't be where we are today. And I say without the slightest remorse, that our economic progress would have been impossible without intervening in the most personal matters—who your neighbor is, how you live, the noise you make, how you spit, or what language you use. We decide what is right. Never mind what the people think." — Speaking to Straits Times newspaper, 1987

The path to a growing identity is not always paved with popular choices. The transformation of a people, the forging of a new identity, and the ascent to national greatness sometimes demand bold interventions, steering the collective spirit toward a shared destiny, even if it means challenging personal freedom. The birth of a nation, like the shaping of its identity, requires a firm hand to guide its course, ensuring that the seeds of progress are sown in fertile ground, regardless of the initial resistance they might face.

Be a light, not a victim.

CIVILITY, DECENCY, AND COMMON ETIQUETTE

Our public conduct will undergo its ultimate test of character. Our trek to liberty is an arduous journey—marked by ugly, thorny betrayals beneath the skin, and a hardship walking on ash-covered burning coal. In a dark frustrated time, we are tempted to let go of the common decency and common courtesy that define our cause.

To meet the ambitions of a growing nation, we can no longer linger in the comfort of milk-drinking infancy or act as emotionally impulsive toddlers—a state fit only for untamed tribal savagery. Maturity is evident in how we speak, act, handle disagreement, and carry ourselves throughout the day, as well as how we manage our time.

Do we spend most of our time idly hanging in a hammock in daytime, letting the hours pass by? Or do we use our finite resources of time productively and with purpose? Do we communicate with a sense of responsibility and empowerment, or do we evade responsibility, speaking insecurely and incapable of facing daily challenges? Our assigned tasks, our chit-chat conversations, and our greetings, work and interaction, must elevate to the level of civic culture, embracing physical, intellectual, and cultural growth in all its forms.

Gentleness in words and courtesy in treatment have long been our nature. Yet, with sudden exposure to a world where irresponsible speech is exalted as freedom, many of our folks find themselves eating the vile fruits of the internet—a realm where unchecked content and sensationalism are monetized. Shame and dignity are left behind.

Bad taste and bad character of tribal sensitivity reinforces the perception that we are nothing more than wild peasants, rude, unsophisticated and incapable of governing ourselves. This narrative, whether self-imposed or perpetuated by external forces, is killing our struggle by a thousand cuts. It casts doubt on our ability to forge a future where we are self-governed and sovereign, personally and nationally.

Freedom of speech, while essential, can also be toxic if misused. Hate speeches, conspiracy theories, and defamation can hurt the state and national cohesion. This is why nations with state authority carefully monitor and regulate its abuse. Laws such as *lèse-majesté*— criminalizing defamation against the head of state or the state itself—are not limited to Thailand or dictatorship regimes but are also enforced in democracies like Germany, Italy, the Netherlands, and Spain, where freedom of speech is highly valued. Reckless speech online spreads vulgar, derogatory, and hateful messages, creating public discord and eroding public morale. A responsible citizen practices self-censorship, using their freedom of speech wisely and with accountability.

Facebook, TikTok, and other digital time-killers can become hazards for those lacking discipline. Without purpose or responsibility, idle hands and minds—young or old—risk being consumed by the untamed world of the internet, where the thumb of impulsive sharing also participates in virtual vandalism.

In fact, these digital platforms are also treasure troves of education and inspiration, with AI-driven algorithms analyzing our browsing patterns to offer content that fosters learning and growth. The time we spend on them either pollutes our minds with sensational junk or enriches us with freely accessible knowledge.

We find ourselves caught in the darker currents of social media sensation where indecency consumes online communities participating in impulsive sharing and resharing of poor taste and poor examples. Some are captivated by the spectacle of cage fighting, where raw savagery is mistaken for glory. Raising a Karen National flag in a kickboxing fight has a lot more social media sharing. Physical brutality is celebrated. Brutal contests cannot offer nourishment for the soul, sharpen neither the mind nor the intellect, and fail utterly in guiding the development of our youth.

Kawthoolei has a high bar, its people cannot adopt the *low* as they please. To pave the path forward, rising above these primal urges is a moral necessity, not a choice. True maturity transcends physical prowess; we need to build our muscle in intellect and decorum as highly as raw physical strength to overcome baser instincts. Without the character of its youth, the nation is unlikely to see progress. Even a rich nation without character will still see its youth broken inside. Our progress is to be measured not by brute force, but by the depth of our ideas and the refinement of our actions.

Making Larger Rooms for Children at Home

Traditional Karen communities are deeply conservative. In many ways, they are the guardians of the moral and social fabric that defines Karen identity. Their cultural life is enriched by elaborate ceremonies—from religious rites like ordaining pastors to social gatherings such as weddings, which announce a lifelong union to the extended Karen community. However, these last stronghold communities discourage children from stepping beyond the norm, stifling experimentation and the valuable lessons that come from failure for education and innovation.

Often, those who venture out leave the community altogether, abandoning the ancestral language, along with social values, and cherished customs passed down through generations. Hence, there is a need to grow to embrace exploration and view experimenting failures as steppingstones toward growth. An environment where learning and experimentation occur within our safe and supportive environment can uphold our moral and social standard while strengthening ourselves with the skills needed to thrive in an ever-changing world—having a safe space at home or always finding a way back home.

We grow by making space—or we wither.

WE ARE THE AMBASSADOR OF OUR PEOPLE

We are all the ambassadors of our people, and everything we do individually matters in representing our people. Our cuisine, our clothing, our social habits, festivity and gathering, our political organization, our work ethic, our treatment of others and each other, our family values, and our moral and ethical standards all shape our reputation, for better or worse. An ambassador must embody elegance in both action and speech, honoring her people in all she represents.

Just a few months before the irreversible national tragedy that would mark the beginning of the first and only Karen Armed Revolution in January 1949, on October 9, 1948, Saw Ba U Gyi engaged in intense negotiations to stabilize the fragile situation in Burma. That night, in a message directed at his people, and heard by other nations, he stated:

> "There are many things of which our fellow Karens should be reminded. And so, let me remind you that, if you desire to have a separate State of your own, you must try to deserve it." (Naw, 2023)

This statement, a mark of his statesmanship, revealed a flaw he recognized within his people—a tendency toward unruliness that risked tarnishing our reputation and weakening the respect of other nations, whose support we need to achieve our aspirations.

As ambassadors of our people, we carry the responsibility to cultivate a reputation of worthiness.

KAWTHOOLEI TO BE KNOWN FOR ITS WORKMANSHIP

Workmanship signals the character of its maker, revealing the heart, mind, and skill poured into the craft. Excellent workmanship earns distinction and trust, while poor workmanship signals a lack of care and integrity. True quality is not defined by advertisements but by the work itself. It embodies moral, ethical, and organizational integrity, showcasing a nation's trustworthiness. Workmanship is the solid foundation of a brand.

Workmanship is not showmanship. Even if no one sees the product we make, doing it with care and attention manifests character. Character, after all, is best measured by what we do when no one is watching. Workmanship is not about seeking a premium for our products; rather, the premium comes as a natural reward for rarity and excellence achieved through superior craftsmanship.

The Karen people often adopt practices from nearby regions. Those near Myanmar tend to mirror local customs there, while those close to Thailand lean toward Thai methods. Quality is infectious, either for better or worse. By and large, workmanship to the west of the Salween River is inconsistent and questionable, while to the east, it is stronger and more refined. Thai products—

from the goods they craft to the food they serve to the service they provide—consistently reflect a commitment to quality.

Thailand's brand extends worldwide, with over twenty thousand Thai restaurants serving as informal ambassadors of Thai culture. Supported by supply networks, a rich culinary tradition, government support, and well-developed ingredient supply chains, these establishments form a national franchise in spirit. Patrons around the world can enter an authentic Thai restaurant and expect a familiar service experience—a taste of Thailand that promotes both trust and tourism. When a product bears the mark "Products of Thailand," it carries an expectation of quality and authenticity. Workmanship is not the effort of a single individual; it is a national culture, supported by government, institutions, and social norms. Every nation, in time, develops its own brand.

We can learn from others, their successes and failures, but need not simply copy those around us. Island nations like Japan, South Korea, and Singapore, without immediate neighbors to emulate, have developed superb workmanship and creativity as their national brands. Taiwan's tea earns high regard for its packaging and quality. Taiwanese packaging creates trust in the quality of the content. Japanese ice cream is crafted with such delicate artistry that it is as pleasing to the eye as it is to the palate. Smooth user experience of a Samsung refrigerator made in Korea shows thoughtful design of art and engineering, from door handles to trays and draws.

Kawthoolei is to cultivate a reputation for workmanship so that "Made in Kawthoolei", "Designed in Kawthoolei", or "Product of Kawthoolei" become synonymous with excellence. Our workmanship should shine in every creation, from the smallest handcrafted items to the advanced products of tomorrow. Kawthoolei should not be known merely for tribal crafts or bamboo utensils, but for ingenuity —one day for high-end design, cutting-edge chips, trusted ethic, and superior services. Product lines are inspected by private and governmental institutions that ensure safety and consistent quality.

It is untrue that the Karen people inherently lack workmanship. The habit of doing things half-heartedly or just for formality—shirking of duty—may stem from a lack of social norms and governmental support that expect excellence. Growing up, my grandfather was strict about workmanship. Every year, he prepared the best harvest baskets in the village. His orchard was organized, with rows of trees in systematic alignment. He had no tolerance for poor workmanship. Entering teenage years, I had to weave three carrying baskets to his satisfaction before he considered me a graduate worthy of conversation.

Elevating dedication to workmanship to a national standard is both a civic duty and a human responsibility. Sloppy workmanship reflects poor character, creating hazardous conditions through neglected details. Sloppiness is costly, inconsiderate, and ultimately unsightly. Poor workmanship is not only unprofessional but also immoral; in grand structures, it can lead to calamity.

If sloppiness is a habit, that habit must be erased—or the nation will be.

To have Kawthoolei as a trusted brand, we must grow beyond mediocre workmanship to the level of excellence admired worldwide, that earns respect and premium value. People must trust our brand enough to put our food products into their stomach.

Trust extends to service as well. Our preservation efforts—our rainforests and the clear waters of our rivers—are a testament to workmanship, too. Japanese drainage systems are known for their water quality, so pristine that fish teem in sidewalk streams. We can aspire to that level of care and quality in everything we build and preserve. Until recently, in the Mutraw Mountains, there was a Karen blacksmith whose knives could slice through 1-millimeter steel with the precision of a Japanese katana. We need to revive that level of skill and spirit of craftsmanship.

THE BUSINESS OF PRIVATE RELIEF

Buildings and architecture in our land are extensions of who we are. They reflect our identity, the reach of our imagination, and the talents that brought them into life. Their consistent design and quality speak to the traditions we uphold.

For an international traveler crossing from Malaysia into Thailand, the humid air remains unchanged, yet everything else under the tropical sky shifts. A new language for wayfinding, a new currency, and a distinct architectural landscape mark the transition. Among these subtle but telling differences is an often-overlooked yet significant experience: the restroom. In Thailand, water is used abundantly, paired with a seated design for convenience—differing slightly from Malaysia, where a pull-flush system prevails. Even the smallest details narrate the values and customs of a nation.

Japan has pioneered the transformation of restrooms from an overlooked necessity into a symbol of thoughtful design and hospitality. Renowned for innovation, it has elevated restroom standards with features like heated seats and bidet-style water sprays, setting a global benchmark. Today, many nations strive to emulate this approach, recognizing the subtle yet profound impact of a clean, pleasant restroom experience.

For Kawthoolei to present a healthy and dignified image to the world, every aspect of our land must reflect care and excellence—including our restrooms. Clean, welcoming, and well-maintained, they should embody the values we wish to project. The smallest details reveal the priorities of a culture. Rather than going overboard with technology, simplicity and pleasant comfort could be an easy relief with Kawthoolei style.

Today, precision engineering has evolved into both a science and an art, holding immense potential to elevate human conditions. To advance in the modern world, the nation must embrace a new culture of precision engineering, meticulous craftmanship, and thoughtful design.

The path forward lies in refining Kawthoolei's national brand—one defined by excellence in workmanship. By showcasing creativity and dedication, we not only uplift our communities but also present our craftsmanship to the world.

GROWING FROM SHYNESS TO ASSERTIVENESS

The Karen people are known for being gentle, shy and quiet, even within their own communities. This quiet reserve, often seen as a virtue of peacefulness and humility, has served its purpose but now calls for transformation. Assertiveness does not abandon humility; instead, it strengthens it, inviting each of us to contribute actively and face challenges with conviction.

In the lower Burma of Sittaung and Irrawaddy valleys, where diverse traits coexist, boldness often paves the way for leadership in business, local administration, and daily affairs. Those who speak with confidence take charge, shaping the direction of their communities.

In the Sittaung River valley—the second most populous region of Karen people after the Irrawaddy Delta—villages once home only to Karen people now see large numbers of settlers from the plains, who arrive with a more confident, vocal presence. They assert control over local businesses and land, regularly using loudspeakers throughout the village for religious and social affairs, while Karen voices are relegated to quiet corners. These new settlers boldly assert their ideas in local administration and are unafraid to argue or quarrel past neighborhoods.

A decade ago, on a bus ride from Chiang Mai to Mae Sarian (Mae Hong Son), I recognized familiar faces among the passengers. These people I know, even in their shadow. I could identify my people from a distance by their movements—these round faces, wide jaws, almost-smiling countenances—quiet, reserved, with no one speaking Karen loudly, cautious not to attract the attention of Thai authorities. Though many of them likely hold Thai citizenship or other legal documents, they remain shy and quiet. The bus was fully loaded with people who probably knew each other and could have busily exchanged friendly greetings of "oh-su-oh-klay," "oh-mu-soet-berr," or "gaw-ler-a-gae", yet the entire bus was eerily quiet.

I have never believed Karen people to be inherently shy or quiet; rather, probably they lack the security and political safety to fully express themselves.

In environments where Karen people feel safe, such as summer camps in the Midwest USA, I have seen Karen youth sang their songs with joy and enthusiasm, as anyone else would. In the new generations growing up in the United States, it is rare to find a shy soul, even among those whose parents inherit a naturally gentle and reserved disposition.

Personally, I was known to be quiet and reserved in my youth, but I grew out of it as I learned to navigate prejudice and discrimination. I survived both death and arrest in my late teens and early twenties. I received uninvited favors because of how I look, and micro-discrimination because of my gender, skin color, or ethnicity. Discrimination can be random—for me or against me. In a small Midwestern town in America, a gas station cashier let me pump gasoline before paying—afterward, I asked why and the answer was simply because I am Asian. I have seen racism and reverse racism; I have witnessed the good, the bad, the ugly, and the beautiful.

Today, I am more at ease speaking with others, delivering public speeches, and sharing my vision for Kawthoolei through a book written in a global language. I organize community gatherings, lead events, and advocate for my views when necessary. In professional settings, offering my perspective and asserting my expertise have become key ways I add value. Though still known as quiet someone who finds energy in solitude, I have come to believe that assertiveness can coexist with—and even strengthen—humility and respect.

To grow as a nation, we must grow from shyness to assertiveness, stepping forward to present our political views and embrace leadership. We have been shy to assert our human dignity and relegate ourselves to being labeled as "ethnic minority."

Social behaviors once widespread have become a political problem; we face land grabs with silence, encroachment with smiles, remaining quiet, and continually being pushed into a corner. Our identity must expand to match that of a growing nation, shedding fear, shyness, and timidity. Our land, our rights, our voices must be heard to be respected.

We can practice our virtues of quietness, politeness, and reserve with dignity only if we are able to protect and preserve what is ours. A nation can grow in identity without losing its virtues. Our identity needs to grow from its core knowing that it is ok to be brave, bold, and saying *no*.

Shy it must not be, for the nation to shine.

NATION GROWING IN PREPAREDNESS

We must grow as a nation in preparedness, not merely reactive to catastrophe. We can no longer afford to wait for disaster to strike and then scramble to respond—that is our usual business, business as usual, and usually does not work. Every country faces the inevitable downpour of challenges of some kinds. In our region, heavy rains fall upon us with definite prior notice, year after year, every year. The real difference lies in those who are better prepared and those who, unprepared, cry for help when disaster strikes.

We live in a world where disasters—both natural and man-made—can hit us without warning. Living in a tropical climate with a long rainy season, it is in our way of life that we are naturally prepared during the dry months. Basic human needs such as food, fuel, and shelter are collected, stored, and built in anticipation of the rains. But this seasonal preparation is often limited to the best-case scenario, the expected. What kills us is not the routine challenges, but the unexpected worst-case scenarios for which we also need to stay prepared.

The worst-case scenario is where true preparedness makes all the difference. As we remain in a state of war, the people of Kawthoolei not only brace for natural disasters but also for the man-made ones, which have become all too frequent. While our region may be fortunate in facing fewer natural disasters, the devastation from bombs and food shortages is no less disastrous.

TAIWANESE PREPAREDNESS

Taiwan, a country that must be constantly prepared for earthquakes that strike without notice, typhoons that can destroy homes and businesses, and the looming threat of invasion from its powerful neighbor, another China. Like Japan, where frequent earthquakes pose a deadly risk due to high-rise buildings and dense populations, environment forces Taiwanese to innovate in design and integrate preparedness into their architecture.

> "Given the high quality of its material resources as well as its human resources, Taiwan is capable of having a first-class system for handling large-scale disasters, potentially a model for other nations to emulate." [Global Taiwan Institute]

Taipei's underground railway stations are indeed designed with multi-functional purposes, including acting as bomb shelters. These stations are built at significant depths, typically around 20 meters (70 feet) below ground, with large multi-layered spaces, creating a vibrant city of their own beneath the surface. These shelters are assigned capacity numbers based on population estimates and are part of Taiwan's broader civil defense strategy, highlighting its geopolitical concerns, the other China (the Republic of China vs. People's Republic of China). Taiwan shows its understanding that resilience must be built into the infrastructure itself—both for natural calamities and the potential geopolitical threats from its powerful neighbor. After all, who faces a more daunting reality than Taiwan, with a billion-strong, often hostile neighbor claiming to swallow them up?

Kawthoolei, with its thick forests and mountains, has long served as a natural fortress for our people, much like Taiwan for its own. The abundance of fruits and vegetables has often lulled us into a false sense of security. Our winters are mild, unlike the harsh cold of the northern hemisphere, where survival demands innovative solutions. There, one winter night without heat can freeze people to death. While other regions innovate under harsher climates, we risk complacency as we allow the blessings of our environment to weaken our sense of urgency. We have the time and the talents to prepare; therefore, we cannot allow our house and our brains to be swept away each year by the floodwaters of a raging cyclone.

Cyclones—fury from the sky—and earthquakes—turmoil from beneath—represent the inevitable wrath of nature. These acts of God cannot be prevented, only mitigated and managed through preparedness. Also, nations must be equally vigilant against other forms of disaster that require readiness and resilience.

SINGAPOREAN PREPAREDNESS

In the modern, overly interconnected and interdependent world, disasters such as global financial crises and pandemics can strike universally, exposing vulnerabilities across nations. Only those nations that are better prepared—both economically and strategically—can withstand these global shocks. Singapore excels in this regard. Despite its dependence on global trade and lack of natural resources, it has demonstrated remarkable resilience.

During the 1997-98 Asian Financial Crisis, many Southeast Asian countries, including Indonesia and Thailand, were severely impacted. These nations struggled for decades to recover, with the assistance of global financial institutions. But this recovery came at the expense of their financial sovereignty, as they were forced to comply with the harsh conditions imposed by the International Monetary Fund (IMF). Singapore, however, with its strong national reserve, weathered the storm of currency speculation, maintaining trust in its economy and financial system.

Despite its inability to produce sufficient food for its population, Singapore wisely diversified its food sources, importing from Australia, China, Costa Rica, Japan, Jordan, Republic of Korea, Panama, the USA, and New Zealand. During the COVID-19 pandemic, this foresight proved critical, as Singapore's integration of food security into its national security ensured that no citizen went hungry. Long before the crisis struck, Singapore had strengthened its supply chains, solidifying its reputation as a nation that prepares for the worst and remains resilient in the face of global upheavals, as demonstrated in 2020.

The nation needs all hands to prepare. Our productive labor is imbalanced, though we are not short of manpower. Many of our youth and adults work tirelessly, while others remain idle. Swinging hammock during daytime workday should be a symbol of shame. Our human resources issue is not the lack of hands but the absence of direction and opportunity, creating a divide between those who labor tirelessly and those who linger aimlessly.

The majority need to learn how to make the most of their youthful years like their peers, many Karen youth around the world who study and work diligently. A strong work ethic is not exclusively valued in East Asian countries; it is a universal principle. The Protestant work ethic and Victorian work ethic in the West once embodied high values that propelled their nations and empires to success.

The growing nation must always be at work, always learn, and always prepare.

Preparedness must be embedded in Kawthoolei's national psyche, reflected in its institutions, governance, talents, and daily life—ensuring that foresight becomes second nature to the nation. Bullets and armors must be mass-produced during peacetime, while physical and cyber infrastructure must always remain missile bunker-strong against malicious attacks. We want to hold peace, we have to hold a strong defense.

The world's most peaceful regions are often the most militarily active, as revealed by the global heatmap from the Strava fitness app. These regions include North America, Europe, East Asia, and eastern South America—places where preparedness is not merely a policy but an ingrained practice.

With a non-confrontational nature, many Karen people prefer to avoid conflict and maintain peace. Carrying weapons and waging war to defend their territories does not come naturally to them. When offered a peace agreement, they run for it fast. When their lands are taken, they can only smile. When invaders rule over them, they can only sing a song in response. That is not a winning instinct. As the saying goes: *"The lion may eat grass, but do not lay down your sword."* For, when the lion comes after you and you search for your sword, it already is too late.

Don't wait for the bombs to fall before digging the ground. Don't wait for the flood to divert the water's course. Don't wait until self-determination is lost to fight for one forever. Rainwater is a blessing—we have it in abundance. But poor preparedness can turn a shower of blessing into a curse of rain. Don't wait till disaster strikes.

The earth may tremble, the sky can fall.

Always must the nation stand tall, prepared.

The Garden of Character Building

Character building is like tending a garden, not the work of a single day or season but a lifelong task of daily care. Young flowers and trees, like fragile dreams, need care. These sprouts can easily be nibbled away by doubt and fear or overgrown of temptation weeds; bad influences threaten to stunt the growth. However, with patience and care, the plants begin to reach for stronger sunlight, their roots deepening, strong against life's storms, the rainy adversity, and the scorching sun. One day, the garden will stand tall, humming with bees and butterflies, with blossoming flowers and fruit-bearing branches, lowly weeds unreached. In this garden of life, character is both soil and seed, flower and fruit—tended not in haste but with steady hands and quiet grace, cultivating beauty that time cannot erase.

A nation is shaped by the character of its people, as each individual's strength contributes to the progress of society collectively. Building character must begin from a tender age in every household.

Let's take a walk in the garden of ideas on character building:

Not only so, but we also glory in our sufferings, because we know that suffering produces perseverance; perseverance, character; and character, hope. [Apostle Paul - Romans 5:3-4, NIV]

Character development, combined with practical skills and education, paves the way for economic stability and social progress, empowering both individuals and society. Traits like integrity, honesty, hard work, and moral virtue are the building blocks of personal success, and they form the very foundation of our country's strength. [Washington, B. T.]

The destiny of a nation is directly tied to the character of its people. Moral development, combined with education and hard work, is crucial for empowering individuals and uplifting society. Character is the foundation of a strong, resilient, and prosperous nation. Fostering it personally while promoting it in others is vital to building such a future. [Washington, B. T.]

Fame is a vapor, popularity an accident, and riches take wings. Only one thing endures, and that is character. [U.S. President H. Truman]

Character, not circumstances, makes the man. [Washington, B. T.]

It is easier to build strong children than to repair broken men. [Frederick Douglass]

I have walked that long road to freedom. I have tried not to falter; I have made missteps along the way. But I have discovered the secret that after climbing a great hill, one only finds that there are many more hills to climb. I have taken a moment here to rest, to steal a view of the glorious vista that surrounds me, to look back on the distance I have come. But I can only rest for a moment, for with freedom comes responsibilities, and I dare not linger, for my long walk is not ended. [Mandela, 1994]

Character, in the long run, is the decisive factor in the life of an individual and of nations alike. [Roosevelt, 1900]

People with high expectations often have low resilience. Unfortunately, *resilience* matters for success. I don't know how to teach you this except to hope that *suffering* happens to you. And I mean it in a positive way. When you refine the character of your company, you want greatness out of them, and greatness is not just *intelligence*. As you know, greatness comes from *character*. Character isn't formed by smart people; it is formed by those who've suffered. If I could wish upon you, I don't know how to do it, but all of you Stanford students, I wish upon you an ample dose of pain and *suffering*. [Jensen Huang, Nvidia CEO]

NOURISHING THE NATION TO STAND TALLER

We, the people of Kawthoolei, have sustained ourselves on diets based on the natural abundance of our land. Our tropical climate offers a rich variety of vegetables, fruits, and herbs, which, combined with rice as a staple, has nourished generations. These traditional diets, balanced and healthy, have given our ancestors the strength to endure physical hardship and remain resilient in the face of adversity.

Yet today, war, displacement, and economic hardship have eroded this stability. Many of our people now show signs of malnourishment. This physical fragility is a symptom of a deeper national instability, reflecting the breakdown of a system that once sustained both body and spirit.

If Kawthoolei is to stand shoulder to shoulder with other nations, this decline in health and stature must be addressed. The goal is to achieve a generation where men average 5 feet 7 inches and women 5 feet 3 inches. A taller, stronger generation will be a visible testament to the nation's renewal, an embodiment of Kawthoolei's desire to reclaim its place in the world.

To achieve this, we must address the foundation of our diet. As our primary staple, rice must be evaluated in terms of the quantities needed for our climate and lifestyle. While it provides essential energy, only rice may be insufficient to support the physical growth we seek. A systematic, scientific study of our dietary habits, particularly rice consumption, is necessary. Supplementing traditional meals with essential proteins, vitamins, and minerals will help rebuild the strength of our population. Government policies must ensure that agriculture supports diverse and healthy food production

Japan's post-World War II transformation provides a powerful model. After the war, Japan faced the challenge of rebuilding not only its infrastructure but also the health of its people. The government introduced fortified school lunches rich in protein, iron, and vitamins, helping children grow stronger and taller. Within a generation, the average height of Japanese citizens increased significantly. At the Paris 2024 Olympics, Japan's athletes won the third-largest number of medals, a testament to how improved nutrition helped produce a physically stronger generation winning on the world stage. (Burmese and the Karen people used to call Japanese people "jer-pan nga-put" and "pu-kor", a derogatory hit on their height.)

China offers a similar example. Once plagued by severe malnutrition during the 1950s and 1960s, resulting in over 30 million deaths, China made food security and nutritional health a national priority. Through scientific planning and targeted government intervention, the nation improved its population's physical stature alongside its rising global prominence. This effort bore fruit— not only in improved health outcomes but also on the world stage—placing China second only to the USA in gold medal wins at the 2024 Olympics. While India, with a population comparable to China's, missed out on winning a gold medal, finding itself far down under the list of medal-winning nations. South Korea followed a successful path, integrating nutrition into its national recovery plan to strengthen its people as the nation rapidly industrialized. Today, these East Asian countries consistently rank among the top performers in international competitions, regardless of their population size.

Similarly for Kawthoolei, national health must be planned with the same attention and strategy as economic development. Schools play a central role in this transformation, offering balanced, nutritious meals to children. Agriculture policies must evolve to ensure a diversity of nutrient-rich foods is accessible. By combining our knowledge in traditional diets and modern science, we can cultivate a population that is not only well-fed but strong and resilient.

A healthy, nourished population will possess not only physical fitness but also overall well-being, with the intellectual and spiritual strength to contribute meaningfully to nation-building. The heights we aim for—5 feet 7 inches for men and 5 feet 3 inches for women—are not arbitrary. They are a marker of Kawthoolei's goal to stand on equal footing with other nations, a reflection of our inner strength expressed through our physical presence.

By ensuring our people are well-nourished, physically strong, and intellectually prepared, Kawthoolei will lay the foundation for a future where our nation stands tall—not only in physical stature but in moral and spiritual strength. A strong, healthy Kawthoolei will lead with confidence, embodying the strength that comes from balanced growth in both body and spirit.

Nation. Nourish and Stand Tall.

ROLE MODELS, NOT BEAUTY MODELS

The nation needs role models, not beauty models. Our youth should look up to figures—not for their fleeting appearance, masked in layers of excessive cosmetics, or for strumming guitars humming hollow tunes—but for their strength of character, resilience, and commitment to the community's well-being. It is through such leaders—those who embody integrity and wisdom— that we shape a generation capable of navigating the complexities of nation-building. These are not superficial qualities; they are the very foundations upon which nations have risen or fallen throughout history.

Among the new generation, countless young Karen in the U.S. and beyond are excelling in music, academics, and community involvement, already well-prepared for college while still in high school. With minds as steadfast as boulders, some are even pursuing a second degree while shouldering the responsibility of caring for their elderly parents. For many, a single degree is not enough; they strive for more. These are true role models—quietly heroic, embodying the Kawthoolei spirit of resilience and dedication, with little need for social media fanfare. Most of these role models possess good looks, but that may be merely a bonus to their talents.

GROWING IN BEAUTY THAT BUILDS

The youth's fascination with beauty trends, over-applied makeup, and over-sexualized images distorts their priorities, pulling them away from the grounded reality that our nation faces. These distractions make us engross in an illusion, one that offers temporary gratification at the cost of lasting fulfillment.

Worse still, some communities have begun to institutionalize this superficiality, promoting beauty pageants, with Karen traditional attires, that emphasize shallow ideals. The rise of these pageants reflects a misguided prioritization of external beauty over internal substance, offering our youth the wrong idea of what it means to succeed or contribute meaningfully to their community.

These organizers may not take time to understand the deeper implications of such events—or there could be a deliberative motive behind systematically ruining youth characters with flashy images away from the urgency of national matters.

Historically, societies that prize vanity over virtue often crumble under the weight of their own illusions. Rome, in its decline, became a society of spectacle, where gladiatorial games and pageantry distracted the populace from the rot within its political and moral institutions. This same danger exists in the contemporary world, whether in the U.S. or China. If an entire youth culture becomes fixated on beauty pageants, it too would face decline. In stable nations, government and institutional guardrails can mitigate excess.

For us, it is fatally dangerous. Kawthoolei sits near a populous giant neighbor grappling with a historical gender imbalance, where many men struggle to find wives. A stateless refugee people cannot afford the luxury of beauty pageants in a region rife with prostitution, human trafficking, and the grip of drug warlords and state-backed mafias. Makeup and trivial celebrities may have their place in selling fish paste, but they offer nothing to a nation fighting to rise above hardship and daily survival.

Nothing is worthy of public display if it lacks character.

Nothing is beauty if makeup lacks virtue.

Nothing is worth pride if it lacks fiber.

Our youth deserve more than the hollow praise of a pageant stage; they deserve the opportunity to become true leaders, guided by principles that have stood the test of time. Role models who embody moral courage, intellect, and self-discipline will inspire them to be the architects of our future. These figures will teach our young people to value substance over style, perseverance over appearances, and responsibility over self-interest.

Many graduates from Thailand universities, the U.S., Australia, Norway, or Netherlands return home, risking their lives and careers to serve their people, spreading knowledge and goodwill, some high profile, some high impact quiet beavers. Coincidentally, they happen to be good-looking people—confident and elegant—who prefer the name "Knyaw." Many more young adults around the world are working hard to lift themselves up and their community. These are our true role models, needing no stage to make their impact. Youths around the world in rising nations work hard, study hard, and have no time to waste their energy on vanity. Our public recognition on national days ought to be these creative talents that have substance.

In place of these superficial public displays, we should promote figures who inspire through their contributions to society, who lead with intellect and vision, and who dedicate themselves to the collective good. These role models will not only serve as guides for our youth but as cornerstones of a stronger, more resilient Kawthoolei.

Beauty, in its shallowest form, fades with time. What remains, what endures, are the values that we pass down—the legacy of integrity, wisdom, and selfless leadership. Kawthoolei's future depends not on beauty models but on role models, whose character will define our nation's strength for generations to come.

East Asia: No Miracle, Only Hard Work and Strategy

The economic success of East Asia—from Japan to the Asian Tigers (South Korea, Hong Kong, Taiwan, and Singapore) and the emerging Asian Dragons (China, Indonesia, Thailand, and Vietnam)—is no miracle. Their achievements are the result of a combination of stable politics, a culture of supreme work ethic and creativity, sound economic policies, and a favorable global environment. If others emulate these principles, similar progress is possible.

Imagine if Japanese, Korean, Chinese, Taiwanese, Singaporean, or Israeli youth spent their days merely singing, dancing, and avoiding hard work or innovation. Their societies would likely resemble ours today, lacking progress in every aspect. Conversely, if we adopt a restless drive to improve, coupled with hard work and a hunger for innovation, we could make meaningful strides—even if not at the same scale as East Asia's meteoric rise.

In Burma, over the past decade, millions of youths have sought opportunities abroad. They line up in droves at embassies, applying to become migrant workers in Japan, South Korea, Singapore, Malaysia, Thailand, Oman, Dubai, and even Laos. After the 2021 military coup, the trend did not slow down. Thousands of to-be migrant workers line up in Yangon Airport to fly for industrial work in distant nations. The irony is poignant: in our grandparents' generation, people fought to expel foreign powers like Japan. Today, their grandchildren queue at the Japanese embassy, seeking work in menial jobs. That is the joke shared around today's Burmese new generation.

There is another joke shared among the youth that captures this irony: "If all Myanmar people went to Japan, Japan would collapse, and if all Japanese came to Burma, Burma would prosper." While exaggerated, the humor underscores a truth: it is not the land's natural resources but the people's work ethic, moral standard, cultural values, institutions, and governance that form the invisible framework driving national progress.

POLITICAL INTELLECT OVER BEING POLITICAL

What the Karen people need is progress in political intellect, not merely more political voices. The rise of social media has given many individuals a platform to express their views, often with great passion. However, passion alone is not enough. While many of these voices are insistent and sincere, they often lack a deep understanding of Burma's complex political realities. Engaging in political discourse without a solid foundation of knowledge and critical analysis can lead to confusion—or, worse, unintended harm to the liberation movement. In navigating Burma's complex political landscape, some generations, lacking a deeper grasp of its dynamics, reduce issues to a simplistic dichotomy—independence versus federal[ism] —missing the nuanced understanding required for meaningful change.

Being political has become easier—social media enables quick opinions and simplified narratives that reach a large audience. But possessing political intellect demands something deeper: the ability to navigate an intricate web of historical context, cultural dynamics, regional power structures, and the hidden forces shaping political landscapes. Burma's political reality is not one to be understood through remote analysis or surface-level engagement. It requires disciplined study of broad history, a nuanced grasp of ethnic and ideological struggles, and a clear vision for moving forward without jeopardizing the cause.

Many of the loudest voices lack this depth; although well-meaning, their statements can sometimes distort issues or fuel unnecessary divisions. In the heat of impassioned debates, they may overlook critical facts or fail to grasp the complexities of alliances, negotiations, and long-term strategies. In doing so, they can inadvertently weaken the movement they may wish to support. Some passionate members were driven to create a government without a clear understanding of constitutional frameworks, institutional foundations, or even a tangible base of constituents. This impatient approach only muddies the waters, hindering progress toward establishing a fully-fledged government. The Government of the Republic of Kawthoolei cannot be established in the air or in exile.

Haste makes waste.

Sincerity, while admirable, is not enough. What we need is a new generation of leaders and thinkers who approach politics with intellect—those who understand what must be done, and how and why it must be done. Simply following foreign advisers without grasping the new world order, regional realities, and the culture of the international system risks falling prey to external powers rather than advancing true liberation. Prudent leaders can analyze situations from multiple perspectives, foresee potential consequences, and craft bold strategies that are both principled and pragmatic.

In the previous century, we befriended missionaries and worked toward our progress, yet colonial politicians viewed us as lacking political sophistication. After the entire Karen nation risked their necks fighting alongside the British, we emerged from a victorious WWII with high hopes for a separate nation. However, during their 1946 visit to Britain, our leaders were simply told to throw their lot in with others. The failure of the 1946 Karen goodwill mission may well have resulted from either meekness or an overreliance on British goodwill (Naw, 2023, 176). Boldness must not lack political intellect, just as loud voices cannot be uninformed.

To progress in political awareness, our entire people need to stay vigilant and let not a single candy by the street beguile them. At its core, the Karen liberation movement depends on the cultivation of political intellect, led by the wisest minds, not the loudest voices.

One day, the Kawthoolei Congressional Assembly must be filled with representatives of political intellect, not with politicized hotheads driven by impulsive, partisan fervor.

Every prudent man dealeth with knowledge: but a fool layeth open his folly. Proverbs 13:16 (KJV)

Behold, I send you forth as sheep in the midst of wolves: be ye therefore wise as serpents, and harmless as doves. Matthew 10:16 (KJV)

GROWTH IN EMOTION

Emotional immaturity prevents large-scale collaboration. It prevents us from addressing the pressing threats to our society. It prevents us from breaking free of the status quo. It prevents us to face each other truthfully. Ultimately, emotional immaturity fails us to be a worthy nation.

Instead of embracing national spirit, we keep attachment heavily on our birthplace district, our township, harming national cohesion and national priority. No nation can be built on parochialism—it verges on tribalism. Breaking fear and suspicion to connect with people beyond one's sphere calls for growth in emotion.

The courage to admit our wrongdoings and shortcomings—and the humility to seek compromise—require emotional maturity. Likewise, the courage to investigate—and to be investigated—as a regular business of a responsible society demand emotional maturity.

To be a nation worthy among nations, we need to grow in emotion, learning to accept criticism with grace so we can correct our shortcomings. We must give criticism constructively and respectfully to ensure it makes a meaningful impact. Too often in our community, personal attachment clouds our ability to resolve disagreements with sound reasoning. We place childlike emotions ahead of reconciling differences in ideas. Diverse talents and diverse perspectives should enrich our growth, yet instead of digesting differences, we allow diversity to become division.

This is not just a political issue—it is widespread in religious organizations as well. In the U.S., many Karen communities and Christians gather in churches, but most cities with a significant

Karen population see at least two churches—not because of distance, but because of personal dislike or ugly fights. We are shy to face one another and resolve differences with maturity. When everyone goes low, it creates only crayons no one can escape.

Relying on reason steadies the mind rather than indulges in the reflexes of childlike emotions. Indeed, intuition and guts, shaped by experience, can guide us, but any judgment we lean toward is to be grounded in reason. Too often, we express opinions in a "Karen-drunken" style, whining, dismissive, and disparaging without base. Years of guerrilla warfare and the demands of constant vigilance have shaped our habits, instilling a reflexive suspicion toward nearly everything. This tribal wariness, while essential for survival, can stifle critical thinking. In small doses, skepticism sharpens our judgment; yet, when left unchecked, suspicion becomes corrosive, eroding trust and open-mindedness.

The Karen people are diverse in political ideologies, religious beliefs, and geographical dispersion, but this is not unique to us. Every nation, even the most established, has faced similar challenges. Yet, they have achieved greatness by uniting people from varied backgrounds under a shared goal, working together to create something extraordinary. Even the drafting of a single document, such as a comprehensive national planning, often relies on the collective efforts of hundreds of scholars collaborating in harmony. For National Planning, Kawthoolei needs many heads, many colors of ideas.

We may not have the abundance of experts that other nations possess, but our greater challenge lies in the absence of emotional fortitude—the strength to meet one another on equal ground, to set aside differences, and to embrace each other as partners in building our future. Too often, the elite look down upon the grassroots, and the highly educated harbor fear, jealousy, or contempt toward others of even ones with similar backgrounds. Ironically, education does not seem to diminish these tendencies; instead, it often amplifies the airing of clever sarcasm and disdain, deepening the divide.

We find ways to get along with others—be it Burmese ordinary, Western scholars, or Chinese businessmen—yet we harbor contempt for our own kind. We are quick to be impressed by mediocrity from others but fail to appreciate the struggles and potential of our own people. Our talents may earn high recognition from outsiders but remain unrecognized and unvalued among our own.

On the ground or cyber space, degradation in moral character and ethical practices breeds distrust and suspicion toward each other. Strong character builds trust, and without it, we risk fracturing the bonds that should unite us. With the aid of group messaging apps, Karen people around the world organize themselves in various topics regardless of the distance. Such energy is admirable. Yet without trust and emotional maturity breaking through fear and suspicion, we cannot organize ourselves on a large scale to a national level, remaining confined to personal, I-know-you-and-you-know-me connections. As a growing national identity, our judgment must grow in reason upholding dignity, not inflating a narrow ego—for, dignity elevates, ego destroys.

GROWING IN ETHICAL STANDARD

To organize ourselves on a national level, we need a clear and consistent national ethical standard. One simple way to test this is through something as ordinary as mailing a letter—sending a message to my elderly mother, who lives in a distant, remote village. Can the mail travel faithfully, untouched by prying eyes, free from interference or breach of privacy? Will the carriers respect its confidentiality, resisting the temptation to open a letter that does not belong to them? In the past, letters have often failed to reach their destination, and those that did arrive came worn, torn, and opened. An uncle of mine (whom I used to play with for a year when we were young) left home in his teenage years to join the revolution in the mountains. The old mother, who still lived in the Sittaung Valley (northern Kawthoolei) scarcely heard from him. But one day, a letter arrived—months after it had been written, ragged, broken, and exposed to anyone who dared look. That letter carried more than just news; it carried a stark reminder of how far we still have to go in building trust and integrity, even in the most basic systems. That was a generation ago, but now, can a private letter be sent with the integrity of the message intact? Behind the scenes, how faithfully we uphold such standards speaks volumes about our standing as members of the nation. One day, Kawthoolei will have its national Kawthoolei Postal Service. How much the world places trust in our mail service will tell of Kawthoolei ethical standards.

As we rebuild Kawthoolei, establishing a reliable postal service will be an essential standard. Postal personnel can be trained to uphold postal standards, but we are a people known for honesty, simplicity, and straightforwardness. It is that these values form the foundation of our national integrity, creating a system that is built on trust, respect, and unwavering ethical standards.

Reputation is the new capital. Brand is the new wealth.

Higher ethical standard is the new Kawthoolei Standard.

GROWING IN MORAL FIBER, RESOLUTE TO HONOR

We are meant to live in harmony with our neighbors, honoring mutual respect and natural sovereignty in alignment with the surrounding nature—without the need for ideologies that are confined like democracy, communism, liberalism, or nationalism, or any made-up-ism. The harsh reality that we must kill neighbors, who come to occupy our land with guns and powder, is a testament we lack honor, the degradation of our character, vigilance, and fiber. The fact that our neighbors dare to harm us signifies their lack of fear or respect for us. The natural order has been tipped out of balance. Our guardian spirit has left us, our soul not worthy to guard.

Even as millions of our people at working age flee the killing business of the liberation movement and seek refuge in Thailand, Malaysia, and Singapore as migrant workers— trapped in the degrading cycle of modern slavery and lingering debt—it does little to help them build integrity, honor, or a worthy human life in foreign soil.

Breaking through the current tragedy calls for leaving behind old habits of complacency, ignorance, and shirking responsibility. Demoralizing as they are, these habits are contagious, spreading to anyone who comes into contact with them. I have seen people from urban areas arrive at the border Karen speaking only areas and quickly adopt this mentality. Too often, our people default to saying, "I don't know," "I can't do it," or "It's not in my control," as a way to resign to circumstances and evade responsibility. This must stop.

> "We are go-getters, change makers, and problem solvers."
> [*a motto of University of California, Davis*]

No nation under the sun is inherently smarter than ours; we are equally endowed with talents by the Creator of all nations. This truth shines in our new generation who, when given equal footing in new lands, rise to compete—and often surpass their peers. What we need now is structure and fiber: a structure to nurture their potential and a fiber to fortify their character.

Unless we despise the harmful habits, we cling to, we remain victims of an unexamined identity, hindering our growth as a nation.

The people of Kawthoolei are not confined by the limitations others impose—we are forging our own path of transformation. Our strength rests in our courage to question, our ability to think critically, and our resolve to face challenges with creativity and purpose. In a world where we compete not with those smarter than us, but with those better organized, our true power comes from uniting and uplifting one another. We are not a nation to be commanded, but to be inspired and to inspire—each of us a go-getter, a change maker, a problem solver. As we grow into the nation we aspire to be—strong in character, emotion, intellect, spirit, and stature—we will build a future where Kawthoolei thrives, led by the wisdom and strength that has always been within us.

> *Arise, shine; for thy light is come.*
> [Isaiah 60:1 KJV]

All boats happily fly the flag after danger of
enemy camps are clear along Salween River.

SawLah@Photography 2023

"No Mountains High Enough to Stop Me." Salween River

SawLah@Photography 2022

Chapter 9

Preservation and Progress

If a tradition pulls us backward, we must let it go—either let go or be left behind while the world ever surges forward. If we do not destroy the harmful traditions holding the nation back, those traditions will destroy the nation.

Among some Karen indigenous traditions, an uncommon practice exists—one that is symbolic yet self-defeating. In certain communities, when an elder reaches old age, a special blanket is woven for them. It is finer than any they have ever owned—beautiful, warm, and worthy. Yet, the elder does not use it. It is carefully stored, reserved not for comfort or celebration, but for the day of their passing. It will be worn only once, then buried with them. In the cold, harsh mountain climate, where warmth is a rare gift, such a blanket could offer dignity to the living. Instead, it is committed to the earth, bringing no benefit to the elder nor to the children left behind.

Another custom, no less troubling, is the destruction of a bronze frog drum upon the death of its owner. These drums—culturally rich and historically valuable as Karen people national heritage— are not preserved or passed on, but often are broken and buried, lost to time. What might have served as a cherished legacy becomes broken metal with the deceased.

These are not merely quaint or poetic rituals. They may not be time-honored customs but rather practices adopted randomly unquestioned for the sake of reverence. Despite their symbolic weight, they become a barbaric burden. They are among harmful practices—awkward preservations that destroy rather than sustain. They reflect a deeper tension in our relationship with heritage: whether we guard it as a symbol of status in death, or live with it, grow with it, and pass it forward for the generations to come.

Tradition exists within the flow of time, shaped and reshaped by human hands. Some of the habits we have recently adopted and mislabeled as traditions are not traditions at all. Likewise, we cannot reduce ourselves to primitive tribes living in a hunter-forager community, preserved for academic study, social experiments, exotic entertainment, or tourist fascination and say it preserving tradition. Humanity has long left the Stone Age behind, rising beyond battles fought with sticks and stones. Nations rise not by clinging to nostalgia but through collaboration, competition, and the strength of talent, industry, and economy.

True progress does not erase culture—it refines and elevates it. Japan transformed into a global power through the Meiji Restoration, modernizing its economy and military while preserving its language, etiquette, and the spirit of Bushido. Britain advanced through the Industrial Revolution and scientific progress, yet the traditions of the monarchy, pageantry, and medieval customs still shape its national character. These nations do not live in the past, but they ensure the better past lives in them.

The new tradition is nation-building—industrious workforce forging institutions, advancing industry, and securing a future through knowledge and skills. Youth study relentlessly. Adults labor, convene, and create to build a nation worthy of its next generation while bringing food to their family tables.

In Korea, a global leader in information and communication technology, worshippers no longer enter churches wearing traditional hats and hanbok. In Japan, no pilgrim ascends the steps of a Shinto shrine clad in samurai armor. And in Taiwan, a powerhouse in microchip manufacturing, ancient Chinese robes are not the attire of a nation that thrives in the modern world.

Good tradition finds its place. At the entrance of Taiwan's National Theater and Concert Hall, classical architecture provides a backdrop for young dancers practicing contemporary movements—a stage for all ages and a global audience attuned to the present. BTS's dances, though not traditional Korean forms, reflect the tastes of a new age and contribute billions to the Korean economy. Progress refines tradition; it does not reject it.

Past sustenance need not define our future. The Karen people's dedication to traditional clothing and dances is commendable, but many young people spend an entire month practicing these performances, investing precious time that could be used for greater pursuits. Nations like Japan, Taiwan, South Korea, China, and Thailand have made remarkable progress while preserving strong cultural identities rooted in their cuisine, craftsmanship, and innovation. Their traditions have not been frozen in time; they have evolved alongside their development, adapting without losing their essence.

A REFLECTION ON TRADITION

Traditions and festivities are the heartbeat of a nation, connecting the past with the present. Traditions are created and recreated, refined and discarded as the nation grows—shedding old skin for healthier growth, yet holding firm to its core. Tradition gifts us stories, rich with lessons and inspiration, from which we build our lives and, in turn, elevate its very essence.

Preservation and growth go hand in hand. Yet currently, most of our efforts lean heavily on preservation without preserving, while clinging to outdated degrading habits that hold our growth.

100 years ago, when our forefathers gained world-class education and were informed about the emerging world order, they gathered among themselves to organize their Karen people as a progressive nation. They pushed for a national day to bring all our tribes and clans and creeds to come together under a national flag so as to rise as a modern nation. Recognition of Karen New Year Day as a national holiday was a victory through collaboration with other nations in a skillful political acumen. The struggle they have gone through is to elevate us, forming a new society embracing a new world.

We will need to rethink and reorganize our approach to festivities and traditions to foster purposeful unity that brings together all tribes, clans, groups, and subgroups as we move toward national progress in the new world envisioned by our forebears. Shifting responsibility solely to the state of war for our current social and educational decline is an inadequate excuse, especially since many gatherings occur in places far from war zones, such as America, Thailand, and even conflict-free parts of Karen State.

Today, we become too comfortable living in the vestiges of an early form of human society. A sign of our organizational decline is in our habitual large gatherings for communal festivals roaming aimlessly in open fields. In large gatherings we bring in bamboo baskets, bamboo sticks, all kinds of tribal artifacts to portray ourselves as primitive beings. Instead of elevating our heritage in national holiday festivities to inspire the nation, we degrade it. We have strayed from the national vision set forth by our forefathers.

We organize festivities that reinforce a stereotype. We are happy when people portray us as tribal. We mistook this for tradition. We built a narrative that we are small people, a tribal people. When we rally ourselves to rise as a nation, not merely a primitive ethnic people, they roll their eyes, they twist their noses. People come to expect tribal colors, tribal sounds, tribal gesture, tribal performance from us, and when some among us do not fit that mold, they want to push us back into it.

Festivities, the Celebration of Traditions

Now, we narrowly define our identity through singing, dancing, and wearing traditional attire in endless festivities, accompanied by one sport tournament after another, inadvertently herding our children to overlook the value of time in a globally hyper-competitive age. Kawthoolei may possess open land and fertile soil, but without the means to defend it with advanced technology and astute diplomacy, our ancestral land risks being owned and managed by those who wield wealth and raw power. This generation is a blessed generation, surrounded by free learning resources in high quantity and quality. Time wasted has turned blessing time into a time inviting curse.

We have a tendency to label any outdated behaviors and tribal-like gatherings as our "Karen Tradition", whether those behaviors belong to tradition or not. Nations rightfully celebrate their traditions, but they do not embrace every backward practice under that banner. Such practices are often merely the made up of a few, not the essence of a heritage.

Our youth also spend an excessive amount of time singing, practicing, and performing. Music is meant to heal, lift our spirits, and renew our strength. But dedicating too much valuable time to it, leaving no space for learning useful knowledge, becomes an overdose of pleasure—numbing our intellectual muscles and blinding us to the progress happening around us. Closing our eyes and singing at the top of our lungs will not bring us liberty; instead, it risks becoming an escape from reality, not a catalyst for change.

A nation cannot sing to seek liberation; a nation seeks liberation first so that it may sing in celebration.

Music indeed has the power to inspire, elevating a nation's spirit to greater heights. The Karen people sing everywhere, every week; it is a defining characteristic of our poetic culture. We can sing together on a global scale and show unity. The largest virtual choir ever recorded featured 17,572 choristers from 129 countries, assembled in 2020 during the COVID-19 global pandemic.

We can. A global Karen choir—one hundred thousand voices strong—joins in a virtual choir, singing glory to Kawthoolei and honoring the land of our ancestors. Musicians and instrumentalists, together with sound engineers, craft a symphony that resonates across borders, calling the entire Karen population around the world to rise and make their voices resound across the universe. The time has come to rebuild our homeland, unleashing the potential endowed by our Creator.

AUGUST 12TH: DAY OF REMEMBRANCE VS. MERE FESTIVITIES

Days of remembrance are designated to honor solemn historical events and the sacrifices made for a nation. No nation of dignity treats such days with disrespect.

Football has become a fixture of every gathering—whether for fundraising, on the solemn August 12th Martyrs' Day, or even the most trivial occasions. Its frequent use as the centerpiece of national days' gathering diminishes the day's deeper significance. Occasional sport activity has become routine, a trend masquerading as tradition. Too often, football is organized by well-meaning yet thoughtless leaders and politicians along the Thai border who see the height of an armed revolution as the perfect time for leisure. This creates the illusion that youth running under the scorching sun somehow advances the cause of liberation. Then, the trend spreads all over the world, in the Americas and in Asia.

To commemorate Karen nationally important days, many organize youth to run aimlessly after a ball called a soccer tournament. Most do not promote friendly competition or sportsmanship, frequently ending in kickboxing of blood-headed tribal savagery. Sport is to bring recreation activities, improve cardiovascular health, and social gathering of personal contact. Ending up in physical fights promotes nothing but shame of incivility. Football tournaments for fundraising are the wrong kind of empowerment. They neither build character in youth nor effectively raise funds to make a meaningful impact.

Impulsively arranging football games on the national day of commemoration—as if forgetting that a moment of silence might serve us better than screaming at good-looking youths chasing an aimless ball. Many of these matches devolve into kickboxing brawls among players and spectators, their blood boiling with passion for the sport—and under the tropical sun. Solemn day turns savagery. Private disputes turn into public spectacles, with these street fighting broadcast on social media for a global audience, transforming disrespect into a public disgrace—a *san-kone-myay-lay* national shame. In computer science terms, it is "garbage in, garbage out."

To Rebuild Kawthoolei, the Nation needs a stronger, finer fiber.

WRIST-TYING CEREMONY VS. FESTIVITIES

During the same month of August where we commemorate those who have fallen, we also celebrate the wrist-tying ceremony—a symbol of unity, binding us together as we seek safety and protection of our spirit during the height of the tropical rainy season, with rain falling daily and floods everywhere. This ceremony serves as a national celebration of belonging, however if we dwell solely in tradition without letting it inspire progress, that tradition risks pulling us backward into a tribal gathering with funny superstition rather than propelling us forward as a nation with reason.

In these formal mass wrist-tying ceremonies, we unwittingly encourage a weak character among our youth, turning the occasion into a social pursuit where boys chase girls and girls are caught up in the distraction, thereby de-sanctifying the ceremony's true purpose as a solemn homecoming.

Sloppy behavior in sacred ritual is an act of disrespect. Instead of bringing health and happiness, our guardian spirits may feel disheartened and distressed. Such a beautiful tradition, born from indigenous belief and rich in symbolism—the sticky rice balls symbolizing togetherness, the sugar cane representing the continuity of life through offspring, the white thread of unification, and the bamboo spatula calling the spirit home—must not be reduced to a meaningless social gathering. The beauty of these practices can be preserved and promoted to inspire progress and unity as we move forward as a nation. If not, such misuse dishonors the sacred practice of spirit homecoming in our native belief.

Public events can reach their highest purpose to celebrate the achievement of youth who excel academically, earn creative accolades, and showcase innovation in national and international arenas. Competitions in essay writing, public speaking, and stage debates on pressing societal issues fosters a culture of rhetoric and critical thinking, empowering voices to guide the nation's causes. Recognition can also be given to young minds who discover ways to harness renewable energy using the land's available resources, promoting a life in harmony with nature. In this context, traditional festivals gain deeper meaning by honoring role models whose abilities uplift the nation.

Ancient mythology and cultural celebration met cutting-edge technology in 2024, as the Lunar New Year (Chinese New Year) was celebrated as a timeless symbol brought to life with modern marvels. Thousands of synchronized drones illuminated the night sky, forming a thousand-foot-long Dragon King—a revered figure in Chinese mythology—that captivated audiences from Nanning in southern China to Singapore's Marina Bay, Dubai in the Middle East, and California on the American West Coast. The night skies of the 21st century have become a canvas for creativity, where the universal language of light transcends geographical boundaries, connecting people through the wonder of drone displays. Thailand held a similar spectacle in April 2024 during their Songkran New Year celebrations. This trend technology use in tradition and festivities is only to go up.

Good roots run deep to flourish; true traditions uplift.

COMPLACENCY OR ENTITLEMENT, NO PLACE IN THE NEW WORLD

We are naturally content, often satisfied with whatever we have. However, our identity cannot remain confined to stagnation but needs to grow to become a worthy nation, even if breaking some of our habits is painful. In truth, every nation must strive continuously to progress, even the most successful, like the United States, rich talents, and far ahead of others. Any hint of complacency will push them out of their place.

In the new Kawthoolei, no citizen should feel entitled. Ancestry alone—specifically, being descendants of the land's original inhabitants—cannot justify special privileges. Such entitlements breed laziness and toxic attitudes. While newer settlers such as the Chinese, Indians, or even the Burmese build their future through hard work in education, business, and industry, the indigenous Karen cannot be content with pastimes dancing, singing, or chasing balls in the fields to win a plastic medal or a brass-coated plastic trophy. Such complacency is as equally destructive as illicit drugs, that wastes the time, dulls the mind and weakens character. Everyone must compete on equal footing—bound by the rule of law—and contribute to the nation's progress through hard work and talent.

A striking lesson of indigenous entitlement is close to home. In Malaysia, millions of Myanmar migrant workers (Karens, Burmese—people from every town in Burma) toil for minimum wage in Malaysia's labor-intensive industries. These laborers enrich that nation. Meanwhile, "sons of the land," the Bumiputera—Malays, Orang Asli, and other indigenous peoples—enjoy special rights, yet many seem to avoid such demanding labor. While *Sons of the Land* enjoy special rights, they lag behind Chinese and Indian settlers in business, economics, and education. Chinese's industriousness fuels the economy; just 20 percent of the population controls 60–70 percent of businesses. Indian Malays excel in education, while indigenous Malays are mainly in government administration. Unlike the Chinese in Myanmar who are largely urban, Malaysian Chinese thrive in both cities and rural areas.

The United States also offers a stark example of how indigenous peoples have struggled to adapt within modern states. Native Americans, the original inhabitants of the land, are granted sovereignty and limited autonomy within reservations—a plot of land in the United States set aside for Native American tribes to live on. However, these territories are often located on non-productive land, leaving many tribes with few opportunities to build sustainable economies. To generate income, some Native American communities rely heavily on gaming, establishing casinos as a primary source of revenue. The creation of the Native American sovereignty system has not resolved the challenges stemming from the historical guilt of European, Asian, and African immigrants who displaced the indigenous population. The system designed to empower them may have disempowered them further.

While gaming does provide jobs and generate income, it does not produce tangible goods or drive innovation. Instead, it operates as a zero-sum game, where the "house"—the casino itself—always wins, leaving broader economic contributions limited. Optimistic tourism, a local dressing up in indigenous attire and asking $5 for a photo post on a tourist does not foster dignity, either. This reliance on a fragile economy remains vulnerable to shifts in consumer behavior and competition. Also, it offers little inspiration for youth to develop skills or create businesses that generate economic value.

The consequences are severe: many Native American communities face challenges such as low educational achievement, unemployment, and social issues like substance abuse and depression. The system has not enabled them to fully reclaim their ancestral lands as thriving spaces where they can compete and excel in a modern, industrialized advanced economy. A critical lesson: sovereignty does not guarantee prosperity.

Sovereignty alone is insufficient for social and economic progress. True nation-building requires more than ancestral pride or territorial autonomy. Physical freedom does not guarantee growth, hence true freedom. Many Karen youth, resettled in wealthy nations, exemplify this, living a life of dependency rather than opportunity. The challenge is to avoid falling into complacency. We must strive to build a nation where all citizens compete equally and cultivate a society defined by hard work, talent, and self-reliance. A vibrant and competitive economy is the cornerstone of a truly sovereign and thriving nation.

While *contentment* is a Kawthoolei's virtue that we should adhere to, we cannot afford to live in a state of complacency, as the U.S. President Obama so powerfully articulated:

> "Even though something inside us tells us that we are not doing our best, that we're avoiding what is hard but also necessary, that we are shrinking from, rather than rising to, the challenges of our age. The thing is, in this new hyper-competitive age, none of us—none of us—can afford to be complacent." [Remarks By The President At Arizona State University Commencement, May 2009]

In this hyper-competitive world, complacency is not just a flaw; it is a danger, a sin. People who ignore it, reject it will be left behind. Therefore, we must push ourselves to do what is difficult but necessary and ensure that we are constantly advancing, even in the face of adversity, not settling until we know in our souls that we have given our very best with our God-given talents.

ANCIENT WISDOM, CONFUCIUS TEACHING

Confucius, the sage of East Asian civilization, taught that cultivating moral individuals is essential for establishing a stable social and political order. By defining and fostering virtuous qualities, a thriving society can be built. He undertook a mission to guide others toward virtue in times of political chaos and moral decline.

We learn our roles within kinship relationships: husband and wife, father and son, older brother and younger brother. Recognizing one's place within these relationships and fulfilling mutual responsibilities within that hierarchy is central to essential moral values. From the family, a sense of loyalty, honesty, duty, respect, and filial responsibility is developed, ultimately teaching us to love those around us. Without teachings brought from offshore, these values are human nature in Asian families.

Many of us speak English as a primary or secondary language, with formal education of Western values shaped by Greco-Roman and Judeo-Christian traditions. Yet much of Karen people's sayings, household wisdom, and daily thought shares its roots with East Asian traditions. I often hear Karen elders say, "tall trees endure more wind". But Keju Jin, a China born economist mentions the same saying in her book, "Tall trees bear the brunt of high wind." The same saying must have had the same origin long before Chinese and Karen people diverged.

Youths give respect to elders and eldest sibling looks after younger siblings are virtues of social cohesion and responsibility of Asia. However, a corrupted version of this dynamic is seen in the concept of the "big-brother relationship," a more cautious, skeptical, and even sinister perspective held by Western views. (A side note: Tracking citizens in every corner with Christmas-tree-like CCTV cameras and assigning them social credit scores has diverted from Confucian values.) Confucius saw the enduring institution of the family as a potent model and a potential solution for society's ills. The family demonstrates how authority can be both exercised and submitted to, fairly and productively through mutual assent, not through intimidation.

> "For Confucius, alongside knowledge and learning, character and moral integrity were highly prized. The emperor held supreme power, yet the day-to-day affairs of the state had to be managed by administrators who were competent, well-educated, imbued with righteousness, self-restraint, and committed to fulfilling their duties" (Jin, 2021).

Under this system, administrators bore immense responsibility to the public. While these values seem rooted in East Asian traditions, the West also emphasizes public trust and institutional integrity. In the U.S., the Supreme Court and the judicial system rely on public trust for the rule of law to function and maintain societal stability. Those in office largely act with restraint to uphold the integrity of their positions.

Everyone knows that the KNU leaders did not fall from the sky, but they grew out of our society. In the current Karen political sphere, there is constant criticism of leadership quality, with many questioning the integrity of those in higher political office, as if those in office were a different breed. In fact, their actions are a reflection of ours. If their capability and moral integrity are poor or lacking, it mirrors a collective state of our society—highlighting a broader issue rooted in our social development, not just the problems with aging men in office. We have strayed too far from our core values that we no longer recognize ourselves, only to be left barking at our own shadow.

Many parts of our society are experiencing social, moral, and political decay, rotting in a decline of etiquette toward the elder for their wisdom and experience. We have respected our elders without the need for fear of them, unlike our neighboring society, like Shan, or Burmese, who created kingdoms and chiefdoms with elaborate strict feudal hierarchies of control. Now, respect for elders and leaders has diminished, leaving behind only fear to authority, and sometimes neither fear nor respect. Elders and leaders, once guardians of the youth and the community's well-being, now find themselves cursed and openly disparaged, a trend fueled by the rise of the dark side of digital technology. As etiquette crumbles, so too does the moral and political order of society, as our societal experience demonstrates. With great power, leaders bear responsibility loaded on their shoulders. Society will not respect their elders when that great power corrupts, not because a respect to elders is inherently bad. To earn respect, elders and leaders also must be worthy of it.

Nowadays, in Karen society, the half-baked adoption of foreign ideologies—such as the right to disrespect authority disregarding the corresponding responsibility of mutual respect—has led some to turn rights into wrongs. A society cannot thrive with disrespect toward its elders; a nation cannot function well without respect for its leaders; nor can it uphold mutual responsibilities without maintaining reciprocal respectful social etiquette.

Leaders define a nation's character; the people's character defines its leaders.

CHASING KOREAN WAVES

Looking up at South Korea's remarkable rise, we see a nation that has not only succeeded economically but has also managed to export its art and culture globally. The "Korean Wave," or *Hallyu*, projects the influence of South Korean music, movies, television shows, fashion, and traditional cuisine as powerfully as its industries of automobiles and technology. South Korea has become an all-round exporter of its culture, reaching every corner of the world.

Yet, while many admire this success, we must reflect on the stark contrast with our own reality in Kawthoolei. For the Karen people, it is rather refugee waves, fleeing hardship and conflict. Despite our fertile land, many of our youth are malnourished, their potential unrealized, while they are caught in the current of displacement and poverty. We admire the beauty and success of Korea, but we must recognize the price South Korea paid to reach this level of global influence.

South Korean parents worked hard, often in the most difficult conditions, to lift their families and their nation out of poverty. Sixty years ago, South Korea was one of the poorest countries in the world. They worked down to the dirt, toiling through hardship, industrialization, and the aftermath of war to create the success their children now enjoy. This was not an overnight transformation, nor was it achieved through superficial pursuits. The strength of Korea's rise is rooted in discipline, resilience, and sacrifice—values we often overlook when dazzled by their cultural exports.

South Korea rebuilt itself from the ashes after the ravage of the Korean War (1950-1953), during which much of the infrastructure established during Japanese occupation was reduced to rubble. It was one of the poorest countries in the world, with a GDP per capita of just $100—poorer than Haiti, Ethiopia, or Yemen at the time. In its early years, South Korea relied heavily on foreign aid from the United States.

Most studies on Korean and East Asian development focus on industrial policies and the strong political leadership of General Park Chung Hee. Yet, a factor often underemphasized is the spirit of its people, what truly sets Korea apart. When General Park promoted an export-driven growth strategy, Koreans had few value-added products to offer. In response, women began selling their long locks, which were made into wigs. By 1970, wigs accounted for 9.3 percent (or $93.5 million) of South Korea's exports. Hair, a personal symbol of beauty, was sacrificed to support the nation's economic recovery.

During the 1998 Asian Financial Crisis, when the government called on citizens to help with the national debt, each family donated an average of 85 grams of gold to repay the IMF loan. This collective effort allowed Korea to repay its $19.5 billion debt three years ahead of schedule. Once, during a lecture in a U.S. Midwest university, a professor asked his students if they would do the same if their government asked—American students responded "no." The unity of the Korean people and their trust in the government were unparalleled. Korean women were loyal to their country's beauty products long before they became internationally renowned and would not choose Western brands even when living abroad.

Now, Korea's GDP per capita ($40,000) surpasses that of its former colonizer, Japan, and several European countries, including Spain and Italy. Whereas, peaceful Thailand could have prospered more but they got stuck at $7,000 GDP per capita, not being able to fix corruption corroding their potential. Now, South Korea excels in advanced electronics, shipbuilding, and semiconductors, reflecting not only strong leadership but also the enduring commitment and sacrifices of its people.

Koreans are not necessarily the smartest people in the world—a Karen man studying and working alongside them observed this well. Nor are Korean women the most beautiful, or those who think so may have only seen them in movies. Good hearted people, naturally adorned Karen (Knyaw) girls can be more beautiful, well-built Karen (Knyaw) boys can be more handsome. On one occasion at a university library entrance in the American Midwest, a Knyaw man walked past a group of Korean students, and the Korean girls turned their heads away from their immediate peers to admire the passerby. Korean students have a habit of gathering in large numbers around the library, a reflection of high social bonds. Many Karens, and Burmese alike, compare themselves to Koreans when they feel confident in their looks, yet this comparison can undermine self-respect. Ordinary Koreans outside of movies look just like anyone else; anyone can appear attractive with meticulous styling, makeup, and flattering lighting on screen on a selective few.

60 years ago, Korea started with 78 percent of the population illiterate. Within 40 years, they are industrialized and catching up with the West (who took more than a hundred years for the process). And in the next 20 years, Korea has surpassed many others, ranking among the nations as an industrial powerhouse. All this happened *not* because South Korea lacked an enemy but because they have a hostile neighbor, the other Korea (DPRK, the North Korea), that gives South Korea no choice but to advance to survive and eventually thrive.

The latter part of 2024 saw the global literary community celebrating Han Kang's Nobel Prize in Literature, awarded for her "intense poetic prose that confronts historical traumas and exposes the fragility of human life." As the first Asian female writer to receive this prestigious honor, Han Kang's achievement sparked a literary fervor that eclipsed even the nation's iconic K-pop and K-drama phenomena. Bookstores faced unprecedented demand, resulting in widespread sellouts, and the government responded with legislative support to encourage writers and foster literary culture. Images of a Korean Nobel laureate on the internet capture a quiet confidence and authenticity that shines effortlessly, without the need for makeup.

Outstanding South Korea's creativity stands out—unashamed, unapologetic, even unflinching enough to depict raw emotions on screen like eating another person's tears and mucus as a gesture of intense romantic love; their craftsmanship is meticulous, their service perhaps exceptional, and their work ethic undeniable, making their nation identity. Korean Air(line) exemplifies this national pride by promoting Korean identity into every facet of its brand: K-pop in safety briefings, K-dramas in in-flight entertainment and cuisines, insightful documentaries, and passenger amenities such as free showers and nap spaces during transit, while airlines around the world compete on services. Korean Air offers competitive fares for Karen expatriates returning to home Kawthoolei. However, some travelers may need to navigate Korean prejudices against Southeast Asians (for having darker skin than East Asians). Koreans are human, who may not always be good at concealing their biases.

Before admiring their success, it is first good to emulate the sacrifices and foundations—mirroring the hard work and creative drive behind it— that make such success possible. While many of our children in Kawthoolei run around in their own land in dusty clothes, struggling with malnutrition, to busily organize Karen beauty pageants outside war zones does not show that our nation grows—it only shows that we are shallow.

Hard work, loyalty to the nation, dedication to learning, bold creativity, and constant innovation— these are the qualities Karen (Knyaw) students and adults should aspire to before mimicking Korea's music, fashion, or style.

If we wish to emulate Koreans, we should emulate their work ethic and tireless pursuit of excellence. Their dedication to education is exceptional: Korean students study rigorously, parents invest heavily in their children's success, and the government continually seeks ways to provide the best resources. Korea is known to have the best internet in the world. Classrooms are designed to foster creativity, aligning with Korea's strengths in electronics and cultural products. Korean students are present in significant numbers across American universities, especially relative to the size of their population.

This disconnect between the admiration for superficial beauty and the harsh reality of our situation is dangerous. It distracts us from what truly matters. We are chasing the wrong tail, pursuing the superficial when what we truly need is to cultivate the qualities that lead to lasting success—adaptability, discipline, and a commitment to uplifting our people from within.

South Korea's success should inspire us, but not to superficial imitation. We should emulate their dedication to craftsmanship, their respect for traditional culture, their strong social bonds, and their unwavering national loyalty. Our path to progress lies not in mimicking beauty standards or pop culture, but in embracing the work ethic, creative drive, and collective spirit that propelled South Korea's remarkable rise. Or do we have mental fiber to match that strength?

For Kawthoolei, the path forward lies not in chasing superficial success but in digging deeper, in understanding that true progress requires innovation, hard work, and a clear vision for the future. Then can we hope to truly transform our refugee wave into a wave of success, one that reflects the full potential of our people.

A nation with a strong spirit can rise to the top within a single lifetime—a reminder to the people of Kawthoolei, if any of us has a hesitant soul.

CLAIMING OUR OWN SOUND

The world still waits to hear a sound that is unmistakably Karen—a genre that boldly declares our identity. Our voices resonate beautifully in homes, churches, and gatherings, now echoing across YouTube, rich with passion and sincerity. Yet much of our music mirrors the rhythms of others—rap, reggae, country, or slow go-go—borrowed from distant origins. While performed skillfully, these genres often lack the signature that would make them truly ours. Most go flat, failing to spark, even among our own.

Talent alone, no matter how abundant, cannot forge a legacy. True artistry demands boldness and authenticity—the courage to innovate, to blend tradition with invention, and to create something that embodies the soul of a people. Imagine a genre alive with the stories, struggles, and triumphs of the Karen—rooted in our heritage yet infused with modern vibrancy. A sound that honors our past while standing among the contributions of the world's musical giants.

The world is not waiting for another echo. It is waiting for the Karen voice to rise, to sing, and to claim its place in the symphony of cultures.

A UNIQUE GENRE FOR KAWTHOOLEI

I once shared a conversation with a Caribbean colleague, a man of striking presence—strong build, curly hair, a slight Creole accent, and Caribbean charm. I mentioned that the Karen people sing beautifully and everywhere anytime, a talent deeply woven into our poetic traditions. Our ancestors recited *Hta*—traditional verses—on quiet nights, at special gatherings, and in daily life. Yet, despite our gift for song, we lack a genre uniquely our own—one that the world would instantly recognize as Karen.

He responded with an inspiring thought: "For a country to be known as unique to the world, it needs only one band to start."

He spoke of reggae, born in the heart of Jamaica. Rooted in local rhythms, reggae became a global force, led by the artistry and philosophy of Bob Marley. His music, beliefs, and unmistakable style transformed reggae into more than a genre—it became a symbol of identity and resilience.

One day, Kawthoolei will create a genre that is authentically its own. Promising efforts already hint at this possibility. Tha Ko Lo and his musical partner have blended rock with the traditional Karen harp, weaving together Pwo and Sqaw dialects while alternating male and female voices—a musical conversation that embodies the richness of Karen identity. Similarly, other songs have begun to integrate both dialects and genders within the same composition.

Meanwhile, the art of *Hta*—though fading—still endures among a few devoted practitioners. Its poetic traditions parallel those of Korea and Japan, whose literary heritage has earned admiration on the world stage. Within such cultural treasures lie the seeds of a genre that could one day bring Kawthoolei into the global spotlight.

The challenge lies in transforming these fragments of culture into something cohesive and revolutionary. A genre born in Kawthoolei would be more than music—it would be an expression of our soul, a declaration of who we are, and a testament to our enduring spirit. Let us aspire to sing, not with borrowed voices, but with a signature of our own.

AUTHENTICITY BEYOND TRADITION

Creating a unique genre does not mean clinging solely to traditional forms or being confined by cultural history. Korea's BTS, a global phenomenon, do not perform in feudal-era hanboks or sing ancient folk songs. Yet their artistry remains unmistakably Korean—blending innovation, cultural pride, and global appeal.

Their influence extends beyond music. BTS have become cultural ambassadors, recognized not only by fans—including many young Karen women—but also by their government and major corporations. They appear in airline safety videos, speak out on social issues, and have even performed at the White House. At Wembley Stadium in London, they became the first non-English-speaking band to sell out the venue, solidifying their global reach.

This example challenges Kawthoolei to dream beyond its borders. An authentic Karen genre does not need to be bound solely to traditional sounds. It can be innovative, forward-looking, and deeply rooted in the creative spirit of our people. The goal is to craft a sound and vision that resonate globally while staying true to the heart of Kawthoolei.

Such a genre would not only introduce the Karen people to the world but also unite our community with a shared sense of achievement and identity. Authenticity lies not in rigid preservation but in fearless creation. Kawthoolei can craft a sound that commands attention, captivates hearts, and tells a story only we can tell.

For a society destined to thrive, clinging to outdated customs often becomes a weight that holds it back. An identity that shows we respect ourselves and deserves respect on the world stage is tethered not to stagnant tradition but emerges from a dynamic blend of heritage, progress, and purpose—an evolution shaped by both the past and the aspirations for the future.

In Kawthoolei, where the echoes of tradition still resonate, the time has come to assess which practices uplift our people and which diminish our standing. Not every custom deserves preservation, nor does every change signify progress. History offers lessons to shape a future where our identity is elevated, not merely preserved, free from the chains of habits that no longer serve us to grow.

A nation that grows finds its healthy roots.

Chapter 10

Growing Nation, Growing Language

As nation aspires to grow, so too must its language. The nation cannot grow without its language growing. Language—a living entity—constantly balances preservation and progress. In linguistic terms, a language features both *retention* and *innovation*. Through *revitalization* and *rejuvenation*, a national language thrives. Revitalization preserves and reawakens core linguistic elements—such as grammar, vocabulary, idioms, and cultural expressions that define the language's identity—primarily through education. Rejuvenation, on the other hand, embraces new words, structures, and usages to reflect societal, technological, and cultural changes, growing the language to articulate an ever-evolving world.

Many of our native expressions—so too our thoughts—are constrained by a vocabulary that holds our psyche hostage. We find ourselves thinking in primitive terms, limited by a language that restricts our ability to fully grasp with the modern world and embrace technological advancements. This lack of comprehension arises from a shortage of vocabulary to express these innovations. Our dictionary includes only a handful of modern terms for physical objects like satellites, missiles, and electricity, but these words see no incorporation into daily usage. The contemporary world needs far more. A nation of ours requires a comprehensive ecosystem of indigenous lexicon to keep pace with progress and speak tongue to tongue, shoulder to shoulder in equal status with other nations, articulating every idea in our native language.

This calls for the revitalization of vocabulary, words, and terms that have faded from use. At the same time, there is a need to continuously invent, adopt, and integrate new words to clearly and elegantly represent the concepts and ideas of the modern world.

In Karen communities resettled in wealthier nations, a small but thriving network of medical translators has emerged, dedicated to innovating medical terminology. This vibrant effort is driven largely by financial incentives, constantly seeking out and inventing new words to meet the demands of their profession. Yet, this represents only a narrow slice of language growth. As these communities integrate into broader societies and new generations grow up, the reliance on such translation services will inevitably diminish, taking with it the vibrancy of vocabulary innovation. This needs a broader, more comprehensive effort to ensure that our language grows holistically across all facets of life on a national scale.

ONE COMMON SCRIPT: UNITING MANY DIALECTS AND SCRIPTS

The nation is overdue for a common script that transcends dialectal boundaries and unifies our fragmented writing systems. Our scattered scripts hinder mutual understanding, with each dialect's script falling short of fully capturing the rich resonance of our Karenic tongues.

Our language has been fragmented into multiple spoken dialects and scattered across a multitude of written scripts and urgently needs bold corrective reform. Instead of fostering a unified linguistic identity, many are—insensitive and uninformed—fortifying scripts for each dialect, some educated deepening divisions by rigidly categorizing each dialect and script as distinct languages—Sqaw, Pwo, Bwe, Geh-bar and so on. Spoken language can be represented in various forms—whether in strokes, Roman-Latin script, or Pyu-Mon script. A written script is merely a tool for representing spoken words and can be adapted in many forms.

Among the different groups, a multitude of scripts has been developed, each shaped by a unique combination of dialects and religious sects, adding significant complexity to our linguistic landscape. Even within the most widely spoken Sqaw Karen dialect, at least five distinct scripts remain in use. The script that serves as the *de facto* national language—employed by the KNU and KBC in official and political contexts—suffers from its hasty creation by missionaries in the 1930s. It was primarily developed out of convenience, utilizing existing Burmese alphabets to accommodate the printing presses of the time. Other Sqaw scripts, such as Ta-La-Kuu, Lee-Kwe-Kaw, and Lee-saw-wet, continue to be developed and used. A Romanized script, used by Catholic Thai Karen communities, also remains in use.

This widely used Sqaw Karen (KBC) script was developed with vowel and consonant structures tailored to a specific dialect of a specific regional usage. While functional, it remains insufficient for fully capturing all the sounds of the Sqaw Karen dialect. The script consists of 25 consonants and 9 vowels and accommodates six tones for a tonal language. However, it struggles to represent some common diphthongs, such as /ai/, /ei/, /uo/, and /ui/, which are frequently used in Sqaw and heavily used in non-Sqaw dialects.

This array of scripts poses a greater obstacle to national unity than it contributes to the cultural richness of variety. Fostering a cohesive national identity and smoother communication requires the adoption of a common script—one capable of fully expressing the full array of our language. Such a script would not only honor our diverse heritage by incorporating the richness of terms, expressions, stories, and folklore but also enable mutual understanding through the ability to read and share across communities, serving as a unifying force that strengthens our nation.

The shortage of expertise to accurately analyze our diverse dialects hampers efforts to make the Karenic language mutually intelligible. Fortunately, there is a linguist community who has studied the Karenic language for centuries. Addressing the challenge requires building a more vibrant community of linguists from native speakers, cultivating widespread national enthusiasm across all dialect communities, and fostering political awareness of a unified script for nation-building. There is hope. Many Karen people with sufficient exposure can understand both closely related Pwo and Sqaw dialects, with some achieving mutual intelligibility despite differences in accents and vernacular variations. Each dialect has exotic vocabulary that can be helpful for building a national vocabulary reservoir.

Without the critical insight to identify commonalities among dialects, efforts toward unification risk exacerbating existing divisions. Without a sensible understanding of the political landscapes in which different Karen groups align, such attempts are more likely to entrench fragmentation rather than foster cohesion.

An exotic branch of our language can illuminate. Among the Karenic languages, Palaychi (Pay-lay-kee) is a distinctive dialect spoken by a small community in northern Kawthoolei. Although these villagers are part of the Karen Baptist Convention, they find the Sqaw Karen script inadequate for representing their unique dialect. In the 1990s a choir group visited my village, coming in December to sing carols. As their host, I guided them around, observing how they used Burmese alphabets to transcribe the sounds of Palaychi for their songs, so that everyone could sing along.

Once, recognizing the distinctiveness of their dialect, one of their religious leaders was asked if he could create a new script specifically for Palaychi. However, the pastor wisely declined, understanding that such an act could deepen divisions within the Karen nation. His decision highlights the crucial role of religious and community leaders who are clear-minded, nationally conscious, and committed to unity. Rather than creating additional scripts that could further fragment our community, we need leaders who champion cohesion and solidarity among our people.

To achieve linguistic unity, we require cohesive, motivated, well-supported experts to delve into the intricacies of our language, examine its dialectal variations, and work toward a cohesive linguistic identity. This expertise is vital to overcoming the fragmentation that threatens the unity of our culture.

Roughly 30 years ago, during the previous generation, Karen community leaders, religious figures, and a few dedicated linguists undertook an ambitious project to create a common script for all Karen people. Their initiative aimed to establish a system similar to the Pinyin notation used for Chinese by expanding the KBC script to include additional consonants, vowels, and other Karenic sounds. This comprehensive script sought to bridge dialectal differences, enabling mutual intelligibility while accurately capturing the phonetic richness of the Karenic language.

The project came tantalizingly close to success, offering a glimpse of linguistic unity within our community. Yet, without the foundation of political freedom, the initiative eventually faltered. The absence of political support, coupled with external interference, eroded the momentum necessary for its completion. Tragically, many of the visionary leaders who spearheaded this effort, such as Tharadoh Saw Lar Bar and Tharadoh Azra, have since passed away, taking with them a vital chapter of our cultural and linguistic aspirations.

Their vision for a unified script serves as a reminder of what might have been and underscores the importance of political freedom in achieving meaningful language reform.

A Common Script in Practice

At a telling occasion of Karen New Year song practice, the need for a common script among the Karen people unfolded before my eyes. The community members with different dialects gathered to rehearse a Western Pwo Karen song, a piece cherished for its melody and cultural resonance. Yet, to ensure everyone could sing along, the lyrics were transliterated into Latin alphabet—a makeshift solution that made participation possible, but not without revealing deeper issues.

At this song practice, the gathering itself reflected the linguistic diversity of our people. Some were Western Pwo Karen speakers, others Eastern Pwo, and many were Sqaw Karen, hailing from both urban and rural areas. Yet, few had been given the opportunity to formally learn the scripts of their dialects, and many were not fluent in the written forms of their language. The younger generation, in particular, was adrift—unable to access the traditional scripts that hold the keys to their heritage.

The song we practiced was familiar, its lyrics echoing across dialects with a shared cultural resonance. But the reality of our fragmented scripts made participation uneven. Some could sing with confidence, reading directly from their respective scripts. Others stumbled, relying on memory. For the younger participants, the Romanized transliteration was a lifeline, allowing them to follow the sounds of the song with ease.

The improvised Romanized script, while practical, was no more than a temporary patch. Yet, it highlighted the potential for a more structured and systematic solution—something akin to a

"Pinyin-style" Romanization—that could unify our scattered dialects and bridge the generational divide.

This is not an unfamiliar path. The Kachin and Chin people, among many other ethnic groups, have embraced Romanized scripts to preserve their languages while adapting to the demands of the digital age. Romanized scripts integrate seamlessly with modern technology, making them accessible on digital platforms and compatible with global communication systems.

However, improvisation cannot be our long-term solution. A thoughtfully developed common script, whether rooted in Roman characters or a synthesis of Karen traditions, is essential. Such a script would not only unify the fragmented linguistic landscape but also empower the younger generation to connect with their heritage, ensuring that the depth and beauty of Karen culture endure in an increasingly globalized world.

This is more than a technical challenge; it is a cultural imperative. Language is the vessel of our stories, our songs, our identity. To leave it fragmented is to allow it to fade. The time has come to forge a common path.

They Like Us to Be Fragmented

Until I grew older and stepped into the reality of a broken world, I was nurtured by songs and stories about the Karen people, the people with a vibrant community of dialects, many tribes and clans—Sqaw, Pwo, Karenni, Pao, P'reh (Ka-Yaw), Kayah Puu, Kayah Moe Pwar, Geh-kho, Geh-bar (Ka-Yan), Pa-Ku, Bwe, and Maw-Nay-Bwa—a common decedents all interconnected by shared cultural heritage, linguistic ties, customs, and ways of life that banging the rain frog bronze drum. As a descendant of the Maw-Nay-Bwa branch, I witnessed my mother and maternal grandparents converse in Maw-Nay-Bwa at home, while Sqaw was used at church and with other Karen communities as the common language. From that region those who attended Karen Bible school in Rangoon, others often found humor in their Maw-Nay-Bwa-influenced vocabulary, usage, and accents.

In 1989, under a new generation of authoritarian Burmese General Than Shwe's rule, the Burmese military not only renamed the country from Burma to Myanmar but also engineered a divisive narrative proclaiming the existence of 135 distinct ethnic nationalities. They positioned themselves as the sole protectors of this manufactured mosaic, promoting this idea to the international community, the educated, Burmese elite, soldiers, and even Burmese citizens, who, while not supporters of the regime, were persuaded of their duty to safeguard the nation. Within this framework, the Karen people were subdivided into 11 ethnic groups and the Karenni into 9, erasing their historical identity as branches of the larger Karen people.

We risk reinforcing the narrative perpetuated by the Burmese military regime positioning itself as the sole guardian of the nation if we fail to reform our language and unify our various dialects. By allowing our dialects to remain fragmented and creating additional scripts, we inadvertently bolster their divide-and-rule strategy, further weakening our collective identity.

Today, it is disheartening to see some Karen highly educated—some with advanced degrees—embrace the narrative of fragmentation. Despite their academic training, many remain politically uninformed and, by conveniently quoting the prevailing narrative, unwittingly acting as agents of division within our people as they take on roles as educators. This narrative has fueled the proliferation of separate scripts for individual dialects, often tied to religious affiliations, further weakening our collective identity.

A century ago, brass-wearing northerners were long-neck Karen, iconic giraffe people to the world. Not long ago in the earlier time on the internet, a signboard at the entrance of a Kayan (Padaung, as a slight derogatory reference by their neighbors) village once read "Long Neck Karen Village" in English. In recent years, the narrative of the "135 ethnic" fabrication has infiltrated our communities, and now the signboard simply reads "Kayan Village," erasing the recognition of Karenic ethno-linguistic connection.

The completion of a Bible translation into the Bwe dialect, using the International Phonetic Alphabet (IPA), is another sign of growing fragmentation. By distancing themselves from the Karen Baptist Convention (KBC), which has historically upheld a unified language as a foundation of Karen solidarity, the Bwe community would be able to read scriptures in their full sound but would less likely use KBC script that is widely used among our people.

To resist these forces of fragmentation, political awareness and linguistic reform take precedence in the pursuit of national cohesion. Only through unity—cultural, linguistic, and political—can we withstand the strategies designed to divide, weaken, eventually erase us.

A PEOPLE WITH NO NAME

The Sqaw do not call themselves *Sqaw* but *Pwar-Ker-Nyaw*, meaning "the People." It is the same for Plone (Pwo), the human. "Sqaw" is the name given to distinguish this group from other tribes, while the Pwo refer to Sqaw as *Shaung*. The term *Karen* is an English re-adaptation, yet we do not have a universally accepted name beyond "the People," such as *Pwarr-Ker-Nyaw Blerr Tee Ker Way Sher* to refer to the Karen Baptist Convention (KBC) that includes many dialects and subgroups. Other tribes do not call themselves *Knyaw*; instead, they identify as *Plone, Kayah, Kyaw, Ke-bah, Kayan*, and others. *Knyaw* represents only a subset of the broader Karen people—a common people that the Burmese elite have ceaselessly sought to dismantle.

In the enactment of Karen New Year, Bill Number 36 of 1937, one can still find its trace in Myanmar's official documents, which continue to uphold certain British-era laws.

The act may be called "The Karens' New Year Recognition Act of 1937.

"Karens" means all races, clans, or tribes forming part and parcel of the Karen People in spite of their castes, creeds, and religions.

A GLIMPSE INTO OTHER NATIONS' GROWING LANGUAGES

Lee Kuan Yew faced fierce resistance from the Chinese community when he introduced English as the working language in Singapore. In a newly independent nation where 70 percent of the population was Chinese, alongside substantial Malay and Indian communities deeply rooted in their own languages, religions, and cultural traditions, the push for a common language met opposition, often toxic. Even within the Chinese community, there were seven mutually unintelligible dialects, complicating communication further. (Notably, many Chinese dialects traditionally spoken in Singapore, such as Hokkien and Cantonese, are linguistically more divergent from one another than Karenic dialects like Pwo and Sqaw are from each other.)

The need for a common language was critical, particularly for national defense. A nation cannot effectively defend itself if its soldiers lack a shared working language, which poses a serious threat to national security. Today, Singapore's success is also attributed to its adoption of English as a working language while maintaining its rich, diverse heritage, teaching bilingual schools. This decision to embrace a global language not only facilitated commerce and trade but also established a legal and regulatory framework that has propelled Singapore's progress and development. English as a working language enabled Singapore to establish itself as a global financial hub, facilitating the provision of financial services on an international scale.

CHINESE LANGUAGE REFORM

The Chinese script, with its roots stretching back over 3,000 years, has long been a symbol of the nation's cultural and intellectual might. From the ancient Oracle bone script to the refined strokes of Kaishu, this script has evolved through countless forms throughout time and space of Chinese civilization. The seeds of language reform were sown during the 1919 May 4th Movement, which ignited a fervor for modernization and sparked a radical push for language change. Ironically, the most patriotic voices were the ones calling for the most extreme measures. Radical intellectuals, in their zeal to save China, proposed that the ancient script that had united the nation for millennia should be eradicated to secure the nation's future.

One of the most vocal proponents of this radical approach was Lu Xun, a prominent 20th-century Chinese author, who famously declared, "If Chinese characters are not destroyed, then China will die" (漢字不滅，中國必亡). To him and his peers, the intricate characters were more than just a writing system—they were symbols of what they saw as childish and barbaric thinking. Lu Xun, alongside linguist Qian Xuantong, believed that the eradication of Chinese characters was essential to dismantling the Confucian thought they blamed for China's stagnation. Qian even argued that only by abolishing Chinese characters would Confucianism be truly uprooted from Chinese society.

The movement gained momentum, and in 1935, the Ministry of Education published a list of 324 simplified characters, a bold step towards simplifying the script. But these changes were just the beginning of a much larger and more contentious struggle.

As the Communist Party rose to power in 1949, the debate over the future of the Chinese script reached a fever pitch. Should China simplify its characters to preserve its heritage, or should it adopt a Latin alphabet to embrace the future? The nation was divided, with scholars and policymakers locked in a fierce ideological struggle. The fate of the Chinese script hung in the balance—this debate was about more than just language; it was a battle for China's soul.

In a dramatic turn, the decision came from an unexpected source: Soviet leader Joseph Stalin. Advising Mao Zedong not to abandon the traditional script, Stalin argued that China's script was not merely a writing system—it was a living testament to thousands of years of history, culture, and identity. Mao listened, and the path was chosen: simplification over eradication.

The result was a compromise—a streamlined set of characters designed to be easier to learn and use yet firmly rooted in the cultural legacy of China. This decision preserved the essence of the Chinese language while making it accessible to a modernizing nation. Simplified characters became the standard in Mainland China and Singapore, while Taiwan, under Chiang Kai-shek Nationalist rule, chose to retain the traditional characters as a defiant statement of cultural and political identity.

The struggle over the future of Chinese characters was not just about reforming a script—it was about preserving a legacy, a heritage, and a sense of self. In the end, the language reform in China was not merely an adjustment of strokes and symbols; it was an affirmation of identity, the enduring power of language to shape a nation's destiny.

THE BIRTH OF AMERICAN ENGLISH

In the late 18th century, America was a fledgling nation, proudly declaring its political independence from Britain. Yet, culturally, it was still tethered to the old world, particularly in its use of the English language. Even as American society rapidly advanced in science, politics, and innovation, the nation continued to rely on British grammar books and dictionaries. The towering authority of Samuel Johnson's *A Dictionary of the English Language*, published in 1755, loomed large, with its thousands of British words shaping the vocabulary of American classrooms. But something was missing—a distinctly American voice, a language that reflected the country's new identity.

Enter Noah Webster, a fiery schoolteacher from Connecticut. Discontented with the British grip on American language, Webster saw the need for a national linguistic revolution. In his passionate writings, he declared that America must be "as independent in literature as she is in politics." He was convinced that the country's language should reflect its independence and evolving culture. His mission was clear: to create a distinctly American form of English, free from the elitism and dead languages of British grammar books.

Webster began his work by publishing *A Grammatical Institute of the English Language* in 1783, known as the "Blue-Backed Speller." This book revolutionized American education, teaching children English in a way that was accessible, practical, and American. It quickly became a staple in schools, selling millions of copies and solidifying Webster's place as a champion of American education. But this was just the beginning of his grand vision.

For nearly 30 years, Webster labored on his most ambitious project: an American dictionary. He traveled across the country, listening to the speech of everyday people, collecting words from Native Americans, settlers, and immigrants. From them, he gathered words like "moccasin," "canoe," and "bullfrog," and created new terms to capture the uniquely American experience. He invented new political terms like "presidential" to reflect the radical break America made with European monarchies, signaling a new political philosophy. He simplified spellings, making words like "color" and "honor" easier to write, and he reshaped American English to reflect the nation's practical, forward-thinking spirit. The language has to grow out of its feudal darkness as the nation born a republic.

In 1828, Webster's *American Dictionary of the English Language* was finally published. It was more than just a book of words; it was a declaration of American cultural independence. It contained 70,000 words, many of which had never been seen in print before. His work was bold and visionary, reshaping the way Americans thought and spoke, giving the new nation a language that matched its revolutionary ideals.

Webster's dictionary sparked outrage in some circles—both in Britain and among American elites who clung to British traditions. But Webster stood firm, believing that language, like the country, must evolve to reflect the people. His vision of a national language, rooted in popular usage and distinct from its British roots, was realized. Webster gave America more than just a dictionary; he gave it a linguistic identity.

In shaping American English, Webster gave the nation its own voice—a voice that would resonate through its literature, politics, and culture for generations. He once said, "A national language is a band of national union," and through his work, he united America with a language that was unmistakably its own. Noah Webster's legacy is not just the words he defined, but the way he helped define a nation.

The English language grows every year. Every year, new words and expressions are added to the Merriam-Webster dictionary. In 2023, 690 words were included. Many of these additions are slang terms that have evolved from niche usage into broader, mainstream acceptance. Others arise from technical necessities or linguistic innovation. Merriam-Webster's lexicographers meticulously monitor a vast array of sources to determine which words warrant inclusion. By doing so, they document new ways of describing the world. Many other English dictionaries also add hundreds of words every year.

HEBREW: A DEAD LANGUAGE REVIVED

As I board a flight bound for home, Kawthoolei, from San Francisco, the airline announcements first echo in the national language of the airline—Korean, Thai, or Mandarin—followed by English, the global lingua franca. On the in-flight entertainment screen, languages are offered for only a select few of the world's major tongues. Among them is Hebrew, a language once considered dead, now revived as the national language of a small nation of fewer than 10 million people in the Middle East. A red dot on the global map, this developed, thriving country speaks Hebrew—a language that has risen from the grave. With a relatively small number of speakers, it nonetheless holds world-class significance.

As I sat there, I couldn't help but reflect on my own language—Karenic language, passed down through countless generations. I speak an ancient tongue that carries the voices of my ancestors, yet it faces an uncertain future. It is not dead, not yet, but it is on the verge of decline. I realize with a jolt: I could be part of the last generation to speak my mother tongue. Unlike Hebrew, my language has not yet reached the point of needing revival—but if we do not act, that day may come. The story of Hebrew's miraculous resurrection reminds me that the future of our mother tongue is still within our hands, but the clock is ticking. For generations, Karen people from urban Myanmar have adopted Burmese as their primary language in speech and writing, already. And they have an attachment to it, already.

Hebrew, considered a dead language for nearly 2,000 years, made an extraordinary comeback and is now spoken by around 9 million people. It stands as the only language ever revived from the dead and is one of Israel's official languages, alongside Arabic. Today, Hebrew permeates everyday life in Israel, from street signs to keyboards to bookstores—a language brought back from the brink.

The revival of Hebrew began with a radical vision. In 1881, Eliezer Ben-Yehuda arrived in Israel determined to make Hebrew the primary language in every Israeli household. His obsession with this dream was so intense that he refused to expose his son to any other language, leading the boy to be mute until he finally spoke his first Hebrew word, "Abba" (father). His son became the first native Hebrew speaker in nearly two millennia, a living symbol of the revival.

This linguistic revolution spread like wildfire, as immigrants from across the world came to Israel, needing a unifying language. Hebrew became the bridge that united a diverse population, and today, millions of Israelis speak it as their everyday language.

The resurrection of Hebrew stands as a powerful testament to the possibility of reviving a language once considered lost to time. As languages disappear at an alarming rate, Hebrew proves that a dead language can indeed be brought back to life. It has united an entire nation and serves as a beacon of cultural and linguistic resilience. Let it be an inspiration to us all, a reminder that we still have the power to safeguard the future of our own languages.

Israel—love it or hate it for its controversial politics—stands as a testament to unparalleled determination. Against all odds, the people of Israel revived a dead language, reclaiming their linguistic and cultural heritage. Yet, as Karen people, we find ourselves in a stronger position when it comes to our native language and land heritage. Our language is still alive, spoken by many, and our connection to our ancestral lands remains legitimate. Time is ticking to ensure that our language and culture thrive before it is too late.

BEAUTY IN KARENIC LANGUAGE AND GENDER NEUTRALITY

Research shows that our native languages shape how we think about many aspects of the world including space and time (Mykhailyuk, 2015). In Karenic languages, this influence also affects how we think about gender, social norms, and even basic things like color.

The Karenic language is notable in its inherent gender neutrality, which contrasts with many other languages, such as Germanic and Romance languages. In these languages, gender-specific pronouns and nouns influence thought patterns and social dynamics. For example, German assigns gender even to inanimate objects, like bridges and the sun, both feminine, while Spanish assigns masculinity to the sun and bridges. This gendered language is prevalent across many cultures, even in Burma, where Arakan people refer to their homeland as "Fatherland," while Burmese people refer to their nation as the "Motherland." Burmese and Arakanese, considered ethnolinguistic close cousins, are more mutually intelligible than the various Karenic dialects. Anyone who understands Burmese can understand Arakan with ease. The Burmese language has an issue with its first-person pronouns, which are deeply rooted in class hierarchy and a feudal archaism. To be polite, phrases like "your good male/female slave" (*kyun-dor, kyun-ma*) reflect this embedded sense of social stratification, reinforcing a slave-master relationship, submissive and servile tone in everyday language. In this aspect, Burmese has not seen its language reform over a century after the end of the feudal system. Their system broke down, the psyche persists.

In contrast, Karenic languages are free from this gender bias. Our pronouns for the first, second, and third person are neutral—similar to "I," "you," and "them" in English, but without the gender-specific distinctions of "he" and "she" or "him" and "her." This neutrality extends beyond pronouns, allowing Karenic speakers to think and communicate without the gendered framework that shapes so many other languages. The current discourse in English-speaking cultures, especially the push from the liberal left, revolves around the need to develop inclusive, gender-neutral pronouns like "ze" and "zir" to address social and moral concerns. But this is a problem rooted in a linguistic structure that Karenic languages simply do not share.

I once casually surveyed young Karen people who grew up studying in the West, asking whether they perceived Kawthoolei, our homeland, as masculine or feminine. Most had no preference. To them, it was neutral—just as it should be in Karenic thought. To Kawthoolei, translating references into English using "he," "she," or "it" strips away the original meaning and values inherently carried in the Karenic language.

It is ironic when outsiders come to our border, insisting on teaching us about gender inclusivity, assuming we face the same challenges they do. In their own societies, they grapple with gendered language and the biases it perpetuates. Meanwhile, we have lived with a neutral, inclusive linguistic structure that is more advanced in this regard. Mothers are respected and capable as fathers, wife and husband are shoulder to shoulder in household and community.

Outsiders teaching us to adopt inclusivity without first understanding what we already possess is not progress—it is ignoring a system that has long been working in ways they are only beginning to explore. In many ways, people in advanced nations are searching for linguistic solutions that Kawthoolei already holds.

GENDER NEUTRALITY VS. GENDER VIOLENCE

Most Karen communities are like one in the region where I grew up, a sane person would never resort to violence against their spouse. Even an unwell person would never think to harm a family member. Domestic violence feels like a foreign disease, alien to the harmony of our community. Life in that region, like anywhere in Burma, is undeniably hard. Yet, husbands and wives bear the yoke of family burdens equally. All absurd, the idea that spouses beating one another as a solution to family hardship is unfathomable.

Among the Karen families, it is not uncommon for one spouse to take on a more dominant role in the household—sometimes the wife, sometimes the husband—but arguments rarely escalate beyond quiet disagreements. In neighboring non-Karen households, one might hear arguments spill loudly into the streets. By contrast, the Karen family holds steadfast to gentleness as its guiding principle. Disputes may arise, and spouses may frustrate one another, but harsh words or actions are a breach of what is expected.

If anyone is on the receiving end of scolding, it is the children—typically from their mother in the morning. These lectures are not outbursts of anger but rather stern life lessons—that no one in the household dares to stop—often spanning the breadth of family struggles, moral expectations, and the importance of behaving as the parents believe they should. This motherly morning's long reprimand is colloquially known as "porridge cooking", children taking it easy on lengthy unpleasant parental disapproval. Outside of home, children usually recount that somber ritual in amusing terms.

KAWTHOOLEI INHERITS HIGH LITERARY CULTURE

I am ashamed to remember that I once spent sleepless nights analyzing and writing papers on Shakespeare's *Romeo and Juliet* and *A Midsummer Night's Dream*, only to later discover a Karen story called *Naw Ser To Paw Dot Kyaw Paw Kyel*, which I listened to more than five times, so far. This tale of two young lovers is more beautiful, more dramatic, more romantic, more humane, and more realistic than anything Shakespeare ever wrote. Told in the Karen language and preserved by elders in the mountains of Thailand, it is a masterpiece of storytelling.

The form and content of the story are so exceptional that the storytellers themselves become part of the narrative. Half-crying or indistinct mourning, whether expressed by the narrator or the protagonist, becomes indistinguishable. The beauty of the tale transcends its medium—it is a treasure that deserves recognition as a national treasure and even as part of world heritage.

At first, I wondered if that Karen tale had drawn inspiration from *Romeo and Juliet*—itself a retelling of an ancient Greek lovers' tale—or if there were cross-cultural influences at play. But after thorough examination, I can confidently vouch that this story is entirely Karen, rooted deeply in our own traditions, ways of life, and with a touch of neighboring contacts.

For those who seek to experience its beauty, the story can still be heard on *Karens All* YouTube channels. This is not just a story; it is a living legacy, waiting to be documented and cherished as part of our intangible national heritage.

There are classic love stories, well-known tales like "Ku Naw Lay and Naw Mu Aye", "Toe Kee Baw dot Naw Thoe Maw", "Thu-Ta-Nu dot Naw Kar Ree" told among geographically diverse places. There many more legends, tales, and poems held in different Karen dialects.

OUR LANGUAGE, OUR HERITAGE

When I speak my mother tongue, I do not merely echo the voice of my mother but also that of my great-great-great…grandmother, who walked on earth thousands of years ago. My mother tongue carries the spirit of my ancestors. My mother tongue is a living language and a language of life. My mother tongue is the language of my lips, the language of my thoughts and the language of my dreams. What could be fairer than the tongue of my sleep.

My maternal great-grandmother, who spoke only Sqaw Karen, lived a simple quiet but busy life into her 90s. In her village in the Sit-Taung Valley (Eastern Bago Region), everyone spoke Karenic until a generation ago, when Burmese education was introduced.

It is impossible to convey the true essence of our national sentiment in another language. Many linguists including Noam Chomsky now emphasized that language is an abstract system for representing thoughts, not a direct reflection of reality. Fully expressing human thoughts and experiences with language is impossible. Translating human experiences and languages is even farther. Translations are verisimilitude. No language possesses a vocabulary vast enough to completely encapsulate the depth of human experience.

Our national experience is shaped by its own unique rationale, a sense of longing and belonging, and the dreams we carry—often expressed through cultural symbolism. In our tradition, dream symbols such as water or fire are interpreted as signs of significant events, much like flying or swimming. Before a final exam or an important life milestone, dreaming of clear water is seen as a sign of success.

Thoughts, symbols, and dreams are perhaps interconnected nationally. In the region I grew up, elder spoke of the meaning of dreams, and to this day I remain attentive to those divine symbols. In 2006 when I was in Chiangmai, a tension was brewing in KNU leadership. A leader I was close to telephoned me saying that everything was resolved now. But I could sense otherwise, since I later dream of the roof of a house consumed by fire while many tried to put it out, helplessly. Dreams spoke of unrest that words had concealed. Hundreds of miles in Yangon, I dreamt of my dearest butterfly cousin had crossed the customary boundary with her boyfriend. Months later when I returned the village, the incident was confirmed—no scientific proof but only did I know that it was the night the dream brought a vivid message. There must be a national language that could barely reflects inexpressible national experiences.

Language is more than a means of communication; it is a vital piece of national heritage, a secret code shared among the members of a community. It binds community together across generations, making the bonds that define a people. Today, many of the world's languages are rapidly disappearing under the encroachment of dominant languages. When a language is lost, everything it embodies—stories, customs, the psyche of its speakers, ways of life, ethos, voices, souls, emotion, spirits of ancestors, underlying beliefs, the worldview, and unique words and concepts—becomes irretrievable. To abandon one's mother tongue is to lose connection to the entire creation and lived existence of the community created by that language.

The Karenic language enriches concepts like Yin and Yang, male and female, Pwo and Sqaw, and the idea of complementarity with poetic nuance. When spoken with the right tone, intonation, and regional accent, Karen becomes a truly poetic language. Male and female words share similar meanings, yet different regions may favor one over the other. However, they are most often used together, and when combined, their meaning does not simply add up but multiply, giving birth to a new richer expression.

Some people confuse spoken language with written script, mistakenly thinking that the Karen people have many languages. This point is crucial: a language can adopt any script to represent its phonemes. The Karen people have already adopted various scripts within the same dialect, influenced by different factors. Sqaw Karen, for example, has multiple scripts. Consider this greeting, which can be written in various scripts:

- Oh chu oh klay
- အိၣ်ဆူၣ်အိၣ်ချ့
- အိဆအိခလေး
- ой Су ой глина
- 哦 蘇 哦 克萊
- 오 추 오 클레이
- オーチューオークレイ

The first three examples are currently in use, while the latter are fictitious—yet they illustrate the versatility of potential script adoption. Cai-Cai, an indigenous language spoken by around one hundred thousand people in Indonesia, has recently adopted Hangul as its writing system. Korean Hangul, developed by King Sejong the Great in 1443, is widely regarded as one of the most scientific and methodical alphabets in the world.

Despite using multiple scripts, speaking dozens of dialects (Pwo, Sqaw, Bwe, Paleke, Mornaybwa, Kayah, Kayaw, etc.), and having hundreds of regional accents, the Karen people share one language, referred to by linguists as Karenic—a distinct branch of the Sino-Tibetan language family proper. A common script is nation building and national cohesion.

The Pwo and Sqaw dialects of the Karenic language are more closely related to each other than Mandarin and Cantonese are within the Sinitic language family. While Mandarin and Cantonese historically share the same writing system, they differ significantly in pronunciation and tonal structure, making them largely unintelligible to one another in spoken form. Traditionally, Chinese characters functioned as a logosyllabic system, representing both meaning and sound. In the 1950s, the Chinese government, under Mao Zedong's leadership, introduced Simplified Chinese to promote literacy, replacing many complex characters used for centuries. However, the traditional script remains in use in Hong Kong, Macau, and Taiwan.

When the Karen people achieve true self-determination, our scattered scripts can and must be unified. What China accomplished within a generation gives us hope that, once political roadblocks are cleared, a similar undertaking is possible for us. A unified script would enhance communication and literacy among our people, fostering national unity through shared stories, inspiration, and spirit—the very foundation that drives a nation's progress.

The Sqaw Karen script, widely used in official communication, has already been adopted by many dialects while allowing people to retain their local variations (Bwe, Paku, Keko-Geba, Kayah Monu, West-Pwo, Mornaybwa). This adoption demonstrates that a unified script is viable, even though the KBC script has limitations in representing the sounds of different dialects and accents.

Though I may reduce my regional accent and dialect (Mornaybwa vocabulary and Moekee accent) to be understood by others, I hold to this precious inheritance passed down through generations of my mothers. Many Karens who, a couple of generations ago, chose not to speak their mother tongue now recognize its value as a heritage of their people.

My mother tongue is the language of my mother, therefore I speak it with respect, honor, and a deep sense of resistance to domination, for it is my heritage. If I can master a foreign language, I can even learn more of my own. I speak, read, and write with respect and pride, not to anchor myself in the past, but to draw strength and energy to push me forward.

Kawthoolei is more than just the Karen people and their numerous dialects, usages, tones, and accents. It is a diverse nation that includes non-Karenic language speakers, and any new script for Kawthoolei must accommodate this linguistic diversity. A growing nation needs a language and script that not only unifies its people but also propels them toward progress. A growing nation requires a language and script that can unify its citizens while driving them toward holistic progress. As it stands, we lack such a script, and the need for a systematic language reform that encompasses our diversity and fosters unity is both urgent and undeniable. This challenge is not technical difficulty, thus making it entirely achievable if people are willing.

RESTORING AND STANDARDIZING NAMES AND ADMINISTRATIVE TERMS

Kawthoolei desires recognition, yet many location names lack standardized spelling and consistency, posing challenges for clear identification, making a huddle for internal and external recognition. To preserve and strengthen the linguistic and cultural identity of Kawthoolei, the following key actions are recommended for implementation by first forming the Kawthoolei Translation Committee and National Language Commission:

1. REVIEW AND STANDARDIZE PLACE NAMES

- Conduct a thorough review of all place names, including villages, towns, cities, streets, rivers, streams, mountains, valleys, and lakes. Restore their original Karenic forms to reclaim cultural and historical authenticity.
- Document each location with its indigenous name alongside corresponding geolocation points to ensure precise identification and usability.

2. REVERSE BURMANIZATION

- Identify and replace Burmanized place names with their authentic Karenic equivalents to restore cultural integrity and reverse linguistic erasure.
- Ensure restored names are consistent across official references, maps, and digital systems to maintain coherence and prevent further loss of heritage.

3. STANDARDIZE SPELLING IN KAREN AND ENGLISH

- Develop and implement a standardized spelling system for all names in both Karen and English, ensuring accurate representation and usability.
- Standardized names should appear on street signs and public signage, accompanied by both Karen and English spellings, to facilitate navigation and integration with international systems, such as computer search and match.

Example: Maw-Nay-Bwar, Mawnaybwa, or (Monnepwa and Monebwa appear in the same linguistic research paper as references to a dialect spoken in a small strip of northern Kawthoolei.)

4. CREATE A CENTRALIZED DATABASE

- Establish a digital repository for all standardized names, linked to geolocation data, to support practical applications in governance, commerce, transportation, energy, education, security, and tourism.
- Ensure the database is searchable, accessible, and integrated into national and international systems to enhance functionality and engagement.

5. Promote Consistent Use

- Mandate the use of standardized names in all official documents, street signs, educational materials, and government communication.
- Collaborate with local communities to foster awareness and encourage the adoption of standardized names in everyday use.

6. Restore and Protect Identity

- Highlight the importance of reversing Burmanization as a symbol of resistance and cultural dignity, ensuring the preservation of indigenous names.
- Educate the public on the significance of restoring original names to maintain a consistent and unified identity.

7. Translation and Naming of Administrative Terminology

Ensure the translation and naming of administrative areas into English are logical, globally relevant, and reflective of Karenic identity:
- Avoid terms like "village tract," which carry connotations of backwardness. Instead, consider modern equivalents like "subdistrict", "county" or "municipality" for relevance and clarity.
- Reassess terms like "township" and "district," which may not align with global naming conventions, hence cause confusion. Alternatives such as "province," "canton," or "prefecture" can be considered for broader recognition.
- Alternatively, use native Karenic terms in English translations to emphasize authenticity and cultural identity, such as Thailand's Tambon: "One Tambon, One Product."

Keeping native terms in one word for administrative areas:

- **Thaworr** for village
- **Kawor** for village tract
- **Karu** for a group of village tracts
- **Kawsar** for township
- **Kawray** for district
- **Kawthoolei** for the collection of districts

This dual approach—using logical English translations or retaining native terms—ensures both global relevance and cultural preservation. Proper translation is not just a linguistic task but a strategic step toward enhancing Kawthoolei's global image and fostering integration into the international community.

These recommendations are for Kawthoolei to restore its cultural heritage, create a unified identity, and establish a strong foundation for progress and global collaboration.

KARENIC LANGUAGE, INDICATOR OF THE KAREN PEOPLE

Linguists have studied the Karen language and its relationships among dialects for centuries. Language serves as a key to tracing the ethnolinguistic identity of a nation. The following is an observation by a Japanese and other linguist specializing in Karenic languages, offering insights into the spread of the Karen population in Burma and its origin.

"Karenic languages constitute the Karenic branch of the Tibeto-Burman family. The ethnic groups that speak Karenic languages (called "Karenic people" here) include several groups, such as the Bwe, Geba, Gek(h)o, Kayah, Kayaw, Kayan, Manu, Monebwa, Mopwa (Mobwa), Paku, Pa-O, Pwo Karen, Sqaw Karen, Thalebwa, Yeinbaw, Yintale, and others (listed in alphabetical order). Today, these ethnic groups live in the eastern, southeastern, and southwestern parts of Myanmar and the northern and western parts of Thailand." (Kato, 2021)

"The Union of Myanmar has two states for Karenic people: Kayin State (Karen State) and Kayah State (Karenni State). These are the only administrative units in the world that are legitimately established for the Karenic people. People speaking Karenic languages are mostly farmers, who make swiddens in mountainous areas and wet rice fields in the plains. The majority of the Pwo Karen and Sqaw Karen population in Myanmar live in the plains of Kayin State, Bago Region, Yangon Region, Mon State, Tanintharyi Region, and Ayeyarwady Region, and some of the population live in urban areas including Yangon and Mawlamyine. However, Pwo Karen and Sqaw Karen in Thailand mainly live in the mountainous areas. Karenic people other than Pwo and Sqaw usually live in the mountainous areas of the southern Shan State, Kayah State, Kayin State, and Bago Region, with the exception of Pa-O, some of whom live in the plains of Kayin State and Mon State. In the plains, people that speak the Karenic languages are usually Buddhists or Christians, whereas in the mountainous areas, they are usually Christians or animists. The majority of Pa-O and Pwo Karen are Buddhists, Sqaw Karen also has a large population of Buddhists, and the rest are mostly Christians or animists." (Kato, 2021)

"The total population of ethnic Karen is somewhere between 6 and 12 million, however, not all ethnic Karen still speak Karen languages. Many now speak only Burmese, especially those living on the plains." (Manson, 2012)

"The English term Karen is probably an adaptation of the Burmese name for these people, but it has been reacquired by the Sgaw to refer to themselves. Other Karen groups rarely use this term to refer to themselves, and refer to themselves instead with an endogenous name, often based on the reconstructed Proto-Karen form *k-ɲaŋA (Solnit 2001), e.g. Kayah, Kayaw, Kayan, Sgaw." ("Sgaw" is a spelling variation of Sqaw) (Manson, 2017)

"The Karen branch has been considered part of Sino-Tibetan for over a century, but only in the last 35 years has a consensus developed that these languages form a distinct branch within Tibeto-Burman rather than a sister to Tibeto-Burman. Benedict (1972: 129) notes that 'morphologically, Karen diverges from Tibeto-Burman almost as widely as does Chinese, especially as regards syntax'. These features lead Benedict to claim that Karen is a sister of Tibeto-Burman proper." (Manson, 2012)

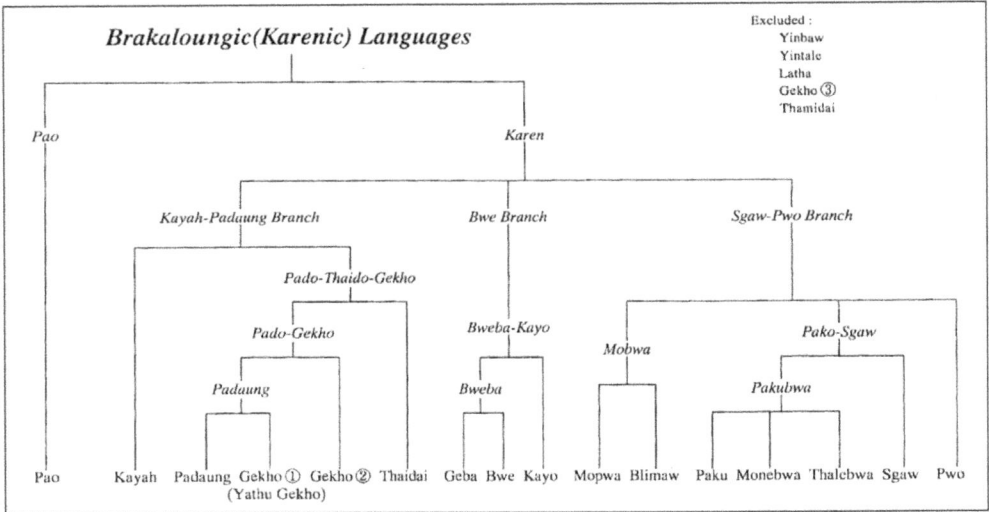

Excluded :
Yinbaw
Yintale
Latha
Gekho ③
Thamidai

Figure 9. Classification of Karen languages: Lexical similarity (Shintani 2002)

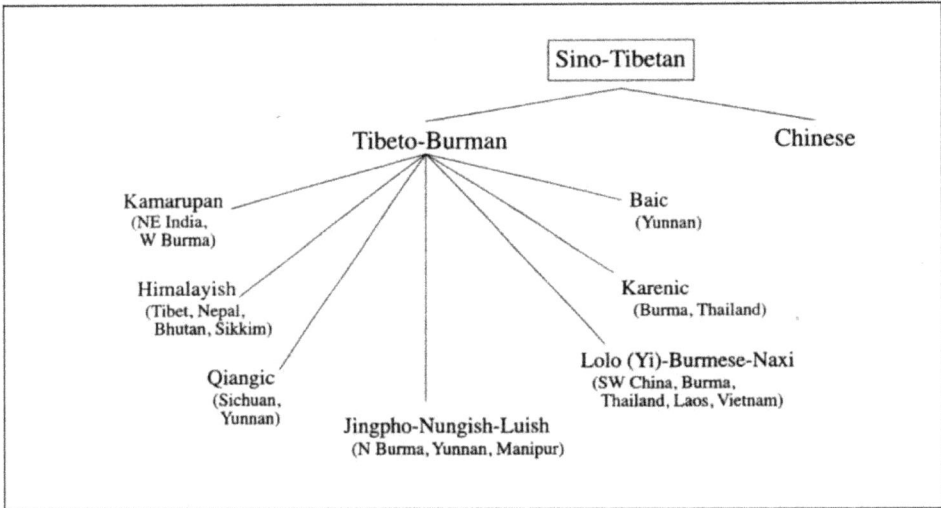

Figure 1. Tibeto-Burman branches (Matisoff 2003)

2

Chapter 11

Ethnic Minority Report

ARTIFICIAL LABELLING THAT HARMS

Words carry meaning. Some words are more loaded than others; some build, some break. Some inspire, some humiliate. They shape perceptions and construct the narratives that define us.

What do people think when they call us "ethnic minority"? Do they refer to our numerical status? What are they ranking us against? Have they conducted statistical surveys on the ground? Such words roll off the tongue with casual ease, their weight unexamined, their impact disregarded—conveniently packaged, yet deeply consequential.

Words have connotations, and they also have collocations. Some words normalize human suffering, others desensitize the wounds of tragedy. The term "minority" is collocated with "persecuted minority," which creates an automatic desensitization. It implies that persecution is normal for minorities—part of their fate—and suggests a helplessness in addressing their plight. Similarly, "marginalized minority" has become a cliché that fails to draw attention to the underlying injustices. Rarely do people consider collocations like "commanding minority" or "influential minority." Such labels are rarely used because the term "minority" is often wielded to convey limitation, not strength—promoting meekness, not empowerment. This labeling becomes a subtle curse placed upon the people, embedding an expectation of diminished status that, over time, becomes normalized for those subjected to it.

For the Karen people in Burma, the label of "ethnic minority" is particularly damaging. It fosters an oversimplified narrative that obscures their struggle for self-governance, recasting them in a way that may attract humanitarian efforts yet seldom empowers their true autonomy. The bustling activity of aid organizations reinforces this label, benefiting from a narrative that perpetuates a cycle of dependency—a self-reinforcing savior-victim tale. Financial support flows to alleviate the symptoms of oppression yet rarely dismantles the deeper structures that sustain their marginalization. This dependency is institutionalized—the documentation of suffering, preparing for the next cycle of tragedy, and setting in place procedures aimed at garnering sympathy. This cycle has persisted across generations, yet with no end in sight.

When the world hears our story, their sensitivity to tragedy has already dulled, worn down by a relentless flow of global crises. To them, the Karen people are just another "ethnic minority" in Myanmar—those small, inconsequential figures on the fringes of a distant frontier. Persecuted by one of the world's most brutal militaries, the Karen's suffering is perceived as a minor, inevitable tragedy within the grand, indifferent sweep of history. Little, it seems, can be done for this "ethnic minority."

Consider, for instance, that Israel—a small nation in the midst of the Arab world—is not labeled an ethnic minority, nor are the Chinese people who make up 20% of Malaysia's population. No one with a sense of human dignity chooses to label themselves as an "ethnic minority."

LABELLING CORRODES INTERNALLY

Accepting the label of "ethnic minority" breeds a sense of incapacity and inferiority, embedding a perception of inadequacy—incapable, incompetent, unintelligent. It does not merely describe; it diminishes. It shackles self-perception and resigns us to lowered expectations. Instead of looking outward with national ambition, it forces a downward gaze, diverting attention from the bountiful opportunities beyond imposed limitations. A nation can achieve whatever it envisions, but an ethnic minority traps itself within the fiction of its own limitation.

That labeling creates a condition—a condition of self-denigration. It instills and spreads a belief that we cannot keep pace with the technological progress of advanced nations. So, let's hold hands together singing "Kumbaya," dressing in tribal attire in festive open fields. The sun shines softly, and rainbows arch above us, leading us to believe that food will fall from the sky.

On a national scale, we cannot organize ourselves, systematically. While large-scale unity remains elusive, small-scale unity under that labeling may thrive under this condition, often leading to clashes and harm among these smaller groups. The term "ethnic minority" suggests a lack of organization and the inability to achieve greatness of a nation on par with those who are well-organized. Unable to organize, we remain defenseless—wild and chaotic, as if the sheer number of us dictates our fate. Our spirit has been stifled, and we begin to embody the labels thrust upon us, trapped in a self-reinforcing cycle of resignation.

Every night we lay our heads to rest, accepting the label of "ethnic minority," we defile our minds and disconcert our dreams. The frightened dreamer awakens with diminished energy, meekness taking hold, burdened by a belief that we are unfit to face the world. It is easier, we tell ourselves, to hide or to appease the forces that have shaped our fate. In doing so, we bury the Creator's gift of power deep within, casting it aside in the backyard of our soul.

MINORITY AND RELATIVITY

Every living human community is ethnic—whether Han Chinese, German, or Indian. Every ethnic group on Earth is a numerical minority except for the Han Chinese, who represent a billion-strong supermajority. "Ethnic" and "minority" are artificially imposed terms that can hardly coexist statistically.

Historically, the Karen population has been counted as the second largest in Burma, following the Burman majority. However, that does not account for all Karen people across various religious affiliations. Population counts during both British colonial rule and after Burma's independence were influenced by ideological and political motives. Karen communities are spread throughout Burma, from the central plains of Mandalay to the northern Kachin valley, the country east Shan State and Wa region, the southern Taunggyi region, and the western coast of Arakan mountains. In lower Burma, particularly in the lower Bago region and west of the Irrawaddy River to the Irrawaddy Delta, Karen people have often concealed their identities to avoid drawing attention, after the Karen revolution was defeated in urban plains. State-led Burmanization for generations also added to identity erasure. These Bago and Irrawaddy regions are among the most densely populated Karen areas—and also, the most populous regions in all of Burma.

Non-Karen individuals either could not recognize the true distribution of the Karen population, did not bother to, or intentionally chose to overlook it. Otherwise, it did not fit into the marginalization narrative.

In 2021, after the military coup, mass protests erupted across Burma, with Karen flags raised by demonstrators everywhere across Burma except in the northwest—Sagaing Region and the Chin Hills—where there is no significant Karen population. Most regions, people tend to popup their true identity in only when fear dissipates and immediate threats overclothed by mass participation. The flag-raising throughout the country could signify solidarity by non-Karens or perhaps reveal the true members of the Karen cause stepping forward at this critical moment.

THE DISTRICTS WHERE TWO CULTURES MEET

In the *Hsaw-Hteet-Taw-Oo* region, where the Karen Hills meet the Sittaung River valley, once there lay the secrets of Kawthoolei—a place in the foothills where its true nature and virtues still breathe.

Growing up on the front lines of the armed revolution in the northern region of the KNU administration, I never felt or labelled as "ethnic minority." The Karen people were indigenous landowners, cultivating farms that yielded abundantly. War and clashes came and went, yet life continued undeterred amid the upheaval. Non-Karen settlers were typically landless, and during harvest, many worked as farm laborers alongside Karen families in a spirit of mutual respect. There was no notion of minority or majority.

However, Karen men were targeted, and Karen villagers feared the Burmese military far more than Burmese-speaking villagers did. Yet, no one saw themselves as victims or sought handouts. The suffering was grave, but there was no foreign humanitarian aid. A blessing in hidden, no disruption to social fabric in those inner districts, away from the border and cities, there were no bustling aid organizations. Not a fertile ground for charitable industrial complex. Everyone had to work, to find their own way of earning a living. The Karen community held a stronger socioeconomic position, grounded in organized religious affiliations, where weekly gatherings reinforced a prevailing refined culture of courtesy and cohesion. Educational opportunities also favored Karen families, likely a legacy of missionary schools from past generations. Karen people were in the position of many school administrators and teachers, serving the population without discrimination.

At the nearest town's high school I attended, Karen students were fewer in number, but I never felt looked down upon. And many teachers had once been taught by Karen educators, including my mother. Academically, I never felt behind; my peers and teachers treated top students with respect naturally. There was no talk of "minority" or "ethnic minority"—such labels held no meaning. Relationships were built on mutual respect, and though all lived under the shadow of an oppressive regime and severe economic conditions under military slavery, there remained a spirit of self-reliance and quiet resilience.

ETHNIC MINORITY: A TRIGGER FOR SYMPATHY

The label of "ethnic minority" is often used to manipulate, whether to garner sympathy, secure funding, or attract donations. This language can also serve as a vehicle for exploitation. In the past decade, as Burma opened up economically, a troubling trend emerged: businesses began branding themselves as "Karen ethnic" to attract funding earmarked for non-Burman ethnic groups. This phenomenon exposes a moral dilemma; while some may genuinely seek to uplift their communities, others exploit this identity for financial gain. The distinction of being "Karen" risks becoming commodified, transformed into a marketable identity rather than a celebration of cultural heritage.

People market products labeled as "ethnic" to evoke consumer sympathy, often at the expense of product quality. If a product is labeled as "ethnic minority," it may indicate that quality assurance is questionable and that the price may not be competitive, a definite signal to consumers that they should exercise caution before purchasing a product marked "ethnic minority".

On roadside billboards, charity organizations that label themselves as helping "ethnic minorities"—often portraying kids with sun-tanned skin, poor hygiene, and inadequate nutrition—should be approached with caution. The good-hearted must be wary of themselves potentially being exploited for sympathy, as these organizations may prioritize fundraising over empowerment.

HERITAGE MISUSED UNDER THE PRETEXT OF GOODWILL

There has been a new wave of abuse. During 2021 the Myanmar Spring Revolution and the events that followed, some impersonators donned traditional Karen attire, waving Karen flags to create a misleading image of support from ethnic minorities. This disingenuous display, often a political maneuver, has long been a tactic used by Burmese military regimes to feign inclusivity and fabricate support, a typical scene of colorful ethnic minority dancing on the stage. Now, it is also aimed at attracting attention and soliciting donations from the Karen community, frequently through online platforms. Such practices should be condemned as blatant exploitation. Just as an unrelated individual cannot don Native American attire to claim privileges from the U.S. government, these actions are not only unethical but also fraudulent.

Karen clothing suffers from misuse rather than genuine appreciation. Celebrated for its simplicity and elegance, Karen attire has become an iconic symbol to be worn everywhere easily, yet it is often exploited by various groups. Burmese ex-military generals—many of whom have orchestrated violence against the Karen people—and politicians don it not as a gesture of cultural respect, but to feign solidarity or make superficial statements. Across the political spectrum, Karen attire is flaunted more as a tool of opportunism than as a sign of genuine regard for Karen heritage.

Some Burmese urban celebrities wear Karen attire not merely to solicit donations, evoke sympathy, or fabricate an indigenous connection. Many Karen are drawn to this spectacle, amplifying it through social media shares and reshares. Over time, donning Karen clothing has become an effortless way to portray the Karen as unsophisticated or impoverished—an insidious distortion that demeans the very people it claims to represent.

In the mythical land of Myanmar, the widespread adoption of Karen clothing by non-Karens largely goes unexamined. Properly, one ought to seek permission from the rightful owners before donning such attire. Ethnic clothing is not merely fabric; it is an embodiment of identity, heritage, and belonging. Identity cannot be assumed or appropriated simply by wearing someone else's attire—it must be understood, respected, and honored.

Many Burmanized Karen descendants supporting Burmese politics enable the misuse of their heritage by wearing Karen clothes, allowing their identity to be co-opted for political gain. The theft of identity is not only normalized but glorified as cultural appreciation. Even in liberated Kawthoolei, ancestral lands face the risk of being seized—not through the force of arms, but through the insidious appropriation of Karen identity itself. Some can wear Karen clothes and, in the same breath, steal Karen lands, simply, if this culture of abuse is unearthed.

No nation can survive such an extended abuse.

ETHNIC MINORITY: A SUBJECT OF RIDICULE

When you are an ethnic minority, confusion clouds your identity. Timidly, you ask for "self-determination," a term that leaves others scratching their heads. People quietly laugh at your request.

Do you mean you want to govern yourself? Do you even understand what self-governing entails? It requires self-regulation, the creation of elaborate rules and numerous institutions to have a functioning society, and the ability to engage with other states on the world stage. With self-rule comes the constant cultivation of self-discipline. As an ethnic minority, you are wild, merely tribal without national level discipline. Hence, your life choices must be dictated by others who are capable.

With great power comes great responsibility. Are you up to that responsibility as an ethnic minority? The label "ethnic minority" means that you are under someone else's rule. You are at the mercy of those in power. You may be granted cultural rights—allowed to dance, sing, and wear tribal attire for others' amusement. In some instances, you may get language rights, but they dictate what and how to teach your own language right. People find you adorable with your funny accent and traditional attire. But political decision-making? That's out of your reach. You are conditioned to think in terms of impossibility. Being an ethnic minority is a self-fulfilling prophecy of stagnation and ridicule. You are to be gradually swallowed into the grinder of a larger machinery of nation-building.

Cultural rights are a temporary soothing balm, choking your potential national awakening. You are expected to be a tiny part of a multicultural nation, where your language and traditional dress are to make others look better—a little spice dressing in a melting pot. Full self-autonomy, a separate governing state, is unthinkable for an ethnic minority. Therefore, you don't have to think about it, so that you don't formulate it in detail since it is deemed impossible because you are an ethnic minority. This reasoning becomes ridiculously cyclical, and you don't bother to question it. After all, you are an ethnic minority because everyone says so.

You can see how disingenuous it is when people label you as an ethnic minority. You are human yet feel dead in spirit, intellect, and dignity. You exist under the rule of others and at the mercy of nations, but that mercy is nonexistent because every nation on earth has the duty to prioritize its own national interests, not yours. Thus, you become merely a subject of ridicule as an ethnic minority.

ETHNIC MINORITY: A TERM OF RECENT USAGE

The term "ethnic minority" has gained usage only recently, particularly after World War II with the rise of nation-states. According to the Google Books Ngram Viewer, the combination of "minority" and "ethnic" began appearing frequently in the 1960s, highlighting a shift in the discourse around identity and representation that reduces certain groups to a lowly status.

At the outset of 1962, when Burmese's General Ne Win seized power through a military coup from U Nu's parliamentary government, army-controlled newspapers portrayed some political figures as villains. However, the Shan people in Burma were referred to as "minority nationals," not "ethnic minorities," as noted in Marti Smith's report, which emphasizes "[P]romotion of the interests of the minority nationals and their states" (Smith, 1999, 196).

In 1959, to address constitutional matters concerning the *national peoples* in Burma, Prime Minister U Nu arranged to convene the "Nationalities' Seminar" in Yangon, then the capital city. At that time, different nations in Burma were not labeled as "ethnic minorities," and even the Burmese government official terminology itself did not hold that designation (Linter, 203).

Later generations of politicians in Burma use the term "ethnic nationalities" and then downgraded to "ethnic minority" by the media to push for a narrative.

In criminology, labeling theory closely relates to concepts like self-fulfilling prophecy and stereotyping. It posits that individuals labeled as deviant internalize that label, leading to behaviors consistent with that identity. This cycle reinforces the label, causing individuals to accept and embody it. By examining how labels affect identity and behavior, labeling theory illuminates the dynamics of social reactions to deviance. Thus, the label "ethnic minority" becomes a tool of disempowerment, confining the Karen people to a life of subservience.

In writings from about 100 years ago, one would not find the Karen people referred to as "ethnic minorities", during the era of our great-grandmothers. Harry Marshall's study on the Karen in the Irrawaddy Valley noted, "Although the Karen have lived for generations in the closest proximity to the Burmese, they preserve their own racial traits, which are quite distinct from those of their more volatile neighbors with whom they have had little in common."

Both the Karen and Burmans (Bamar) were viewed as indigenous people of Burma, without distinction as "ethnic minorities." They were all sons and daughters of the land, often seen as similar to outsiders, with brown faces and sunburned skin serving the pale faces of colonial masters. Their labor and lives, their talents and blood were siphoned by foreign invaders from faraway lands to fuel the machinery of colonial empires, so that "the sun never sets on the British Empire." In that context, everyone looked alike and equally exploited, and there were no classifications of numerical majority or ethnic minority. In many parts of the land, Karen and Bamar people lived side by side, coexisting in various villages despite their cultural differences like in many parts of Burma still today in most communities.

Without labels, rights and agency cannot be stripped from a people so easily. The term "ethnic minority" may well be the root cause of the stagnation in our political path and the normalization of social challenges. Labeling creates its own ecosystem, reducing the struggles of a national liberation to "identity politics." No politicians of our kind dare to speak to inspire people to be a rising nation. Any effort by our leaders to assert dignity and preserve identity is dismissed as "narrow nationalism," leaving them hesitant to make bold political moves that the people aspire to. While the label "ethnic minority" denies us the status of a nation, our armed struggle is reduced to "ethnic conflict," our nation is labeled a "rebel group," our service members as "ethnic rebels," and our commanders as "rebel leaders." This imposed identity stifles our aspirations, reducing our pursuit of autonomy to an inconsequential footnote in a narrative that refuses to recognize our legitimacy.

THE CURSE OF MISLABELING

The label of "ethnic minority" leads to a curse that stifles our rise. We witness too many activists but experience too little transformative change. We are helped by too many saviors under many banners yet enjoy too little liberty. Countless donations pour in to alleviate our plight but yield too little empowerment. Too many heroes have we lost in sacrificial Kawthoolei yet secured too little liberation. Everywhere, youthful spirits loiter in sports fields yet too little manpower for nation building. Every year, we celebrate too many graduates, yet we find ourselves with too few human resources. In the political arena, we read a constant stream of political statements, yet we see little meaningful impact. There are too many talents among the Karen people across many nations, yet too few have the chance to contribute to their own nation's progress. There are too many critics and skeptics yet too little constructive to divert the effort. The movement has too many seasoned politicians yet too little political vision that inspires the public, too many promises, yet too little hope for the ethnic minority.

It is all vanity under the sun.

As long as degrading labels are passively accepted and the stature of a true nation remains unrealized, we remain trapped in a life unworthy of our potential—a life not worth living as human beings or as a nation. Endowed with strength and promise, we must cast aside all labels that diminish our fleeting existence in this universe, ceasing to dishonor the blessings we embody as a nation.

The seemingly harmless designation of "ethnic minority" carries with it a quiet sentence of neglect. If the Karen people's story truly understood, this story is not one of minority suffering but of a people yearning for the basic respect and freedom that every nation claims to cherish.

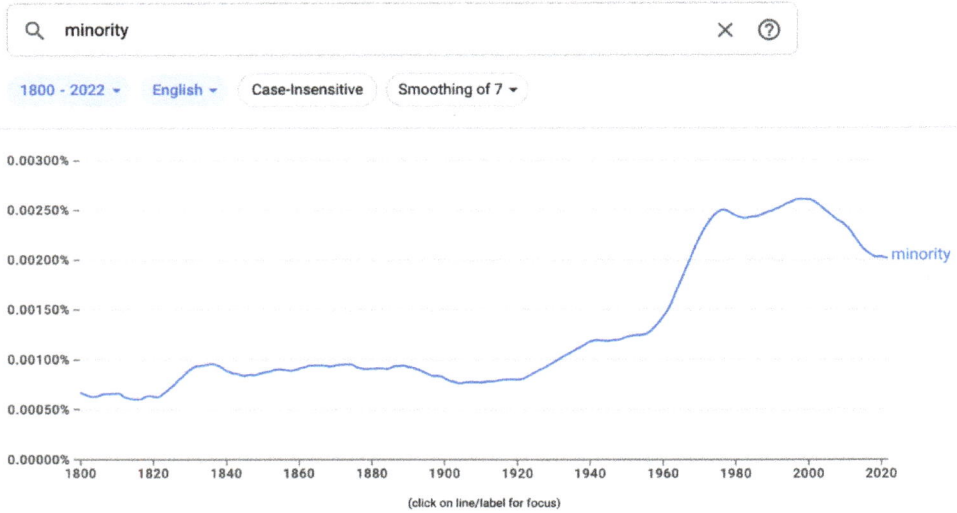

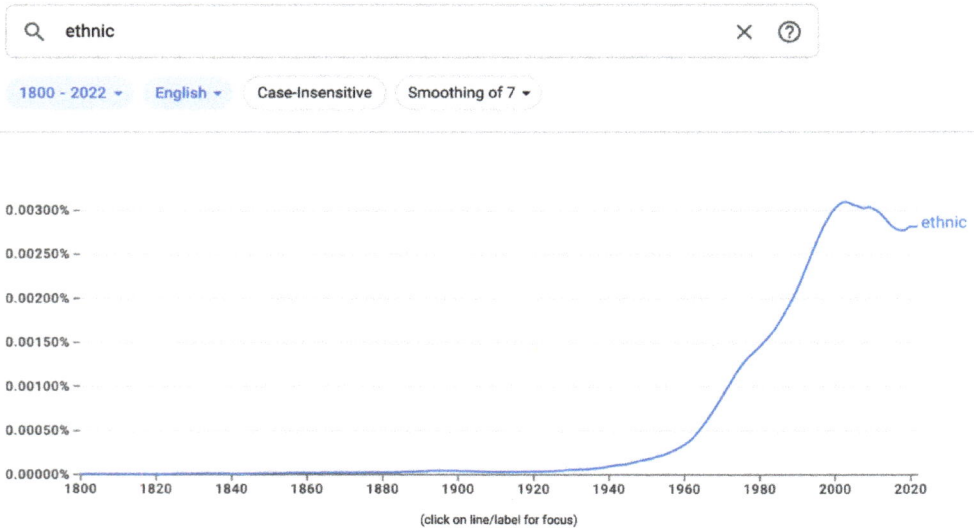

WE ARE WHAT WE ARE TO BE

Our commanders may not yet live in the comfort of an electrified city, but they are leaders with military intellect, mental resilience, courage, and true battle experience, driven by a clear purpose. Our national liberation soldiers wear the hat of dignity, the badge of bravery, the belt of valor, and are dressed for victory and honor. Progressive in thinking and unwavering in endurance, embodying the spirit of an emerging nation, the people of Kawthoolei will walk toward their destiny, forging the path forward.

Salween River, After the fall of all enemy camps along Kawthoolei Salween banks, boats fly Karen People flags high to display freedom and happiness.

SawLah@Photography 2023

Peh-Hta, Salween River at Karenni Border

SawLah@Photography 2023

Chapter 12

Education Educates

KAWTHOOLEI NATIONAL EDUCATION TO BE

A nation's future begins in the classroom, where its youth are prepared with both confidence and competence. National education fosters self-respect without ignorance, independence without isolation, and patriotism without pretense.

A strong national education never teaches its citizens to see themselves as ethnic minorities in someone else's story. It makes no room for imported ideologies—however flashy, trendy, or well-funded—that seek to override local values and dismantle existing social cohesion. It prepares a workforce that strengthens the national economy, not one destined to serve abroad as migrant laborers. To thrive on the global stage, a nation will first be fortified from within. National education, above all, builds the nation.

A good education teaches people their history—not as a tale of victimhood, but as a mirror of both glory and grief. It draws on strengths to inspire and failures to refine, shaping a future that avoids repeating old mistakes. Through legends, lived experience, and ancestral memory, it binds generations into a shared identity rooted in continuity.

Most of all, education sharpens the mind to question—not merely to absorb. It invites the young to wrestle with ideas, apply reason to their surroundings, and remain open to the world beyond. In classrooms guided by national purpose, civic virtues are not recited—they are practiced: integrity in honest effort, justice in fair dealings, courage in truth-telling, humility in the art of listening. Here, the freedom of thought walks hand in hand with responsibility to restrain and the duty to serve—raising citizens who stand upright in both conviction and conduct.

A confident national education informs its citizens about its neighbors—not to instill fear or hatred, but to promote understanding and prepare them for cooperation and regional progress.

Kawthoolei's education system will need to undergo a transformative shift—one where its leaders have faith in its excellence by enrolling their own children in the schools they oversee.

Committed to excellence, Kawthoolei's education system is to be a model of rigor, quality, and inclusivity—so exceptional that administrators responsible for the education system enroll their own children in the schools they oversee. Even those in positions of power and privilege in Kawthoolei choose these schools for their academic excellence. Even more so, Kawthoolei's schools inspire Karen families abroad to send their children home to study, drawn by the outstanding educational standards and the opportunity to reconnect with their roots and foster a sense of belonging.

Guided by Kawthoolei's humanistic values, the education system provides a holistic approach, nurturing not only academic excellence but also the character, well-being, and moral development of its students.

True education empowers and elevates the people.

EDUCATION IN REFUGEE CAMPS

Students spend their youth in a 12-year education system, yet if graduates are less prepared than middle school students in other nations, those years waste youthful potential. Moreover, it is a moral imperative that education does not become a business enterprise driven by external forces. Good education focuses on uplifting the people, not merely benefiting the agenda of others. Curriculum development and teaching methods is a continuous improvement, evolving with new scientific discoveries and the ever-changing global context.

In the Maela refugee camp in 2005, once the school asked a seventh-grader Karen student to memorize a poem in Burmese depicting the life of the Karen people: "A simple mountain Karen dweller, he carries a chopper to his farm." The student did not comprehend the words, as Burmese was neither spoken at home nor used in her community. Perhaps this worked to her advantage, sparing her from the poem's demeaning portrayal of her people as if unsophisticated and primitive. Such education was neither national nor empowering. Rather than uplifting students, it diminished them, offering neither meaningful knowledge nor learning another language.

In fact, if utilized effectively, refugee camps can offer students an optimal environment to focus on their studies—unlike students in Kawthoolei homeland, whose education is often hindered by war or household chores such as collecting firewood for cooking, assisting on the family farm, or foraging for food. The constant fear of threats from the sky takes a toll on learners.

In refugee camps, students' abundant free time is frequently spent playing volleyball, cane ball, football and many other balls. The time spent in playing comes at the expense of the time for studying. The lack of structure and purpose can lead to just restlessness in the confined camp environment. Ironically, these days, refugee camps have more books and better libraries than the environment my generation grew up in on the frontline districts. With safety, stability, abundance of free time, and access to resources, refugee camps present ample opportunities for students willing to study and work hard to make the most of their time.

KAWTHOOLEI'S KAREN EDUCATION IN 1980S

During the Mar-Ner-Plaw Era (1975–1994), Karen education instilled a strong sense of nationalism in its youth. While the war raged in frontline areas, Mar-Ner-Plaw Headquarters remained relatively safer due to its fortifications. The educational focus was primarily on fostering political resistance. Key moments, such as the 1949 Karen uprising—a unifying struggle against oppression—were presented as powerful symbols of inspiration, with terms like "Burmese chauvinism" and "military dictatorship" serving as rallying cries.

Under the pressures of war, the approach leaned heavily toward resistance, leaving little room to explore broader political realities or to cultivate a deeper understanding of Burma's political dynamics. As a result, most students had limited opportunities to develop the political awareness needed to navigate the complexities of military rule across Burma or to assume political leadership—unlike the previous generation, which had risen to confront their adversaries.

In another dimension, to learn what is useful, we must avoid wasting time on what is not. In the 1980s, Kawthoolei's education system included Shakespeare in its English curriculum. While Shakespeare represents the pinnacle of classical English literature, it offers little practical value for students navigating the demands of professional or everyday English. Shakespeare is a cultural luxury—rich and enlightening—but it does not equip students with the skills needed to master contemporary, formal English. Every subject introduced into secondary education comes with an opportunity cost—the loss of a potentially more valuable subjects for the nation's future.

During the Mar-Ner-Plaw era, British-educated Karen leaders continued to shape the education system. However, their focus on the war effort left them disconnected from the global linguistic evolution of the 1960s and 1970s, a period marked by the rise of American English as the dominant language of global business, technology, and international affairs in the U.S.-led world order.

For real-world communication today, Kawthoolei schools must prioritize practical English—language that reflects how it is spoken and written in modern contexts. American English should serve as the foundation, with British, Australian, and Canadian variations as complementary flavors. Let literature inspire, but let language prepare.

Nurture to Grow, Not Punish to Hold Potential

The purpose of education is to nurture potential and foster growth, yet the Karen education system in the Kawthoolei-Thailand border is widely trapped in outdated paradigms that prioritize rigid assessments over meaningful learning. Instead of being a pathway to empowerment, education often becomes a mechanism that constrains and suppresses.

In the current pedagogical model, students are required to pass every subject to advance. A single failure—often in a subject with little relevance to their future aspirations—forces them to repeat an entire academic year, revisiting every subject including the one they already excel at. This one-size-fits-all approach undermines the diversity of individual strengths and ignores the broader goals of education.

There was a case of a diligent student who struggles in one particular subject. Year after year in three years, this one weakness prevents them from advancing, eventually stopping them from getting the diploma for secondary education.

Education must not be a system of punishment. It should find ways to support students who struggle while celebrating their unique strengths. Instead of focusing on failure that punishes students, it should focus on helping every student succeed. A good education system helps young people grow by addressing their weaknesses and building on their abilities. The focus must shift from punitive practices to a growth-oriented pedagogy that empowers students to thrive in a variety of fields, both practical and intellectual.

If the education model continues to punish rather than nurture, it will hold back an entire generation.

Safeguarding Academic Spaces from Ideological Influence

Colleges are meant to be sanctuaries for intellectual exploration and the pursuit of higher knowledge. They thrive on freedom of thought, critical inquiry, and the exchange of diverse ideas. To subject higher-ed institutions to ideological control undermines their sacred purpose of advancing knowledge. Such control reduces them to instruments of indoctrination.

In Kawthoolei, post-secondary schools and junior colleges are scattered across the region, offering valuable opportunities for education. When institutions are forced to adhere to specific ideological agendas, they lose the ability to nurture independent thinkers and innovators. Such control stifles creativity, diversity, and the very spirit of higher education.

Instead of imposing ideological conformity, a robust accreditation body should oversee these institutions, ensuring they meet minimum standards of academic excellence. This body would focus on tangible metrics, such as requiring a certain number of faculty members with advanced degrees, alongside qualified teaching assistants, to maintain a high standard of instruction. It could also establish guidelines for essential subjects that should form the foundation of any college curriculum, fostering well-rounded and forward-thinking graduates.

Colleges should be spaces for discovery and intellectual freedom, not arenas for indoctrination.

KING CHULALONGKORN'S LEGACY AND THAILAND EDUCATION

King Chulalongkorn's reign (1868–1910) marked a decisive shift in Thailand's history, as the kingdom navigated the delicate balance between preserving tradition and embracing modernity. A typical feudal society faced with the growing pressures of Western colonialism, Chulalongkorn embarked on an ambitious program of reform, determined to protect Thailand's sovereignty and secure its place among the world's powers. Thailand was fortunate to have the timely forward-looking King when European empires roamed the globe, seizing territories under the banner of civilizing their inhabitants and expanding markets.

The king's reforms were sweeping and transformative. Chulalongkorn began by abolishing slavery, signaling his commitment to progress and equality. He restructured the judicial and financial systems, introduced legislative councils, and gradually overhauled the country's administrative framework. Despite opposition from conservative factions, his persistence paid off, and by the late 19th century, the king had established a modern bureaucratic state.

Central to his vision for a new Siam was the reform of education. Understanding that an educated populace was vital for the country's long-term prosperity, Chulalongkorn made primary education compulsory, planting the seeds of a national identity grounded in knowledge and civic duty. This move was more than a mere policy change; it was a strategic act of nation-building that aimed to foster citizens who could lead Thailand into the future.

In 1892, Chulalongkorn expanded his reforms by creating twelve ministries modeled on Western lines, responsible for key areas such as defense, foreign affairs, and education. These reforms helped eliminate arbitrary governance and ensured that the rule of law extended across the entire country, solidifying his commitment to justice and national unity.

However, Chulalongkorn's modernization efforts were not blind imitation. He carefully navigated foreign influence, engaging in diplomatic negotiations that preserved Thailand's independence while managing unavoidable territorial concessions. His skillful diplomacy earned Thailand respect on the global stage, and by the time of his death in 1910, he had left behind a modern, independent nation capable of standing tall in a rapidly changing world.

King Chulalongkorn's legacy is a testament to his vision and the critical role education played in shaping Thailand's destiny. Through his reforms, he ensured that Thailand remained a sovereign nation in an era where many neighboring feudal countries fell to colonial rule. His leadership left an enduring mark on the country, one that continues to inspire future generations.

MEIJI IMITATION

On July 8, 1853, American Commodore Matthew Perry led four ships into Tokyo Bay, marking a pivotal moment in Japan's history. His mission was to re-establish regular trade and diplomatic relations between Japan and the Western world after over two centuries of isolation. Perry arrived with a small squadron of U.S. Navy ships to demonstrate the technological and military superiority of the West. He and others believed that showcasing advanced firepower was the only way to persuade Japan to open its ports to Western trade and influence.

After facing humiliation by the West, 19th-century Japan embarked on the transformative Meiji Restoration, determined to rise and assert itself as an independent nation capable of standing alongside global powers. However, the path it pursued was one of imitation yet strategic. To compete with the West, Japan adopted a more flexible social structure, embraced a constitutional political framework, and prioritized advancements in science and technology. Ironically, even as Meiji Japan sought to reject Western dominance, it found itself mirroring the systems and structures that defined Western power. Japanese imitation of the West was to *adapt*, not to *adopt*.

CALIFORNIA'S EDUCATION: PREPARING FOR THE FUTURE

As the birthplace of Silicon Valley, California has shaped its education system to remain competitive in the global race for technological leadership. With the U.S. losing ground in semiconductor manufacturing and increasingly reliant on Taiwan—a hub for advanced chip production—California's focus on tech education has never been more critical.

The stakes could not be higher. Taiwan's cutting-edge microchips power everything from smartphones to defense systems, making them indispensable to U.S. interests. Geopolitical tensions threaten this fragile supply chain, exposing vulnerabilities in the U.S. tech industry. In response, California has intensified efforts to equip the next generation with the skills needed to navigate an increasingly technology-driven world.

Between 2016 and 2018, California introduced rigorous standards ensuring that even young students grasp the fundamentals of computing and its societal impact. In classrooms, children program robots and design school projects fueled by imagination. By their mid-teens, they have spent hours tinkering with circuits and writing code—not just learning to program, but critically analyzing AI ethics, questioning data privacy laws, and evaluating the societal effects of automation.

Stepping back from their screens, they see the intricate web of technology shaping human lives. They begin to understand the policies that govern it and the responsibilities that come with such power. Their curiosity extends beyond how technology works to how it should be used.

California's K-12 Computer Science Standards, a model for Kawthoolei's education, emphasize computational thinking over mere technology use. A simplified progression of student learning includes:

- Grade 2: Understand basic hardware and software.
- Grade 5: Troubleshoot simple hardware and software problems.
- Grade 8: Analyze how changing variables affect computational models.
- Grade 12: Debate software-related laws and regulations, examine network scalability and reliability, and explain the Internet's influence on systems.

California defines computer science as more than typing, word processing, or basic computer repair. It emphasizes the "Four Cs"—collaboration, critical thinking, creativity, and communication—integrating theory with practice. By fostering creativity, problem-solving, and innovation, the curriculum empowers students not just to use technology but to shape its future.

SINGAPORE'S EDUCATION: PREPARING FOR THE FUTURE

The world is learning from Singapore what they are doing right. Any politician uttering to "catch up" with Singapore must first study its education system. Kawthoolei's education leaders—both today and tomorrow—can benefit greatly from Singapore's approach to education.

Singapore consistently outperforms the OECD average in Mathematics, Reading, and Science. (The Organisation for Economic Co-operation and Development, or OECD, is an intergovernmental organization of 38 member countries, primarily composed of the world's wealthiest and most developed nations. Notably, Singapore is not an OECD member but participates in key assessments such as PISA.)

Singaporean students also excel in International Baccalaureate (IB) diploma exams, consistently outperforming their international peers. In November 2023, students in Singapore achieved an average score of 37.76 out of 45, well above the global average of 29.06. Remarkably, they also maintained a 100% pass rate, with every student who attempted the IB Diploma successfully earning it.

Singapore's education system fosters a culture of competitiveness, deeply ingrained in educators, parents, and students alike. Mediocrity has no place in a world of high standards, and Singapore's collective commitment to excellence ensures its continued success on the global stage. For Singapore, excellence is not just an aspiration—it is a necessity for maintaining its liberty and prosperity.

> "If you are going to reach out to the kids, you need to be savvy with technology. If you are not savvy with technology, you are going to lose them soon."
> — *Ho Peng, Director-General of Education at the Ministry of Education (2012)*

Adrian Lim, Principal of Ngee Ann Secondary School, emphasized the importance of creating an engaging learning environment:

> "I think it is important to make school fun. And when school is fun, kids wake up with no problems in the morning. When kids are engaged, when they are interested, that's where learning takes place."

Lim also highlighted the impact of technology on learning:

> "Web 2.0 with Wiki, with your Facebook, your blogs—you find that it's a very participatory culture. It calls for a lot of collaboration. They no longer become just consumers of knowledge. They actually produce knowledge."

The adaptability of Singapore's teachers plays a key role in the nation's success:

> "The world has changed, and teaching cannot stay stagnant. Teachers recognize that they cannot teach the way they were taught ten or twenty years ago. They must adapt their methods."
>
> — *Adrian Lim*

Professor Lee Sing Kong, Director of the National Institute of Education, described the evolving role of teachers in a digital world:

> "Today, knowledge is no longer monopolized by teachers. Students can access knowledge from a myriad of sources. The role of the teacher today is facilitation— helping students find the right knowledge, synthesize it, and discern the quality of the information they encounter."

One of the key factors behind Singapore's educational success is ongoing professional development. Many schools form professional learning communities where educators share best practices and critique lessons—both within their own schools and with peers around the world. (Edutopia, 2012)

KED's 2015 Education Policy

Meanwhile Karen Education Department (KED, now KECD) has its policy focus.

In 2015, the Karen Education Department (KED) introduced an education policy built on four foundational principles aimed at fostering a sense of identity and respect for both Karen and other ethnic cultures.

1. "Every Karen shall learn his own literature and language."
2. "Every Karen shall be acquainted with Karen *history*."
3. "The Karen culture, customs and *traditions* shall be promoted."
4. "Our own Karen culture, customs and *traditions* shall be made to be respected by the other ethnic nationalities, and the cultures, customs and *traditions* of the other ethnic nationalities shall mutually be recognized and respected."

At all educational levels, the curriculum emphasizes Karen history, literature, poetry, and global history, creating a well-rounded history focus education system.

LESSONS FROM SINGAPORE

Heaven and Earth. It may be discouraging to see how far we have fallen behind, but it is equally inspiring to remember how others have risen from humble beginnings. Singapore, though now a shining star, is not an unreachable sky. There are Karens from the current generation who have thrived in Singapore's education system, excelled in professional careers, and built families there, resettling and contributing to this tiny yet thriving nation. We must learn to break free from the belief that success belongs only to others.

"Learn from every country in the world," declared Deng Xiaoping when he came to power in 1978, amidst the ruins of China's economy. During his visits to Thailand and Singapore later that year, Deng was impressed by Singapore's rapid progress and efficiency under Lee Kuan Yew's leadership. One of China's key takeaways was *meritocratic governance*, including high pay for civil servants to reduce corruption—lessons that helped transform China's own progress.

What can Kawthoolei learn from this tiny island nation with no natural resources? Singapore's story is one of transformation that defied all odds. In less than a lifetime, it rose from a struggling port city to a global financial powerhouse, surpassing nations that spent centuries industrializing. Today, Singapore boasts the world's top-ranked airport, one of the busiest seaports, and the most powerful passport on Earth.

At the heart of this remarkable journey lies one key factor: education. As Lee Kuan Yew admitted, Singapore's success was not due to its people being inherently smarter, but to its determination never to settle for mediocrity in education and its firm stance against corruption in governance. A government free of corruption fosters trust, and trust, in turn, strengthens the effectiveness of governance. A clean government is the bedrock of an efficient and capable nation.

If a nation without forests, minerals, or farmland can compete with global giants like the United States and China, surely are there valuable lessons for us. In the following sections, we will explore how Singapore's education system continues to navigate the complexities of the modern world. These lessons are more than academic—they are about how a nation preserves its independence.

THE SINGAPORE'S EDUCATION FOCUS: TEN-POINT LESSONS

The following are areas Singapore has adopted over the years that are worth learning from.

1. *Reducing the overemphasis on high-stakes exams*

In many countries, high-stakes exams remain the cornerstone of secondary education, determining a student's future path. China's *Gaokao*, the National Higher Education Entrance Examination, epitomizes this system. (Evidently, China has not yet taken lessons from Singapore in rethinking its reliance on high stakes testing.)

Each year, high school seniors nationwide prepare for this grueling exam that dictates their college admission, field of study, future career, and ultimately, their life. The entire society revolves around this two-to-four-day event. The Gaokao is a pathway to opportunity—particularly for students from underprivileged backgrounds—offering a chance to rise in a system upheld as a meritocracy. It is a yearly national ritual. Cities slow down. Taxi drivers volunteer their services. Workers near exam sites pause their activities. Parents wait outside, soaked in the rain. Communities rally to give students every possible advantage.

Preparation for this exam is an all-consuming, year-long endeavor, with the test itself treated as a public spectacle. For Chinese students, the Gaokao is not merely an academic test—it is a mental and emotional battle, a competition against tens of millions of peers nationwide for a place at the most prestigious universities. It is nothing short of a *mental military training*, producing generations who are both mentally resilient and academically rigorous.

Similarly, in Burma, the tenth-grade matriculation exam served as a gateway to higher education. Students dedicated an entire year to preparation, while families eased their responsibilities to enable focused study. During exam week, cities across Burma grew quieter. Local businesses scaled back operations. Communities showed respect for those sitting the test.

Despite this intense preparation and the communal support, such high-stakes exams often fail to capture the full scope of a student's abilities. A few stressful hours cannot always reflect a year's worth of learning or a student's overall aptitude. External factors—such as illness, fatigue, or a fleeting memory lapse—can derail performance, producing results that do not accurately represent a student's true potential.

2. *Creating a more student-centric and* **values-driven education system**.

The keyword here is "values-driven". Time spent in learning ought to have values. Our high school students spend countless hours each week in classrooms, year after year. Yet, when this time fails to equip them to stand among their peers in the world nurturing their own growth, it becomes time misspent—a routine of learning that leaves little of lasting worth. Memorizing facts that are partial, outdated, and lack relevance, loses its purpose, leaving students unprepared for the competitive future they face. Students need to learn various subjects and connect those pieces to make sense of a full picture making sense of the world. Memorizing a selected fact is less likely to help prepare them for the future.

Every hour in class is to enrich students' ability, igniting curiosity, building character, and preparing resilient minds for an unpredictable future. What students need is the ability to evaluate information and make sound decisions through critical thinking. This focus on creating value extends beyond the classroom: every practical endeavor—whether personal, professional, or a national sacrifice— gains purpose when it adds lasting value.

Education is to equip students to use resources for the practical benefit of their society. Resourcefulness is the essence of education—not merely adhering to what textbooks dictate. Characteristics such as problem-solving, adaptability, creativity, efficiency, and initiative define resourcefulness, creating real value.

Singapore has adopted instruction further away from rote memorization and repetitive tasks and toward deeper conceptual understanding and problem-based learning. Teachers or students or the education system as a whole has a moral duty not to waste years of human lives in learning that fails to build understanding.

3. *Having transformed into a world-class model known for its* **rigour, quality, and inclusiveness**.

Our education system needs *rigor*. Students build understanding from constant engagement, whether through homework or projects that lay the groundwork for future learning and real-world application. There should be little room for idleness after class. If students take rest, rest with purpose. But, when students have excessive free time for leisure activities in the evenings and on weekends, it signals a lack of rigor in their education. Homework, group projects, and personal projects should fully engage student life.

Excellence in mathematics builds step by step, mastering each level's fundamentals before moving to more abstract concepts. College-level success relies on a foundation laid in secondary school, which, in turn, rests on a solid understanding from primary years. Educational rigor cannot be reserved solely for later part of secondary stages; it must be embedded from the earliest years.

Likewise, developing strong reading skills demands continuous engagement. Reading, too, is a skill that grows with practice; the more students read, the more they enjoy and comprehend, preparing them for future learning. A broader understanding of context develops through consistent reading.

Among the Karen people, the culture of a love for reading is still weak. This could not merely be laziness but largely stems from a lack of intensive reading practice during school years. Reading is a form of mental exercise. Without regular engagement, the skill fades, making reading difficult later in life and often deterring individuals altogether. This gap in early development leads to limited reading proficiency, restricting broader comprehension and lifelong learning. Mastering reading and writing are the key that unlocks the door to greater knowledge and growth.

To see more graduates in Kawthoolei with a competitive edge on the global stage, every level of education must be infused with rigor (rigour), world-class quality, and inclusivity, ensuring that no son or daughter of Kawthoolei, regardless of ability, is left behind.

*4. "**Teach Less, Learn More**" initiative in 2005, encouraging schools to focus on quality teaching and deeper learning rather than quantity.*

The virtue of education can often be better defined by what it is not. Education cannot simply be handed over as mere instruction; true learning happens when one willingly absorbs knowledge on their own and thinks. In Kawthoolei, our goal should be creating an environment that encourages learning, complete with available tools, resources, and an adaptable structure. While world-class labs may be lacking, every available resource can become a tool for learning.

While formal education provides structure, excessive rigidity can stifle true learning. However, for fields like engineering, including computing software engineering, a systematic foundation is essential to ensure thorough, methodical learning.

In response to the need of learning more and teaching less, universities have introduced the *learning-by-doing* approach, integrating practical, hands-on experiences into their curricula. This is an approach that Kawthoolei must take seriously. Practical learning fosters deeper understanding, bridges theory and real-world application, and equips students with the confidence to innovate and solve real problems.

5. The Character and Citizenship Education (CCE) curriculum focuses on values, social-emotional competencies, and civic consciousness.

Schools are training grounds for civic values, spaces that enrich young minds with knowledge, national character, humanistic values, and social-emotional maturity. A nation's education system is often a reflection of its character, and in Myanmar, generations have witnessed a decline in civic and ethical standards. In the City of Yangon, streets littered with trash reflect the state of civic responsibility, civic education, and the effectiveness of municipal services. Trash is discarded without thought, left to be carried by tropical downpours through clogged and undrained streets. A similar scene unfolds along the Salween River of Kawthoolei, where plastic bags and bottles drift endlessly, polluting its once-pristine waters.

Ranked by Transparency International as one of the world's most corrupt countries, Myanmar's culture of corruption would not confine within the military but to the society, communities in Kawthoolei cannot escape such infestation. Character and moral compass are closely connected. Who can escape from a country in ruin dragging down everyone in it. Every day public behavior has normalized corruption, gradually desensitizing people to compromised moral standards.

Civic education teaches its citizens to prioritize the nation first. A Singaporean Chinese does not identify herself as Chinese, but Singaporean. Kawthoolei education must educate the principle that Kawthoolei as a nation comes first, while ethnic identities—Karen, Burmese, Shan, Pa'O, or Hindu Indian, Chinese—are secondary. Everyone is equipped with civic responsibilities and national duty working toward the greater good of the whole nation. It is an education that prioritizes national unity above all.

6. Smart Nation initiative in 2014, heavily invested in integrating technology in education. digital literacy, blended learning, and online platforms for education.

While Kawthoolei may not yet have the infrastructure to adopt fully integrated technology in classrooms, understanding these advancements and recognizing how others are moving forward can inspire us and guide our effort.

7. Continuing to evolve, guided by the principles of meritocracy, equity, and adaptability.

Meritocracy and equity must be balanced, ensuring no corner of Kawthoolei is left without access to basic education.

8. Nurturing future-ready learners who possess not just academic skills but also the character, resilience, and adaptability to thrive in an uncertain, complex world.

National education cannot afford to neglect building character and leadership skills. Adaptability is a virtue to be pursued constantly.

9. Driven by the vision to create a cohesive society, a competitive economy, and a future-ready population.

Our obsession often entangles in the past—narrowly fixed on the Karen people history. A lesson Singapore has is that it achieves successful multicultural nation building with minimal reliance on historical narratives. Our education materials should rather be constantly revised to help Kawthoolei citizens future ready, not anchored on outdated information and irrelevant past.

10. Make students learn based on their bands rather than age.

While students take most of their classes within their bands, they can take classes in other bands depending on their aptitude and interest in a given subject, such as Grade 5 to Grade 8 students who are enthusiastic in robotic programing.

One may retort that what works in Singapore may not work in Kawthoolei. We should learn to make things work, rather than being quick to excuse our shortcomings or dismiss new ideas.

NEIGHBORLINESS THROUGH A SHARED LANGUAGE OF PROGRESS

Our neighbors, Thailand and China, continue to advance their industrial revolutions, powered by science and technology. If we do not speak the same language—the language of science and technology—we risk being treated as subhuman, much like we were centuries ago by colonial powers who saw us as mere servants, subject to the mercy, will, and ideology of foreign powers. Now some have begun learning Chinese, yet instead of raising their status, it often entrenches them in roles of servitude. Similarly, many Karens at the border speak Thai, but without the language of empowering knowledge, it remains a tool for basic communication, reinforcing subordination rather than opening the door to progress.

Currently, it is estimated that about 10 percent of Myanmar-born reside in Thailand, with most working as low-wage migrant laborers. When thinking of migrant workers, images of urban factories or low-skill, labor-intensive industries like textiles often come to mind. However, migrant workers are employed across a range of sectors, from plantations to service industries such as hotels and restaurants. Many Karen people from Kayin (Karen) State find themselves working as undocumented laborers on plantation farms in the mountains of Mae Hong Son Province. These workers live in cramped, overcrowded huts, often sharing the space with a dozen others. In such harsh living and working conditions, women along with working men are left without safety, privacy, or basic human dignity. They are vulnerable to various forms of abuse, not only from local landlords (many of whom are non-Thai), but also from Thai immigration authorities, who subject them to searches, arrests, and treatment worse than that of slaves.

Just as millions of people from Burma find themselves working as low-wage laborers in Thailand, so too will China press harder to expand its influence. China, with its global ambitions to compete as a top superpower and maintain its status as an economic powerhouse, relies on the expansion of its influence. Under the banner of the Belt and Road Initiative, railroads and highways are bound to crisscross Burma, making it a predictable client state. Burma, lying right beneath China's belly, will see China weave its presence through infrastructure. Chinese customs, language, and business ventures will tighten its grip on this fragmented country—the land of Burma would have been set as a manifest destiny for China. In this new dynamic, mafia-like Chinese businessmen would become the bosses, while native, indigenous people in Burma could find themselves reduced to the role of obedient servants, dependent on foreign control for their livelihoods.

If our education fails to prepare us with knowledge and skill as equal partners with our neighbors, Kawthoolei—and all the nations within Burma—will be regarded with little respect. When primary and secondary education is focused solely on memorizing facts from a version of opiated culture and opinionated history, the nation will continue to struggle envisioning its future.

BE RESTLESS FOR CONTINUOUS IMPROVEMENT

Education reforms are a continuous effort, both at the national and program levels, to ensure progress and relevance. A culture of reviewing and improving teaching methods and content is essential for vibrant, meaningful learning. Learning comes not from rote memorization of historical facts—that only dull imagination and creativity. The days of students spending their time memorizing stale historical facts are fading when Google already democratizes memory with search. Learning is an active pursuit, where students engage in exploration, experimentation, and synthesis, driven to uncover solutions and best practices rather than passively absorbing inherited knowledge.

Unredeemable youthful years wasted on excessive playing and singing should be yielded back to intellectual contests like writing competitions, debates, and hands-on projects that sharpen the minds. A four-day school week focuses on structured learning, while weekends hustle with practical projects—building, experimenting, and exploring new possibilities. While students in Singapore, Taiwan, or America are still studying late at night, Kawthoolei students should not go to bed before midnight. To that spirit, Kawthoolei students spend 14 hours a day, 7 days a week, their evening hours delving into established principles and practices, using every time to refine their skills and expand their knowledge, raising themselves to be ready for the challenges of the modern world.

Hustle and learn—the universe holds knowledge boundless.

Living in the severely underdeveloped regions of Kawthoolei, youth may feel isolated from the competitive global landscape. However, competition has been global for generations, driven by the interconnectedness of institutions, economies, and talents across the world. Software programmers around the world are collaborating in github.com. Even something as simple as a pair of jeans could involve contributions from ten different countries, from cotton production to sewing, decorating, and washing. High-tech tools like drones, now used on Kawthoolei battlefields, consist of microchips and raw materials sourced from multiple nations, with software created by programmers from around the world. In a newer model of car—the one running in Kawthoolei soil included—thousands of microchips are embedded for vehicle functions. We cannot guarantee our safety with total ignorance of what is underneath our seats.

In every aspect of life, humanity depends on global collaboration. Nations collaborate and compete at the same time. Microchips are not solely made in Taiwan, they just rely on machines, materials, and designs from other countries, mainly from the U.S, Korea, Japan, Netherland, and China. Overwhelmingly, the most value-added aspect—the one that costs the most or makes the most money—is the *design*, the sophisticated machines at the edge of science are the secondary.

Without a competitive edge, we risk being left behind. We survived without being cutthroat in the past, but we will not survive in the future without being competitive. We did not do well in the past with a laid-back culture either. Our education must prepare us to meet this challenge. In today's interconnected age, having natural resources is no longer sufficient—the true competitive advantage lies in our ability to transform these resources through human ingenuity.

Currently, we rely heavily on physical labor, even for tasks as simple as mixing concrete for construction, breaking the backs of many able-bodied men. What we need is a *seismic shift*—a habit of making tools and utilizing machinery to ease our work and be more productive. This calls to first engage our minds—using our fingers, eyes, ears, and imagination—before resorting to muscle strength. This shift in mindset is essential for building creativity and efficiency.

We may feel no hunger to learn from the world beyond our borders. Meanwhile we find ourselves with nowhere to hide in our own land, shamefully wondering why the world does not come to our aid, we lose sight of the natural drive of a nation that lives with dignity and capability.

Learning can be painful. Life is hard. Embrace challenges and grow.

World-class education lies at our fingertips, just a click or swipe away. With the same data and bandwidth spent watching TikTok dances and live streaming funny Karen eating fishpaste videos, surely, we have data and connections for learning online. The doors are wide open to many of the most prestigious academic institutions in the world. For secondary education, Khan Academy (khanacademy.org) alone provides more than enough resources in many subject areas, offering highly accessible and quality teaching. For college level, free courses from Yale, Harvard, Stanford, MIT, University of Cambridge, University of Chicago, University of California and many other top universities on a variety of subjects—from building bridges to debating ethics—once reserved for the wealthy and academically privileged, are now accessible to anyone with an internet connection. Ours is a generation of unprecedented opportunity, but it will only be a blessing if we choose to seize what's before us. Otherwise, if we abuse this abundance it can turn to a curse.

In this era of boundless opportunity, scarcity is no longer an excuse. The barriers that once restricted access to education have crumbled, leaving a world of knowledge open and within reach. If the glow of mobile screens reflects entertainment rather than enlightenment, countless possibilities for learning are untapped. No space for complacency while the world moves forward.

LIFELONG LEARNING

Education is about learning, and learning must happen within an education system. However, learning is not confined to formal education—it can occur anywhere, at any time. As the term *lifelong learning* suggests, it is the continuous process of acquiring knowledge throughout one's life. It also reflects a dynamic exchange: anyone can learn from anyone, at any stage or level. Even Bill Gates, former CEO of Microsoft, once shared that he continued learning through Khan Academy, a platform initially designed for secondary education.

It is unwise to harbor disdain for what lies beyond our understanding. True learning begins by engaging with the unfamiliar. In a rapidly evolving world, new models of social and economic organization—such as investing, cryptocurrency, social media, e-commerce, and emerging technologies—have profoundly shaped our communities and personal lives.

A few years ago, parts of the Karen community were drawn into the allure of cryptocurrency investment schemes. Unfortunately, within close-knit communities like the Karen, reliance on word-of-mouth recommendations often bypasses research and critical evaluation, primed for Ponzi scheme. As a result, many investors failed to discern legitimate opportunities from sophisticated schemes in cyberspace.

Lifelong learning is both a practical necessity and moral duty. Above all, it can even be seen as a meditative practice—a fulfilling lifestyle, living a rich life, constantly seeking understanding the universe while living briefly here on Earth.

RECOMMENDATION FOR KAWTHOOLEI EDUCATION SYSTEM

1. English as a Bilingual Language and a Working Language

This policy is already in place at the high school and post-secondary levels, with all subjects primarily taught in English—except for mother tongue language courses. English opens the door to a wealth of global literature across all fields of study. The primary reasons for adopting English as a working language are as follows:

- **Primary Education Feasibility**: Nowadays, accessible online resources make English learning feasible for elementary students to build a strong foundation from an early age.
- **Global Engagement**: English, as the global lingua franca, raises Kawthoolei's status as a community fluent in the language of the world, prepared to engage with advancements in global culture, norms, ethics, innovation, and trends.
- **Science and Technology Access**: Proficiency in English empowers students to understand technical terminology, access scientific research, and participate in competition and collaboration in fields of technology and innovation.
- **Cultural Exchange and Higher Education**: English fluency facilitates educational exchanges and partnerships with international institutions, elevating the quality of education and research in Kawthoolei. (Singaporean universities has been integrated with Ivy league in the U.S. for decades)
- **Industrial Integration**: Machinery and tools are universally standardized and labeled in scientific terms, which are predominantly in English, its fluency is essential for industrial progress. (ISO - International Organization for Standardization has standardized on health and safety standards, time and date format, language code, environment, health, tools, food and safety management, currency code, country code)
- **Digital Literacy**: English gives access to coding, programming, AI tools and ecosystem, and other digital resources, vital for the digital economy and modern skill-building.
- **Tourism Development**: English-speaking service providers enhance the tourism experience. (As current state, Kawthoolei should not attract tourists for security and environmental reasons, for tourism can put a stress on security and environments before regulation has fully developed.)
- **Social Cohesion and Efficiency**: As a common language, English improves collaboration, knowledge-sharing, and teamwork across Kawthoolei's diverse communities.

2. Integrate Hands-On STEM curriculum in Secondary Education

- **Practical Engineering Concepts**: Introduce foundational engineering concepts in secondary school. Students should engage in hands-on projects, Lego blocks, learning electrical components, robotic control, and practical applications alongside theoretical studies.

- **Real-World Construction Experience**: High school students should participate in community construction projects—such as homes, meeting halls, bridges, and hydro-power initiatives—gaining valuable hands-on experience with nails, hammers, saws and bricks and wooden planks, and power tools that reinforce classroom learning.
- **Advanced Technological Proficiency**: Middle and high school students should become proficient with microcontrollers, circuit boards, solar and battery-powered projects, and basic drone operation, preparing them for technical crafts and multiple engineering principles into a practical application.
- **Global Competitiveness**: Equip secondary students with skills that meet international standards—reading, writing, arithmetic—ensuring they are well-prepared for both technical education and liberal arts in post-secondary schooling.

PROPOSAL FOR KAWTHOOLEI REAL-WORLD CLASSROOM

No more than four days a week should students be in a structured classroom for instructional learning.

Their late afternoon, evenings and Fridays would be dedicated to personal homework and group projects, allowing weekends to be reserved for exploration, experimentation, prototyping, hacking, tinkering, reversed engineering, troubleshooting, testing, and development. Students then present a written or demonstration report, earning grades based on their engagement in these activities and the learning outcomes they achieve.

Students learn best when they are genuinely interested, and real-world environments spark interest. With Kawthoolei's rich biodiversity, students could gain far more by learning outdoors, combining firsthand experiences with textbook knowledge in biology. Science becomes more meaningful when students can experiment, see, smell, and even taste their discoveries, experiencing sensory learning.

All secondary students should engage in hands-on projects with real-world applications relevant to Kawthoolei. They must explore engineering concepts to understand why some structures withstand the test of time while others fail. Practical projects could involve tinkering with batteries and microcontrollers to understand electronic components, experimenting with electromagnetic waves to uncover the invisible forces of physics, and writing code to develop software that controls robots—bridging theory with practical innovation.

With Kawthoolei's mountainous terrain and abundant streams, there is a practical need for bridges to support transportation. Students could gain practical engineering experience by constructing small bridges over streams and overcoming uneven surfaces. Kawthoolei's warmer climate also calls for simpler building designs compared to colder regions with elaborate heating, cooling, and water systems. By engaging in masonry—the craft of building with brick, stone, and metal bars—

students would develop essential skills that serve both their communities and their education, strengthening their muscles and minds in the process. Facts and figures may fade quickly from memory, but practical, service-oriented projects create lasting, lifelong memories.

KAWTHOOLEI'S COMMITMENT TO AMERICAN ENGLISH STANDARDS

The Kawthoolei education system and official communications should favor American Standard English over British English as the primary dialect.

- This choice enhances linguistic clarity carrying the spirit of the republic.
- With simpler spellings (e.g., "catalog" rather than "catalogue"), American English is widely understood, embodying a modern, clear, and concise style that aligns well with technological progress, global trade, and international diplomacy.
- Due to the natural adoption of American English through digital interactions —especially among Gen-Z youth, even in countries like Thailand, where British English is traditionally taught—American English has become a practical choice for communication and education in Kawthoolei.

PRESERVING TRADITION, EMBRACING MODERNITY

National education fosters national unity by promoting legends, teaching folktales, and reciting ancient poems that bring heritage to life and build appreciation for shared cultural identity.

Despite efforts, our rich literary heritage is at risk of being diminished. The label of "ethnic minority" consigns Karen literary culture to the margins, portraying it as substandard and undeserving of recognition. This marginalization is further compounded by the detachment of many educators, trained in other languages, away from the Karen way of life and its vibrant literary traditions.

While scattered Karen written scripts are relatively new and dialects are diverse, our oral traditions and poetic culture are reservoirs of immense value. **Hta** (pronounced with a high tone "taa") stands as a cornerstone of this heritage, encompassing proverbs, prophecies, teachings, stories, divine, rituals, legends, practical knowledge on health and agriculture, social norms, courtship exchanges, riddles, and vernacular expressions. These traditions are not just cultural artifacts but living embodiments of our history and identity.

The urgent task of national education is to preserve these treasures. Our literary heritage is fading as elders—the custodians of this knowledge—pass away, and formal education continues to neglect its significance. In the northern districts of Mutraw, Hsaw-Hteet, and Taw-Oo to the southern districts of the Taw-Naw mountainous regions, this culture is making its final stand.

Elders recognize the fragility of their traditions, threatened by the destruction of the way of life they represent, the ravages of war, and the encroachment of external cultural forces.

The last stronghold is crumbling. Without immediate action, Karen literary culture may see its final generation. This is a call for national education to fulfill its duty: to safeguard, promote, and celebrate this irreplaceable legacy before it is lost. We can never fully express the depth of our heritage in another language. Even this book, written in English to reach global language readers, cannot fully capture the nuances and richness of our mother tongue.

The path forward, rejuvenating our language to achieve equal status among the world's languages will require dedication, innovation, and the courage to embrace modernity without losing our roots, a step toward securing our identity with style claiming its place in the modern world.

HARD WORK ISN'T GLAMOROUS

Hard work may not be glamorous, but its rewards are. Kawthoolei education should prioritize creating an environment where students are encouraged to work hard, engage deeply in learning, and enjoy the process of exploration and experimentation.

Learning is an active pursuit—a process of taking, not receiving. Teaching, on the other hand, is about giving. While teachers can work tirelessly to provide knowledge and guidance, learning happens only when students put in the effort to learn for themselves.

In the United States, Asian Americans consistently excel academically and outperform Whites, Blacks, and Hispanics socioeconomically. Their success in academics and technical fields has become so pronounced that it has given rise to the stereotype that their achievements are the result of natural talent rather than hard work. However, Thomas Sowell, an esteemed American economist, social philosopher, and political commentator, shared a different perspective based on his experience while teaching at UCLA, one of California's and the nation's top universities. He recounted the following:

"The question of why Asian Americans consistently outperform their peers has been asked for years, and the answer is not as complicated as you might think. Let me take you back to a moment I had while teaching at UCLA. It was a Saturday night, and while most of the campus was quiet, I found myself heading to the research library. I expected it to be nearly empty—it was the weekend, after all—but when I walked inside, I was surprised to see it buzzing with activity. Almost every student I saw was Asian American, deeply absorbed in their books, typing away at their laptops. I did not see many Black students there, not many White students either, just row after row of determined, focused Asian Americans. They were not wasting time; they were working. It was no surprise to me that come Monday morning, these were the students who came to class the most prepared.

There is no great mystery to their success. It is not about natural talent or luck. It comes down to one simple thing: work. They worked harder than everyone else. Imagine this—while most of their peers were out enjoying their weekend socializing or relaxing, these students were putting in the extra hours. It is not glamorous, it is not easy, but it is that quiet, persistent effort that sets them apart. In the end, it shows in their results.

Success in academics, or in life for that matter, is rarely handed to you; it is *earned*. That night in the library, what I saw was not just a group of students studying—I saw the makings of future success. Hard work overtime beats talent when talent doesn't work hard. It is not about being smarter; it is about being consistent. These students were not born with a head start; they created it. Day by day, assignment by assignment, they built the foundation that allowed them to excel when it mattered."

This phenomenon is not confined to a single American university—it unfolds wherever Asian students are present. Whether they are international students from Asia or Asian Americans, they consistently populate the libraries of mainstream universities across the United States. Beyond American campuses, the same dedication is evident among students in Taiwan, Korea, Singapore, China, and even Thailand. Their university libraries remain hubs of focused effort, filled with students determined to maximize their time. This commitment to learning—persisting even when others embrace leisure—reflects a deep-rooted culture of education and hard work that transcends borders.

During my time at an American university, I regularly went to the university main library late at night to study in a dedicated atmosphere. I expected to find a few sleepy souls in the quiet hours' past midnight. However, even at two A.M., the 24-hour library was alive with wide-awake night owls—I wondered if some were hanging out at the library for leisure—but most fully immersed in their work. Studying hard in teens and early twenties is not viewed as an extraordinary sacrifice—it is simply normal, a necessary passage of life. This collective ethic of hard work is what drives national progress. When all young and old citizens embrace diligence and dedication, the entire nation moves forward.

In its *2022 National Development Plan 2030, South Africa* reflected on 18 years of democracy and the lack of progress made. A critical conclusion emerged: the greatest shortcomings were poor-quality education and a lack of work opportunities for youth and adults. This lesson is universal—hard work transcends talent, climate, race, geography, political ideology, and economic policy.

For Kawthoolei to advance, quality education and hard work are not just essential; they are the foundation and a moral imperative. These pillars will not only lift us up but propel the nation forward.

No loitering, no time killing—stay sharp, stay driven, keep learning.

CHILDREN LEARNING WORK IS NOT CHILD LABOR

Growing up on the frontlines of Kawthoolei, my summers and weekends were occupied with chores—collecting, chopping, and stacking firewood, preparing for the rainy season, assisting my grandfather in his orchard, clearing weeds, and digging drainage for irrigation. In our region, every able-bodied child contributed to the daily workload at school, home, and farm.

From primary to high school, there were only teachers and students—no janitors, no additional staff. Students took full responsibility for cleaning classrooms and fetching drinking water. Born out of necessity, this practice instilled discipline, responsibility, and a strong work ethic—values still admired in other cultures. In Japan, for instance, primary school students uphold similar traditions, cleaning classrooms, communal spaces, and even assisting in meal preparation.

Child labor becomes problematic only when it involves exploitative or physically unfit industrial workloads for tender youth. In some U.S. communities, such as the Amish, able-bodied children contribute to their parents' farms and family businesses, cultivating responsibility and a sense of community. Developing a work ethic from a young age is not a burden but a natural part of human growth and learning. Students in Kawthoolei should not shy away from work. Among the Karen, elders speak of a deeply held belief that life finds meaning through labor.

The perception that Karen people are lazy is far from accurate. I grew up watching my grandfather, a man of diligence, wake up at 3 A.M. to cook breakfast for workers before they set off for the fields in the pre-dawn hours. When the harsh tropical sun was high in the horizon, they completed the first half day of work. Afterward, he would return home cooling off for afternoon. In the evening, he continued working, weaving baskets or preparing bamboo slices, laboring under candlelight until bedtime. He labored ceaselessly until the end of his life. Happy working, happy living.

NATIONAL EDUCATION EDUCATES. EDUCATION MUST EDUCATE.

National education is a moral imperative—a fundamental duty of the state to provide meaningful and transformative learning. No hours, days, or years should be wasted. Classrooms must be spaces of exploration, where students engage with real-world challenges. The focus shifts from rote memorization to critical understanding, preparing students with the confidence and competence to navigate an ever-changing world.

In the pursuit of technical excellence, Kawthoolei's humanistic values provide guidance so that progress is tempered by civic responsibility and measured by both intellectual growth and national character. This blend of skill and integrity shapes generation leaders capable of guiding their nation forward with wisdom and virtue.

1. *Surrender is out of the question.*

2. *The recognition of the Karen State must be complete.*

3. *We shall retain our arms.*

4. *We shall decide our own political destiny.*

We shall retain our arms—among them, education, our strongest weapon—we shall hold firmly and wield steadfastly.

Tha-Nu Hset Lar Culture School, Mutraw District

SawLah@Photography 2023

Zerr-Thwal-Thaw New Generation School, Mutraw District

SawLah@Photography 2022

PART IV

REBUILDING WORLD-CLASS EXCELLENCE

How can we dance or sing the songs
among our ancient poetry
in the land of our ancestry,
if we cannot secure our way of life —
standing strong, respectable, and capable
among our neighbors,
both near and far?

Chapter 13

Rebuild Kawthoolei, Embrace the STEM

The usual way of doing things is neither the only way nor the right way; nor have the old ways yet led to triumph for us. It is irresponsible to seek solutions for 21st-century challenges with 20th-century tools.

The First Way or the Second Way—both have trapped generations in endless political debates, clinging to outdated paradigms while real progress remains elusive. To move forward, the nation needs not a dichotomized black-and-white worldview, but a broader vision—one that asks not only why a nation rises, but how.

Sheer will alone is no longer the defining measure of progress; *clear logic* has become its maker. In the modern era, nations rise through science, innovation, and bold ideas. STEM shapes not only societies and economies but also warfare and geopolitics.

The field of **s**cience, **t**echnology, **e**ngineering, and **m**athematics (STEM) is the universal language of material progress, built upon the syntax of logic that powers the heartbeat of a thriving, independent nation. STEM enables us to harness the energy of our rivers, transforming back-breaking labor into productive enterprise. It allows us to design structures, railways, and ports that not only drive commerce but also show the marvel of human ingenuity. It empowers us to build bridges, roads, and stations that both connect distances and bridge divides. Science equips us to verify assumptions and refine our understanding. STEM transforms vision into reality, missions into accomplishments, and imagination into innovation, turning the magical into tangible outcomes. With national mastery of STEM, our defense becomes not just formidable but admirable for excellence.

At its core, STEM—or perhaps more accurately, MSET (Mathematics, Science, Engineering, Technology)—follows a natural hierarchy: technology builds on engineering, engineering relies on science, and science is governed by the universal laws of mathematics. This is the natural progression where each discipline reinforces the next.

Although excelling in one area without a solid foundation is possible, real breakthroughs demand firm ground of knowledge. Cross-disciplinary computer engineering will require a strong grasp of physics, chemistry, and general scientific principles. Mathematics itself is a discipline of layered abstractions, where higher-order concepts rest on the mastery of previous ones.

For Kawthoolei students to thrive in STEM, they must build this foundation early, mastering mathematics in primary and secondary school to prepare for the college-level rigor that fuels research, innovation, and creative work. Wasting time on constant merry-making and tribal dancing on Refugees' Day or Valentine's Day festivities will not pave the way forward. Adults, teachers, or organizers who encourage such distractions among students deserve scrutiny, as their motives may not align with the pursuit of excellence and national advancement.

It is easy to dismiss science and technology as irrelevant, weighting that we are an agricultural society and should therefore focus solely on familiar ground—farming and meeting basic needs. Enough excuses are at our disposal. Some may claim a lack of interest in STEM within the Karen community, rejecting high-tech innovation as unrealistic. While formal education may compartmentalize knowledge into distinct subjects, the world does not.

We often resist, ignore, or even despise what is unfamiliar—but a lack of understanding does not make something unimportant. Dismissing what lies beyond our grasp does not diminish its significance. What we reject remains unchanged. The unfamiliar may hold the power to transform us, while the familiar may lead us nowhere. To grow, we must learn to be comfortable with the unfamiliar.

The power to reshape our future lies within our grasp. In this digital age, information is more accessible than ever, and learning materials, made abundant by mass production, have never been more affordable. Our moment calls for us to equip the younger generation with technological skills while the older generation also supports and values these advancements.

THE LOGIC OF FORCE VS. THE LOGIC OF WILL

Modern warfare has shifted from a "logic of will" to a "logic of force," Johnathan Bi noted in one of his lectures. In the past, war was driven by sheer determination, resilience, and bravery. Today, however, conflicts are increasingly defined by technological superiority—by who wields the most advanced tools, from precision missiles to autonomous drones. A profound example of this shift took place during World War II, not only remembered for its human toll but for its scientific rivalry between two brilliant minds—Werner Heisenberg and J. Robert Oppenheimer.

Heisenberg, a quantum mechanics pioneer, led Nazi Germany's nuclear weapons program with the goal of developing an atomic bomb. Opposing him was J. Robert Oppenheimer, the American physicist directing the Manhattan Project, where the first atomic bombs were developed at Los Alamos. These men were more than scientists; they represented their nations' quests for technological dominance. The contest between Heisenberg and Oppenheimer exemplifies the ultimate shift to the "logic of force." If Heisenberg had succeeded first, the world we live in would have unfolded very differently. This competition was no longer about vast armies but about a few elite scientists whose knowledge could reshape global power. In the modern age, the influence of a select few experts has become critical to national security.

The development of nuclear weapons did more than introduce a new tool of warfare; it redefined global order. Today, nations with nuclear capabilities maintain a delicate balance of power, often at the cost of justice—suffering of smaller communities is ignored for the sake of world peace—an uneasy peace held by technological force.

For Kawthoolei, embracing STEM is essential not only for material progress but for security in a world where scientific knowledge, not will power alone, determines the strength and sovereignty of nations.

FROM CONSUMERS TO PRODUCERS

Some of us might dismiss STEM, presuming that Kawthoolei is incapable of grasping such advanced concepts. But that unfounded assumption would be the language of defeat—an ethnic-minority mindset resigned to limitations and blind to possibilities. Yes, we are an agricultural society. Yes, still, we can become efficient and productive. Israel, a nation of arid deserts where water is scarce, the sun hotter than our tropical sun, mastered STEM to transform its land into agricultural powerhouse, exporting products including citrus fruits, tomatoes, and beans, to neighboring regions. During the winter months, Israel serves as Europe's greenhouse, supplying melons, tomatoes, cucumbers, peppers, strawberries, kiwis, mangoes, avocados, and various citrus fruits. To its neighbors, their exports have become their diplomacy. Their AI-powered robotic harvesters not only pick fruits and vegetables but have themselves become prized technological exports.

The United States, too, was founded on agriculture but revolutionized productivity by driving tools and machinery. Today, only 2% of the U.S. workforce remains in agriculture, yet their efficiency feeds 350 million people and supports trillions of dollars in exports. The difference between typical farms in Asia and those in America is stark: while Asian fields are dotted with laborers toiling under the sun, American farms are nearly empty—machines and technology do the work. Kawthoolei, too, cannot linger on toil with human muscle and crude shovel under the burning sun but must rise to the grace of tractors and ride with precision controllers.

> The desert nations bloom with abundance, while rain-fed lands hunger in silence. Where arid sands yield harvests with ingenuity, why is fertile soil bound by scarcity?

At this stage, the producer culture within our community remains weak. Even for basic agricultural needs, we often buy what we could easily grow or produce ourselves, despite Kawthoolei's fertile land and abundant resources. Innovation is rarely visible. We default to buying from other for events and special occasions. For instance, wedding preparation on the west side of the Salween-Moei River often involves buying goods from the east, a break from the tradition of yearlong family efforts to prepare for such special occasions.

To bring food to the table, we still rely heavily on manual labor. In many areas, rice is still pounded with leg-press mortars instead of using engine-powered mills—a reminder that we have yet to fully embrace the tools capable of transforming our productivity. While such practices served us well in the past, they will not sustain us in the future. Our limited labor resources are needed to maximize productivity for the nation's progress.

A nation that makes economic progress is one that produces and exports, not merely consumes. Competitive advantage lies not in the gold or minerals beneath our feet but in the skills, we cultivate and the innovation we seek. Gold mines scatter across the seven districts of Kawthoolei, yet the children running above them in worn, dirty clothes, their hair dusted grey, tell a different story. Wealth of a nation is not measured by natural resources but by what we build, create, and produce—by the strength of our human resources and the depth of our ingenuity.

Kawthoolei used to have abundant hardwood and renowned, magnificent teak forests. However, the intricate wooden decorations, premium furniture, and elegant interior designs crafted from its prized teak are found not in Kawthoolei, but in distant lobbies and luxury rooms across the world. Our teak sits gracefully abroad, while Kawthoolei is left with rotten stumps—laughing at us, mourning for us—a haunting reminder of its once-vibrant forests and the truth that precious raw materials alone cannot build prosperity in a war-torn country.

In today's world, nearly every consumer product is shaped by value-added processes. The smartphone in your pocket functions as a gateway to the vast power of the internet, the ultimate supercomputer. Its raw materials hold little inherent value but are transformed into high-priced technologies through creativity, innovative design, and the mastery of nature's secrets. Abundant silicon rock, refined by human ingenuity, and cobalt sourced from distant lands are crafted into cutting-edge devices.

STEM is the driving force of progress when humanity oversights. Kawthoolei—or any nation—will thrive when its people are creators, producers, and builders, not merely buyers or consumers, and certainly not beggars. As a nation, as communities, or as individual human beings, it is not a life worth living if all we do is consume what others have produced.

Through a sleepy valley at dawn, resonating the rhythmic thud of leg-press rice mortars echoes up-and-down "klak-klak-dud." This is more than a labor-intensive time-consuming tradition—it has become an alarm bell in 21st Century. The rooster's call before sunrise stirs the community, awakening us to the boundless possibilities awaiting Kawthoolei.

ISRAEL AND THE KAREN PEOPLE AT ODDS

There is a disconnect. While the older generation of Karen people admires Israel, their admiration does not extend to the science and engineering fields that are central to Israel's success. Alas, the aging souls have collected excuses, uninformed reasoning, or outdated narratives of Jewish people over actionable insights.

We have yet to embrace the scientific rigor and innovation that propelled Israel to global leadership in this area. With one of the highest ratios of scientists per capita in the world, Israel invests 4.5% of its GDP in Research and Development (R&D), far surpassing the United States (2.8%) and the European Union (1.9%). The country is a global leader in scientific output, boasting 6,500 start-up technology companies.

Israel's journey, marked by the leveraging of technological progress against overwhelming odds. Many Karen conservative Christians—and their Buddhist counterparts alike—admire Israel deeply, despite Israel's pragmatic relationships, including its historical alignment with Myanmar's military. Israel's strategic alliances, like that with Myanmar, reflect the contradictions of international politics, where pragmatism often supersedes moral consistency, unfortunately. General Khin Nyunt, a member of the 1988 military coup and one of Myanmar's most prominent military intelligence figures, reportedly received training in Israel. The irony is that this intelligence master failed to sense the moment he became the hunted—defenseless as he was escorted from his home on the night of October 2004, stripping him from the title of President of the country.

The people with a history of persecution—Israel and the Karen people—should have been on the same side. For the Karen people engaged in the struggle for autonomy, Israel's ties with the Burmese military may appear disheartening. Nonetheless, the spirit of Israel—its perseverance, innovation, resilience, and pragmatism—continues to inspire. Israel's transformation from a small, embattled nation to a global technological powerhouse attests to the power of will, innovation, and foresight, lessons that should resonate with the Karen community even when geopolitical alliances do not align.

Cultivating scientific talent is a strategic necessity. For emerging nations, Israel offers valuable lessons—its success is built on both military strength and strategic investments in STEM. In Israel, these fields are not merely academic pursuits but essential to national security and prosperity. Its journey demonstrates that real power and autonomy are not preserved by tradition alone but secured through bold innovation.

Behold—the resilience of the Karen people stands unmatched, a people nothing to be compared. Facing annihilation by both force and assimilation—driven from our land or absorbed into foreign cultures—we have endured without the backing of any global power. In contrast, Israel has survived with sustained support from the world's leading superpower, the United States, that has consistently defended Israel at the UN Security Council and provides billions in annual aid, alongside close security cooperation.

FROM RESILIENCE TO LEARNING

Our people possess remarkable endurance, having withstood a long national tragedy that has tested the limits of human strength. The challenge now is to channel this resilience into learning, experimentation, and exploring new possibilities in STEM—embracing small failures and adopting the fail-fast principle as essential steps toward progress. The world is waiting to see products proudly marked with "Designed in Kawthoolei," "Made in Kawthoolei," and "Product of Kawthoolei."

To achieve this, we are called to fundamentally change how we view experimentation. Our conservative culture may discourage us from taking risks, paralyzed by the fear of making mistakes. Often, failure is met with ridicule, and its cost is not just monetary but also social, with embarrassment and reputation at stake. This fear suppresses innovation and discourages daring experiments that could lead to extraordinary breakthroughs. It is crucial to distinguish between failures rooted in moral shortcomings and those born of calculated risk.

In a technologically advanced world, experimentation and small failures are seen as stepping stones to greatness. The willingness to try, fail, and try again drives innovation. To create something excellent, the determination to overcome societal judgment must be stronger than the fear of failure. The hunger to explore must be stronger than the shame of being ridiculed. What we need is a fearless mindset—an attitude that embraces challenges not just for personal good, but with a mission for the greater good.

We cannot continue to rely solely on buying weapons or machines produced elsewhere, leaving us helpless when they break down. The lack of understanding of the appliances we buy and the lack of skills to build for ourselves are what we should be ashamed of—not the act of failing while trying to create something of our own. Buying ready-made solutions without the ability to innovate or repair creates a dependency that holds us back. Buying products with community donations and when donations dry out, we are left helpless is what we should be ashamed of. Realization to the addiction to humanitarian aids is what should be ashamed of.

Relying on military products made by others creates a security vulnerability. The makers possess the knowledge of the product's secrets, while we ready-made buyers remain in the dark. In today's era of advanced technology, many devices are designed to work with micromagnetic waves. Even something as simple as a night vision binocular can contain a microchip, potentially enabling external tracking or interference.

Many of our youth are drawn to artistic pursuits—guitarists and soloists who find meaning in the expressive, emotional world of art. Yet Kawthoolei does not need more dreamers in front of microphones; it needs minds at research laboratories, drafting the blueprints for a brighter future. No nation has risen by the echo of performance alone. Indeed, artists can inspire the public to rally for Kawthoolei, but, for now, the nation needs fewer celebrity figures of limited substance who attract attention to seek donations or sell fishpaste. Kawthoolei needs more inspiring scientists, not more inspired artists.

Having endured so much tragedy, we should be comfortable with small failures that push us toward progress. Failure is not the enemy—it is the pathway to growth. Theoretical frameworks are the foundation, and experimentation gives understanding to mastery. The path forward is to rise with hunger to learn, the courage to experiment, the resilience to fail, and the determination to succeed.

SAFE SPACE FOR EXPERIMENTAL PLAYGROUND

Sandbox environments, testing grounds, and innovation labs are designed as controlled spaces to embrace failure, allowing for experimentation and testing without incurring significant risks.

American universities house laboratories that conduct cutting-edge research, such as testing the speed of moving bullets, analyzing the behavior of novel viral strains, and studying radiological materials for scientific insights. These labs inherently involve extreme hazardous conditions, yet they operate safely through a combination of engineering controls, administrative oversight, and strict regulatory compliance. Multiple layers of safeguards ensure that these experiments are not only possible but conducted responsibly, advancing science while minimizing risk.

This is not a novel idea for Kawthoolei, who is at war and constantly experimenting out of military necessity. Testing explosions is normal in Kawthoolei. What remains crucial is fostering an environment that encourages experimentation while ensuring safety through proper controls. These controls are not just about mitigating risks—they are about encouraging experiments while preventing serious harm, such as damage to human health, loss of eyesight or limbs, or, most importantly, human lives.

Beyond military necessity, Kawthoolei will need to develop world-class R&D friendly spaces—innovation parks, research parks, technology hubs, and industrial zones—starting small and growing into a full-fledged ecosystem where these spaces become ecosystem supporting one another to advance the land of Kawthoolei, its economy, and the whole society.

LEARN UNIVERSAL, INNOVATE LOCAL

Scientific discoveries and engineering principles can be applied universally, but effective adoption requires careful consideration of the local context. Conducting our own research and development in ways that align with our unique climate, economy, and cultural context is crucial.

In the United States, for example, California has widely adopted solar technology on an industrial scale, with solar panels installed across businesses and residences. This approach makes business sense due to California's high fuel prices and is practical because the state's year-round blue skies provide abundant sunshine. However, this same approach would be far less effective in Washington State, where frequent rain clouds limit solar panel efficiency—despite both states sharing the West Coast facing the Pacific Ocean.

Similarly, while Kawthoolei and Thailand share the same tropical skies, their differing economic conditions, industrial stages, and cultural contexts call for innovations uniquely tailored to their needs. For progress to be sustainable, technology adoption in Kawthoolei will need to stay attuned to local realities and traditions to minimize harm while maximizing benefit. Kawthoolei will need to adopt gentle *industrialization*—in everything we design, build, and create, we are kind to overall environmental wellbeing, humans and animals, streams and water, and mountains and lands.

Thailand is now actively exploring the development of Small Modular Nuclear Reactors (SMRs) as part of its strategy to achieve net-zero greenhouse gas emissions by 2065. After discovering natural gas in the Gulf of Thailand in the early 1980s, the country relied heavily on this resource. However, Thailand is a good example of how a nation can recognize the limits of its natural resources and take early action to prepare for the next era of green energy before those resources are depleted. Kawthoolei must learn from this principle that natural resources are exhaustible, therefore start preparing for the next phase of national development while weighting on its natural resources.

As we innovate and bring new creations to the land, the guardian spirits of rivers and forests must be honored, ensuring their happiness as they watch over. Fish in the streams must keep swimming; creatures in the forest must continue hustling. Our happiness and health are intertwined with theirs, for we drink from their waters and thrive on the abundance they provide.

TECHNOLOGY TRANSFERRED, LEARNING FROM NEIGHBORS

Thailand has long demonstrated its potential in applying technology and engineering principles, innovations that emerge from universal knowledge yet are tailored to its unique environment. From road designs and bridges built to withstand tropical downpours, landslides, and floods, to its strong presence in the global technology supply chain, Thailand has a strategic approach to technology. For example, the 2011 floods in Bangkok caused a 30% drop in global hard disk drive (HDD) production, as Thailand was a major producer of storage memory for computers. This disruption highlights the nation's pivotal role in global manufacturing, backed by a solid foundation of skilled engineers. As Kawthoolei shares its longest border (over 2000 km) with Thailand, there is much to learn from its neighbor's achievements—though not from its challenges with corruption and inefficient management.

Thailand's economic products and telecommunications have already flowed into Kawthoolei, but the real lesson lies in Thailand's workmanship and mass production capabilities. Without skilled labor and quality-focused manufacturing processes, Kawthoolei cannot hope to scale up its industries or participate in the competitive global marketplace where a nation that cannot compete is a nation that cannot thrive.

Thailand has growing momentum in the global technological landscape, having a hunger to grow. In May 2024, Microsoft pledged significant investments in Thailand's cloud infrastructure, followed by Google's $1 billion investment in September, aimed at expanding data centers, cloud technology, and artificial intelligence. These are not mere financial boosts—they represent the arrival of cutting-edge technologies and, more importantly, the introduction of a culture of software development that demands technical and intellectual rigor far beyond the monetary value itself. With these advancements come new governance practices rooted in accountability, the checks-and-balances of U.S. practices, multiple layers of verification, and rigorous quality assurance—elements of a system that Kawthoolei has yet to fully embrace.

Business software used in daily operations—whether for banking, shopping, or registration and application, managing data—does not come directly from the software developers who write the code. Before reaching end users, it passes through multiple layers of review—technical assurance, user experience testing, and formal business approval. While the engineers who design and build the system form its core, critical enterprise applications undergo rigorous evaluation tested in various testing and staging environments to ensure functionality, reliability, and usability before release.

We cannot introduce a rigorous quality production system into our land without its whole ecosystem. Quality has to become a society norm, accompanied by a professional culture backed by legal accountability. Without legal consequences for damages caused by substandard work, quality assurance will remain difficult to sustain. In the U.S., the term "checks and balances" is mostly associated with political arrangements, but in reality, it is a daily cultural norm applied in every domain. It is already in the culture to double check (multi-layer checks), verifying another person's claim or work in every enterprise. For example, U.S. regulations require that two people must always be present in the airplane cockpit, while European airlines only adopted this rule in 2015 after a tragic incident in which a co-pilot crashed the plane in a suicide while the captain was out of cockpit. From the production of home appliances to software development, multiple-step verification and formal checks are ingrained practices in the U.S. The U.S. workers may not always excel in craftsmanship, but the system itself ensures quality, therefore, consumer trust.

Adapting to a culture of large-scale operation, where various specialized knowledge collaborate, will be an unfamiliar uphill challenge—but it is the mountains we can climb—just as any nation can. A hydroelectric power plant, for example, requires the seamless integration of expertise from multiple fields. Mechanical engineers design the turbine machinery, electrical engineers manage the flow and distribution of electricity, and chemical engineers handle the storage systems. Software engineers are needed to develop monitoring and control systems, while knowledge of the local environment—climate, rainfall patterns, and landscape—becomes crucial. Mathematical precision is also essential for accurately gauging the landscape and ensuring efficiency. Only when these diverse specializations come together can such a basic infrastructure be realized effectively.

A thoughtful design is a technical and moral necessity, for a lack of it can harm. A student project in Kawthoolei to generate electricity from a stream was washed away during heavy rainfall, highlighting the need for a comprehensive design that accounts for multiple moving factors and best-case and worst-case scenario.

Technology transfer involves both sharing technical knowledge and embedding a culture of efficient implementation. It includes a developmental approach of iterative trials and errors, rigorous research and testing, quality assurance procedures, and attention to intuitive user experience. This culture develops and maintains systems that produce high-quality, globally competitive products. In this new culture, no one can satisfy at raw quality as finished products. No one can rest but hustle. No one can swing in the hammock during work hours.

In fact, our expertise, though diverse, remains dispersed, and we lack a culture of cohesive, large-scale collaboration that creates something remarkable. Mastering the art of collaboration—where distinct fields of knowledge are integrated—is a culture of cross-disciplinary teamwork. This culture of collaboration opens up the possibility. By studying Thailand's approach and beyond, Kawthoolei can learn how to harmonize local needs with universal principles. The path forward is not one of imitation, but adaptation—learning and innovation that respects our social values, honors our land, and shapes our future.

Latecomer Advantage

We can leap from sticks and stones to digital dominance, even as the underdog.

The U.S., a technological and industrial giant, often struggles to leapfrog into new technologies. Latecomers, in contrast, have a unique advantage in adopting innovation. As Economist Keyu Jin aptly puts it, less developed economies can often adopt the latest technologies directly from advanced nations, bypassing the long, slow, and costly intermediary steps. In contrast, the U.S., with its entrenched infrastructure, frequently lags in embracing lightweight, cutting-edge innovations.

By the early 2000s, people in Thailand, Malaysia, Taiwan, and Korea had already carried mobile phones, while widespread cell phone usage in the U.S. remained limited. The U.S. relied on its robust broadband infrastructure, landlines, and pagers. Additionally, its low population density in rural areas made investing in mobile networks less economically viable. By the late 2000s, the U.S. caught up as mobile technology became indispensable.

Adoption of Mobile phones also triggered a cascade of digital advancements. Countries with lightweight mobile networks quickly embraced mobile banking, e-commerce, delivery services, remittances, and digital transactions. Many also adopted off-grid renewable energy solutions, such as solar panels, which required minimal infrastructure compared to costly centralized grids.

International travelers arriving at New York's JFK or Chicago O'Hare airports encounter historic architectural designs that reflect a different era. While these airports remain efficient in processing passengers, they lack the technological sophistication of newer Asian airports. JFK, for instance, opened in 1948 as a state-of-the-art facility, while Beijing was still operating a military airfield for domestic travel. Today, Beijing's Daxing International Airport uses facial recognition for security checks, geothermal heat pumps for renewable energy, and RFID baggage tracking. Airports in Taiwan, Singapore, and Korea have adopted advanced technologies, allowing outbound travelers to pass through security and immigration without human immigration officers behind the glass.

For the U.S., facial recognition reflects broader priorities in the U.S.—privacy concerns, complex legislative processes, and a preference for human oversight. While these safeguards uphold essential values, they also slow the pace of innovation compared to nations unencumbered by such constraints. U.S. Immigration also let its citizens reenter into the country with a face photo without a need to open up the reentry passport.

In January 2025, the Chinese startup DeepSeek gained significant attention by developing an AI model that rivals those from the U.S.-based companies like OpenAI. DeepSeek's innovative approach has led to the creation of advanced AI models at a fraction of the cost and time typically required. This development raised concerns among investors about the future demand for high-end AI training chips, leading to a 17% drop in Nvidia's stock price overnight. DeepSeek's success shows that latecomers can still excel in AI development, proving that innovation and efficiency can help new players make a significant impact.

Progress does not always require incremental steps through outdated systems. By embracing innovation directly, Kawthoolei can leapfrog into a future defined by technology and efficiency, proving that even humble beginnings can lead to transformative growth.

Kawthoolei is seeing solar panels and satellite mobile technology usage, bypassing the need for extensive traditional grid infrastructure. These lightweight, cost-efficient solutions pave the way for the new wave of rapid progress, enabling Kawthoolei to catch up quickly and excel in future technological adoption.

AUDACITY BEYOND SURVIVAL

If we work as if our lives depend on it, we will make a difference. And our lives depend on making a difference from the status quo. Kawthoolei has already witnessed a surge in drone development and usage following the Myanmar Spring revolution. New generations—Gen Z and beyond—are innovating out of necessity, to survive and prevail. This rapid adoption of drone technology mirrors developments in Ukraine, where they have mastered and mass-produced various types of drones since the 2022 Ukraine-Russia War.

Countries like South Korea and Singapore have advanced their own defense technologies and artillery in response to regional threats. Singapore military expenditure is insane, the smallest nation having the highest militarily active, but which neighbors bother to threaten Singapore these days? Today, South Korean weapons are in high demand across Europe for their quality and competitive pricing. Survival breeds expertise.

The odds against Kawthoolei are formidable. The real battle lies not only in resisting external forces but in overcoming doubts and fears within. Challenges press in from every side, tempting us with quick fixes and foreign promises ashore that only deepen our struggles. War and poverty surround us, yet the greatest threat is internal—our own resistance to embrace audacity that progress demands.

NATIONS WORTHY TO LOOK UP

Faced with challenges far greater than those of today, visionary leaders like Park Chung Hee, Chiang Kai-shek, and Lee Kuan Yew chose transformation over stagnation, steering their nations toward industrialization and modernization.

When Park assumed leadership of South Korea, the nation was an agricultural backwater, its economy worse than that of many African nations at the time. The country had been ravaged by war, left with virtually no infrastructure or industrial capacity. At the same time South Korea has another Korea (North Korea - DPRK) that constantly threatens to obliterate South Korea's existence. Park could have focused on rebuilding South Korea's subsistence farming, and few would have questioned him. But he knew that agriculture alone would not secure South Korea's future. Park launched bold policies to drive the nation into heavy industries like shipbuilding, automobile manufacturing, and electronics. His vision laid the foundation for the South Korean economic miracle, turning the country into one of the world's most advanced economies.

In 1950 Taiwan, Chiang Kai-shek confronted a similar situation. Taiwan's economy was predominantly agricultural, and much of its infrastructure was a relic of Japanese colonial rule. Taiwan (Republic of China) was threatened by the other China (People Republic of China) with a population of a billion strong. Chiang understood that relying on farming would not protect Taiwan's sovereignty or create sustainable prosperity. His focus on industrialization, particularly in textiles and later in electronics, transformed Taiwan into a global leader in semiconductor manufacturing, a crucial sector in the modern world economy. Taiwan's path to technological dominance was born from necessity, not luxury of choice.

Lee Kuan Yew faced an even starker reality when he took charge of Singapore. This small city-state had no natural resources, was surrounded by hostile neighbors to squeeze Singapore lifeline getting external resources. Culturally, they were just a tiny minority in the lands of Malay Archipelago. Lee could have succumbed to the belief that Singapore's size and lack of resources would always limit its ambitions. Instead, he redefined the nation's trajectory, investing heavily in education, technological innovation, and creating a business-friendly environment that attracted global investment. Today, Singapore is a global hub for finance and technology, admired for its resilience and strategic foresight.

These leaders—Park, Chiang, and Lee—could have used their countries' agrarian economies, lack of resources, or war-torn pasts as reasons to remain stagnant. But they understood that technological progress and industrialization were the routes to true national security and economic strength. And they broke through it. Their stories are not just historical curiosities; they are living proof that nations at a crossroads can choose a path of innovation and transformation, in one lifetime, no matter the starting point.

Clinging to subsistence agriculture will not build the defenses needed for self-determination, nor will it create the economic prosperity essential for a secure and independent future. Just as South Korea, Taiwan, and Singapore used technological advancement as a foundation for their nation-building, so too must Kawthoolei recognize the power of science and technology as the cornerstone of its progress.

The youth of Kawthoolei need not be discouraged by the seeming distance between their current realities and the high-tech world they aspire to join. Kawthoolei's new generation of sons and daughters, both at home and all over the world, are competent and capable of standing shoulder to shoulder with peers from any nation. Have the courage to take steps like the footsteps of leaders like people of Park, Chiang, and Lee, or risk being left behind in an increasingly technological world. This is not just a call to action—it is a call to survival and to thrive.

COMPLACENCE TO HUNGER

Kawthoolei cannot afford the luxury of complacent passivity, nor can it seek refuge in the comfort of old defenses. In an era defined by technological warfare with rapid innovation, relying on outdated methods is a dangerous illusion. The enemies of tomorrow will not be deterred by the rifles and strategies of yesterday. The modern battlefield knows no borders; it thrives in cyberspace, within the silent algorithms of artificial intelligence, and in autonomous systems capable of striking with deadly precision from thousands of miles away.

History is unforgiving to nations that fail to adapt. Those that neglect STEM fields—science, technology, engineering, and mathematics—may hold land, but they may surrender their sovereignty. In the 19th century, the once-legendary Qing Dynasty of China could not withstand a smaller but technologically superior and better-organized British force. It was compelled to sign the Treaty of Nanking, surrendering its sovereignty and opening its commercial ports.

Without a robust technological infrastructure, a nation becomes vulnerable, not only to military invasion but also to cyberattacks, diplomatic coercion, and economic exploitation. For Kawthoolei, which aspires to true autonomy, defense and security will be built on the indomitable foundation of technological advancement.

Complacency is the quiet poison that corrodes our ambitions, creeping into the deepest corners of our national psyche and inuring us to the belief that mere survival is enough. Comfort is no luxury; it is a trap—one that seduces us into stagnation while the world surges ahead. This mindset of being satisfied with subsistence betrays the future Kawthoolei must strive for in a world that demands innovation and resilience as the true measures of progress.

If we allow ourselves to be satisfied with the status quo, we will remain vulnerable, easy prey for those ready to exploit our weaknesses, either becoming slave workers in our land or driven out of our land. To settle for comfort is not only shortsighted—it is a step toward irrelevance. Survival is not progress. We ought to push ourselves beyond mere existence to claim our rightful place in a world that rewards those who are bold, innovative, and forward-thinking. For a nation to thrive, it has to become a nation equipped not only with traditional defenses but with the intellectual and technological prowess needed to defend and advance in the digital age. In the wars of tomorrow, cybersecurity, artificial intelligence, and general technological superiority will be the defense that determine sovereignty. Beyond the fields of subsistence, there is a future where knowledge and innovation are our greatest shields. Innovate or perish.

ISRAEL, AGAIN, HOW IT SURVIVE

In 2024, it is not an ideal time to look up to Israel as a model while it remains perpetually entangled in conflicts with its neighbors, facing widespread international condemnation for state-led atrocities that have resulted in significant civilian suffering to Gaza in the south and Lebanon in the north. Its head of state, along with a former defense minister, faces warrants from the International Criminal Court (ICC) as of November 2024. Regardless , there are lessons to be learned from how Israel continues to survive.

Israel's survival hinges on its technological edge, with investments in defense, cybersecurity, and R&D transforming it into a global leader. Initially driven by necessity, Israel's technological advancements, such as the Iron Dome missile defense system and cybersecurity innovations, have evolved into powerful economic assets, attracting international customers seeking similar protection.

In *Start-Up Nation*, Dan Senor and Saul Singer explore how Israel, despite its small size, ongoing conflicts, and limited resources, has become a global leader in start-ups, producing more companies per capita than much larger nations. Key factors behind this success include:

> Military Training and Innovation: Israel's military, particularly elite units like Unit 8200, instills problem-solving skills, risk-taking, and teamwork, essential traits for entrepreneurship.

> Cultural Traits and Immigration: A culture of *chutzpah* (boldness) encourages risk-taking and boundary-pushing, while Israel's diverse immigrant population brings a range of perspectives that fuels creativity.

> Government Policies: Pro-innovation policies, such as tax incentives through the Yozma program and R&D grants, create a supportive environment for entrepreneurship.

> Education and Research Network: Institutions like the Technion and Weizmann Institute drive technological advancements, laying the groundwork for many start-ups.

> Global Perspective and Resilience: Israel's need for survival has fostered resilience and a global outlook, motivating entrepreneurs to pursue international markets.

Together, these elements form a unique ecosystem where innovation thrives, despite Israel's challenging circumstances.

Kawthoolei ought to establish a STEM-focused education system allocating at least 5% of its national wealth to nurture a culture of R&D and build innovation hubs. This is not about building weapons; it is about cultivating the intellectual and technological capacities needed to deter threats, neutralize risks, and defend our nation against the complex challenges of the 21st century.

We cannot sing the songs of our ancient poetry in the land of our ancestors if we cannot secure our way of life—if we cannot stand as a capable friend to neighbors, both near and far, while guarding against the forces that threaten our future.

San Fransico Bay Bridge, California   *SawLah@Photography 2023*

UKRAINE-RUSSIA CONFLICT: SHOWCASING NEW WEAPONS

The ongoing Ukraine-Russia war has demonstrated the transformative power of drone technology in modern warfare. Both Ukraine and Russia have made extensive use of drones, fundamentally changing battlefield dynamics. For Ukraine, drones have become crucial for defense and a key area of innovation, with Ukrainian engineers rapidly advancing drone technology.

Ukraine's "Army of Drones" program exemplifies how drones have leveled the playing field. Early in the war, Ukraine deployed larger drones like the Turkish Bayraktar TB2, which proved effective against Russian armor and artillery. However, as Russia's defenses evolved, Ukraine shifted focus to smaller, more agile drones. These drones, often retrofitted commercial models, have been essential for surveillance, artillery spotting, and precision strikes (Given Ukraine's open geography, Russian tanks have little shelter for concealment). Ukraine's ability to adapt and innovate has been pivotal to its resistance. By 2023, Ukraine had over 80 domestic drone manufacturers—a remarkable increase from just seven the previous year—fueling the production of these critical tools of warfare.

On the other side, Russia has also ramped up its use of drones, including increased reliance on Iranian-made Shahed-136 kamikaze drones. In 2023 alone, Russian forces deployed over 140,000 drones, with plans to expand production significantly. These drones are primarily used to target Ukrainian infrastructure and military positions, illustrating how drones have become key components in both offensive and defensive strategies.

What is particularly remarkable is how Ukraine has mobilized local talent to excel in drone innovation. From building small, first-person view (FPV) drones guided in real-time by operators, to crafting custom UAVs for reconnaissance and offensive missions, Ukrainian engineers have shown that necessity truly is the mother of invention. This conflict shows that drones are no longer just tools of war—they are *force multipliers*.

For Kawthoolei, the lesson is clear: mastering technology is essential not only for defense but also as a business opportunity. By leveraging local innovation, Kawthoolei can both secure the nation and open new avenues for economic growth. Just as today's internet and GPS, now used by consumers worldwide, began as military research, Kawthoolei's advancements could similarly pave the way for broader applications and prosperity.

DRONES IN MYANMAR CONFLICTS

In Myanmar's northeast in 2023, the Three Brotherhood Alliance—comprising the Arakan Army (AA), Ta'ang National Liberation Army (TNLA), and Myanmar National Democratic Alliance Army (MNDAA)—has made extensive use of drones as part of its military strategy. These ethnic armed groups have reportedly deployed hundreds, if not thousands, of drones to target Burmese military bases in their ongoing conflict with the Tatmadaw (Myanmar's military).

The alliance's use of drones has escalated as part of a broader guerrilla strategy, employing them for both surveillance and direct strikes, including the dropping of explosives on military outposts. These tactics align with global trends in modern warfare, where commercially available and custom-modified drones provide an accessible yet powerful tool against more conventionally equipped forces. The ability to strike from a distance with precision has allowed the alliance to seize strategic positions, especially in challenging terrains where traditional assaults are difficult.

Local manufacturing and modification capabilities within the region have bolstered these tactics, mirroring trends observed in the Ukraine-Russia war independently. Reports suggest that the Three Brotherhood Alliance has effectively integrated drones to disrupt and damage Tatmadaw infrastructure, achieving significant impact through relatively low-cost yet high-impact strikes and inflicting heavy losses on the Tatmadaw (Myanmar military). The Tatmadaw, in turn, has quickly learned from these tactics and adopts similar drone technology for counterstrikes.

THE FUTURE OF WARFARE AND DEFENSE

The future of warfare will rely far more on mechanization and technological prowess than on traditional soldiers with assault rifles. The dominant tools of combat will no longer be heavy artillery, reminiscent of World War II, with their crude, large projectiles. Instead, warfare will pivot toward intelligent missiles equipped with autonomous decision-making (localized AI) capabilities and low-or-high flying machines outfitted with GPS, sensors, and advanced microchips. These devices will gather intelligence with unmatched precision while offering offensive and counteroffensive capabilities. In this new era, firearms like the AK-47 and M-16 will seem as primitive as sticks and stones from the Stone Age.

A U.S. soldier no longer needs to fly a fighter jet risking her life but sits in front of computer monitors in a comfortable room controlling an unmanned aerial vehicle (UAV) carrying out an assigned mission.

The best defense system of today becomes vulnerable for tomorrow's attack. Drones (quadcopter, a different kind of UAV) possess a much smaller radar and thermal signature compared to traditional missiles, making them harder to detect and track. Unlike crude missiles that follow predictable trajectories through the visible sky, drones can maneuver unpredictably, change course, and even rest in hidden locations before striking at the most opportune moment. Their versatility in "hide-and-seek" tactics makes them far more elusive and dangerous. Future weapons can fly, rest and hide, and then fly again and complete its mission by itself.

Even advanced defense systems, such as Israel's renowned Iron Dome (considered one of the best air systems in the world), have struggled to counter this evolving threat. The attack in October 2024 on an Israeli army base, where inexpensive drones bypassed defenses and caused casualties, highlights the growing vulnerability even in highly fortified military systems. This serves as a stark reminder that drones are reshaping the modern battlefield, making traditional defenses increasingly obsolete. Defense system needs to constantly adapt.

SECURITY AND INTELLIGENCE

The future of intelligence gathering is no longer exclusive to military-trained personnel. Advanced nations recognize that national intelligence relies on individuals with specialized skills and talents suited to working in technical environments. In reality, U.S. intelligence personnel are far from the dramatic portrayals of movie spies—buffoons running around, dangling from airplanes, or frequenting a good-looking dude hiding a gun under shirt.

The U.S. intelligence community is staffed with engineers, scientists, accountants, and analysts who excel in fields such as applied mathematics, computer engineering, data science, electrical engineering, physical sciences, bathymetric data analysis, geodetic survey, cartography, and systems engineering. Intelligent community is filled with people who are not only technically proficient but also deeply knowledgeable in evolving international affairs, threat analysis, and early detection.

Nation-states engage in espionage in cyberspace. High-profile nations like Iran, North Korea, Russia, and China are known for competing with the West, yet Western countries also spy on one another. For instance, the revelation of U.S. surveillance on Germany caused significant embarrassment. Meanwhile, Israel's advanced intelligence and cybersecurity capabilities have even become a profitable industry.

However, intelligence is not only about technology; it is also about understanding people, cultures, regional dynamics, geopolitics, and the international system. Most of us, gaining formal education systems focus on Western history, culture, and values, often taught through the medium of the English language. This creates a gap in understanding the perspectives and thinking of neighboring countries, like Thailand and China, or India.

China, for example, systematically studies mountain peoples and ethnic connections as part of its nation building and national security strategy. Their intelligence apparatus likely knows more about us than we know about them, especially since much of our knowledge is filtered through media in languages like English. If we are to compete on the global stage, we must develop the capacity to understand our neighbors in their own languages and from their own perspectives.

Without a deep understanding of the nations around us, we cannot craft effective diplomatic strategies. Relying on the flawed belief—biased narratives—that larger nations will come to our aid is a dangerous trap. No nation is morally obliged to protect our interests, nor do we have binding treaties to guarantee such support. If they appear to offer help, it is likely because their own larger interests are at play. Accepting such assistance without caution could lead us into an even more precarious position.

Intelligence gathering today demands precision and intellectual acumen, far removed from the daring, larger-than-life field operations portrayed in mid-20th-century spy movies. It is a disciplined, often mundane, daily endeavor rather than the high-octane theatrics of a James Bond film. In the 21st Century, a patriot can defend her nation from her laptop.

INTERNATIONAL POLITICAL SYSTEM AND DEFENSE

The lack of technological understanding and awareness of the international political system was starkly displayed during Burma's recent Spring Revolution. Many in the public genuinely believed that by donating money, they could help revolutionaries purchase weapons to shoot down SAC fighter jets, which have been deliberately bombing villages, schools, and hospitals. Public enthusiasm was sincere, but their efforts bore no fruit. The public's goodwill turned sour when they realized that their donations were not secure for air defense—that is not as simple as buying a gun over the counter to shoot down planes.

Air defense requires a sophisticated, integrated system involving radar detection, control mechanisms, and advanced weaponry like the U.S.'s Terminal High Altitude Area Defense (THAAD) or other surface-to-air anti-aircraft systems. It is not a single weapon that one can point and shoot, but an elaborate system designed to detect, track, and neutralize airborne threats. Even with that sophistication, sometimes, it misses.

Moreover, in the international relation system, nations do not sell advanced weapons to just anyone with money. Weapons transactions are governed by alliances, treaties, and agreements, and are only accessible to countries within certain diplomatic frameworks. The virtues of sincerity and generosity, while noble, are insufficient to equip revolutionary forces with the capability to counter SAC's aerial bombardments. Without the necessary political alliances and technological know-how, challenging such advanced military power is a far more complex endeavor than many had initially believed.

NEW AGE DEFENSE STRATEGY

Defense strategies, too, will shift. They will depend increasingly on digital infrastructure and cyber capabilities. Warfare will move from steel and gunpowder to the realm of electric circuits and programming, where preemptive strikes can be carried out to neutralize threats before they materialize. Digital security, network infiltration, and software manipulation are fast becoming the backbone of modern defense systems—enabling the interception, disruption, and control of hostile operations in ways once thought unimaginable.

Even in localized conflicts, such as the ethnic armed resistance across Burma, drones play an increasingly prominent role. Hundreds of drones are deployed in operations against the SAC's (State Administration Council) resource-heavy military bases, with each unit relying on anti-jamming technology to maintain operational capability over long distances.

These demands call for adaptation and excellence. It is not enough to merely adapt; we must excel. Adaptation alone will leave us vulnerable, as adversaries with greater resources will always adapt faster. To truly excel, we must cultivate deep, foundational knowledge in key areas.

To design, or even to buy already designed and to apply, microchips tailored to our specific needs, we require a comprehensive understanding of how electronic components function. To control our devices effectively, we must be deep-dive, in-and-out, well-versed in harnessing electromagnetic forces. To program the software that controls these machines, we require not only programming skills but also multiple engineering principles, the experience that can bend imagination and be brave to experiment, research, and develop solutions suited to our particular challenges. Without this foundational knowledge, we risk falling further behind, and the compounding effect of this gap will make it increasingly difficult to catch up.

This path toward excellence demands an education system that prioritizes STEM disciplines. Electronic components are mass-produced and becoming affordable every day for classroom use. Public appreciation in STEM equips us with the intellectual tools necessary for survival and success in an age defined by technological warfare.

ARTIFICIAL INTELLIGENCE, FORGING THE FUTURE

The name Artificial Intelligence (AI) remains shrouded in mystery. It is neither particularly "artificial" nor truly "intelligent"; it is still software—many kinds of AI as a variety of software, though now capable of learning from data, hence the term "Machine Learning" (ML or AI).

With data, the software recognizes and builds patterns; without data, AI is still powerless. In the case of translating our Karenic language, AI cannot yet translate between major languages like English and any Karen scripts due to a lack of sufficient training data.

In 2024, John J. Hopfield and Geoffrey E. Hinton, the godfathers of AI, were honored with the *Nobel Prize in Physics* for their foundational work in neural networks, bringing AI's transformative power into sharper focus.

AI has raised as many questions as it has provided solutions. It has stirred philosophical debates—such as who holds responsibility when a machine makes independent decisions. Gratitude and accountability become complex. When dining in a restaurant where a robot serves you, whom do you thank? The engineers who programmed it? Whom do you tip? Could a software or hardware malfunction spilling a hot pot on a customer lap? Is this progress to be feared or embraced?

When software can drive a vehicle more safely than humans, as cars in newer models equipped with advanced safety features, what becomes of the driver's license test? Our generation starts riding in smart cars that can drive themselves, but our children will only know cars that do. These vehicles will eventually know where we want to go, learning from our patterns of movement and preferences. Behold, they already start knowing and controlling us.

One way to think of AI is as a personal guardian, tapping on your shoulder to help you avoid embarrassment or injury. Previously, software was thought to be capable of syntactic understanding but now advanced to semantic understanding, generating insights at speeds far beyond human capability. In a different perspective, AI can be seen as a vehicle that amplifies productivity, taking one further on tedious tasks and working fast and tirelessly on behalf of its user. One telling example is that AI has helped humans crunch data to find Covid-19 vaccine in one year, the task of traditionally a decade-long quest.

Like machines can travel autonomously, missiles now feature intelligent guidance systems, and soon, weapons themselves will possess advanced intelligence. Control centers may eventually rely on a network of AI software. Whereas, humans could become powerless if software takes full control.

Betting our lives on software may seem peculiar, yet it has become a routine part of modern existence. Autopilot systems control our planes and cars, while hospitals, energy grids, and financial institutions all depend on computer algorithms. As software increasingly takes on decision-making roles without conscious intent, the human obligation for careful, deliberate oversight becomes essential. Software cannot run loose in the wild.

Intelligent yet sentient human beings still need to monitor, control, and validate generative AI outputs. Machines may act intelligent, but machines are still machines. Machine could cut you in half and it wouldn't feel a gag.

Now, with large language models (LLM) drawing from global data sets of trillions, software can outperform humans in many areas, able to generate human-like language and perform related tasks. Machines do not tire like humans, who are bound by flesh and blood and metabolism. Still, there persist challenges in AI capturing the subtle nuances of idiomatic expressions.

With AI as data-crunching software, data becomes so valuable that NVIDIA CEO Jensen Huang remarked, "A country's data becomes its natural resources." China exemplifies this; with its massive population and structured data systems, it has gained a competitive edge in AI, leveraging it for commerce, transportation, government administration, security, finance, and manufacturing.

Advancement of AI is unstoppable, which raises essential questions for Kawthoolei how to harness this new power. First, Kawthoolei will have to start from a blank slate—as with everything else. The nation needs structured and organized data to be usable in training models. Even our naming conventions, spelling, accents, and tones must be standardized. Our locations and place names must also be consistent. If we hope to use AI in infrastructure, our roads must meet engineering standards and precise geolocation. We need to lay the groundwork for success in agriculture, administration, and commerce. For small-scale data management, Excel spreadsheets suffice. However, the next step lies in leveraging large-scale data to extract patterns and insights, driving business growth with the power of AI.

Those who control machines will wield power, while those who lack control may come to fear. AI can make independent decisions within a limited framework, but Artificial General Intelligence (AGI)—capable of multi-tasking and self-teaching through a series of decisions across various contexts—remains on the horizon yet to be feared. Machines cannot surpass human morality when they learn from humans. They absorb human data and mimic behavior, sometimes displaying wisdom, yet at other times reflecting human folly.

Humans often think they are *in* control but *under* control. Most software today is embedded with AI. Our social media, searches, views, politics, networks, intellectual content, purchasing habits, and even our thinking are already shaped by AI algorithms. If humans find pleasure in sensation, AI will deepen that immersion. If humans seek intellectual content, AI will provide material that elevates them toward higher ground. Machines grind on, as always, without remorse or empathy. For us, remaining detached offers no protection either. Is doom or bloom, the road to be taken.

The future is one of human-machine collaboration—a partnership that has always characterized technological progress. Those who harness this collaboration will thrive, while those left behind will, as always, fall victim to the progress of others. This time, however, we have access to the transformative power of technology; it is up to us to start learning, experimenting, and making the most of this progress to shape our nation's future.

To embrace technological progress, we do not need to start from scratch; we can stand on the shoulders of many giants whose work has paved the way. Many open-source software programs are freely available, and numerous models can be trained. Generational energy and institution funding flow into AI development, and the energy of our youth must match and excel in this field to be competitive. Entry barriers are low in terms of knowledge access and available tools, a blessing in this age of software propagation.

A NOTE TO STUDENT EXPLORING FIELD OF STUDY

I may be biased. But I hope to see the new generation of Karen students with opportunities to study at world-class universities boldly consider pursuing Computer Science or some engineering fields that tie back to software. Learning the foundations of computing and engineering principles can unlock a promising future, especially for those with a natural curiosity, a flair for design, artistic and creative imagination, and a solid STEM foundation.

Law and policy are increasingly being translated into code. Business workflows become algorithms. Code becomes law. Those who control the code hold the power to multiply force and influence. Today, learning to code is easier than before---AI can generate syntax, and tools and resources are abundant. In this new landscape, coders hold the power akin to modern-day wizards.

Engineering is more than just a career or skill—it is a way of life that can play a vital role in rebuilding Kawthoolei and securing its place on the global stage. While classical programming may no longer be in high demand, rapidly growing fields like AI engineering present incredible opportunities. Working as a software architect, for example, can be challenging and exhausting, with many lives and businesses relying on such expertise. Yet, it is a highly rewarding path, especially for those ready to seize this generational opportunity.

Students selecting a major can explore Computer Engineering, Data Science, and Robotic Engineering—fields that shape the future of innovation and creation. While AI may handle simple coding, humans are still essential for designing and communicating with AI to build meaningful solutions. AI will improve in software creation but physical engineering, AI will still lag behind since software code are in text format that AI can learn from but physical engineering are not. Even if one cannot pursue engineering as a full-fledged major, people could still learn to be tech savvy. The ability to command and control powerful machines remains a timeless axiom of power.

Kawthoolei needs a broad spectrum of engineering expertise—technocrats with deep knowledge in fields often overlooked within our community. Chemical and materials scientists will be vital for developing new products; biologists, for managing our rich biodiversity; and geologists, for uncovering and understanding the resources beneath our land—not so outsiders can discover and control our treasures, but so we ourselves can take ownership and manage them with wisdom and skill.

THE FUTURE IS DIGITAL

Banking, healthcare, commerce—nearly every industry has embraced the digital shift. Both public and private institutions now interact with their customers through digital platforms. Investment, and everything financial, has already gone Fintech (computer programs and other technology used to support or enable banking and financial services). Transactions, contracts, and trades now flow seamlessly through digital systems. In the U.S., while cash remains an option, the majority of transactions occur digitally. Fiat currency, traditionally controlled by centralized nation-states, has largely moved away from physical form; only 25% of the U.S. monetary supply exists as paper money, with the rest circulating digitally. Governments no longer print money to expand supply— they simply adjust zeros, a process that is as technical as it is political.

Also, a new movement is emerging called Web3, where users can read, write, and own their content on the web. Decentralized finance enables peer-to-peer, bankless transactions, while decentralized social platforms will allow users to own their data and identity. This tokenized economy represents a potential paradigm shift in the new interconnected world.

Enter cryptocurrency—a revolutionary monetary system independent of nation-states. Unlike fiat currency, cryptocurrencies operate on decentralized blockchain technology, ensuring transparency and security through immutable digital ledgers. These currencies are not just digital in nature but inherently designed to challenge the monopoly of centralized monetary systems.

For Kawthoolei, an independent monetary system is no longer a luxury—it is a necessity. Such a system must withstand external pressures, uphold dignity, and enable robust commerce and trade both domestically and globally. Cryptocurrency offers a promising solution, but trust is essential for its success. This trust must be built on a foundation of solid technology and guided by experts with deep knowledge of monetary systems and blockchain innovation—and definitely backed by a worthy economy.

A trusted cryptocurrency system has the potential to empower Kawthoolei, securing its economy, facilitating trade, and safeguarding its sovereignty. With thoughtful implementation, it could elevate Kawthoolei's role in the global economy, proving that independence and progress can thrive in the digital age.

The adoption of digital and cryptocurrency bypasses traditional barriers like physical infrastructure, making them especially appealing for regions with limited resources. Thailand, for instance, is rapidly embracing digital money, and its public has adapted comfortably to digital transactions. At a casual night bazaar of mountain town Mae-Hong-Song, you can easily buy a bag of coffee using Line (app) credit, where vendor could not bother with the hassle of making change for cash. Similarly, in many African countries, mobile money systems have thrived overcoming limited infrastructure. These systems reduce costs, streamline transactions, and extend financial access to remote areas. However, caution remains crucial to safeguard against scams and ensure security.

Kawthoolei has an opportunity to learn from these successes and challenges, crafting a monetary system that is not only innovative but also resilient and inclusive, paving the way for a digital future empowering dignity and sovereignty.

The future is already at our doorstep, ready to help us embark on the path forward.

FROM HESITATION TO CUTTING EDGE COLLABORATION

Shaped by a combination of limited exposure in those fields and reluctance to learn out of their comfort zone, the hesitation of many Karen people toward science and technology perpetuates a cycle where fear and unfamiliarity feed each other. Not knowing how to control a machine breeds fear, and that fear turns into a dismissive attitude toward learning to master it. Yes, like much of the modern world, most Karen people rely daily on the power of science and technology.

We eat the fruits of science every day, so have we yet to appreciate it. To break free from this paralyzing cycle, we must summon the courage to embrace the advances that science offers and cultivate a clear, logical thinking in Kawthoolei. Without industries and forward-thinking approaches, we remain trapped in a constant state of hardship—a recurring cycle of misery, natural and man-made disasters that repeat season after season.

Many of our youth have already embraced the pursuit of scientific knowledge; yet what is needed is a shared, connected, widespread enthusiasm that can dissolve lingering hesitations. In mass participation, we move together toward a future defined by security, progress, and prosperity.

Not everyone needs to pursue the same field of STEM, or even a STEM major, for Kawthoolei to progress. A thriving society requires a diversity of expertise—designers, architects, environmental specialists, user experience experts, psychologists, and even those in sports science—all working together to address human needs, environmental sustainability, animal welfare, and water health while incorporating aesthetics to ensure holistic progress.

In technology firms, the workforce is not limited to software engineers; professionals from a wide range of disciplines contribute to marketing, service support, design, user experience, and requirements gathering. During my years in a global technology consulting field, I worked alongside individuals from diverse academic backgrounds—ranging from aerospace, electrical, and civil engineering to computer science, sports management, social sciences, and even divinity studies. These varied talents collaborated as a team, each bringing unique strengths to create innovative solutions. Kawthoolei's progress will be built on the same foundation of diversity and collaboration.

What we need is the spark of widespread enthusiasm to ignite large-scale collaboration.

Breaking the Chains of Nonsense

Excessive and widespread superstition harms. A nation striving for progress cannot afford to be consumed by irrational beliefs. When we embrace nonsense, it reinforces itself through confirmation bias—our tendency to selectively gather evidence that aligns with preexisting beliefs, even if those beliefs are entirely unfounded.

For example, if one is convinced of the existence of UFOs in the 80s and 90s, they will inevitably "see" them in the sky—an occurrence often reported predominantly in the United States. Similarly, if one believes in half-human, half-devil creatures lurking in the forest, their senses may create "confirmations" of such fearful imaginations. Over the internet, there will be plenty of data will confirm our bias. When weekend assemblies teach nonsense every week, they do harm, instead of fostering spiritual empowerment.

To break free from this cycle, we will need to cultivate critical thinking and nurture scientific curiosity. Otherwise, we will be a people of gullibility, easily fooled from left and right—the left and the right. Our progress depends on engaging with the body of globally validated scientific knowledge and building on proven discoveries rather than falling prey to superstitions.

The path forward rests on intellectual rigor and a commitment to evidence-based understanding —not on clinging to comforting illusions or fearful nonsense.

Test and verify to know; be humble to and learn the unknown.

PONDERING OUR EXISTENCE THROUGH ASTRONOMY

Beyond the hard, cold realms of technical subjects, STEM brims with excitement and profound philosophical questions about existence. Among its fields, Astronomy stands out as a window offering glimpses that transcend worldly affairs. As one of the oldest disciplines, Astronomy has long sparked curiosity, inspiring ancient seekers in their quest for the divine.

My intellectual journey was marked by an introduction to the history of the philosophy of science, where ancient thinkers gazed up at the starry night sky, seeking answers to the mysteries of the celestial realm. From the ancient Greeks, who laid the groundwork for systematic observation, to the quiet yet significant preservation of scientific principles in the Islamic world, and then to the West with Copernicus and Isaac Newton, the study of celestial bodies has always sparked spiritual questions that led to the pursuit of natural science.

During medieval times, alchemists dreamed boldly, but their visions crumbled without the foundation of scientific principles—yet in their failure, they laid the groundwork for the scientific method to emerge.

From the musings of ancient thinkers to the breakthroughs of Copernicus-Newton's classical physics, and Einstein's theory of relativity, humanity has uncovered nature's deepest secrets, including the immense power locked within the atom. This revelation, first unleashed during World War II in Hiroshima and Nagasaki, Japan, not only redefined the boundaries of science but also forged a new world order—one in which we find ourselves entangled today.

While the ancient Greeks looked to the skies to count stars and chart their movements, the ancestors of the Karen people watched the heavens, embedding their observations in ancient poems.

derr mu du har tha lay lah (အမှၢ်ထူၣ်ဟါသလ့ၤလါ)

Marking the arrival of the first month of the year with the *Pleiades* (clustered stars) stay above head at dusk.

These verses, still recited today, guide the marking of calendars for sowing and harvest seasons, celebrations, and divine commencements. The People watched celestial revelations through distant stars, connecting the divine to the natural world.

Astronomy teaches us that humanity resides on a peculiar planet orbiting a typical star in a quiet corner of the Milky Way—one among billions of stars, in countless galaxies of a universe whose end remains unknown. This perspective humbles us, revealing Earth as an infinitesimally small and fragile "A Pale Blue Dot", as an American astronomer and planetary scientist Carl Sagan made the phrase, inspired by an image of the earth taken from 6 billion kilometers away. Humanity's physical insignificance is a stark reminder to live lives of dignity, courage, and virtue, leaving a legacy of good on this planet. Though small in the cosmic scale, our unique existence on this Earth calls for a life worth living—a testament to the greatness possible within our fleeting moment in the universe.

Astronomy tells the story of the universe, the cosmos, and the history of Earth itself—a grand narrative of every chemical element, seen and unseen, organic and inorganic. It tells a complete story of creation.

Do we limit our horizons to teachings shared casually in weekend assemblies, or do we open ourselves to the vastness of the universe through the lens of scientific exploration? The cosmos, immense and ungraspable, invites us to expand our perspective and ask larger questions about who we are and who we can become and what memory we leave after our end of time here.

As we contemplate the vastness of the cosmos, we are also called to reflect on our identity and purpose as a people. Will we let the label of "ethnic minority" define us, or will we rise beyond it to claim our rightful place in history? Shall we shine brightly like a star, only to glow into eternity, leaving a fleeting moment yet brilliant legacy, like the light of a supernova? Shall we embrace the divine power bestowed upon us—the courage to rise, to lead, and to guide humanity forward? Kawthoolei virtues are worth shining to the world.

Our ancient folktales tell of a people of the first born we are (Poe-Wal-Koe), a kinder nation chosen since time immemorial. We are no less capable than any other nation to rise, to lead, and to be an example for others. We are not ashamed of who we are, but instead embrace our potential with dignity, honor, and purpose. The choice is our generation to keep living as a flicker of dim light or to stand as a beacon of hope on the hill for the generations to come.

A world without Kawthoolei is deprived. A universe without Kawthoolei is incomplete.

A Worthy Path for Kawthoolei's Go-getters

To create a culture of go-getters and trailblazers, we invest in education that encourages creativity, innovation, and STEM fields—empowering our people to not just follow paths but to forge new ones—knowing that every great nation rises not only from its resources but from the indomitable will of its people to solve problems, innovate, and lead.

Kawthoolei stands at a pivotal moment in its journey, and to achieve true progress, it needs a new generation with a can-do attitude—a spirit that embraces challenges, solves problems, and blazes new trails. The old mentality of "*mar-ta-thay-bar*" or "*per-terr-klerr-eh*"—expressions of doubt, uncertainty, or passivity—must be shed. These phrases, which roughly translate to "I can't do it" or "I don't know how," reflect a mindset that no longer serves a community striving for self-determination and growth.

Kawthoolei must rekindle an inner yes-I-can spirit—a mindset of resilience and bold action. Embrace challenges with determination, and nurture the entrepreneurial, problem-solving attitudes that will guide our future. Just as nations have harnessed the energy of their young talent to build high-rise, tech-driven, modern societies, Kawthoolei, too, fosters a generation that believes nothing is beyond their reach.

Kawthoolei needs more engineers, more builders, more inventors—creative minds skilled with their hands and rich in imagination, capable of solving problems with the resources at hand. Kawthoolei needs more technocrats, more technically sound thinkers, and more technology-savvy talents who understand and appreciate the direction in which the world is moving. We no longer dwell in the 18th century, at the margins of humanity.

To not let our people from sinking further, our vision of innovation must rise beyond the coordination of receiving aid. Kawthoolei is not only a land of memory and struggle—it is a land of possibility, worthy of becoming a hub of ingenuity, a center of intellectual pursuit, and a beacon of progress. Let us not wait to be lifted by others. Let us rise—by the strength of our minds, the skill of our hands, and the courage to build what has never been built before.

Chapter 14

Rebuild the Nation with Diverse Talents

The talents that rebuild Kawthoolei do not need to be born in Kawthoolei. A thriving nation attracts minds from all corners of the world, recognizing that innovation and leadership transcend borders. We must create an environment that welcomes and nurtures talent, regardless of origin, if we are to strengthen our nation's foundations.

The U.S. economic powerhouse epitomizes the art of talent attraction. Top-tier talents are not always U.S.-born. As of this writing, seven of the world's eight most valuable companies—each worth trillions—are based in the United States. Remarkably, four of their CEOs are foreign-born: Satya Nadella of Microsoft (India), Jensen Huang of NVIDIA (Taiwan), Sundar Pichai of Alphabet-Google (India), and Elon Musk of Tesla (South Africa). Their leadership is a testament to the power of diversity and openness in nation-building, demonstrating that talent, when given the right environment, can flourish anywhere.

If we aspire to unlock our potential on the global stage, we must consider embracing a similar openness. However, for the Karen people, the issue has rarely been about exclusion; if anything, it is the opposite—a people of *hospitality*, officially enshrined in our national anthem. Historically, we have been open—too open—welcoming everyone without proper discernment. Time and again, our generosity and trust have been exploited, yet our compassion remains steadfast, undeterred by these hard-learned lessons. Perhaps, the Karen people naturally err on the side of compassion.

Openness must be paired with wisdom. If we wish to be a respectable host having good guests in our house, we must first build a strong fence, a secure gate, and a reliable gatekeeping system. True openness is not boundless vulnerability; it is a balance between hospitality and safeguarding the integrity of our home so that our property and our personal space are not constantly violated.

With that understanding, the talent to rebuild Kawthoolei should not be restricted solely to descendants of Karen people. The opportunity extends to anyone who honors and is committed to the vision of rebuilding Kawthoolei, regardless of their ethnic origin or place of birth. History shows us that greatness is achieved by embracing those who share a common purpose, not simply a common ancestry. Kawthoolei is open and welcoming as the Karen people are.

Team USA, a powerful example found in the 2019 International Mathematics Competition, who secured first place was primarily composed of individuals of Asian descent, with one member of mixed Caucasian heritage. The group photo circulated online, sparking humorous comments about the irony of an Asian-looking U.S. team defeating the Chinese team.

The students are younger than 23 years old. Their success demonstrates the value of diversity when unified by shared ambition and dedication. Those who can contribute to Kawthoolei's resurgence, whether Karen descents or otherwise, should be welcomed if they embody the spirit of renewal and commitment to our cause.

True strength lies in the collective force of those who share our values and dedication, rather than merely bloodlines.

The ideals of Kawthoolei inspire progress through an openness that welcomes talent and new citizenship. This inclusive vision is rooted in the belief that building a strong nation requires contributions from diverse minds, regardless of origin. As President Ronald Reagan once observed, "You can go to live in France, but you cannot become a Frenchman. You can go to live in Germany or Turkey or Japan, but you cannot become a German, a Turk, or a Japanese. But anyone, from any corner of the Earth, can come to live in America and become an American."

Kawthoolei embodies this principle of inclusivity. True progress comes not from closing doors, but from creating a space where all those who honor the ideals of Kawthoolei—politically, socially, morally, spiritually, and intellectually—can contribute, regardless of their background. In doing so, we build a nation that thrives on the diversity of talent and shared purpose.

Anyone who dedicates their life to Kawthoolei can be a citizen of Kawthoolei—much like Ruth, the gentile who became the mother of ancient Jewish people. As Ruth proclaimed, "Please do not insist on my leaving you or forsaking you. Wherever you go I will go, and wherever you live I will live. Your people will be my people, and your God will be my God. Wherever you die, I will die and be buried there" (Ruth 1:16 CNB). This kind of commitment is what binds a people and builds a nation—where belonging is rooted in shared values, purpose, and sacrifice.

Wherever you go I will go, and wherever you live I will live. Your people will be my people.
Wherever you die, I will die and be buried there. [Ruth 1:16 CNB]

In Kawthoolei, after the 2021 uprising against the Burmese military's coup, many Burmese urban dwellers have joined the ongoing revolution as members of the People's Defense Force (PDF) under the command of the KNLA (KAF), sacrificing their limbs, lives, and talents. Their contributions—whether in tactical operations, engineering innovations, or acts of unmatched bravery—are reshaping the future of military engagement. Witnessing their hometown friends turned comrades fall in battle—a soldier's brain falls off by ambush attack, intestines busted by bullets—yet they still march forward with unshakable courage. Their sacrifices and dedication will forever be remembered in the history of Kawthoolei, a testament to the spirit of resilience and unity that defines the revolution.

A Karen commander officer leading the battle seeing the bravery and sacrifice of the youth from the cities, he noted that we, the Karen fighters, are embarrassed by the superior bravery of PDF, the new generation fighters from urban areas.

Again, the United State thrives in making space for talents around the world. Weeks before the 2024 Paris Olympic torch was lit, there was a lesser spectacle: the 2024 International Mathematical Olympiad (IMO) in Bath, England, where the United States claimed first place. This victory marked the first time the U.S. had taken the top spot in 25 years, a remarkable achievement driven by a diverse group of talents.

The USA six-member winning team—Lefkowitz (17, Connecticut), Pothapragada (18, Illinois), Wan (18, Florida), Wang (16, New Jersey), Qiao (Tiger) Zhang (16, California), and Tang (18, California)—came from a variety of backgrounds, yet all distinguished themselves in the American Mathematics Competitions (AMC), organized by the Mathematical Association of America (MAA). Their last names tell a story of cultural diversity, with two of European origin and the others of East Asian descent, names that may have once been the target of teasing as "funny." Yet, their collective achievement speaks not only to their individual brilliance, but to the power of dedication and talent that transcends geography, origin, and the stereotypes attached to names. Their success is a testament to the boundless potential found in diversity.

The coach, Po-Shen Loh (Chinese: 罗博深; born June 18, 1982, the name sounds like Karen/Knyaw name), is an American mathematician known for his expertise in combinatorics (the field of mathematics concerned with problems of selection, arrangement, and operation within a finite or discrete system). He is a professor at Carnegie Mellon University and served as the national coach of the United States International Mathematical Olympiad (IMO) team from 2014 to 2023, leading them to numerous victories on the global stage.

Born in Madison, Wisconsin, U.S.A., to Singaporean immigrants, Loh's success exemplifies how diverse backgrounds strengthen national achievement. Singapore may have lost one of its fine talents in Po-Shen Loh, but it has also gained many from its neighboring countries, including sons and daughters of the Karen people, many of whom are working in the services and tech industry of Singapore. If Kawthoolei can make a proper space, there would be Karen talents eager to serve Kawthoolei under good leadership.

Singapore's strategic openness to talent drawing in minds from across the region fuels its progress. Ten of thousands of college graduates from Burma are working in Singapore contributing to its progress without the need of Singapore nursing those talents during their tender age. Scholarship programs in Singapore universities also attract bright minds from the region. Remarkably 25% of graduate students at National University of Singapore (NUS) are international students. They contribute to research and innovation while universities also profit from providing higher education as a service. By offering opportunities and creating a nurturing environment, Singapore has turned into a hub where talent from diverse backgrounds can thrive, contributing to its rapid development and global standing.

R&D Investment Per Researcher: 2009 – 2016
Constant 2012 dollars

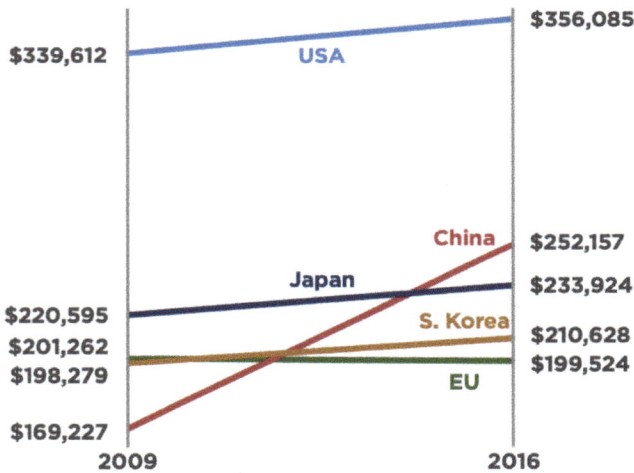

USA — $339,612 → $356,085

China — $169,227 → $252,157

Japan — $220,595 → $233,924

S. Korea — $201,262 → $210,628

EU — $198,279 → $199,524

2009 — 2016

.7000

National Science Foundation
ncses.nsf.gov/indicators

The United States has long reaped the benefits of an inflow of foreign-born scientists and engineers, who bring invaluable skills and knowledge. This broad category includes both long-term U.S. residents with deep roots in the country and recent immigrants who still maintain strong ties to their countries of origin. In 2017, half of the foreign-born individuals in the U.S. with the highest degrees in science and engineering (S&E) were from Asia, with India (23%) and China (10%) leading the way. Among foreign-born holders of S&E doctorates, China provided the largest share (24%), followed by India (15%). These trends have been consistent since at least 2003. Go to a U.S. hospital, you will meet a specialist or MD from China or India.

In academia, nearly half (49%) of U.S.-trained postdoctoral researchers are foreign-born, and 29% of full-time S&E faculty are also from overseas.

Kawthoolei stands to gain immensely from individuals with varied backgrounds, expertise, and experiences who are committed to its progress. By welcoming both locally rooted and foreign-born talents, Kawthoolei can tap into a vast reservoir of knowledge and innovation, driving development forward and ensuring its future is shaped by the most capable minds, regardless of their origins.

At the University of California's 12 campuses, in 2023, 44% of postdoctoral scholars were of Asian descent. Diversity and talent drive research and innovation within California's higher education institutions. Each year, scholars in California are awarded Nobel Prizes for groundbreaking discoveries in fields such as chemistry, biology, and other scientific disciplines.

The Kawthoolei Government could establish a diaspora talent program modeled after successful international examples. India's Overseas Citizen of India (OCI) initiative offers individuals with Indian ancestry (parents or grandparents) the opportunity to reconnect through special residency rights, while Israel's Birthright program invites young members of the Jewish diaspora to visit and experience their ancestral homeland.

Plenty of success stories offer a powerful lesson for Kawthoolei: attracting diverse talents—honest, skilled, and visionary individuals—while strictly rejecting thieves, scammers, gamblers, and lechers. By welcoming scholars from all backgrounds, Kawthoolei should cultivate an environment that fosters research, innovation, and collective knowledge.

Embracing diverse talents is essential to rebuilding a nation; to ignore this is both shortsighted and irresponsible.

A Glance at Global Talent Strategies

The United States: A Melting Pot of Innovation

Kawthoolei could emulate aspects of the U.S. approach by establishing a highly selective visa program for skilled workers in fields critical to its development in technology, education, or health. However, Kawthoolei must also guard against the pitfalls of an unchecked system. The U.S.'s lottery-based H-1B selection process has often led to an oversupply of applicants, and there have been instances where it has been critiqued for displacing local talent. For Kawthoolei, the focus must remain on targeting the skills that will directly contribute to the growth and sustainability of its unique context.

While we find ourselves beneath an insecure sky, where the threat of bombs looms overhead, attracting talent might seem our least priority now. Likewise, this sense of insecurity is mirrored in our leadership and authority—hesitant in its resolve and lacking confidence to openly invite its people. Yet, overlooking the wealth of potential talent within our reach would be irresponsible, unworthy of leaders who fail to look outward and forward.

Singapore: A Strategic Balance of Local and Global Talent

Singapore offers a different but equally compelling model. Known for its strict yet pragmatic immigration policies, Singapore attracts talent by focusing on high-value industries such as biotechnology, information technology, and finance. The government's *Employment Pass* system is carefully calibrated to balance the influx of foreign professionals with the protection of local employment. Singapore's rigorous focus on education, coupled with its robust support for startups and research through grants and tax incentives, makes it a destination for innovation.

Kawthoolei could learn much from Singapore's strategy of selective immigration. A specialized employment pass system that focuses on sectors such as green technology, public health, or education could help develop a highly skilled workforce without overwhelming the local economy. Singapore's reliance on education as a backbone for its talent policy also offers an important lesson: Kawthoolei should invest in building top-tier educational institutions to nurture homegrown talent and attract foreign scholars who can work together.

Israel: Cultivating Talent from Within and Abroad

Israel's success as a "Startup Nation" is often attributed to its ability to integrate military service with the development of technological expertise. Unit 8200, the Israeli military's elite intelligence unit, has produced some of the world's leading tech entrepreneurs. But beyond its internal cultivation of talent, Israel also employs immigration as a nation-building tool. Through the *Law of Return*, which grants any Jew the right to settle in Israel, the country has continuously attracted a global diaspora eager to contribute to the nation's security, culture, and economy.

The Israeli model demonstrates the importance of marrying national identity with a global outlook. While Kawthoolei's path may not involve a formal military structure, it can foster institutions that encourage technical and leadership training. More importantly, Kawthoolei could also create pathways for its diaspora to return and contribute, whether through streamlined residency options or offering incentives for those with valuable skills in governance, education, or industry.

CHINA: HARNESSING FOREIGN TALENT FOR NATIONAL AMBITIONS

In recent decades, China has transitioned from being a manufacturing hub to a global leader in technology and innovation. Central to this transformation is the *Thousand Talents Plan*, a program designed to attract top foreign researchers and entrepreneurs to China. The country has aggressively invested in research and development (R&D) while offering attractive financial incentives and cutting-edge infrastructure to lure foreign talent.

Yet China's success in attracting talent goes beyond monetary incentives. By building world-class educational institutions and cultivating an ecosystem of innovation, China ensures that both domestic and foreign talents can thrive. For Kawthoolei, this points to the necessity of creating an ecosystem that not only attracts talent but also nurtures it. A comprehensive strategy might include establishing partnerships with international universities, developing technology hubs, and offering R&D grants to encourage innovation in areas critical to the nation's development.

CRAFTING KAWTHOOLEI'S PATH FORWARD

Kawthoolei stands at a crossroads, where it must decide how to shape its future in a rapidly globalizing world. The success stories of the U.S., Singapore, Israel, and China each offer valuable insights, but Kawthoolei's unique cultural, political, and economic conditions mean that its path must be carefully tailored.

A talent-attracting strategy for Kawthoolei should:

- **Develop Selective Immigration Policies**: Looking forward, Kawthoolei should focus on training, attracting, and retaining local professionals in high-value sectors while maintaining a clear policy framework to protect local employment.

- **Nurture Homegrown Talent**: Inspired by Israel's focus on internal development, Kawthoolei must prioritize building world-class institutions to train local leaders in technology, governance, and education.
- **Leverage Diaspora and Regional Talent**: Kawthoolei can take a page from Israel's Law of Return, encouraging its diaspora to return and contribute. In addition, it could attract talent from nearby regions that share similar values and aspirations.
- **Invest in Education and Innovation**: Learning from China's massive investment in R&D, Kawthoolei could create research hubs and innovation zones that drive economic growth and place the nation on the global map.

BUILDING A FUTURE OF INNOVATION AND TALENT

The key to Kawthoolei success stands at its ability to attract and cultivate talent from around the world. By drawing on the experiences of nations that have harnessed the power of immigration and innovation, Kawthoolei can create an environment where the best minds thrive and where the future is crafted now.

In defining skilled workers, particularly within the field of Science and Engineering (S&E), the U.S. National Science Board adopts a broad classification that encompasses a wide array of professions. According to their framework, the S&E workforce includes:

- Biological, agricultural, and environmental life scientists: Professionals working in fields related to the study of living organisms and ecosystems, focusing on areas such as biodiversity, environmental conservation, and agricultural innovation.
- Computer and mathematical scientists: Specialists in software development, data analysis, artificial intelligence, cryptography, and computational modeling.
- Physical scientists: These individuals work in fields like physics, chemistry, astronomy, and material science, driving innovation in industries ranging from healthcare to aerospace.
- Social scientists: Experts in psychology, economics, sociology, and political science who analyze human behavior and societal trends to inform policy and organizational strategy.
- Engineers (all types): This broad category includes civil, electrical, mechanical, chemical, and industrial engineers, among others, who design, build, and improve systems, structures, and products.
- S&E Postsecondary Teachers: Educators and researchers at universities who contribute to the advancement of knowledge in these scientific and engineering disciplines.

This broad classification emphasizes the diverse nature of the S&E workforce, encompassing both research-driven and applied professions that contribute to various sectors of the economy. Kawthoolei, in seeking to attract talent, could apply this broad framework to identify and target skilled individuals in these critical fields for national development.

NURTURING HOMEGROWN TALENT IS A PRIORITY

Many of the Karen new generation may lack good internet access, but that is not an excuse. There are many others who live outside the war zone, with the ability to access resources and educate themselves. The opportunities exist for those willing to seek them out. The challenge is clear: adapt, learn, and prepare, or be left behind as the world surges forward.

Some parents have failed to instill in their children a meaningful path, leaving them adrift without a sense of responsibility or purpose. Yet, there are also parents who have guided their children well, raising them to contribute positively to society and take responsibility for their future. The difference lies in the values imparted at home, and the next generation must decide which path they will follow.

HUMAN CHAMPION VS. MACHINE INTELLIGENCE: A HUNDRED MILLION CAPTIVATED

What were our youth doing while a hundred million others stayed awake past midnight?

More than 100 million people, primarily from the younger generation, were riveted by the power of artificial intelligence during the historic 2016 match between Google DeepMind's AlphaGo and South Korean Go champion Lee Sedol. This event was more than a competition between human and machine—it was a wake-up call for the world, a demonstration of how AI—a software that learns from patterns— is reshaping the future and challenging human intelligence. The future is unfolding rapidly, and those who are unprepared will be left behind.

The game of Go, an ancient strategy game over 2,500 years old, was once considered too complex for any machine to conquer. Even AI experts believed that a computer would not defeat a top Go player for at least another decade. But AlphaGo changed everything. Through deep learning and neural networks—a computing system that uses interconnected nodes to process data and learn from it—AlphaGo defeated Lee Sedol, one of the greatest Go players in history, winning four out of five games. This was not just a triumph of technology; it was a resounding statement about how quickly progress can overtake those who fail to prepare. Fast forward eight years 2024, now AI is permeating in every aspect of our life in consumer application and industrial automation.

The younger generation in countries like Israel, Singapore, South Korea, and Taiwan are building their nations by pushing boundaries, mastering technology, and preparing for the future. The Karen youth cannot afford to be aloof, nor can the educated remain unappreciative. A lack of appreciation diverts resources into unproductive spaces. Seeking temporary distractions while assuming Kawthoolei will always remain unchanged—or failing to equip oneself with critical skills—will lead only to irrelevance and demise.

While many young people across the world are mastering AI, programming, and technology, few among the Karen youth are stepping into this new frontier. It is easy to blame poor internet access in war-torn regions, yet many young Karen are outside the conflict zone with full access to online resources. Still, many remain distracted, disengaged, or unaware of the immense opportunities at their fingertips. The tools to expand their horizons are within reach—but the will to pursue them is lacking. Appreciation of STEM is weak and sometimes disingenuously hostile among the older generation. Likewise, the highly educated show little enthusiasm and appreciation on what lies ahead with technology potentially rearranging from finances to political economy to geopolitics.

The defeat of Lee Sedol was not just a symbolic moment in the competition between human and machine—it was a warning. Those who rest on tradition, without adapting and evolving, will be overtaken by progress.

The Karen youth should recognize that without developing skills, acquiring knowledge, and engaging with the future, they will not only be outpaced—they will be replaced.

And not a single bullet will need to be fired.

GREAT REPLACEMENT WARNING

Some Karen, bearing the deep trauma of Burmese atrocities, viewing all Burmese as "Ber-yaw" (a derogatory term used to describe Burmese military and the people alike), may find it difficult to accept the idea of Kawthoolei embracing non-Karen people in large numbers. This resistance stems from the pain of oppression and the fear of dilution of their identity. However, this insular mindset could hinder the progress of rebuilding Kawthoolei.

In the U.S., a similar fear exists among certain groups, notably among white supremacists, who believe in the "Great Replacement" theory—a conspiracy claiming that white people are being systematically replaced by non-white populations. In August 2017, during the "Unite the Right" rally in Virginia State, this belief was loudly proclaimed when demonstrators marched with torches, chanting, "YOU WILL NOT REPLACE US." From an outsider's perspective, — especially I for one among many Asian observers—this spectacle of fear and defensiveness can seem both ironic and misplaced. People with a misplaced belief will be misplaced and eventually replaced.

Karen people must also recognize the risks of complacency. With ongoing war and mass immigration affecting Kawthoolei, without obsession to learn, invent, innovate, and the willingness to adapt, they(we) too could face their own form of replacement—not by external forces, but by a lack of progress. Kawthoolei will not survive on stagnant identity and endless tribal festivities alone. If the Karen do not develop the skills, acquire the knowledge, and build the capacity to rebuild their homeland, others—whether through migration or external intervention—may take their place. Slowly, but surely, the very notion of Kawthoolei could fade, not through conquest, but because of stagnation.

When there comes stability in Kawthoolei, mass immigration into Kawthoolei will happen. The good, the bad, the ugly will be carried into Kawthoolei. Even with the ongoing war, natural migration has happened for decades in search of natural resources east of Sit-Taung River, overwhelming the local population.

Meanwhile, many in the new generation of Karen youth spend their time singing, dancing, practicing songs, loitering and roaming in groups, running around soccer fields, mis-Karen competition, and posting meaningless images, pursuing wild appetite of festivities, while their peers around the world are immersed in learning technology, working with microcontrollers, betting their energy in crypto blockchain ecosystem, or testing electronic devices with robotic programming. While a significant number of Karen youth are indeed studying and working hard, dedicating themselves to various fields, it is not enough to rely on a few hands. To truly rebuild Kawthoolei, there needs to be a critical mass—a collective, upward trend—where the entire generation focuses their energy on learning and building.

If the Karen youth fail to adapt, if they remain complacent and distracted, idle, laziness will ultimately get replaced. In a fast-evolving world, the consequence of neglecting growth and education is replacement—not through invasion or oppression, but by the slow erosion of their relevance and capacity to lead their own future. One can be in her ancestral land but be a slave to an offshore global corporation or to a local exploitative boss.

To avoid this, the new generation of Karen must rise to the challenge, channeling their creativity and enthusiasm into skills that will equip them to rebuild Kawthoolei. The key to survival is not only in preserving culture but also in embracing progress, adapting to new realities, and working tirelessly to secure a place for themselves in a rapidly changing world. Otherwise, they will be left behind, replaced by those who have the drive and vision to move forward.

The Final Case for Attracting Global Talent

Openness, not fear, must guide Kawthoolei's approach—tempered always with thoughtful care. Yet, a persistent fear lingers among our people: that Karen educated abroad may return and impose themselves as masters. Ironically, this fear is less pronounced toward non-Karen internationals. At the same time, genuine talent within Karen communities worldwide often finds serving Kawthoolei unappealing, distaste by the state of its leadership lacking vision and competence. Old heads simply lamenting the absence of returning talent is neither wise nor productive. Instead, there must be a sincere reflection on *why* this is the case and *what* barriers have been created—whether by mistrust, governance, or lack of opportunity. Many fear that their service to the homeland will be exploited by leaders who fall short on displaying integrity.

Asking for unreasonable sacrifice is open for exploitation, as history has shown. Volunteering without recognition or reward is not a model to uphold. Even if it is morally justifiable, it is not economically sustainable. The arrogance of believing we do not need talent is destructive and runs counter to true public service.

This dual challenge—a mistrust of our own and the reluctance of our brightest to contribute— underscores the urgent need for leadership that inspires trust, values talent, and fosters unity.

Talent is neither defined by skin color, upbringing, nor diet. Furthermore, not every individual educated abroad can be presumed to embody true talent. Addressing these challenges requires deliberate investment in talent acquisition and a robust vetting process to identify genuine ability. Equally important is the creation of an environment where talent feels valued, empowered, and inspired to contribute meaningfully to the nation's progress.

Human resources are far more precious than gold and silver mines. Kawthoolei must prioritize investing in its people before natural resources are depleted or extraction industries leaving the land scarred with irreversible environmental damage. Kawthoolei should allocate approximately

5-10 percent of its national wealth to developing both home-grown and international talent. The foundation for progress that relies on human ingenuity and resilience rather than finite resources is to build a sustainable and prosperous future.

In the formative stages of nation-building, leaders often focus inward, cultivating the strength and identity of their people as a foundation for future progress. However, as history has repeatedly shown, the most prosperous nations are those that embrace the outside world—not with open arms to every passerby, but with a discerning mind, focused on attracting the best and brightest.

For Kawthoolei to build a successful, prosperous nation, it must consider encouraging the entry of creative, innovative, and skilled individuals from around the globe, while maintaining its cultural integrity and political sovereignty. From scientific innovation to cultural preservation, from disciplined leadership to artistic expression, each contribution holds value in the grand mosaic of national renewal.

The path forward reaches beyond survival, toward the creation of a thriving, self-sustaining homeland, where every individual is empowered to contribute their best regardless of their ancestry. The strength of Kawthoolei rests in the harmony of its diversity where talents bloom.

The talents who pledge:

With all my strength and all that I am, I pledge my allegiance

to the progress of Kawthoolei and honor the virtues of this land.

From a refugee camp to an education advocate

You can't choose where you were born, but you can choose where you're heading.

"FROM REFUGEE TO DESTINY."

I was a "nobody,"
Fenced in like a bird in a cage,
I was a refugee.

Through trials and tears,
I found my voice,
From silence to strength,
I made a choice.

To rise above,
To pave my way,
From shadows deep,
Into the day.

A journey hard,
A path unknown,
From "nobody,"
To "somebody"

From refugee camps,
To classrooms bright,
I advocate,
For every right.

To learn, to grow,
To break each chain,
To show the world,
What's in a name.

No longer caged,
My spirit free,
From refugee,
To destiny.

By Naw Manger Baw

Moei River, Kawthoolei.

SawLah@Photography 2022

262

——————

Chapter 15

National Symbols

DIRECTION, AESTHETICS, AND SPIRIT

From the soaring eagle to the humblest insect, National symbols distill the essence of a nation—its land, people, and heritage. Whether drawn from nature, forged by human hands, or rooted in historic achievements, these emblems are more than mere ornamentation. They embody the character and ideals of a nation, inscribed on seals, woven into flags, and etched into the public consciousness. When chosen with care and upheld with purpose, they do more than signify; they unify, instill pride, and project the nation's identity with quiet strength upon the world stage.

Some symbols are native to the land—endemic—while others are born of imagination. The American bald eagle is more than a bird native to North America; it reflects the national psyche of freedom and dominance that has shaped its history. In contrast, Singapore's Merlion—a mythical blend of lion and fish—has no ecological roots in the region but symbolizes the nation's maritime heritage. Whether natural or mythical, symbols encapsulate a nation's identity and aspirations. At a glance, a flower, bird, or landmark can evoke a shared sense of belonging and unity among its people.

For Kawthoolei, there are many shared cultural and natural symbols to unify and represent the nation, but they require official recognition to formalize their significance. A well-chosen national symbol has the power to embody the values of which we cherish—simplicity, honesty, and purity, bravery, and resilience—that resonate deeply with the Karen people.

NATIONAL BIRD

Many nations designate national birds, but few achieve the prominence of the American bald eagle. Its commanding presence soars far beyond its ecological role, embodying the U.S.'s national psyche of strength and leadership at the top of the food chain.

In Asia, Thailand's Siamese Fireback (Lophura diardi) and Japan's Green Pheasant (Phasianus versicolor) are beautiful and rare, yet they are less prominent in public consciousness. A national bird, to be truly inspiring, must transcend its biological classification and take on a broader cultural resonance, becoming a visual and symbolic shorthand for the nation's story.

Within the United States, states assign symbolic birds to reflect local pride. The Northern Cardinal, Indiana's state bird, is both cherished and legally protected. A Karen individual in Indiana State once faced legal consequences, a series of court visits and fine for hunting hundreds of cardinals, out of ignorance on the State's designation. Similarly, California's California Quail (Lophortyx californica) is more of a token designation often overlooked in the state's public narrative. Symbols carry meaning only when society collectively upholds their value, requiring a concerted effort to elevate them to national prominence.

As Kawthoolei contemplates its national bird, it must look for a species that not only thrives in its forests but also mirrors the character and aspirations of its people.

KAWTHOOLEI NATIONAL BIRD - A PROFOUND CANDIDATE

Among Kawthoolei's rich cultural and natural heritage, the Asian Fairy Bluebird has potential to have the title of the national bird.

Known by various names across Kawthoolei, the Asian Fairy Bluebird bridges the cultural and geographical divides between the plains and the mountains. In the plains, it is colloquially called Toe-Thoo-Lah ("black blue bird"). Among the Pwo Karen, it is known as Pee-Bee-Yaw ("Grandma Beeyaw"), and the Sqaw Karen call it Toe-Buu-Grar ("rice pest manager bird"). These diverse names reflect the bird's prominence and its resonance with people across the land.

In a sample survey, a few communities also support this bird, accepted as a good candidate for its practical, esthetic, and cultural significance.

GUARDIAN SPIRIT OF RICE

The Asian Fairy Bluebird is entwined with the cultural fabric of Kawthoolei through the national fairy tale of the Guardian Spirit of Rice. This tale, cherished by both Pwo and Sqaw Karen communities, narrates how the bird protects rice, a sacred crop and staple of life, from pests and misfortune. The bird's bravery is legendary, fighting off snakes, rodents, and pests that threaten the rice in the fields and barns, despite its relatively small size. Rice paddies, vulnerable to fast-growing and multiplying caterpillars, benefit from the bird's vigilant nature for snacks.

AESTHETIC AND ECOLOGICAL SIGNIFICANCE

Native to the entire Indochina region, the Asian Fairy Bluebird connects Kawthoolei to its ancestral lands, historically known as Kaw Lah (the Green Land). Its vibrant blue and black plumage symbolizes the natural beauty and enduring spirit of the nation. Beyond its aesthetic appeal, the bird plays an essential role in its ecosystem as a protector of crops, aiding the farmers.

Adopting the Asian Fairy Bluebird as Kawthoolei's national bird will provide more than a mere designation; it offers a tangible representation of the nation's values. The bird's bravery and role in protecting rice highlight resilience and gratitude, while its wide recognition across Pwo and Sqaw Karen communities emphasizes unity.

More than a prominent beautiful bird, the Asian Fairy Bluebird is a cultural and ecological treasure that embodies the spirit of Kawthoolei. By elevating this bird as a national symbol, Kawthoolei can unite its people under a shared banner of courage and hope, qualities essential for building a strong and harmonious nation.

The National Flower

National flowers are more than mere botanical symbols; they embody the identity, aesthetics, and aspirations of a nation. Across the world, countries have carefully chosen blooms that reflect their unique cultural and natural heritage. Some flowers transcend their botanical roots to become emblems of national identity, woven into stories, traditions, and even the national psyche. From the regal cherry blossoms of Japan to Malaysia's resilient hibiscus, these floral symbols stand as quiet yet powerful ambassadors of a nation's spirit.

The Blossoms of Other Nations

Malaysia's national flower, the hibiscus (*Hibiscus rosa-sinensis*), known as *bunga raya* in Malay, is an example of how a flower can shape a country's identity. This bright red bloom is featured on coins, government seals, and official documents, embodying the nation's vibrant spirit and cultural pride. The hibiscus is a botanical symbol that transforms into a visual representation of Malaysia's unity and diversity.

South Korea's national flower, a variant of the hibiscus with light pink blooms, reflects the country's enduring beauty and resilience. Known as the *mugunghwa*, it appears in art, architecture, and public spaces, reminding Koreans of their rich heritage and the value of perseverance. The flower's prominence reinforces its status as a symbol of national pride and identity.

Similarly, Hawaii has adopted the hibiscus as its state flower, linking the bloom to the islands' natural beauty and tropical identity. Despite sharing the hibiscus with other nations, Hawaii has cultivated its own unique association with the flower, using it to enhance its image as a paradise destination and a symbol of its distinct cultural identity.

Toward a National Flower for Kawthoolei

For Kawthoolei, the choice of a national flower must resonate deeply with its people and reflect the core values of simplicity, honesty, and purity. An endemic white flower, easily recognizable and culturally significant, captures the essence of the people's psyche while connecting to the land's natural beauty. This symbol not only honors the region's biodiversity but also serves as a tangible representation of its people's aspirations and unity. The national flower is still being sought and yet to be nominated—a quest of a national symbol shared by all.

THE NATIONAL SACRED MOUNTAIN, THAWTHIKHO

Thaw Thi Kho, a majestic peak rising to 2,620 meters, dominates the northern landscape of Kawthoolei, straddling the border between Karen State and Karenni State. As one of the highest summits in the Karen Hills Mountain range, ThawThiKho is more than a towering geographical feature; it is a sacred site, celebrated in poems, literature, and legends, and deeply intertwined with the history and struggles of the Karen people.

For the Indigenous Karen, ThawThiKho is no ordinary mountain. It is believed to be the seat and resting place of **Ywa**, the Spirit of all Guardians. Once, a sacred stream was said to flow from its peak, carrying profound spiritual significance. Ancient poems, traditional songs, and sacred prayers extol the mountain's beauty and divine essence, inspiring deep reverence among the people. This admiration is reflected in the widespread adoption of its name by individuals and entities across the northern regions, *Taw-Oo, Lerdoh, Hsaw Htee,* and Karenni.

Just as Thailand venerates Doi Inthanon, its highest peak at 2,565 meters, preserved as a national park; the United States honors Mount Rushmore as a national monument; and Japan's indigenous religion, Shinto, reveres Mount Fuji as a sacred mountain and dwelling place of gods and spirits, ThawThiKho holds a divine and symbolic place in the hearts of the people of Kawthoolei. Its towering presence and profound cultural significance make it more than just a natural wonder— it is a cornerstone of the Karen identity and spirit.

ThawThiKho, alongside its sister mountain *Pwgor Gaw Kho*, deserves to be celebrated as a sacred landmark. Dedicating the surrounding area as the *Kawthoolei National Park* will preserve its breathtaking natural beauty and spiritual importance for future generations. Such a designation will protect its unique flora and fauna while solidifying its role as a unifying symbol for the Karen people.

In the Kawthoolei National Park, there shall be no commercial, sectarian, or military activities allowed. Visiting the park must be carefully managed according to its carrying capacity to prevent environmental damage. Measures could include issuing permits to regulate the number of travelers, limiting the duration of their stay and the activities allowed within the park, and monitoring what visitors can bring to avoid pollution. By enforcing these safeguards, the park can remain a pristine sanctuary for nature and a place of spiritual reverence for the Karen people.

The cultural, spiritual, and geographical heritage of ThawThiKho makes it an outstanding candidate for recognition as a UNESCO World Heritage Site. Such a status ensures its legacy endures on the global stage, highlighting its significance as a sacred site and a natural treasure of universal value.

Kawthoolei is a mountainous country. There are iconic and culturally important mountains like *Kwal-Ka-Baw* Mountain and *Taw-Naw* Mountains that can be among nationally important mountains.

Thawthikho Mountain from Mutraw View   *SawLah@Photography 2023*

KAWTHOOLEI DOLLAR

Forty years ago, during the Mar-Ner-Plaw era, the Kawthoolei Government made an attempt to introduce the Kawthoolei Dollar. Stamps were issued as part of this initiative. However, the venture faced technical hurdles and the realities of an unorganized economy. Fast forward 40 years, what was once a distant aspiration has now become a technical possibility. As the Karen saying goes, *the elders will dream, the young will see.* In the modern world, the nature of currency has evolved—from paper cash to digital transactions that flow across cyber networks, connecting businesses, governments, and individuals without the need for physical transfers.

We have arrived at an era where old dreams are becoming reality. Blockchain technology has made it possible to establish an independent national banking system without the need for costly and sluggish central banks. This system could be implemented using a selected token—potentially called Kawthoolei Coin—backed by the solid value of a stablecoin, such as USDT or USDC, both pegged to the US dollar, which is, in turn, backed by the world's largest economy.

A reliable and independent financial system is the lifeblood of a nation's economy. A healthy economy cannot exist without a stable and trustworthy financial backbone. Likewise, a currency cannot carry value—nor inspire trust—without being backed by a robust and functional economy.

Currently, some people in Kawthoolei rely on the Myanmar Kyat out of necessity. Yet, the currency loses nearly a quarter of its value every year due to rampant inflation. So far, it has not yet plummeted to the catastrophic levels of the Venezuelan Bolívar, which has experienced inflation rates exceeding 10,000% in some years. Not yet, thus far. Many accumulate wealth in some way in Myanmar. But no sane mind entrusts their savings to the Myanmar Kyat.

In one telling incident, a frontline district brought stacks of Kyat to the Thai border to purchase goods. However, they had to return home with bags of paper money since no merchant accepted the currency—the value was simply impossible to gauge. A paper money without trust is adrift without the weight of integrity.

Kawthoolei cannot afford to depend on fragile or externally controlled financial systems. Relying on currencies whose value consistently declines, economically rotten, politically ignominious— "Kyats - the lion notes"—leaves the Kawthoolei's economy exposed to external forces. Using the Thai Baht or any foreign currency as a medium of exchange creates vulnerabilities, including economic blockades and institutional freezes on funds. Even small remittances from abroad often face restrictions, delays, or confiscation—outcomes that Kawthoolei has no power to prevent or control. That is entirely up to their discretionary power. In fact, there is no inherent issue with nations prioritizing the protection of their own financial systems and setting policies to safeguard their economies and national security. Those are the duty of the state institutions.

A sound government policy can transform this vision into reality. Without an independent monetary system for a self-sustaining national economy, the hard-won freedom, paid for by the countless sacrifices of our brave men and women, risks becoming hollow. Sovereignty is not merely political—it is also economic.

A SYMBOL OF STABILITY AND DIGNITY

For Kawthoolei, establishing its own currency is not merely an economic necessity but a statement of sovereignty. Unlike traditional fiat currencies that rely heavily on centralization, modern decentralized digital currencies provide an alternative. Kawthoolei can make a hybrid model, the benefits and best of both worlds.

While money was once minted, printed, and tokenized in physical form, digital currencies can be mined, tokenized, and even printed if desired. Kawthoolei could honor its historical and cultural heritage by featuring iconic leaders on its currency—figures like *Saw Ba U Gyi* or *Dr. San C. Po*, who laid the foundation for Karen people's self-governance nation state. People of Kawthoolei around the world can carry that currency with grace, having their national leaders ranking among other those of other nations.

The Kawthoolei Dollar would be more than just currency—it would serve as a national instrument of dignity and economic freedom. People would transact without fear of external interference devaluing their assets or freezing their funds. Backed by a functioning national economy, a trusted reserve, and strong public and private institutions, the Kawthoolei Dollar could withstand global financial storms. A well-managed currency will project strength and stability to the world, staying above harm from hedge fund speculators. A small but rising nation like El Salvador has been using Bitcoin as a legal tender. Estonia, a small nation in Eastern Europe also has made some attempt to adopt crypto currency.

Mystical and mountainous Bhutan, under the leadership of its forward-thinking king, has been accumulating Bitcoin as part of its national reserves. The country harnesses its abundant hydroelectric resources to power Bitcoin mining operations, amassing significant cryptocurrency holdings. As of November 15, 2024, Bhutan's state investment arm, Druk Holding & Investments (DHI), had mined over 13,000 Bitcoin, valued at approximately $750 million. This strategic move positions Bhutan among the world's largest governmental Bitcoin holders, surpassing even El Salvador. A blockchain token for Kawthoolei can now be generated easily and adopted into the financial system when most households start using mobile phones.

Whether through a decentralized block-chain digital currency or a carefully managed fiat currency, the Kawthoolei Dollar can symbolize a new era of self-reliance and prosperity—a currency not only for transactions but for national honor, economic stability, and freedom from external economic pressures.

KAWTHOOLEI STANDARD TIME

The current Kawthoolei Standard Time traces its origin to the awkward colonial legacies of the 19th century. While operational a century ago, it is now an outdated anomaly, incompatible with the modern world's time zones, which are commonly divided by the hour rather than half-hour increments.

At present, the seven districts under the KNU administration fall under the same solar time zone as Thailand. Commonly, nations have adopted time zones slightly ahead of their actual solar time because waking early confers advantages—from economic productivity to maintaining a competitive edge.

In many traditions, the guardian spirits frown upon their subjects who rise late. We have been late for so long and left so far behind. The ongoing misfortunes our nation endures may have stemmed from prolonged neglect of our guardian spirits and the natural order around us that are longing for us to wake up on time. Could generations of our tardiness have been a natural curse?

Time zone offset from UTC+07:00 (in light blue)

Source: commons.wikimedia.org PlatonPskov 2017(public domain)
https://commons.wikimedia.org/wiki/File:Timezones2011_UTC%2B7.png

The Misalignment of Time in Kawthoolei

The global time system divides the Earth's 360-degree rotation into 24 time zones, each spanning 15 degrees of longitude. The prime meridian at Greenwich, England, marks the starting point for what was once known as Greenwich Mean Time (GMT), now referred to as Coordinated Universal Time (UTC). Each 15-degree increment represents one sun hour.

Kawthoolei, however, adopted Burma Standard Time, which is 6.5 hours ahead of UTC to match Yangon's time zone. Yet geographically, Kawthoolei lies to the east of Yangon—the sun rises earlier. Natural order around us—roosters crow, birds chirp, insects awaken, and animals stir—follows the sun hour but Kawthoolei remains half an hour behind its natural rhythm. This misalignment has contributed to the perception of people in Kawthoolei as late risers, a sentiment once observed by Karen communities in Thailand who associated Kawthoolei people waking up late with laziness.

Learning from Neighbors

Kawthoolei, Thailand, Malaysia, and Singapore share the same time zone. Yet, *Malaysia* and *Singapore* made strategic decisions to advance their clocks by an hour—aligning their time with Hong Kong, Asia's former financial center of the world. This decision helped these nations synchronize with global trade and economic activities. Even Thailand's parliament has considered advancing its time to match Malaysia and Singapore, though practical concerns, such as children traveling to school in darkness among other, have delayed implementation.

While neighboring nations move forward to maximize economic and social opportunities, Kawthoolei remains shackled to an outdated artificial time standard.

Some geographically vast countries have unique ways of defining standard time, with stark contrasts evident between nations like the United States and China. In the United States, time zones reflect both practical and political considerations. While most states adhere to a single time zone, some—such as Indiana—are divided between Eastern and Central Time Zones to align with neighboring regions. States such as Texas and Nebraska straddle Central and Mountain time zones, while others adjust for Daylight Saving Time to maximize daylight hours in spring and summer. These decisions are adopted to balance regional needs, economic activities, and political realities.

By contrast, China, which is geographically as vast as the United States, uses only a single time zone—Beijing Time—for the entire country. As a result, the western regions experience sunrise and sunset much later than the official clock time.

Four time zones in the contiguous United States.

The territory of the 50 US states extends over eight standard time zones, from UTC (GMT) −4 to −11 hours. There are six designated US time zones; and there are four time zones in the contiguous USA.

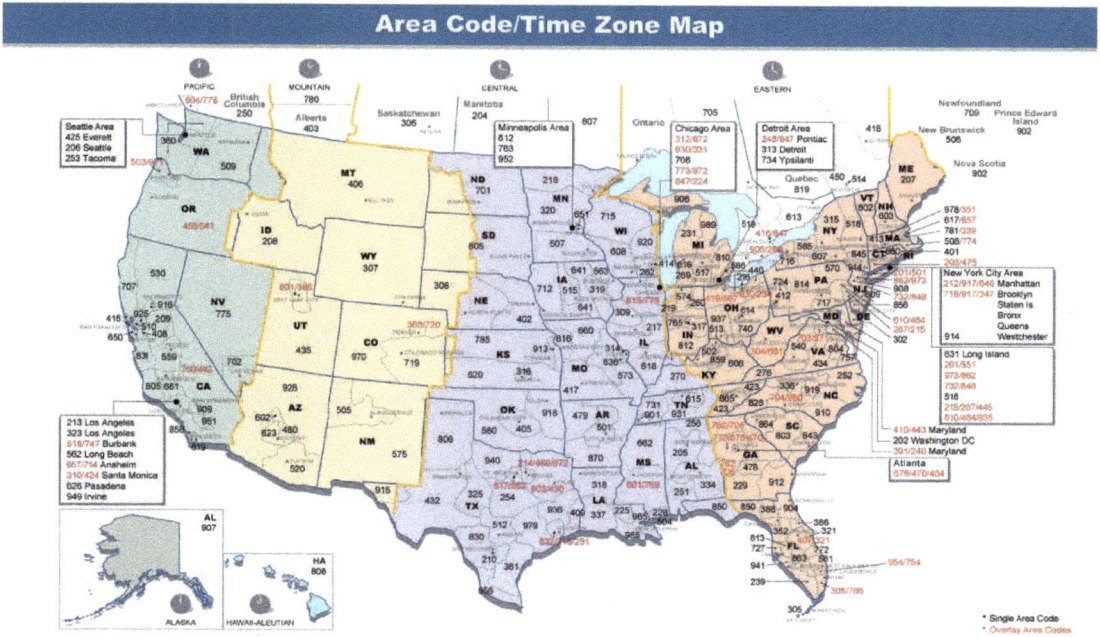

Magog the Ogre, 2011 (public domain)
https://commons.wikimedia.org/wiki/File:Area_codes_%26_time_zones_US.jpg

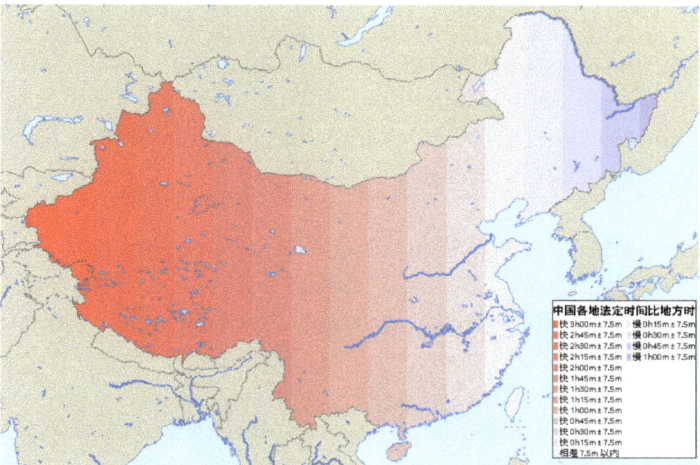

By 片桐研太 - Own work, CC BY-SA 4.0,
https://commons.wikimedia.org/w/index.php?curid=127306218

This map shows the difference between legal time and local mean time in China. Northeast China is significantly behind, and western parts of China are significantly ahead of local solar time as a single standard time offset of UTC+08:00 is observed across the whole of China, even though the country spans almost five geographical time zones (73°26'E - 134°46'E).

273

THE KAWTHOOLEI STANDARD TO BE

Kawthoolei Standard Time serves as a symbol of early-rising, punctual national character, not only does the correct time reflect the geographical reality of its eastern position. Aligning time is more than a technical adjustment—it is a commitment to productivity, order, modernization, and competitiveness.

The adoption of a new standard time could serve as a rallying point for broader standards—standards that define Kawthoolei's identity:

A Standard of Ethics and Conduct: Upholding honesty, integrity, diligence in all endeavors. People hustle in Kawthoolei Time and Kawthoolei standard.

A Standard of Excellence in Design and Products: Establishing Kawthoolei as a brand of reliability and craftsmanship. The reputation of quality is the ads itself. Kawthoolei Standard is the brand itself.

A Standard of Intellectual and Cultural Excellence: Kawthoolei upholds the development of both mind and soul as a national standard. Intellectual curiosity, critical thinking, and lifelong learning are embedded in public life. Arts, literature, language, and oral traditions are preserved and refined—not as relics, but as pillars of identity and progress. Kawthoolei's cultural and intellectual standard is one that nations admire and aspire to—this is the Kawthoolei Standard.

A Standard of Infrastructure and Cleanliness: From safe buildings to clean and dignified public restrooms, Kawthoolei can set benchmarks for public health and hygiene. For one, public restrooms—going relief in elegance is a new Kawthoolei's standard.

A Standard of Early Wakefulness and Punctuality: Rising with the sun, embracing the natural rhythm of work and life. The people of the East align their worth with the Star of the East. To be on time, to work in harmony with others, is a gesture of respect—punctuality, a virtue, and the mark of Kawthoolei.

The adoption of true Kawthoolei Standard Time is more than a technical adjustment; it is a declaration of intent. It is a shift toward a forward-looking nation that embraces its natural rhythm, aligns itself with global standards, and inspires its people to rise early, work diligently, and uphold a standard of excellence.

Karen people around the world constantly have personal or organizational contacts with people in Kawthoolei and the half hour time zone becomes an inconvenient confusion as it is backward and awkward. Kawthoolei's time should reflect its values, aspirations, and readiness to meet the challenges of the modern world.

When people from the western regions enter Kawthoolei territory, their cell phone clocks will adjust to the local standard time. That will also be a declaration of sovereignty that they are entering the land of Kawthoolei that has its own law, regulation, standard, and virtues that all visitors must abide by.

This time zone will need to be registered with organizations such as the IANA (Internet Assigned Numbers Authority), which map and maintain global time zones. These mappings ensure that telecommunication networks and mobile services adjust seamlessly to the correct local standard time.

When we adopt, we adopt forward, not backward.

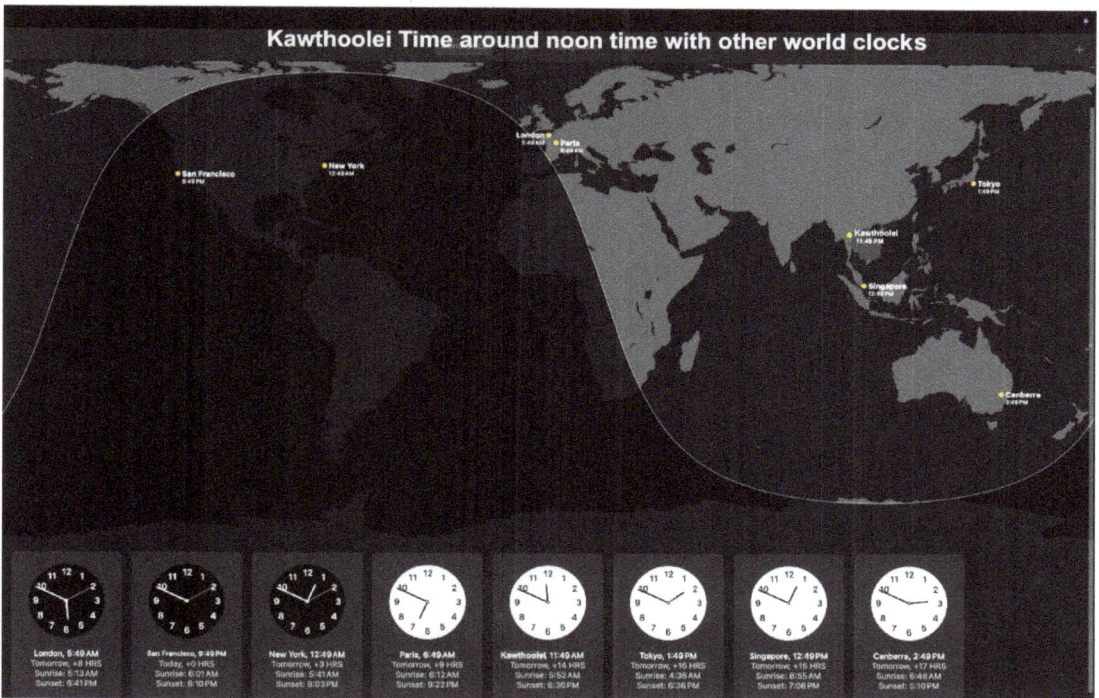

Figure 5. International Time Zones

Apple World Clock

KAWTHOOLEI NATIONAL UNIVERSITY

National universities transcend their role as institutions of teaching, research, and awarding degrees; they stand as symbols of a nation's highest academic aspirations, intellectual strength, and cultural identity. Cultivating knowledge and wisdom, universities project a nation's reputation globally as beacons of academic excellence and pillars of national progress. These priceless intellectual jewels, more valuable than gold or silver, build a national workforce with expertise and skills essential for a nation's advancement. Often, prestigious, high-ranking universities become economic assets, attracting foreign students and generating revenue. Moreover, their alumni serve as academic ambassadors, carrying the intellect and cultural essence of the nation that nurtures them, from its ideas to traditions to local diets.

Kawthoolei University is not confined to a single campus. Across the nation, it will function as a network of interconnected campuses, each loosely aligned yet firmly committed to the highest standards of research, codes of conduct, and academic ethics set forth by the University. These campuses will specialize in different fields of study, benefiting from shared resources, funding, discoveries, cyber networks, software applications, and best practices among students, faculty, staff, and administrators. The university campuses hold high quality standards—not the proliferation of campuses—for Kawthoolei no longer has a taste of the low quality of universities and colleges.

Across the globe, national universities have set benchmarks of excellence. Taiwan has National Taiwan University; South Korea boasts multiple flagship national universities like Seoul National University. Israel is home to Hebrew University, while Singapore's National University of Singapore is ranked among the top in Asia and the world. National universities are designed to serve their nations; therefore, academic freedom bears academic responsibility and respect for the nation.

Nations take pride in their thinkers, even those who are provocative and challenge authority, as great thinkers illuminate society and drive progress. Professor Yuval Noah Harari, a historian and lecturer at the Hebrew University of Jerusalem, is a notable example. Though his criticism may trouble Israel's leadership, Harari remains a source of national pride for his academic prominence and global influence. His books, which have sold over 45 million copies in 65 languages, have cemented his reputation as one of the world's most influential public intellectuals. Nations take pride in the intellectual bedrock on which they build their future—where academia holds the treasure of the nation's brain power and projects its soft power.

In the United States, most states have a state university system, which is publicly funded and primarily supported by the state government. In Indiana State, where many students from Burma have attended, Indiana University (IU) operates nine campuses and is renowned for its library system and a picturesque Bloomington campus.

In California, the University of California (UC) system exemplifies how academic institutions drive innovation and inclusivity. Comprising 10 campuses, five medical centers, and managing three national laboratories, UC leads in research across various disciplines. Campuses such as UC Berkeley, UCLA, and UC San Francisco consistently rank among the world's best. To date, 83 out of 976 Nobel laureates worldwide have been affiliated with California institutions. This underscores California's significant contribution to global academia. Additionally, more than half of UC's graduate students hail from abroad, enriching its diversity and fostering global research collaboration.

If we dare to dream, Kawthoolei University will excel in academic pursuits that achieve breakthroughs worthy of Nobel recognition—discoveries and research that benefit all of humanity. Supported by a network infrastructure and exceptional instructors, Kawthoolei University focuses on three key areas: science, engineering, and humanities. Its motto, "Kawthoolei Ingenuity Advancing Humanity." Kawthoolei University is to be a beacon of both groundbreaking research and virtues in living and practice—championing progress in human goodness and common progress. Home to one of the last strongholds of rainforest, its research discoveries in biodiversity will benefit not only the nation but also the broader global community.

In the libraries and laboratories of Kawthoolei University, the sons and daughters of Kawthoolei work tirelessly—day and night, through weekdays and weekends— driven by a relentless pursuit of excellence through tinkering with electrons, modeling with software, designing robotic automation process, innovation, and research, all in service to their nation's progress. Youthful laughter and idle chatter now hum with the rhythm of keyboards, making gadgets and gears, tapping out essays and sparkling intellectual debates—a symphony of minds crafting a brighter future.

In today's world, the wealth of university library resources no longer resides solely on physical shelves; it proliferates in cyberspace. Affiliated members can access vast collections from anywhere—literally at their fingertips—whether from their bed or kitchen table, at any hour, without the need to shower and makeup to physically step into a library. Beyond institutional resources, the internet opens doors to elite research papers, virtual experiences, and cutting-edge knowledge, often at little to no cost. The barriers to learning have been dismantled for those who want to learn.

Kawthoolei University has the power to embrace this digital revolution and leapfrog traditional limitations. Partnering with world-class institutions can amplify its reach. For instance, since 2007, the National University of Singapore has collaborated with the Massachusetts Institute of Technology (MIT), enabling students in Singapore to virtually join lectures alongside their American peers. This concept, once futuristic, is now the standard for forward-thinking education.

Without costly architecture but with a bold vision, Kawthoolei University can build an intellectual country with good internet connection and innovative approach to education. Salman Khan, founder of Khan Academy, advocates for a reimagining of in-person class time, suggesting it be devoted to Socratic dialogue, collaborative assignments, and individualized support for student work. Traditional lectures are no longer the most effective use of classroom hours, as technology now enables lectures to be delivered more efficiently through online platforms (Khan, 2024).

With minimal infrastructure but maximum ingenuity, the University can become a global player, delivering transformative education and research. Kawthoolei University can redefine what it means to learn, proving that the most powerful tools for progress are not brick and mortar but ideas, collaboration, and mission to seek knowledge. Kawthoolei University is one of the top ten universities in the world. Kawthoolei is to be an intellectual hub, a talent-rich nation.

Kawthoolei University – Bamboo Campus [CONCEPT *AI Assisted*]   *SawLah@Imagination*

KAWTHOOLEI AIR

A national airline is far more than a system of transportation. It is a projection of the national image—a testament to technological mastery, engineering marvels, and exceptional service—an immersive national symbol that a passenger can sit and eat and fly in. Airlines are ambassadors of a nation's culture, cuisine, and tourism, offering the world a glimpse of its identity and achievements.

Kawthoolei already had an airport built in the last century that was recaptured recently by our daring soldiers. Today, we have the opportunity to rebuild not just an airport, but an advanced aviation system. This includes a national airline, a robust logistics network, engineering services, and administrative oversight. International airline system encompasses secure immigration protocols, efficient customs operations, and policies integrated with international air traffic management. It must uphold both security and seamless service for travelers. In the contemporary world, aviation is driven as much by digital infrastructure as by physical infrastructure. Airline networks depend on intricate software systems that synchronize operations across continents, ensuring efficiency, security, and global connectivity.

With a national airline, Karen people across the world could fly directly to and from Kawthoolei, free from the inconvenience of transiting through neighbors' lands. More than just a mode of transport, it would stand as a symbol of sovereignty and progress—connecting Kawthoolei to the world while grounding its people in their national belonging.

Kawthoolei Air will set a global standard—far from mediocrity. More than an airline, it will be a gateway, hosting transit services for international carriers and positioning Kawthoolei as a vital hub in global aviation. While every nation aspires to be the center of the world, Kawthoolei holds this advantage by nature—it sits at the crossroads of continents, where the East greets the Pacific dawn across the ocean from the Americas, while the West stretches toward the markets of South Asia, the Middle East, and Europe. Airlines traversing Kawthoolei airspace will do so on its terms, adhering to its regulations and fee schedules, affirming its place on the world stage.

A prime example is Singapore, the so-called "tiny red dot," which has positioned itself as the center of Southeast Asia. Changi Airport, consistently ranked among the world's best, stands as a testament to this ambition. Lacking natural resources, Singapore's leadership understood decades ago that its airline could not afford to be mediocre. Today, Singapore Airlines, paired with its world-class airport, generates billions in revenue, proving that a talent-rich, hardworking nation can thrive through excellence and strategic vision.

Similarly, Korean Air is not just an airline but a global ambassador of Korean culture and technological prowess. It generates billions dollar revenue annually while showcasing South Korea's cuisine, beauty industry, and entertainment—from high fashion and skincare to the twirling and leaping of BTS, seamlessly weaving soft power into its aviation success.

When a service is excellent, it commands a premium, not a discount.

The fine sons and daughters of Kawthoolei—those who want to look their best, dress their best, and serve with purpose—can help shape this vision by contributing their skills to Kawthoolei Air. The first words passengers hear on board will be in Plone-Shaung, the mother tongue of Kawthoolei, followed by other international languages. This airline will not only transport travelers but carry forward the hopes, dreams, and aspirations of an emerging nation.

Kawthoolei Air will be built and operated by the hands of Kawthoolei talents: The skilled sons and daughters of Kawthoolei—mechanics, architects, engineers, pilots, software specialists, and service crews—will bring this vision to life. The stern-looking Kawthoolei immigration officers, and young good-looking customs officers will establish the security and flow of goods and travelers. With technology-assisted vigilance, officials will oversee operations, protecting the homeland and ensuring a smooth, secure experience for all travelers. The ground crew and the air crew communicated scientific technical terms yet in their full mother tongue, the Karenic language. The world knows this airline by the ingenuity, service, and diligence of its people.

Kawthoolei International Airport will offer a seamless and pleasant walking experience, where travelers naturally navigate toward their destinations without the clutter of wayfinding signs or the stress of rushing between terminals. The interior design embodies Kawthoolei's minimalist charm, showcasing its soothing landscapes, vibrant way of life, and warm welcoming smiles.

The airport will feature thoughtful amenities: showers, lounges, nap rooms, meeting spaces, quiet corners, prayer rooms, culture exhibition, and a language room dedicated to the Karen language and its ancient poems. A *healthy food exhibition* will introduce travelers to *bar-ker-err*—a traditional dried fermented mustard packed with essential nutrients, vitamins A, C, D, E, K, folic acid, riboflavin, calcium and manganese, B6, B12, and probiotics, celebrated not only for its health benefits—enhancing circulation, providing antioxidants, and promoting skin health—but also for its bold symphony of sour, bitter, punchy, and umami flavors. It can be enjoyed in many ways: as a soup, a hearty stew, a stir-fried dish, a porridge enhancer, or paired with meat as *Ka-paung*.

Stepping into Kawthoolei International Airport will feel like entering a carefully crafted, human-made park—an oasis where waiting for a flight becomes an experience in itself. Travelers will not grow bored waiting but will instead feel reluctant to leave this healing space.

The architecture embraces natural light above and cutting-edge technology underneath—a-hike-in-a-park-like airport. The design prioritizes the look and feel of a humanistic, nature-inspired aesthetic over the sterile feel of ultra-modern airports. Kawthoolei International Airport will serve as a gateway to both the soul of its people and the beauty of its land.

Behind the scenes of this engineering grandeur, the people of Kawthoolei work tirelessly—designing, testing, and crafting—while seamlessly collaborating. Designers, who obsess over every pixel and every shade of color, work alongside engineers, who pour their sweat into perfecting every millisecond of screen responsiveness and every nanosecond of data flow in the elegant Kawthoolei-signature system design. Together, they bring Kawthoolei's artistry, ingenuity, and hospitality to breathing life.

Somewhere in the world—at an airport whether in San Francisco, Buenos Aires, Amsterdam, or Taiwan Taoyuan International Airport—a voice will echo across the terminal: *"Kawthoolei Air Flight KLA-709 to Kawthoolei City is now boarding at Gate G7."* Travelers will rush toward the gate, happy to fly to Kawthoolei City, the beating heart of national governance, cultural expression, and an intellectual hub.

That may be the near future we have to build, but even somewhere in the world right now, an airplane airborne is already serviced by a skilled Karen mechanic or software engineer, or flown by Karen pilots who can speak, read, and write Karen fluently. Experts in the aviation industry worldwide are ready to bring that excellence back home to rebuild everything together from the ground-zero scratch.

Kawthoolei Air will not just transport passengers; it will carry the spirit and character of a nation— lifting a new generation who no longer hides in fear but fly to the boundless heights of the skies with no fear.

KAWTHOOLEI AIR at Kawthoolei City International Airport [CONCEPT *AI Assisted*]   *SawLah@Imagination*

KAWTHOOLEI SQUARE

National squares serve as both spaces and symbols of national unity and identity. Every nation treasures a central public space—an iconic landmark that serves as a stage for political and cultural expression. Kawthoolei National Square will embody this purpose, coming together in an open physical space to rally for Kawthoolei. It will host historic moments such as presidential inaugurations, national celebrations, and gatherings that reflect the collective spirit of the nation. Beyond its physical presence, the Square will symbolize Kawthoolei's values, projecting its aspirations and ideals to the world.

Across the globe, national squares have become synonymous with the character of their nations. Taiwan's Liberty Square echoes the island's journey toward democracy, while China's Tiananmen Square is a symbol of centralized power. The United States' National Mall hosts events of monumental significance, from protests to presidential inaugurations, including the historic gathering of 1.8 million people for President Obama's inauguration. Russia's Red Square and Thailand's Democracy Monument stand as reminders of political transitions, while South Korea's Gwanghwamun Square has been a space for citizens to rally against injustice, as seen in the massive protests that led to the impeachment of a president in December 2024.

Kawthoolei Square will aspire to this legacy—a place where public gatherings affirm the nation's democratic values and cultural identity. Whether celebrating political milestones or expressing the collective voice of the people, the Square will represent Kawthoolei's national commitment to political freedom, unity, and progress.

Kawthoolei Square will span 1,000 acres of flat land, surrounded by hills that take full advantage of Kawthoolei's natural topography. It will be designed as a park where the public can gather for leisure or explore the nation's history, endeavors, and achievements with museums and exhibitions around the perimeter of the Square. It will stand as a testament to the enduring power of public spaces to shape history and reflect the soul of a nation.

U.S. National Mall, Washington, D.C.
AI generated

Accommodated 1.8 million attendees during President Obama's Inauguration.

NATIONAL FISH: KAWTHOOLEI SALMON

Kawthoolei, with its lush rainforests, dense jungles, and fast-growing trees, hold many untold secrets of the land. Its multi-generational war and lack of open access for business and research have left much of its biodiversity undocumented. Hidden within its pristine environment are unique plants, animals, and fish that could one day symbolize the spirit of Kawthoolei.

Among these treasures is the Kawthoolei Salmon, a freshwater species found only in the rivers of Kawthoolei. Unlike its ocean-dwelling relatives, this salmon lives, spawns, and hatches entirely in freshwater. In favorable years, these remarkable fish lay their eggs in abundance, with the riverbeds teeming during the spawning season. Their eggs provide sustenance for squirrels and other wildlife, contributing to the delicate ecological balance of the region. However, the Kawthoolei Salmon is ecologically sensitive, thriving only in specific conditions—crystal-clear freshwater at specific temperatures.

This unique species could be elevated as the National Fish of Kawthoolei, a symbol of its natural heritage and environmental wealth. Its image could grace national emblems, documents, and official signage, promoting awareness of Kawthoolei's biodiversity.

Additionally, Kawthoolei is home to other rare and extraordinary creatures that could also serve as national emblems. However, their recognition and preservation require proper conservation capacities and regulatory frameworks before they can be formally committed to the nation's natural treasures and national symbols.

The River in Kawthoolei Where Salmon Run Free   *SawLah@Photography 2022*

KAWTHOOLEI PASSPORT

For decades, many of our people have lived in subhuman conditions, stateless and unrecognized by any nation-state. They are as bright and capable as anyone in humanity yet denied the freedom to pursue their dreams or travel freely because no state has acknowledged their existence—hence stateless. It is a sorrowful state to be deprived in a life so brief in the universe. Those offering them foreign passports often do so at the cost of erasing their identity altogether.

The Kawthoolei Passport issued by the rightful government of Kawthoolei changes everything. It is not just a travel document but a declaration of dignity and legitimacy—a badge of honor for a people who have risen from the shadows killed at gun point to claim their rightful place on the global stage. This passport will enable citizens to travel the world with pride, whether attending international conferences on biodiversity, presenting groundbreaking research, or advocating for equitable economies or indigenous knowledge that the world longs for at global forums like the United Nations and the World Economic Forum.

This navy-blue passport, embedded with a secure microchip and integrated into global profile systems, has a seamless passage through immigration checkpoints worldwide with pre-screening priority pass. Kawthoolei citizens will walk with grace as a representative of the nation celebrated for its values of liberty, virtue, and progress.

It has been settled. Kawthoolei is a nation of peace—with no enemies or adversaries—only friends and partners across the globe. From the Middle East to Europe, from the Americas to Africa and Australia to Canada, the Kawthoolei Passport is welcomed as a symbol of goodwill and honor. Nations will see in its holders as ambassadors of freedom, unity, and the enduring spirit of a people who have overcome multi-generation-long adversity.

Humble in its past and proud of its character, Kawthoolei shines as a beacon of humanity, offering hope for the world to emulate. The Kawthoolei Passport is not merely a document for travel; it is a gateway to opportunity, connection, and progress, embodying the hopes and dreams of a nation that inspires humanity itself.

Kawthoolei Passport [CONCEPT AI Assisted]
SawLah@Imagination

KAWTHOOLEI ARMED FORCES

Kawthoolei has many symbols of unity and cultural soft power, yet it must confidently project its strength through the emblem of crude military capability. The Kawthoolei Armed Forces (KAF) will serve as a concrete foundation of Kawthoolei stand to shake hands for diplomats, not only as a force of defense. A nation of peace requires a formidable armed force—not only to be the keeper of its own peace but also to broker peace for others. The KAF is not only formidable but also admirable, ready to serve its people and deploy to help nations in crisis internationally.

In its inception, the Kawthoolei Armed Forces were envisioned as a modern, comprehensive military force encompassing an army, navy, and air force. Before Burma gained independence in 1948, Karens constituted a significant portion of the British Armed Forces in Burma. The Karen made up over 35% of the armed forces in Burma, despite being only 10% of the total population (Callahan, 2005). After Burma gained independence, Karen officials still took leadership roles in Burma: Lieutenant General Smith Dun served as Commander-in-Chief of the Burmese Army, and Wing Commander Saw Shi Sho led the Air Force. During the early days of the Karen Revolutionary War, Karen forces displayed remarkable restraint, leaving captured air bases and aircraft untouched, showcasing their discipline and respect for military assets.

As the 1949 revolution unfolded, specialized units from the Burmese Armed Forces—including Marines, Signals, Artillery, Armor, and Engineers—joined forces with the Karen National Defense Organization (KNDO) and the Karen Rifles. Together, these groups formed the backbone of the revolutionary forces. By 1956, the Kawthoolei Armed Forces were officially recognized under the Kawthoolei Governing Body (KGB) during its Congress, laying the foundation for a unified command.

The modern KAF aspires to be an integrated, cutting-edge military organization, modeled after world-class forces such as the U.S. Armed Forces, the Israel Defense Forces (IDF), and the Singapore Armed Forces (SAF). These organizations operate under a single command, encompassing ground forces, air power, naval capabilities, intelligence, and specialized units. Similarly, the future KAF will be structured to ensure the security and well-being of Kawthoolei.

PROPOSED STRUCTURE OF KAF AFTER THE LIBERATION WAR

As a professional, world-class military operating under a unified command in the new Nation, the Kawthoolei Armed Forces (KAF) will comprise specialized branches and divisions, each designed to address distinct strategic and operational objectives.

1. Kawthoolei Special Forces
2. Kawthoolei Navy
3. Kawthoolei Air Force
4. Kawthoolei Coast Guard
5. Kawthoolei Army
6. Kawthoolei Border Guard
7. Kawthoolei Cyber Force
8. Kawthoolei Army Corps of Engineers
9. Kawthoolei Civil Defense Forces
10. Kawthoolei Space Force
11. Kawthoolei Secret Service
12. Kawthoolei Military Intelligence
13. Kawthoolei Navy Seals
14. Kawthoolei Viper Force
15. Kawthoolei Centipede

1. KAWTHOOLEI SPECIAL FORCES

The Kawthoolei Special Forces serves as an elite force, specializing in rapid deployment and precision combat operations across diverse terrains. Unlike conventional ground forces, the Special Forces are highly mobile, trained for swift, coordinated assaults. They excel in expeditionary warfare, conducting both offensive and defensive operations in urban, jungle, and littoral zones.

2. KAWTHOOLEI NAVY

Tasked with safeguarding Kawthoolei's extensive maritime borders along the Bay of Bengal, the Kawthoolei Navy is a critical branch responsible for maritime dominance, security, and surveillance. It patrols territorial waters, ensures freedom of navigation, and protects commercial and civilian vessels operating legally in these waters. Its strategic focus lies in securing sea lanes, deterring piracy, and responding to maritime emergencies.

3. KAWTHOOLEI AIR FORCE

The Kawthoolei Air Force commands the skies with a focus on air space security, air superiority, and rapid mobility. Equipped with advanced aircraft, surveillance drones, and aerial defense systems, the Air Force conducts reconnaissance, air interdiction, and humanitarian missions. It ensures the protection of national airspace and supports joint operations with ground and naval forces.

4. KAWTHOOLEI COAST GUARD

The Kawthoolei Coast Guard operates as the amphibious frontline defense for coastal security, with a focus on law enforcement, search and rescue, and environmental protection within territorial waters. It plays a vital role in preventing smuggling, illegal fishing, and human trafficking while ensuring maritime safety and disaster response. The Coast Guard works closely with the Navy, leveraging smaller, more agile vessels to conduct patrols and maintain order along Kawthoolei's coastlines.

5. KAWTHOOLEI ARMY

As the backbone of national defense, the Kawthoolei Army is responsible for ground operations, territorial integrity, and national security. It consists of highly trained infantry, armored divisions, artillery units, and logistics support teams, prepared for conventional and unconventional warfare. The Army focuses on strategic defense, counterinsurgency operations, and humanitarian assistance during crises.

6. KAWTHOOLEI BORDER GUARD

The Kawthoolei Border Guard is tasked with protecting and securing land borders from external threats, illegal crossings, and smuggling. Operating in remote and challenging terrains, the Border Guard conducts patrols, monitors cross-border activities, and collaborates with intelligence units to detect potential threats. Its primary objective is to maintain territorial sovereignty while fostering safe and regulated border interactions.

7. KAWTHOOLEI CYBER FORCE

In an era of digital warfare, the Kawthoolei Cyber Force stands as a frontline defender against cyber threats, espionage, and information warfare. Securing national networks, countering cyber-attacks, and developing offensive cyber capabilities, the Cyber Force also engages in intelligence gathering, electronic warfare, and protecting critical infrastructure from digital vulnerabilities.

8. KAWTHOOLEI ARMY CORPS OF ENGINEERS

The Kawthoolei Army Corps of Engineers is responsible for military construction, infrastructure development, and emergency response. From building military bases and fortifications to constructing bridges and roads in conflict zones, the Corps ensures logistical and structural readiness for military operations and provides engineering expertise during natural calamities and humanitarian missions.

9. KAWTHOOLEI CIVIL DEFENSE FORCES

The Civil Defense Forces act as a localized militia network, designed to protect civilian populations and maintain order during emergencies or crises. Comprised of trained volunteers and local leaders, this force bridges the gap between military and civilian defense, empowering communities to remain resilient and facilitating effective civilian rescue operations.

10. KAWTHOOLEI SPACE FORCE

The Kawthoolei Space Force is a strategic branch dedicated to safeguarding national interests in outer space. It focuses on satellite deployment, space surveillance, and developing technologies for communication, navigation, and intelligence gathering. In an increasingly contested space domain, this branch ensures Kawthoolei's ability to monitor space-based threats and secure technological competence. During the nation's early stages, before Kawthoolei can deploy its own satellites, the Space Force will collaborate with allied nations to access space technology for both civil and defense services.

11. KAWTHOOLEI SECRET SERVICE

The Kawthoolei Secret Service operates in the shadows, conducting covert intelligence gathering, counter-espionage, and high-stakes security operations. Its agents are highly trained in infiltration, surveillance, and data analysis, working to neutralize threats before they materialize. The Secret Service also provides protection to key national leaders, critical assets, and sensitive operations.

12. KAWTHOOLEI MILITARY INTELLIGENCE

The Kawthoolei Military Intelligence branch serves as the brain of the armed forces, focusing on gathering, analyzing, and disseminating critical intelligence. It operates across all domains—land, air, sea, cyber, and space—to provide actionable insights for military strategy and operations. Its role is to anticipate threats, assess enemy capabilities, and guide decision-makers with accurate and timely intelligence. Its analysts are well versed in international relation and geopolitics to analyze and report holistically on security issues.

13. KAWTHOOLEI NAVY SEALS

The Kawthoolei Navy SEALs are an elite special operations unit trained for high-risk missions in hostile environments. Operating on sea, air, and land, they specialize in counter-terrorism, reconnaissance, and direct-action missions. The SEALs are renowned for their exceptional physical and mental toughness, executing missions with precision and secrecy under extreme conditions.

14. KAWTHOOLEI VIPER FORCE

The Kawthoolei Viper Force is a specialized rapid-response unit designed for covert deployment in high-stakes scenarios. Operating with stealth and agility, the Viper Force excels in counter-insurgency, hostage rescue, and sabotage missions behind enemy lines. Its members are trained to operate independently and adapt to unpredictable challenges with minimal support.

15. KAWTHOOLEI CENTIPEDE

The Kawthoolei Centipede is a clandestine operations unit, specializing in intelligence gathering, infiltration, and unconventional warfare. Known for operating deep within enemy territory, Centipede agents are experts in psychological operations, asymmetric warfare, and disruption of enemy logistics and communication networks. Their operations are often classified, with missions aimed at destabilizing adversaries while remaining undetected.

The Kawthoolei Armed Forces (KAF) can be organized into four primary branches, offering both short-term and long-term goals to establish a modern, adaptable, and versatile defense strategy. This structure allows flexibility, ensuring alignment with the availability of resources and evolving national priorities.

KAWTHOOLEI GROUND FORCES:
1. Kawthoolei Special Forces
2. Kawthoolei Army
3. Kawthoolei Border Guard
4. Kawthoolei Viper Force

KAWTHOOLEI NAVY:
1. Kawthoolei Navy
2. Kawthoolei Coast Guard
3. Kawthoolei Navy SEAL

KAWTHOOLEI AIR FORCES:
1. Kawthoolei Air Force
2. Kawthoolei Space Force

KAWTHOOLEI INTELLIGENCE:
1. Kawthoolei Secret Service
2. Kawthoolei Military Intelligence
3. Kawthoolei Cyber Force
4. Kawthoolei Centipede

KAWTHOOLEI NATIONAL GUARD:
1. Kawthoolei Civil Defense Forces
2. Kawthoolei Army Corps of Engineers

These divisions reflect Kawthoolei's commitment to not only defend its sovereignty but also lead in innovation, security, and global peacekeeping efforts. Whether patrolling its borders, securing its waters, or advancing into new domains such as cyberspace and outer space, the KAF will embody the discipline, strength, and values of Kawthoolei.

In the new Kawthoolei Armed Forces, every citizen will dedicate at least 18 months to national service when they turn 18, tailored to their capacities and interests. This training extends beyond preparing for defense or understanding military protocols during crises—it serves as a crucible for forging national character. The benefits of compulsory military service are evident in nations such as Singapore, Taiwan, South Korea, and Israel, where it has become a cornerstone of national cohesion. Youth emerge from service not only disciplined and resilient but also firmly committed to contributing to their nation's growth across businesses, institutions, and society at large.

Those who have served in the KAF become the face of our nation, representing its diverse regions, cultures, and stories. They embody a unity forged through shared purpose, bringing their unique backgrounds into a collective effort to defend Kawthoolei's way of life. Driven by an innate sense of duty, a commitment to victory, and an unshakable purpose, the KAF stands as a symbol of Kawthoolei's strength, capable of winning not just battles on the field, but also the hearts and minds of the people they serve.

The Kawthoolei Armed Forces will not only protect the homeland but also stand as a symbol of the nation's resolve and its aspirations for liberty, progress, and peace. Through professionalism, advanced capabilities, and adherence to ethical principles, the KAF will forge a legacy as one of the most admired military forces in the world.

Kawthoolei will be known not only for its physical symbols and institutional projections, but for the intellectual vitality it cultivates. One day, the world will gather for the *International Rainforest Summit* and sign the *Kawthoolei Accord*—a milestone in the preservation and promotion of rainforest diversity and its enduring benefits to humanity. *The World Liberation Forum*, a *Symposium on the Theory of Knowledge*, and the *Forum on Virtue and Human Progress* will all find a space on Kawthoolei soil.

In Kawthoolei, national symbols are not mere emblems—they are the soul of the nation made visible. The sight of Kawthoolei Flower finds our hearts at peace; likewise, Kawthoolei Armed Forces, we find release. All the symbols fuse the essence of Kawthoolei's identity, history, and aspirations into tangible forms that unite its people across generations and borders. These symbols—whether seen on a flag fluttering in the wind, heard in the song of a national bird, or felt in the weight of a sovereign currency, or an intellectual bustling at national university— serve as mirrors reflecting Kawthoolei's inner spirit and windows projecting its virtues, resilience, and dignity to the world. In them, the people see not only themselves but also the promise of a nation that rises, unyielding, towards liberty, virtue, and enduring progress.

Chapter 16

Entering the International Community

PRACTICAL RECOGNITION,

REAL INSTITUTIONS,

AND INTERNATIONAL STANDARDS

In the grand theater of statecraft, where sovereignty and legitimacy are often measured by a seat in the chambers of the United Nations, many movements for self-determination fixate on political recognition as the ultimate prize. Yet, such recognition, while symbolically hallowed, risks becoming mere hollow if not underpinned by institutions capable of interacting meaningfully with the international community. A flag raised in New York does little to alleviate poverty, strengthen public health systems, or educate the next generation if the foundation of governance remains fragile.

For a nation to establish relationships with others, it must have the necessary functioning infrastructure, robust institutions, and reliable systems. Meaningful and enduring international relations require a state to demonstrate credibility, built upon a reliable and integral institutional foundation. Can it manage essential services, like a postal system? Does its passport have a guarantor institution, such as an immigration or interior department, to affirm its legitimacy? Most importantly, is that document recognized as valid by other nations? Can its health institutions govern policy, workforce development, and deployment? These are critical questions that underscore the importance of robust institutions and systems in supporting both domestic operations and international standing.

Practical recognition—the capacity to engage with global institutions across finance, health, education, security, and technology—is not merely an alternative to political recognition but a prerequisite to it.

Organizations like the World Bank, the International Monetary Fund (IMF), the World Health Organization (WHO), and the United Nations Educational, Scientific and Cultural Organization (UNESCO) serve as gateways to participation in the global community. Participation in these organizations does not demand full statehood but does require institutional sophistication, transparency, and administrative competence.

Kosovo—a landlocked country in the Balkan region of Europe—despite limited recognition by United Nations member states, has nonetheless established itself within global institutions such as the World Bank and IMF. This practical recognition facilitates financial assistance, policy consultation, and integration into global trade and investment mechanisms. Similarly, Taiwan—a nation with contested political recognition—has flourished economically and technologically through its participation in international economic organizations and specialized agencies.

East Timor (Timor-Leste), after gaining independence in 2002, faced immense institutional fragility. Despite international institutional support playing a crucial role in the early stages of nation-building, significant challenges remain. Through partnerships with the United Nations Development Programme (UNDP) and the World Bank, it established basic governance structures, improved healthcare, and initiated economic stabilization, demonstrating the power of practical engagement even with limited formal recognition.

However, no nation can rise sustainably unless its own people are equipped to build, operate, and sustain its institutions. While international aid provided a crucial foundation, it took nearly two decades for East Timor's new generation—educated and empowered—to assume these responsibilities and drive the nation toward self-reliance. This highlights the enduring importance of investing in human resources to ensure lasting progress and independence.

In contrast, Somaliland, despite functioning as a de facto independent state since 1991, remains unrecognized internationally. Yet, it has managed to secure partnerships with international health and education networks, significantly improving healthcare systems and access to education. By collaborating with agencies like WHO and UNESCO, Somaliland has shown that institutional engagement can yield results even without formal recognition.

The primary goal of collaborating with global organizations must be to empower Kawthoolei to chart its own course in alignment with its political and cultural values. Such partnerships should prioritize building Kawthoolei's capacity for sustainable growth and self-reliance, rather than allowing international bodies to exploit its name for career advancement or profit. International collaboration should be a tool for Kawthoolei's empowerment, not a vehicle for external agendas that compromise its autonomy.

Building Institutional Readiness

Kawthoolei should prioritize building institutions that meet international standards. While UN organizations offer valuable collaborative opportunities to nations regardless of UN membership, engagement should extend beyond the UNHCR. Over-reliance on the UNHCR reinforces a narrow narrative that may not serve Kawthoolei's long-term interests. Our goal is not perpetual refugee status; we will rebuild our nation and live with dignity.

For emerging nations, the path to practical recognition requires a deliberate strategy. Financial institutions, for instance, demand fiscal responsibility, transparency, and sound economic planning. Public health partnerships with WHO necessitate data-sharing capabilities, epidemiological infrastructure, and compliance with global health standards. Engagement with global education bodies requires policies aligned with international best practices and demonstrable investment in human capital.

Active participation in international research collaborations, academic conferences, professional networks, global festivals, and sporting events should form an integral part of Kawthoolei's strategy for meaningful and forward-looking engagement.

Building a Financial System

A resilient financial system is the backbone of any nation. Kawthoolei must establish a central banking organization to regulate the financial sector, ensure fiscal responsibility, and facilitate economic transactions. Partnerships with institutions like the Asian Development Bank (ADB) and the International Monetary Fund (IMF) will provide critical financial assistance, policy guidance, essential expertise and financial tools. Moreover, exploring digital currencies and stablecoin exchanges through blockchain technology could offer innovative financial solutions. A thorough policy formulation is needed to govern against malicious actors while financial crimes increase globally disregarding national boundaries.

Financial regulations, public audits, and transparent taxation systems are vital for fostering trust and accountability. Participating in international financial institutions requires comprehensive monetary understanding and fiscal discipline. Otherwise, big institutions can bring big problems, where nations fall to the heel of the institution backed by the rich and the powerful.

Engagement with Non-State-Friendly UN Agencies

Historically, regions and territories lacking full statehood have turned to non-state actor-friendly U.N. agencies as practical pathways for global collaboration. Palestine, for example, has bypassed the political gridlock of state recognition through partnerships with FAO, UNESCO, and WHO. Likewise, Somaliland has engaged with international health and education networks to improve its human development indices. This path is not merely symbolic; it is a practical necessity.

To effectively collaborate, establishing specialized liaison offices for each agency, staffed with professionals trained in the specific mandates of these organizations is a work to-do. The Food and Agricultural Organization (FAO) will require expertise in sustainable agriculture and food security programs. Collaboration with the International Civil Aviation Organization (ICAO) will demand adherence to global aviation safety protocols. Partnerships with the International Labor Organization (ILO) will necessitate well-documented labor laws and enforceable workforce protections. Similarly, cooperation with the International Maritime Organization (IMO) will require standardized shipping and environmental protection practices.

These engagements are not ceremonial. They demand sustained effort, transparency, and measurable outcomes. Kawthoolei must prepare detailed proposals, compliance reports, and periodic reviews to maintain credibility and secure continued support.

Participation in Professional Associations and International Competitions

Active participation in professional and international networks will significantly bolster Kawthoolei's global engagement. Key areas include:

- **Academic Associations:** Collaborating with global scholars in history, anthropology, and related disciplines will position Kawthoolei as a contributor to international research and intellectual discourse.
- **Cultural Exchanges:** Participation in music, dance, and other cultural festivals will promote Kawthoolei's rich heritage and showcasing its soft power.
- **Sports Participation:** Kawthoolei should aim to compete in international sporting events such as the Olympics, the Fédération Internationale de Football Association (FIFA) World Cup, and regional competitions like the Southeast Asian Games. Sporting diplomacy can foster unity and visibility on the global stage.
- **Other International Competitions:** Participation in global events like the Commonwealth Games, Paralympics, and youth championships creates opportunities for emerging athletes.
- **Scientific Networks:** Engage with international scientific bodies such as the Convention on Biological Diversity (CBD), the International Union for Conservation of Nature (IUCN), and the Convention on International Trade in Endangered Species of Wild

Fauna and Flora (CITES) to contribute to and benefit from conservation efforts. Some work on this area is ongoing and gaining momentum of international collaboration.

- **Geology and Nature Networks:** Collaborate with organizations focused on natural resource management and environmental science to build expertise and develop sustainable policies.
- **International Mathematics Competitions**: Competing in global mathematics Olympiads will highlight Kawthoolei's intellectual potential and inspire young talent to pursue excellence in STEM fields.
- **International Poetry Competitions**: Participation in global literary contests will emphasize Kawthoolei's creative and artistic contributions, enhancing its cultural presence.

HEALTH PARTNERSHIPS WITH THE WORLD HEALTH ORGANIZATION (WHO)

Collaborating with WHO offers Kawthoolei an opportunity to strengthen its health infrastructure, improve public health, and contribute to global health initiatives.

BUILDING A ROBUST HEALTH INFRASTRUCTURE

To collaborate effectively with WHO, Kawthoolei must develop a health system that meets international standards by focusing on:

- Healthcare Facilities: Establish modern hospitals, clinics, and laboratories equipped with advanced technology.
- Epidemiological Tools: Implement disease surveillance and outbreak tracking systems for accurate monitoring.
- Workforce Development: Train healthcare professionals to provide skilled, ethical care aligned with WHO guidelines.

KEY AREAS OF COLLABORATION

- Pandemic Preparedness and Control: Strengthen early warning systems, immunization programs, and pandemic response capabilities, including medical stockpiles and isolation centers.
- Research and Development: Participate in WHO-led research on regional health challenges, such as malaria and tuberculosis, for targeted interventions.
- Health Policy and Standards: Align policies with WHO standards, focusing on public health campaigns, sanitation, disease prevention, and addressing non-communicable diseases.
- Universal Health Coverage (UHC): Work toward ensuring affordable, quality healthcare for all citizens without financial hardship.

LEVERAGING WHO RESOURCES

WHO provides critical support through technical expertise, funding, and global health networks. Kawthoolei can leverage these resources to:

- Access Essential Medicines: Ensure affordable, life-saving medications.
- Strengthen Maternal and Child Health: Improve outcomes with prenatal care, vaccination, and nutrition programs.
- Combat Health Inequities: Bridge healthcare access gaps in rural and underserved areas.

DATA SHARING AND GLOBAL INTEGRATION

Effective collaboration requires robust systems for data sharing and communication:

- Health Information Systems: Develop digital platforms for collecting, analyzing, and sharing health data.
- Transparency and Accountability: Build trust through reliable and ethical data practices.

LONG-TERM BENEFITS

By partnering with WHO, Kawthoolei can:

- Improve public health outcomes, enhancing life expectancy and quality of life.
- Build resilience to health emergencies, mitigating the impact of pandemics.
- Gain international recognition as a capable participant in global health efforts.

Through strategic collaboration, Kawthoolei can develop a sustainable health system that addresses immediate challenges and integrates into global health initiatives, ensuring a healthier future for its people.

PRESERVING CULTURAL HERITAGE WITH UNESCO

By engaging with UNESCO, Kawthoolei can actively safeguard its cultural identity, transform its education system, and earn international recognition for its unique heritage.

SAFEGUARDING CULTURAL HERITAGE

Kawthoolei's rich traditions and historic sites are foundational to its identity. Through UNESCO, efforts can focus on:

- Recognizing Cultural Landmarks: Nominate sites like Thawthikho for UNESCO's World Heritage List to preserve their historical significance and highlight Kawthoolei's contributions to global culture.
- Protecting Intangible Heritage: Document and preserve traditional songs, dances, festivals, and indigenous knowledge under UNESCO's Intangible Cultural Heritage program, fostering cultural pride and continuity.

STRENGTHENING EDUCATION

UNESCO's educational initiatives can help Kawthoolei align with global standards while maintaining cultural relevance. Priorities include:

- Fostering Literacy: Develop literacy programs tailored to Kawthoolei's diverse linguistic and cultural context, improving access for underserved communities.
- Preserving Indigenous Languages: Collaborate with UNESCO to document and integrate local languages into the education system, ensuring cultural continuity.
- Promoting Inclusivity: Implement educational policies that prioritize access for marginalized groups, including rural populations and women, in line with UNESCO's goals.

ADVANCING SCIENTIFIC COLLABORATION

UNESCO's global networks and resources can support Kawthoolei in addressing critical challenges, such as environmental conservation and sustainable development, by fostering scientific research and innovation.

This partnership will strengthen Kawthoolei's identity and position it as a valued contributor to the shared heritage of humanity.

ENVIRONMENTAL COLLABORATION WITH THE UNITED NATIONS ENVIRONMENT PROGRAMME (UNEP)

Environmental sustainability is no longer optional but a requirement for global engagement. Through collaboration with UNEP, Kawthoolei can establish an Environment Protection Agency dedicated to conservation, biodiversity preservation, and combating environmental degradation. Building on existing partnerships, such as with the International Ranger Federation, Kawthoolei's Forestry Department can play a pivotal role in sustainable forest management.

COMMUNICATION INFRASTRUCTURE DEVELOPMENT

Reliable communication infrastructure is a cornerstone of international engagement. Securing an Internet Top-Level Country Domain Name through the Internet Corporation for Assigned Names and Numbers (ICANN) or the International Telecommunication Union (ITU) is a critical step toward enhancing Kawthoolei's digital presence and facilitating global connectivity. Examples of existing country domains include ".uk" for the United Kingdom, ".th" for Thailand, ".it" for Italy, and ".sg" for Singapore.

Additionally, establishing a telephone country code through ITU would solidify Kawthoolei's integration into global communication networks. For instance, Canada and the United States share the country code +1 under the North American Numbering Plan (NANP) without compromising their distinct national identities, providing a potential model for Kawthoolei to consider. Standardized codes for country and language, as maintained by ITU and the International Organization for Standardization (ISO), are essential for ensuring seamless global communication and representation.

PRACTICAL STEPS:

- Research and apply for a unique Internet Top-Level Domain (e.g., **.kt** for Kawthoolei).
- Secure a telephone country code through ITU.
- Adopt standardized language and country codes from recognized international databases (e.g., https://countrycode.org/).

To maximize the impact of these initiatives, investments should also be made in public internet access, digital literacy programs, and robust cybersecurity protocols. These measures will support Kawthoolei's economic, educational, and administrative activities, while ensuring its secure and effective integration into the global digital community.

AIR TRANSPORT AND CONNECTIVITY

Taiwan has several international airports, including Taoyuan (TPE), Kaohsiung (KHH), Taichung (RMQ), and Taipei Songshan (TSA), which receive numerous direct international flights. Similarly, Somaliland operates Egal International Airport (HGA) in Hargeisa and Berbera International Airport (BBO), both handling direct flights from various countries in Africa and the Middle East, facilitating international travel to these territories.

Air connectivity is a critical enabler of trade, tourism, and diplomacy. To establish a robust presence in global aviation, Kawthoolei must prioritize the following steps:

- Establish a National Airline: A national airline would serve as a symbol of sovereignty and a driver of economic growth through increased trade and tourism.
- Secure an IATA Airport Code: Obtaining an International Air Transport Association (IATA) code for Kawthoolei's primary airport is vital for its integration into the global air transport system.
- Obtain an Air Operator Certificate (AOC): Ensuring compliance with international safety and operational standards through an AOC is crucial for credibility and operational legitimacy.
- Collaborate with ICAO: Partnership with the International Civil Aviation Organization (ICAO) will enable Kawthoolei to align with global aviation regulations and safety protocols, facilitating seamless integration into international aviation networks.

By achieving these milestones, Kawthoolei can foster economic development, enhance its connectivity with the world, and ensure the safety and security of its air transport systems.

UNIVERSAL POSTAL UNION (UPU) AND BORDER MANAGEMENT

Establishing a robust postal system that meets Universal Postal Union (UPU) standards is essential for connecting Kawthoolei to global postal networks. This effort requires:

- **Physical Infrastructure**: Developing well-equipped post offices and logistics facilities.
- **Institutional Infrastructure**: Implementing training programs for postal workers, ethical standards, and operational policies to ensure efficient and reliable service.

A regulated and efficient Kawthoolei Postal Service would enhance communication, support commerce, and elevate the nation's international reputation.

CREATING A POSTAL CODE SYSTEM FOR KAWTHOOLEI

Kawthoolei can establish a 5-digit postal code system aligned with international standards to enhance mail delivery and global integration. The system would build on existing governance structures, with the first digit representing the district, the second digit for townships, and the third digit reserved for Karuu (village groups). The last two digits would specify villages or delivery zones, ensuring precision and scalability.

This structured approach improves efficiency, reduces logistical friction, and facilitates e-commerce and international shipping. Implementation would require mapping postal zones, public education, and collaboration with logistics providers for seamless adoption. For example, a postal code 12500 could indicate Mu Traw District (5), a specific township (2), and a designated Karuu (4), with room for village-level precision (00). Example as follow:

Naw Lah Moo
472 Shae Lo Street, Dwe Loe
Mutraw, 52400
Kawthoolei

CUSTOMS CONTROLS AND BORDER MANAGEMENT

Effective border and customs controls are equally crucial for security and trade. Aligning with World Customs Organization (WCO) standards will:

- Streamline the movement of goods under cross-border management.
- Prevent smuggling and other illicit activities.

Investments in shipment tracking technologies and training for customs officers are necessary to ensure secure and efficient border operations, strengthening Kawthoolei's ability to manage its borders and promote lawful trade.

COLLABORATION WITH INTERPOL

Integrating with INTERPOL is crucial for Kawthoolei to combat transnational crimes like human trafficking, drug smuggling, and other illicit activities. This participation will strengthen collaboration with global law enforcement agencies and enhance regional security.

BUILDING A PROFESSIONAL LAW ENFORCEMENT FRAMEWORK

For international law enforcement integration, Kawthoolei needs a professional, well-trained police force operating under a clear legal framework. This framework must define roles, responsibilities, and accountability, aligning with international standards.

KEY TRAINING AREAS FOR LAW ENFORCEMENT

- Proficiency in INTERPOL Standards: Officers must understand INTERPOL's operational frameworks, communication systems, and data-sharing platforms to enable seamless global cooperation.
- Sensitive Information Management: Robust protocols for handling and protecting classified information are essential to maintaining security and credibility.
- Ethical Enforcement: Training must prioritize human rights and the ethical application of laws to maintain public trust and meet international norms.

ENHANCING REGIONAL COLLABORATION

INTERPOL membership enables Kawthoolei to collaborate with neighboring nations on joint operations, intelligence sharing, and coordinated responses, strengthening regional security. Building trust and communication with these partners will further enhance Kawthoolei's international standing in law enforcement.

PROTECTING CREDIBILITY AND REPUTATION

Kawthoolei's INTERPOL collaboration demands adherence to the organization's rigorous standards. Continuous investment in training, infrastructure, and oversight is essential for a robust and trustworthy law enforcement system. Meeting these standards will establish Kawthoolei as a credible international partner, effectively combating transnational crime and enhancing global security.

ADOPTION OF INTERNATIONAL STANDARDS

Adopting international standards is a crucial step for Kawthoolei to align its systems with global practices, ensuring compatibility, efficiency, and credibility in trade, governance, and technology.

TRANSITION TO THE METRIC SYSTEM

Kawthoolei must fully adopt the metric system, the global standard for measurements, to streamline operations and enhance international collaboration:

- Facilitate Trade: Metric units eliminate conversion errors, aligning exports with global markets.
- Support Infrastructure Development: Standardized measurements ensure consistency in engineering and construction, promoting collaboration with international partners.

STANDARDIZATION ACROSS KEY SECTORS

Beyond measurements, adopting international standards can transform vital sectors:

- **Quality Management**: Align with ISO 9001 to ensure products and services meet global benchmarks, enhancing market competitiveness and consumer trust.
- **Environmental Policies**: Implement ISO 14001 to integrate sustainability into projects, demonstrating responsible resource management and attracting international funding.
- **Health and Safety**: Apply ISO 45001 to safeguard workers, reduce hazards, and enhance foreign investment appeal.
- **Energy Efficiency**: Leverage ISO 50001 to optimize energy use, improving sustainability and security.
- **Food Safety**: Adopt ISO 22000 to ensure agricultural exports meet global food safety standards, building trust in international trade.
- **Information Technology Security**: Use ISO/IEC 27001 to protect digital infrastructure, ensuring cybersecurity and fostering trust in Kawthoolei's digital economy.

BENEFITS OF STANDARDIZATION

Adopting global standards offers key advantages:

- **Global Compatibility**: Seamless integration with international systems enables cross-border collaboration.
- **Expanded Trade Opportunities**: Standards-compliant products and services access larger markets and inspire consumer confidence.
- **Attracting Investment**: Compliance with global standards signals professionalism and reliability to foreign investors.
- **Enhanced Efficiency**: Uniform practices reduce inefficiencies and improve resource management.

IMPLEMENTATION STRATEGY

To ensure successful adoption of international standards, Kawthoolei should:

- **Establish a National Standards Body**: Create an institution to manage the adoption, promotion, and regulation of standards.
- **Invest in Training**: Equip industry professionals with skills to implement and maintain standards effectively.
- **Encourage Public-Private Collaboration**: Foster partnerships between government, businesses, and international organizations for smooth transitions.
- **Monitor Compliance**: Develop systems to assess and enforce adherence, ensuring consistency and credibility.

WORLD METEOROLOGICAL ORGANIZATION (WMO)

Collaboration with the WMO is crucial for Kawthoolei to enhance disaster preparedness, mitigate climate risks, and build resilience against unpredictable weather patterns. With extreme weather events and climate change posing increasing threats, robust meteorological systems are essential for both national security and sustainable development.

STRENGTHENING METEOROLOGICAL INFRASTRUCTURE

To engage effectively with the WMO, Kawthoolei must prioritize the development of its meteorological infrastructure:

- Weather Monitoring Systems: Install weather stations, radar systems, and satellite data receivers to ensure accurate and timely data collection across the nation.

- Data Sharing Protocols: Establish systems to share real-time meteorological data with the WMO and regional networks, enhancing global weather monitoring and collaboration.
- Forecasting and Early Warning Systems: Develop advanced capabilities to forecast weather and issue timely warnings for disasters such as floods, cyclones, and droughts.

CAPACITY BUILDING

By investing in the training of meteorologists, climate scientists, and technical staff, Kawthoolei can build a skilled workforce capable of addressing complex climatic challenges. Collaboration with the WMO provides access to specialized training programs, workshops, and international expertise to support this crucial investment.

DISASTER PREPAREDNESS AND CLIMATE RESILIENCE

Leveraging WMO resources can enhance Kawthoolei's disaster preparedness and climate resilience through:

- Risk Mapping: Utilize meteorological data to identify high-risk areas prone to disasters, guiding infrastructure development and resource allocation.
- Community Education: Educate the public on disaster preparedness, evacuation procedures, and climate adaptation strategies.
- Sustainable Development Planning: Incorporate climate and weather data into national planning to ensure future development is resilient to climate impacts.

REGIONAL AND GLOBAL COLLABORATION

Participation in WMO-led initiatives, such as the Global Framework for Climate Services (GFCS) and the Severe Weather Forecasting Program (SWFP), will allow Kawthoolei to benefit from international advancements in weather forecasting and climate adaptation. Regional cooperation through the WMO will strengthen disaster risk reduction and climate resilience.

ENHANCING CREDIBILITY AND RECOGNITION

Active engagement with the WMO will demonstrate Kawthoolei's commitment to global meteorological standards and disaster management. This collaboration addresses immediate climate-related challenges while reinforcing Kawthoolei's credibility and international recognition.

By integrating advanced meteorological practices and aligning with WMO standards, Kawthoolei can protect its population, enhance climate resilience, and contribute meaningfully to global efforts against climate change and weather-related risks.

KAWTHOOLEI TOURISM, WORLD TOURISM ORGANIZATION (UNWTO)

Tourism offers immense potential for economic growth, cultural exchange, and global recognition. By partnering with the United Nations World Tourism Organization (UNWTO), Kawthoolei can position itself as a premier destination, leveraging its cultural, historical, and natural treasures to attract visitors while fostering cross-cultural understanding and enhancing its international reputation.

HIGHLIGHTING KAWTHOOLEI'S ATTRACTIONS

Kawthoolei's unique appeal lies in its:

- Scenic Landscapes: Verdant forests, cascading waterfalls, and mountain ranges ideal for ecotourism and adventure activities like trekking and wildlife observation.
- Cultural Festivals and Traditions: Annual events showcasing traditional music, dance, crafts, and cuisine celebrate Kawthoolei's heritage while attracting tourists.
- Historical and Spiritual Sites: Landmarks such as Thawthikho, Kwekabaw, and other culturally significant sites draw visitors interested in history and spirituality.

BUILDING INFRASTRUCTURE FOR SUSTAINABLE TOURISM

To support a thriving tourism industry, Kawthoolei must invest in:

- Transportation Networks: Reliable road, air, and water systems to improve access to tourist sites.
- Eco-Friendly Accommodations: Lodges and homestays that align with sustainable tourism principles and benefit local communities.
- Visitor Services: Visitor centers, guided tours, and multilingual information to enhance tourist experiences.

Collaboration with UNWTO will provide access to expertise, training, and global promotion platforms, enabling Kawthoolei to:

- Develop Tourism Strategies: Create plans that integrate sustainability and local needs into tourism development.
- Build Capacity: Train local communities to benefit from tourism, fostering economic growth and cultural preservation.
- Promote Globally: Showcase Kawthoolei at international tourism fairs and through UNWTO's networks to attract global visitors.

EMBRACING SUSTAINABLE TOURISM

Kawthoolei must prioritize sustainability to protect its natural and cultural assets:

- Eco-Tourism Programs: Encourage responsible tourism that minimizes environmental impact and supports local conservation efforts.
- Cultural Sensitivity: Ensure tourism respects local customs and offers authentic, meaningful experiences.
- Environmental Conservation: Collaborate with organizations like UNEP to safeguard biodiversity and landscapes.

Tourism is more than an economic driver—it is a tool for shaping national identity and increasing global visibility. By showcasing its unique attractions and adopting sustainable practices, Kawthoolei can position itself as a destination that values its heritage, natural beauty, and hospitality.

Through strategic investments and partnerships with UNWTO, Kawthoolei can unlock tourism's potential to drive economic prosperity, preserve culture, and enhance its global standing, sharing its treasures with the world while fostering appreciation among visitors.

PROTECTING AND PROMOTING INTELLECTUAL PROPERTY

WORLD INTELLECTUAL PROPERTY ORGANIZATION (WIPO)

The protection and promotion of intellectual property (IP) are vital for fostering innovation, encouraging creativity, and building a strong economy. Collaborating with the World Intellectual Property Organization (WIPO) will enable Kawthoolei to safeguard its intellectual assets, support creative industries, and integrate into the global knowledge economy.

ADDRESSING GAPS IN IP AWARENESS

In Kawthoolei, respect for intellectual property remains limited, with practices such as downloading and resharing content without acknowledgement being common. While the community values honesty and non-stealing, a lack of awareness risks ethical erosion. Education and awareness campaigns are urgently needed to align local practices with modern IP norms.

Respect for intellectual property (IP) remains weak in our community, and the concept itself is often alien to our people. Practices such as downloading and resharing content without acknowledgment being common. A community rooted in values of honesty and non-stealing risks becoming unwitting participants in intellectual theft if it remains disconnected from the evolving norms of the modern world. Ignorance of these changes can erode the ethical foundations we hold dear. Education and awareness campaigns are urgently needed to align local practices with modern IP norms.

THE IMPORTANCE OF INTELLECTUAL PROPERTY

IP covers inventions, literary and artistic works, designs, symbols, and trademarks. Protecting these assets is essential to:

- Encourage Innovation: Legal protection incentivizes research and development.
- Support Creative Industries: Protecting music, film, crafts, and other works ensures creators can benefit economically.
- Foster Economic Growth: IP rights attract investment, promote entrepreneurship, and facilitate international trade.

DEVELOPING IP INFRASTRUCTURE

TO BENEFIT FROM WIPO MEMBERSHIP, KAWTHOOLEI MUST BUILD A COMPREHENSIVE IP FRAMEWORK:

- Legal Protections: Draft and enforce laws for patents, copyrights, trademarks, and geographical indications in line with international standards.
- Institutional Capacity: Establish an Intellectual Property Office to handle registrations, monitor compliance, and educate the public.
- Judicial Framework: Develop specialized courts or mechanisms for resolving IP disputes efficiently and fairly.

COLLABORATION WITH WIPO

Through WIPO, Kawthoolei can access resources and expertise to strengthen its IP system:

- Training and Capacity Building: Workshops and technical assistance for legal experts, government officials, and business leaders.
- Policy Development Support: Guidance in creating IP laws tailored to Kawthoolei's cultural and economic needs.
- Global IP Systems: Participation in frameworks like the Patent Cooperation Treaty (PCT) and the Madrid System for trademarks to simplify international IP protection.

PROMOTING CREATIVITY AND INNOVATION

A robust IP framework will unlock Kawthoolei's creative potential by:

- Preserving Traditional Knowledge: Protecting indigenous practices, crafts, and cultural expressions through geographical indications.
- Encouraging Technological Advancement: Empowering inventors to commercialize innovations and attract funding.

- Building a Creative Economy: Ensuring artists, musicians, and writers receive fair compensation and thrive in global markets.

INTEGRATING INTO THE GLOBAL KNOWLEDGE ECONOMY

Engaging with WIPO and international IP agreements positions Kawthoolei as a competitive player in the global economy. Respecting and enforcing IP rights attract investment, foster international partnerships, and support technological and artistic collaboration.

IP AS A PILLAR OF NATIONAL DEVELOPMENT

By aligning with WIPO frameworks, Kawthoolei can make intellectual property a cornerstone of its national strategy. This will preserve cultural identity, empower creators, and ensure the nation's intellectual contributions are recognized globally. A strong IP system will drive innovation, strengthen the creative economy, and enhance Kawthoolei's prosperity and global standing.

A PATH TOWARD GLOBAL INTEGRATION

By adopting international standards, Kawthoolei positions itself as a forward-thinking and globally integrated nation. This commitment to excellence not only enhances the nation's economic prospects but also reinforces its reputation as a reliable and competent member of the international community. Standardization enables Kawthoolei to develop the infrastructure, trust, and capacity necessary to thrive in a highly interconnected world.

Practical recognition also carries the weight of accountability. International funding and technical support are not merely handouts but investments in stability and progress, and as such, carry reciprocal responsibilities. With them come obligations—to manage resources prudently, to uphold human rights, and to ensure equitable distribution of benefits across society.

Ultimately, political recognition might confer prestige, but practical recognition builds substance. It is the difference between being invited to a banquet and having the capacity to contribute meaningfully to the feast. A nation that focuses on building strong institutions, fostering technical expertise, and integrating itself into the operational frameworks of global systems will find that political recognition follows as a matter of inevitability rather than ambition.

The road to becoming a recognized member of the international community is paved not merely with diplomacy but with competence, credibility, and contribution. For any aspiring nation, the lesson is clear: build the house to raise the flag.

Chapter 17

Economy of Growth

The strength of a nation rests in the vitality of its economy—the backbone of progress, the anchor of stability, and the lifeline of national well-being. Breaking free from traditional economic models is no longer optional; it is the gateway to sustainable growth and the foundation of self-reliance.

Burma stands as a poignant example of what happens when economic opportunity collapses and religious institutions proliferate in its place. Monasteries, Bible schools, spiritual sayers, and religious icons multiply—not always as signs of rising virtue but as refuges. If the country offered earning paths for honest labor, able-bodied men and women would not be compelled to wear robes for survival or carry bibles for social mobility. In times of economic hardship, the *spiritual-industrial complex* flourishes: pastors are well-dressed and well-fed, preaching and singing from the stage, while many in their congregations on the floor endure hard labor, weary eyes, and torn clothes. Without economic dignity, even faith risks becoming a livelihood rather than a light.

Meanwhile, war consumes what remains. Most estimates suggest the Myanmar military retains a force of half a million. Civil conflict and military buildup have drawn hundreds of thousands into uniforms—on both sides. Working-aged men are now carrying guns instead of laptops. Youth who might power factories are instead entrenched in armed camps, producing weapons and ammunition instead of wealth. To sustain this machinery, the military has transformed the state into a vast industrial apparatus under its control. Burma's human capital is trapped within the *military-industrial complex*, leaving the economy starved of the hands that build, make, and sustain.

New World, New Economy

No modern marketplace thrives on the clinking of gold and silver coins anymore. No nation fuels its economy with horse-drawn carriages in the name of preserving tradition. No enterprise flourishes by wielding the tools of the past in homage to history. Tradition, with all its beauty and wisdom, is a lantern that illuminates our path—but it must never become the shadow that dims the light of progress.

For generations, Kawthoolei's economy has relied on subsistence farming, resource extraction, and traditional trade—pragmatic yet poorly managed remnants of an old-world system built for survival. Meanwhile, the global economy has transformed in many layers, driven by technology, innovation, and connectivity. Digital industries and knowledge-based markets now lead the charge. Kawthoolei's advancement depends on the emergence of a modern economic framework—one that fosters new industries, harnesses technological progress, and thrives within an interconnected world.

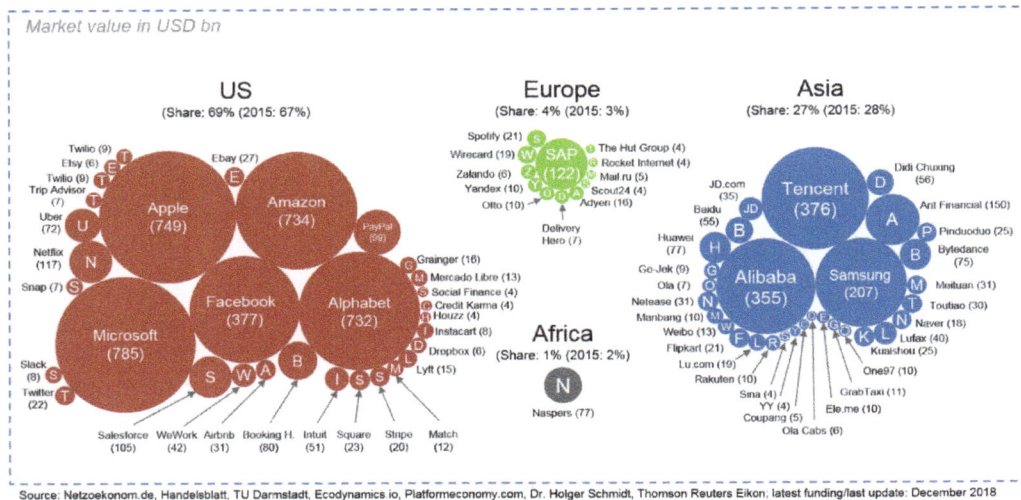

Source: Netzoekonom.de, Handelsblatt, TU Darmstadt, Ecodynamics.io, Platformeconomy.com, Dr. Holger Schmidt, Thomson Reuters Eikon; latest funding/last update: December 2018

When the Suez Canal opened in 1869, it revolutionized global trade, turning the Irrawaddy Delta into a rice-exporting powerhouse. Global demand surged, fetching high prices, and during the British colonial era, Karen communities in lower Burma prospered as landowners, rising with the tide of rice exports. That prosperity, however, was tied to an industrializing world that no longer exists. While the traditional trade economy remains relevant, it is no longer sufficient. The new economy demands innovation over production, ideas over commodities, and transformation over preservation.

The Karen State in Burma remains a region where rice is both a staple food and the backbone of household economies. Rice farming has endured as a way of life, even as the whole Burma grapples with the scars of generational war and the harsh legacy of forced rice rationing and exploitation. While subsistence farming has provided resilience in times of hardship, it cannot serve as the foundation for Kawthoolei's future as a thriving nation.

Wealth is not conjured from the soil alone. Nations do not grow prosperous merely by sitting atop natural resources. It takes adaptation. Take Saudi Arabia and Nigeria both with lots of oil reserves, for instance: Saudi Arabia's trillion-dollar wealth was not built solely on its oil fields but on mastering innovation, managing global enterprises modeling after the U.S. market mechanism, and embedding itself seamlessly into the world economy by adopting modern market mechanisms and technology.

VOCABULARY, SERVICE INDUSTRY, NEW NATURAL DEFENSE

The terms *economy*, *commerce*, and *business* lack clear definitions in the local language, and their concepts are often indistinct and poorly differentiated. When the term *economy* is mentioned in Kawthoolei, the general understanding tends to default to activities such as cutting down trees to sell logs or digging into the earth to extract minerals for mining companies. This narrow perspective reveals a critical need for broader education and discourse on the true scope of economic development, which extends far beyond the mere exploitation of natural resources.

Modern economic concepts, such as commodity, security, exchange, credit, tokenization, derivatives, liquidity, government bonds, liabilities, and assets, will gradually enter Kawthoolei. While their general ideas are understood, the precise terminology and working mechanisms have yet to be fully developed. To establish a functional economy, these terms need to be adapted, coined, and taught in the local language to practice effectively.

Ironically, those who among the loudest voices advocate for preserving tradition often lack a strategy to defend and sustain it. Preservation without preserving. Instead, they misplace human talents and exploit natural resources in ways that undermine the livelihoods and way of life they claim to protect—causing harm both in the short and long term.

Advanced economies thrive on service industries, generating significant wealth through sectors like finance, technology, healthcare, education, and entertainment.

While a nation's natural resources often invite conflict, its human resources are its true wealth and defense. China covets Taiwan's advanced microchip ecosystem, recognizing its irreplaceable value for economic and military dominance. Yet, an invasion would risk the destruction of the semiconductor industry it seeks to control—risk killing the golden goose for the golden eggs. Taiwan, with its mountainous terrain, is fortified not only by geography but by the ingenuity of its people.

Similarly, Singapore, one of the wealthiest nations per capita in the world, lacks natural resources, making it an unlikely target for invasion, for there is nothing to extract once its population is removed. Singapore's treasure lies not in inanimate minerals beneath the ground but in the living talents walking its streets and driving its industries. This understanding forms the foundation of Singapore's *Total Defense* strategy, where Economic Defense stands as one of its five essential pillars: Military, Civil, Economic, Social, Digital and Psychological Defence.

In contrast, a country rich in natural resources but lacking the human capital to manage them becomes a magnet for external exploitation. China has already tightened control over its rare earth extraction at home and increased imports from Kachin State in northern Burma. For four decades, China has been the manufacturing powerhouse of the world, but at a steep environmental cost—its air, water, and soil bearing the scars of industrial activity. Now wealthier and more environmentally conscious, China is shifting towards advanced manufacturing with minimal environmental impact and a focus on green energy. Its manufacturing base will endure, but much of the heavy industry will relocate beyond China's borders, particularly to Southeast Asia, Central Asia, Eastern Europe, and Africa. Myanmar, lying directly under China's geopolitical belly, is set to bear the brunt of this industrial migration.

The high-value specialized services that a nation provides to the world often become their natural defense. There are few nations on Earth that the wealthy have no desire to see invaded— Singapore and Switzerland chief among them. These nations have become sanctuaries for global wealth, attracting vast financial reserves from elites worldwide. Even Myanmar's oligarchs and crony capitalists are known to safeguard their fortunes in Singapore, recognizing its stability and financial security.

VALUE-ADDED ECONOMY: CRAFTING WORTH FROM WHAT WE HAVE

In building Kawthoolei's economy, we must embrace the principle of value addition— transforming raw resources into refined products that command higher returns. Whether it is bamboo sticks and leaves, banana fronds, stones scattered across river yards, pristine mineral water from mountain streams, raw honey, or naturally grown rice and beans— no-chemical-no-pesticide-no-fertilizer-but-natural-better-than-organic products—every resource must be elevated before it is exported or sold.

The gold beneath our soil must not leave Kawthoolei in its raw, unrefined form. Instead, our gold mines must aspire to produce 24-karat, 99.9% pure gold, minted to global standards. Today, we may lack the tools, skills, and infrastructure to achieve this. But, we must set a clear five-year target to export world-class gold products that carry the mark of Kawthoolei—a symbol of trust, precision, and excellence. Products with standard carry a premium.

Knowledge is the first resource we must extract. Having a structure that allows talents and skilled resources to participate in managing our resources is the first step for this. There are individuals who understand the intricacies of mining, refining, and managing these ventures. Yet, all too often, raw minerals and precious materials are extracted under the radar, their true value obscured, and their wealth siphoned away without our knowledge. If we do not know what lies beneath our feet, we cannot craft policies to protect it, nor can we stop those who exploit our ignorance.

Understanding our natural wealth is not merely an academic exercise—it is a safeguard. When we know what minerals we possess, we can negotiate fair terms with investors, implement sustainable extraction policies, and prevent theft disguised as commerce.

The future of Kawthoolei's economy lies not in selling unprocessed gold dust or raw timber but in exporting premium products—gold minted to perfection, bamboo crafted into premium merchandise, rice packaged for international markets, and mineral water bottled with pride. Every resource holds potential, but its value must first be unlocked by knowledge, skill, and vision.

Kawthoolei is to be known as a nation that understands, refines, and commands respect in the global marketplace, not as a land of untapped riches. Every product should not leave our land without having value-added through skill, ingenuity, and craftsmanship.

INFESTATION OF DECEIT

In pockets of Kawthoolei, businesses have emerged that starkly defy its core ideals of honesty, compassion, and truth. Political instability and the absence of law and order have created fertile ground for exploitation by foreign agents, turning these areas into breeding grounds for moral decay. Among the most egregious is the scamming industry—an enterprise with global reach that produces nothing, adds no value, but preys on the trust and livelihoods of others. It is a stain on humanity, a betrayal of Kawthoolei's aspirations, and a sobering reminder of the price paid when justice and integrity are neglected.

The Karen people are no less intelligent or capable than any other race. It is sorrowful to witness some among us allow this infestation to thrive in our land under the guise of survival. Kawthoolei deserves better—its people are destined for greater things than complicity in industries that corrode dignity. This infestation compromises the image of Kawthoolei in long term. No human should live in a world where preying on others is normalized.

Kawthoolei's path forward must reflect its highest ideals, reclaiming integrity and purpose for its people and its nation. A rising nation cannot live on begging for donations, scamming on people, cutting down old forest, or gutting the land for minerals.

Building an Ethical Entrepreneurial Spirit in Kawthoolei

In the relentless tide of globalization, Kawthoolei cannot afford to be in a corner of isolation from the global market, or worse getting to know it only superficially and getting to gamble. The market is no longer confined to Wall Street or the gleaming towers of financial capitals. With a smartphone and an internet connection, someone huddled under a house thatched roof in the jungle, rain pounding above and shadows of creeping creatures below, can access the same investment opportunities as a hedge fund manager with suite and tie in New York. The gates of the global marketplace are wide open, decentralized, and democratized. But an open gate is not an open invitation to easy riches.

Participation in the new money without comprehension is a recipe for ruin. The seamless flow of digital capital across borders demands more than casual curiosity—they require a rigorous understanding of economic systems, financial markets, and the anatomy of business cycles. Without this, our people will not only fall prey to the cunning schemes of external actors but also risk becoming predators themselves, preying on their own communities out of ignorance masked as ambition.

Karen communities have seen it before. A seemingly sincere figure emerges, dripping with confidence and cloaked in the language of "financial freedom," "personal development," and "growth mindset." They set up a Ponzi scheme under the illusion of progress, feeding on collective dreams and insecurities. Thousands of Karen families in richer countries from hard earned wages pooled their savings into this mirage, whispering tales of quick riches from mouth to mouth. And then, as night follows day, the bubble busted. Dreams turned to nightmare, and families were left grappling with despair and losing their savings.

Markets do not work that way. Investments are not magic spells cast on financial charts. If wealth were that effortless, no one would work for W2 salary wages, but every person on earth would be lounging in a penthouse. Real markets operate on cycles—booms and busts, risks and returns.

The sky has opened clear. Our younger generation does not wish to live in deprivation. For too long in the past and in the dark, we the Karen people in the traditional community have romanticized satisfaction with little—assuming it for a moral high ground. I grew up in the Karen community where songs were sung and sermons preached about being a people satisfied with what we had, material wealth and scientific progress was badly evil. But that glorification falsified when the new generation met a wider world. When they see a bigger open water, they sail for a bigger fish. Some are in the business of sale and some financial services, some owners of traditional retail and wholesale, some dream millionaires to billionaires. They dream of financial freedom, of breaking the chains of poverty, of being contributors rather than beggars at the table of the global economy. Some dream big for Kawthoolei economy in a daring entrepreneur spirit.

Kawthoolei needs a growing community of risk-taking business entrepreneurs to be in the world of businesses that make a world-class economy. Yet, ambition without understanding is like fire without a hearth—it burns indiscriminately. We need entrepreneurs, risk-takers, and business leaders who are not seduced by surface-level success but are grounded in the deep knowledge of market systems. We need salespeople who recognize the weight of their promises, who carry integrity as their most valuable currency, and who refuse to exploit the trust of their community for short-term gain.

A generation of shallow entrepreneurs chasing glittering illusion cannot sustain, therefore we must build a community with a foundational grasp of global economic principles—one that understands the cyclical nature of markets, the fragility of financial bubbles, and the moral responsibility that comes with wealth. We can better defend ourselves against the storm of the global economy or have freedom to choose how much we want to participate or if we want to participate at all.

The road ahead demands courage, knowledge, and discipline. The coffee-hype and crypto-mirage that once swept through our community must serve as lessons, not precedents. We will need to educate ourselves and our people—not just the sharp few but a good entire community—on the intricate workings of political economy, financial markets, and ethical entrepreneurship. Only then can Kawthoolei step boldly into the global marketplace—not as gamblers hoping for luck, but as daring entrepreneurial of sustainable prosperity.

FROM BAMBOO TOLLGATES TO GOLDEN GATEWAYS

Kawthoolei is a land blessed with abundant riches—precious resources lie beneath its soil, fertile fields stretch wide above, and the skies open generously with life-giving rain. These are nature's gifts, overflowing with promise. Yet, amidst this abundance, a tragic irony is that vibrant, capable youth, driven by survival or the lure of greed, stand at bamboo toll gates, automatic rifles slung over their shoulders, demanding cash from passing travelers. This stark image reveals more than material poverty; it reflects a deeper poverty of vision.

One traveler, driving from Yangon to the border town of Myawaddy in Karen State, counted more than fifty tollgates—most of them collecting cash with rifles on their shoulders. This practice—whether born from desperation or systemic failure—must not stain the face of Kawthoolei's future. No citizen of a rising nation should have to earn a living through coercion and intimidation, outside the boundaries of law and policy. Such makeshift bamboo tollgates are not symbols of governance but of governance absent, and of dignity and vision absent.

In a nation founded on principles of fairness and collective progress, if there is to be a tollgate, let it stand with legitimacy. Let it be built not from desperate bamboo sticks but from policies well thought out, infrastructure safely engineered and legally sanctioned and systematically designed for the benefit of the entire community.

Tollgates—whether literal or metaphorical—are not inherently unjust. Around the world, they symbolize organized governance, infrastructure maintenance, and communal benefit. When a toll is paid, it must not vanish into unaccounted pockets but flow back into society—to build roads, fund education, and strengthen healthcare systems.

The youth of Kawthoolei must not be left to wander in survival mode, their ambitions narrowed to the next bamboo gate. They deserve better—an access to quality education, vocational training, and pathways into agriculture, industry, and entrepreneurship. Every tollgate incident is not just an economic failure—it is a moral failure. The proliferation of bamboo toll gates indicates a nation at failure morally and economically.

We can and must rebuild Kawthoolei with a system where prosperity is earned through effort, innovation, and participation in a robust and well-regulated economy—not through bullying, extortion, or fear.

In the new Kawthoolei, no one should have to choose between dignity and survival. The wealth of this land—its resources, its fertile fields, and its abundant rain—must be channeled through thoughtful policies and clean governance.

This is not just an economic priority—it is a moral imperative. The bamboo tollgates of desperation must be replaced with the gates of opportunity, where every payment made is a contribution to a shared and brighter future.

BALANCING FOREIGN INVESTMENT AND SELF-RELIANCE

Kawthoolei's economic development welcomes foreign investment while maintaining self-reliance as the bedrock of national economic growth. The vision is not one of isolation, nor of blind dependence, but of a balanced relationship where external support serves as scaffolding, not as the source of our economic house.

Foreign investment brings capital, technology, and access to global markets, but it is a double-edged sword. Even nations as economical stable foundation as Thailand have felt the tremors of over-reliance on foreign capital and global markets. *Thailand's Thirteenth National Economic and Social Development Plan (2023–2027)* explicitly warns against excessive dependence on external forces, highlighting vulnerabilities such as limited bargaining power in global value chains and reliance on foreign capital and exports:

> "Problems relating to structural factors—namely the excessive reliance on foreign countries for capital, technology, production, and exports, as well as limited bargaining power in the global value chain—are ongoing issues for Thailand."

Thailand's heavy dependence on foreign capital left it vulnerable, and the collapse of that capital triggered the Asian Financial Crisis of 1997. Before the crisis, the country experienced a large inflow of short-term foreign investments, which fueled rapid economic expansion and speculative activities, particularly in the property sector. However, when foreign investors began withdrawing their capital due to concerns about Thailand's economic stability, it triggered a currency crisis. The Thai baht collapsed in July 1997 after the government was forced to float it, unable to defend its peg to the U.S. dollar. This marked the beginning of the Asian Financial Crisis, which quickly spread across the region.

Foreign aid is to be viewed as temporary accelerators, not permanent crutches. The role of foreign aid must constantly be calibrated. It must not create dependency but act as a catalyst for building a local economy resilient to external shocks. Humanitarian assistance, when it arrives, should not merely address symptoms but help construct systems that can outlast the aid itself. A sudden cut off of USAid in January 2025 exposed the vulnerability of dependency. When the aid runs out, the community should be able to function independently. Aid should fund schools, not fleeting events; infrastructure, not temporary relief; knowledge transfer, not perpetual handouts.

Moreover, foreign investors often come with their own policies, agendas, and visions for "development." Kawthoolei must engage with these stakeholders from a position of dignity and strategic clarity. Cooperation should be guided by clear national interests, ensuring every penny of investment aligns with the broader vision of economic independence. A good example of a nation that managed aid effectively after war is South Korea, which built its economy in the years following WWII with sole reliance on U.S. aid. By the 1960s, it had gained enough momentum to continue its growth even after the aid ceased.

Investors and aid organizations are not adversaries; many bring goodwill and expect a return on their investment (ROI) through social impact. The greatest return they can witness is a Kawthoolei standing tall—an economy that thrives not because of perpetual handouts, but because of its ability to harness both internal strengths and external opportunities with foresight.

Likewise, in education, military affairs, and socio-political culture, Kawthoolei must discard the habit of seeking external approval—especially when certain rankings and endorsements are hollow. Trophies for being a genecon generous soldier do not bring us any closer to liberation. True sovereignty lies not in being recognized by others, but in being self-determined and self-sustaining capability. Otherwise, other may ridicule us on we, in a distant corner, blindly following the rules they set in a distant tower.

In the end, dignity must remain the lodestar of Kawthoolei's economic journey—a nation capable of welcoming the world while standing firm on its own two feet.

CRYPTOCURRENCY AND CAPITAL INFLOW

Some corner of Kawthoolei has been scarred by the scamming industry, exacerbated by the high potential, near frictionless, unregulated cryptocurrency. This suffering stems from unawareness, compounded by fragmented organization and political instability, which exploit the absence of a regulatory framework and ignorance of local authority.

Among those pursuing political self-determination, cryptocurrency remains largely undiscussed. By combining traditional ledger-based blockchain technology, mathematical cryptography, and financial innovation, it has risen to decentralized finance (DeFi)—a system that may accelerate global integration while simultaneously expanding financial autonomy, an ironic paradox.

Traditionally, nation-states position themselves to attract foreign direct investment (FDI) from large institutions, a process often fraught with friction and long-term commitments to national economic development. Cryptocurrency and its broader technological ecosystem eliminate many of these barriers, enabling faster and more fluid capital inflows. As of this writing, the global cryptocurrency market is valued at approximately three trillion dollars—a figure still tiny compared to total global liquidity. However, the growth trajectory could become parabolic as major institutions and state governments adopt this new technology. This offers a promising opportunity for nations with underdeveloped infrastructure and institutions to access global financial markets. Nevertheless, sustaining such investment requires robust governance structures with strong expertise to ensure stability, security, and long-term economic growth.

The United States has the Securities and Exchange Commission (SEC), which regulates the securities markets and protects investors—an essential framework that entrepreneurs and investors must navigate when raising capital or offering public securities. Thailand also maintains its own Securities and Exchange Commission to oversee financial markets and safeguard the nation's economic stability. Kawthoolei, likewise, must establish such an institution—out of necessity and a commitment to best practices in financial governance.

SELF-RULE ECONOMY AND SECURITY

Security and commerce are intertwined in preserving the nation's sovereignty.

Two agencies of Kawthoolei's Government must oversee the nation's economy and security: the Kawthoolei Economic Development Board and the Kawthoolei National Security Council. Other bodies should actively work for commerce and environmental protection such as the Kawthoolei Chamber of Commerce and the Kawthoolei Environmental Protection Agency.

The *Kawthoolei Economic Development Board* may fall under the Department of Commerce. It is responsible for developing strategies to enhance Kawthoolei's business, industry, innovation, and talent. The Board will formulate both short-term and long-term economic plans for the nation, ensuring the effective allocation of the country's natural and human resources.

The *Kawthoolei National Security Council* will be responsible for the prevention, warning, resolution, and suppression of threats, as well as the maintenance of national security. Kawthoolei may constantly face security threats, both now and in the future. National security is a vital foundation for the nation's progress, prosperity, resilience against challenges, and effective preparedness. Without national security, other aspects of the well-being of the citizens cannot be secured.

National security encompasses multiple aspects, including physical security, military security, economic security, food and energy security, natural and environmental security, and border security.

Kawthoolei Environmental Protection Agency is to protect human health and the environment. Its responsibilities include developing and enforcing regulation, studying environmental issues, sponsoring partnership, and educating the public about environmental concerns.

KAWTHOOLEI CHAMBER OF COMMERCE

The Kawthoolei Chamber of Commerce is an organization that represents and promotes the interests of businesses in Kawthoolei at the national level. This association should be organized at grass-root level for training and strengthening culture of commerce, starting from Ker-ru to Kaw-sar to Kaw-ray to whole Kawthoolei. Some of the key functions are as follows:

Advocacy: The Kawthoolei Chamber of Commerce advocates for policies and regulations that support the interests of businesses.

Networking: The Chamber provides opportunities for businesses to connect with each other, fostering networking and relationship-building among members through mixers, conferences, symposiums, and seminars.

Business Support: The Chamber offers various services to support businesses, such as training programs, workshops, resources on topics like marketing, finance, legal matters, and mentoring services to help businesses grow and succeed.

Information and Resources: The Chamber provides information and resources to businesses, including market research, economic data, a business directory, insurance and discount information, and advertising opportunities for their members.

Promotion and Marketing: The Chamber promotes the interests of its members and the business community through various marketing and promotional activities. This can include advertising campaigns, business directories, and participation in trade shows and expos.

Policy Development: The Chamber engages in the development of policies and initiatives aimed at improving the business environment, economic development strategies, infrastructure improvement, and workforce development programs.

Training and Education: The Chamber provides training and educational programs to local and small businesses at the district and township levels, covering best practices in quality assurance, supply chain networks, and procurement.

AN INDUSTRIAL POLICY TAILORED FOR KAWTHOOLEI

Market economy should not be an official economic policy since the market system is not Kawthoolei ideal. Kawthoolei ought to refrain from opening its economy to market-driven resource extraction until comprehensive policies and regulations are established.

Kawthoolei can adopt a balanced *Industrial Policy*, avoiding the extremes of rigid central planning on one hand and unregulated laissez-faire economics on the other.

- **Central Planning (Rejected, too strict):** A Soviet-style command economy leaves no space for innovation, private ownership, or entrepreneurial spirit.
- **Laissez-Faire (Rejected, too loose):** Unfettered market liberalization risks exploitation, crony capitalism, and unsustainable growth patterns.
- **Industrial Policy (Adopted, guiding hands for growing balance):** Kawthoolei must nurture and prioritize key industries, establish regulatory safeguards to ensure healthy competition, and protect state-owned enterprises while fostering responsible private sector growth and gradually releasing ownership to private hands with public policy.

Premature liberalization risks disastrous consequences. Without robust regulatory frameworks, Kawthoolei could face resource plunder, land degradation, and community exploitation. Instead, economic liberalization must proceed gradually, with clear policies and institutional oversight. The duty of government is not only to regulate business but also to subsidize, promote, incentivize, and oversee strategic industries.

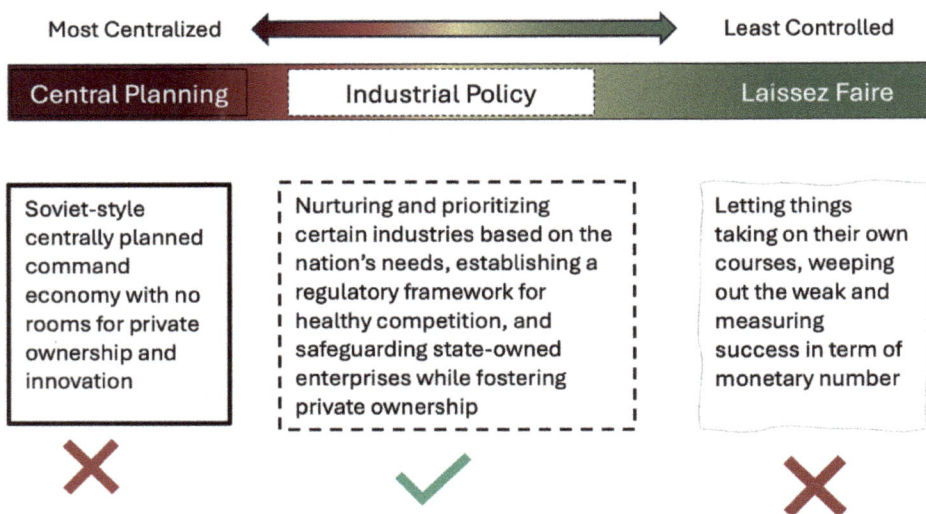

Most Centralized		Least Controlled
Central Planning	**Industrial Policy**	**Laissez Faire**
Soviet-style centrally planned command economy with no rooms for private ownership and innovation	Nurturing and prioritizing certain industries based on the nation's needs, establishing a regulatory framework for healthy competition, and safeguarding state-owned enterprises while fostering private ownership	Letting things taking on their own courses, weeping out the weak and measuring success in term of monetary number
✗	✓	✗

Figure 6. Industrial Policy in the Economic Spectrum

KAWTHOOLEI'S SIX STEPS TOWARD AN ADVANCED ECONOMY

Building a world-class economy begins with strengthening its foundations and progresses toward innovation-driven industries. This model outlines six interconnected steps, each building on the last, to reflect economic theories while addressing Kawthoolei's unique aspirations.

1. **Agriculture: The Foundation**

   Agriculture is the cornerstone of Kawthoolei's economy, providing food security, employment, and raw materials. Modernizing the sector through sustainable practices, precision farming, and climate-resilient crops can unlock its full potential. Investments in irrigation, storage, and transportation infrastructure will reduce waste and improve market access. By transitioning from subsistence farming to market-oriented agriculture, Kawthoolei can create the surplus needed to fuel industrial growth.

2. **Resource-Based Industries: Leveraging Natural Wealth**

   Kawthoolei's abundant natural resources—forestry, minerals, and energy—offer a unique opportunity to drive early economic growth. Resource-based industries can generate revenue, create jobs, and fund infrastructure development. However, sustainability must be at the forefront to avoid environmental harm and overexploitation. Developing local value chains, such as processing raw materials into finished goods, ensures lasting economic benefits while building industrial capacity.

3. **Infrastructure: The Backbone of Development**

   A robust infrastructure network—roads, power grids, water systems, and digital connectivity—is essential for linking people to markets and industries to opportunities. Strategic investments in sustainable and green infrastructure, such as renewable energy and efficient transportation systems, will future-proof Kawthoolei's growth while attracting domestic and foreign investment.

4. **Manufacturing: Adding Value**

   Manufacturing represents the transition to value-added production, transforming raw materials into higher-value goods. By starting with labor-intensive and resource-based industries, such as textiles, food processing, and construction materials, Kawthoolei can create jobs, diversify exports, and reduce reliance on imports. Over time, technical training and investment in machinery will enable a shift to more complex manufacturing industries.

5. **Services: Broadening Opportunities**

   The service sector offers tremendous potential to elevate Kawthoolei's economy. Banking, education, healthcare, tourism, and logistics provide employment while improving quality of life. Digital services, such as IT and e-commerce, can tap into global markets, fostering innovation and creating opportunities for young talent. Kawthoolei's cultural and natural heritage also makes tourism a promising sector, capable of driving sustainable community-based development.

6. **Advanced Manufacturing and Innovation: Reaching Global Competitiveness**
The pinnacle of economic development lies in advancing into high-tech and innovation-driven industries, such as electronics, pharmaceuticals, and renewable energy. Achieving this requires investments in education, research, and development to build a skilled workforce and foster creativity. Partnering with international technology firms and creating innovation hubs will position Kawthoolei as a competitive player in the global economy.

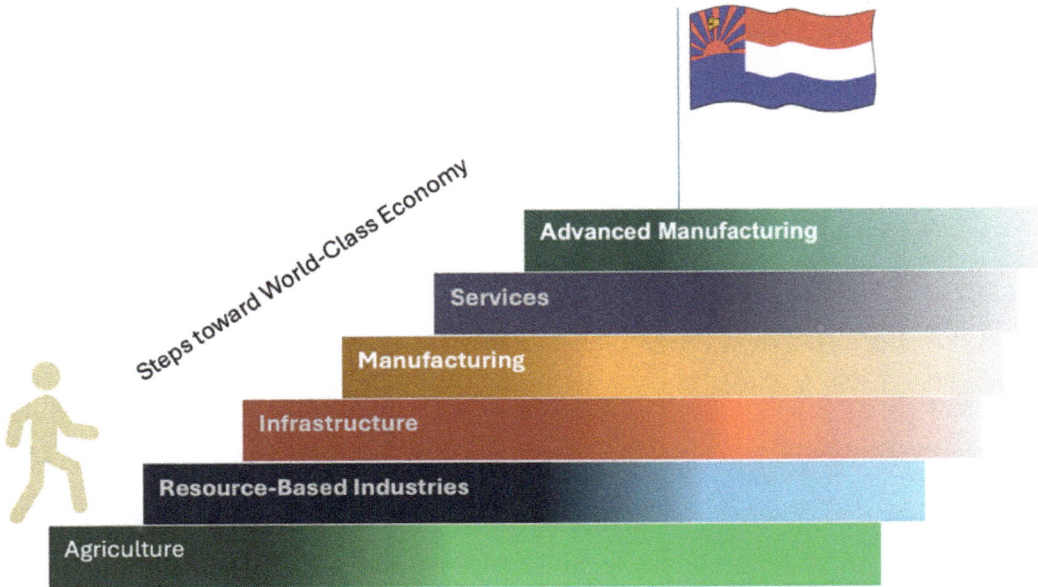

Figure 7. Kawthoolei's Six Steps toward World-Class Economy

Practical Considerations:

- *Education and Human Capital*: Each step depends on a skilled and healthy workforce. Parallel investments in education, vocational training, and healthcare are critical.
- *Governance and Stability*: Political stability, transparency, and effective governance are foundational to managing resources, infrastructure, and industrial growth efficiently.

Challenges to Address:

- *Sustainability*: Resource-based industries and infrastructure projects must prioritize environmental and social sustainability to avoid long-term harm.
- *Funding*: Infrastructure and industrialization require significant capital. Partnerships with development banks, foreign investors, and public-private collaborations will be key.
- *Economic Shocks*: Resilience to external shocks, such as climate change or global economic downturns, should be built into the strategy.
- *Cultural Context*: Economic development must respect and incorporate Kawthoolei's cultural values, ensuring that progress enhances rather than erodes its identity.

PRINCIPLES OF ECONOMIC GOVERNANCE FOR KAWTHOOLEI

There are various economic models that Kawthoolei can learn from the success and failures of others. In shaping Kawthoolei's economic destiny, we are not tasked with reinventing the wheel but with adapting global economic lessons to our unique soil, our people, and our aspirations.

At the heart of national economic policy lies a triad of principles: *Control*, *Allocation*, and *Mobilization*.

Control. The foundation of any economy lies in its governance of resources—land, finance, and policy frameworks. Kawthoolei must not mistake unregulated markets for freedom, nor unrestricted ownership for prosperity. Singapore offers a lesson worth noting: a fiercely business-friendly nation where the government owns 90% of the land and controls 80% of housing projects. Ownership is not merely possession; it is stewardship. Our land cannot become a marketplace trophy, sold to the highest bidder without regard for collective well-being.

Allocation. Every organized economy begins with priorities, not promises. Agriculture has sustained us, but it cannot build our future alone. Kawthoolei must learn to pivot strategically, advancing from subsistence agriculture to manufacturing, and from manufacturing to services and advanced industries. An economy tied eternally to low-tech agriculture is not a national economy—it is a cycle of survival. At least 5% of the national budget is considered for research and development and national wealth is incrementally invested in national education that prepares for the nation's economic growth while defense and stability as the highest priority.

Mobilization. Knowledge without application is like a tool rusting in the shed. Kawthoolei must mobilize its people and expertise towards national priorities with urgency and precision. History offers striking examples—the Manhattan Project, the Apollo Moon Landing— moments when entire nations aligned their brightest minds and resources toward singular goals. During WWII, Ford automobiles turned their mass production to making armored vehicles for battle when their nation is in need. Every year, tens of thousands of youth graduate from local institutions, border high schools, and universities abroad. Without strategic mobilization, their talents risk scattering into a global wind, leaving behind echoes of potential unmet.

These ambitions cannot take root in corrupted soil. A nation's economy is only as strong as its governance. Without integrity in leadership, even the most brilliant economic blueprint becomes a hollow document. Resources mismanaged become liabilities; trust squandered becomes an irreparable chasm between the people and their government.

We are not building an economy for the sake of wealth alone, but for resilience, dignity, and progress. Kawthoolei must not aim to merely survive in the global marketplace—it must learn to thrive, to adapt, and to lead. The task ahead is to control with wisdom, allocate with vision, and mobilize with purpose.

Political liberty sets the people free, nation' economic prosperity dresses the citizen with well-being and crows the nation with dignity.

Night Sky over Kawthoolei, looking up at Orion Belt

SawLah@Photography 2023

Life. Limited internet access. Winter morning, unforgettable youth chat by bonfire.

SawLah@Photography 2023

PART V

LEGACY & REFLECT

The Moonlit December Night Over Kawthoolei

SawLah@Photography 2023

One day,
the Sun will no longer rise,
the Moon will cease to shine.

To ashes and dust
shall return the Earth.

In Heaven shall Memories sing,
recounting the brave hearts
who won victorious
the land of no more darkness.

Chapter 18

The Legend of Ageless Being Returned

There are many tales of the Karen people's origin. Some say they emerged from the depths of a primordial cave, molded by the divine matriarch *Mu-Khra*, the guardian spirit who stirred the first life from the primordial soup, mixing it with her reproductive blood. Others speak of Ywa-Doh, the Benevolent Creator, who brought them forth as Poe-Wal-Koe, the first nation among human families.

Among them, the tale of Totmaeba traces the roots of the modern-day Karen people—every branch, tribe, clan, creed, and subgroup—who recall their migratory journey through him, with him, and ultimately because of him. His story is more than a legend; it is the grand narrative of the Karen people, the wellspring from which all their stories flow.

Totmaeba (tɒ:.'mɛə.bɑ: / TOT-MAE`-BA/) is believed to be the original leader of all branches of the Karen people. Immortalized in folklore and poetry, his legacy has endured for generations.

Elders across every community speak of tradition—how Totmaeba was inadvertently separated from his followers during their migratory journey. For centuries, each generation kept his memory alive, awaiting his return. Yet now, this ancient tale is fading. Or still, the ageless being may yet walk among us.

As the rich practice of transmitting national memory through oral tradition diminishes, a question arises: *Will Totmaeba survive in the hearts of generations to come?* While other nations celebrate their legends with grand festivities and elaborate monuments, the legendary leader of the Karen people walks into obscurity, fading into the mythical affair.

This redeeming story invites us to walk alongside Totmaeba and his followers—the ancient Kann-Yan people of antiquity. Remembering the ancients rekindles a nation's confidence and pride in its roots. It opens a door to ancient wisdom, offering us a chance to investigate our history, understand our existence, and renew our hope.

The following is a personal story, yet a nation's tale—of every corner casually alluded to by elders, whispered by grandmothers, and woven into the literature. It is the story of the ancient ageless being whose legend endures, passed down from generation to generation, a thread binding the past to the present.

Long, long ago… in a faraway land, there lived an ageless being named Puu TotMaeBa.

It was a time when nature reigned supreme. Brittle human souls wandered beneath its overwhelming forces. Restless wild beasts raged and roared. The earth swarmed with creatures that crept and crawled. Venomous serpents slithered, giant and small. Killer birds gilded and soared, while heaven and thunder blasted and poured at will.

In that age, mortals could scarcely distinguish the power of nature from the supernatural. Mother Nature was revered, and her wrath struck fear deep into the hearts of humankind.

In this ancient world, Totmaeba was a man of ordinary physique yet extraordinary strength. One day, during a hunting expedition in the borderlands between the mortal and the immortal realms, he encountered a giant wild boar—an unstoppable beast with tusks like spears, ready to gore him. The beast charged with all its fury, but Totmaeba stood firm. With a single, fateful punch, he wrestled the wild boar to its death.

The next day, when he returned to retrieve his game trophy, the beast's body had vanished. In its place, he found a single mystical tusk—a hunting souvenir unlike any other. From that tusk, Totmaeba crafted a comb to tidy his long, curly hair.

But this was no ordinary comb.

Whenever he ran it through his hair, the gray strands darkened and gleamed with youthful brilliance. Wrinkles faded from his face, and his body returned to its prime. The comb held the magic of rejuvenation, turning him into an ageless being. From that day on, Totmaeba—*the father of the wild boar tusk*—became immortal, forever young.

That is the legend of Totmaeba, the magnificent ageless being, whose story lingers on through the whispers of time.

The Great Migration

Over three-to-four thousand years unknown, a commanding leader named Totmaeba gathered families for an unprecedented endeavor—a journey southward from the sand-flowing river *Tee-set-met-ywaa* toward the equator. What may be known today as the Gobi Desert marked the starting point of their migration into the fertile lands of Indochina.

The migratory path was no straightforward journey from point A to point B. It was a generational quest into the unknown—an exploration for fertile soil and refuge from hostile city-states and rival tribes. Progress was slow and often marked by stop-and-go advancements, where generations passed before the next leg of the journey could continue.

Temptation and Distraction on the Journey

When Totmaeba's followers first entered the subtropical rainforests, they found themselves in a strange and bewildering environment. Rivers and lakes teemed with life, but the abundance brought new challenges. Prawns and crabs, when cooked, appeared bloody and raw, confusing this ingenuous tribe. Travelling families tried to prepare water snails and mussels, only to discover that these stubborn creatures refused to soften no matter how long they cooked. They argued, waited, and debated over the proper way to cook their newfound delicacies.

But indulgence was a distraction. The rainy season was approaching, and time was short. People may tarry, but the monsoon was relentless and unforgiving. Totmaeba urged his followers to hasten. A few families stood up, ready to follow, but most remained, seduced by the mystic comfort of their surroundings. Seeing the delay, Totmaeba gathered the willing and led them forward, slashing through the undergrowth with his long machete to blaze a trail.

Lo and behold, they entered a *musa* paradise, where banana trees and other plants regenerated with astonishing speed. By the time others tried to follow, the cut plants had already regrown, blocking the path once again.

Some whispered, believing Totmaeba possessed a regenerative power that caused the plants to sprout in no time. Under the impenetrable rainforest canopy, they shrugged and murmured, "We cannot catch up with Totmaeba. The trees have regrown, and there is no path left for us."

And so, Totmaeba trekked southward and disappeared. His followers, left without their guiding force, became disoriented. Ever since that fateful day, our ancestors—and we, their descendants—have wandered without direction.

Lonely, the Green Land

During the long migration, our ancestors witnessed the rise and fall of dynastic kingdoms and feudal city-states. They avoided the chaos of warring civilizations, choosing instead to follow rivers through rugged terrain where no trace of human habitation could be found. Their journey continued until they discovered a valley vast enough to shelter the wandering families—a land they could call home.

When our ancient ancestors finally settled in this newfound, virgin land, the world was quiet but for the sounds of nature. Life was serene, though loneliness lingered in the air. The land was lush and green, rivers teemed with life, and the dark, fertile soil promised abundance. Aptly, they named it Kaw Lah (gɔːˈlɑː / GOR-LAA), *the Green Land*, a place of vast valleys, rolling hills, and towering mountains carved by rivers and dotted with lakes and springs. At that time, even the Irrawaddy's deltas had not yet fully formed.

To mark their new homeland, our ancestors raised a red garment atop a long bamboo pole, a declaration of settlement—proclaiming to all who might come that this land was theirs, the first settlers. They lived happily, yet every generation continued to hope for the return of their ageless leader, Totmaeba.

These quiet, gentle people led steady, uneventful lives for many years—in a land without thieves, without greed, and, above all, without man-made grief. Time passed, and their peaceful existence remained undisturbed … until strangers began to arrive.

At first, some arrivals were decent and respectful. Others were boisterous. Our ancestors, being people of goodwill, accepted them all. But not all came with honest intentions. Into the land of kindness, shadows crept.

At night, dogs barked uneasily, and household animals stirred with alert noises as strange spirits seemed to lurk in the darkness. The land where there was no stealing, no quarreling, and no lying began to change. Over time, the purity of Kaw Lah diminished, and with it, the simple, harmonious life of its first settlers faded into memory.

The Great Spread

The story of this migration explains the great geographical spread of our people across what is now modern-day Thailand and Burma. Multiple waves of migration gradually divided our ancestors, until some regrouped and settled near each other throughout the Green Land. Over time, they developed distinct dialects and regional accents, shaped by their new environments and evolving experiences.

Some families journeyed all the way to the sea, settling in the fertile lowlands of the Irrawaddy Delta, while others remained in the highlands, becoming mountain dwellers with their own unique ways of life. Some tracked the leader southward until they reached the shores of the ocean, while others stopped in what is now Chiang Rai and Chiang Mai in Northern Thailand. Some settled in Phekhon (Shan State), others in Demoso (Karenni State), and still others ventured as far as the Tenasserim Coast, at the southern tips of modern-day Burma and Thailand. A few pushed westward, reaching what is now the southern region of Arakan (Rakhine State), while many found refuge in the fertile Irrawaddy Valleys near modern-day Pyay (Prome)—until later arrivals forced them out.

It took over a millennium for our ancestors to complete this monumental journey from the sand-flowing river to the Green Land. They arrived in multiple waves, each one shaping the land and leaving a legacy. The last great wave marked the beginning of the Karen Era, 2,764 years ago—counting from the year 2025.

A Family Scattered, Yet Whole

Given the great diversity among the Karen people, some have speculated that distant relatives might still live in Southern China or other parts of Southeast Asia. But the evidence tells a different story. Linguistic traces reveal that all Karenic-speaking peoples settled exclusively in what is now modern-day Thailand and Burma. Despite the vast distances separating them, they remain one people, bound by shared roots, language, and history and the moral tradition—the grand migratory journey that brought them to the Green Land.

The Rain Frog Drum

The Karen rain frog drum, also known as a Heger Type III bronze drum, is not merely a musical instrument but a powerful symbol of Karen heritage. Used in rituals and festivities, it connects the present with the distant past—a surviving artifact from the time when our ancestors journeyed through territories rich in bronze at the peak of the Bronze Age.

Among the hundreds of varieties of bronze drums found across Asia, the distinctive shape of the Karen rain frog drum sets it apart. It is believed that these drums were specially commissioned by our ancestors, reflecting their unique cultural identity. While similar bronze drums are found in different countries, the rain frog drum belongs unmistakably to the Karen people. This enduring legacy is honored in the flags of many Karen branches, where the drum stands as a central emblem.

> "Today, the Karen are among the most populous hill tribe groups in Burma. They occupy a broad area extending from Taunggyi and the Shan State in the north, along the Salween Valley, to the southern border of Burma. Other Karen groups live in the Arakan Yoma and the Irrawaddy Delta. The people in this study, referred to as Karen, do not form a homogeneous group, as numerous subgroups differ remarkably in language, customs, and name. However, one cultural trait has remained across all Karen groups: the use of the bronze frog drum in various religious rituals and as a medium of exchange." (Cooler, Richard M., 1995. *The Karen Bronze Drums of Burma*)

A Living Connection to the Past

The bronze drum is more than an artifact; it is a living connection to our ancient beliefs, practices, and way of life. While much of our indigenous heritage has been corroded by time and neglect, the rain frog drum has survived—thanks to bronze's remarkable resistance to rust and decay. Unlike the alterable nature of oral traditions or perishable symbols, the drum endures, allowing us to see, touch—even taste and smell—and hear the same resonant sounds that echoed through the lives of our ancestors thousands of years ago.

In a modern world where much of our ancient heritage fades away, the rain frog drum remains. It is a tangible link to the past, reminding us of who we are and where we came from, its deep, resonant hum a timeless song of our people.

Karen artisans continued to reproduce this bronze heritage until the 19th century. However, the mastery of the lost-wax casting technique, essential for crafting the intricate patterns and fine decorations of earlier centuries, gradually disappeared in the 20th century. Attempts to revive this ancient art largely ended in disappointment. The reproductions of the past century reveal unsteady workmanship, a stark reminder of the untrained hands that struggled to replicate what had once been a refined and highly skilled craft.

Remembering the Ancients in the Contemporary World

Remembering ancient figures is not an exclusive affair of the Karen people. Many cultures honor their ancestors and literary giants whose legends left no direct messages but whose legacies were reconstructed by later generations. Often, the influence of such figures transcends the boundaries of a single nation, becoming symbols of universal wisdom and timeless values.

These ancient figures—whether leaders, poets, or philosophers—are less about the words they spoke and more about the stories we tell to give meaning to their lives. Their enduring presence shapes our understanding of heritage, helping us bridge the distant past with the present.

King Arthur, the Perfect King

Throughout British history, King Arthur—the mythical yet perfect king, eternally dwelling in the national psyche—has been celebrated as the ideal monarch, leading noble knights on holy quests. His legend evolved through countless retellings, merging multiple versions into a singular mythic figure.

By the sixteenth century, King Henry VII harnessed the Arthurian legacy for his own ends, commissioning the Round Table to be repainted with the Tudor rose at its center and depicting Arthur in his own likeness. The Victorians later enshrined Arthur as the pinnacle of medieval English knighthood, reimagining Camelot as a timeless medieval court.

During the 1870s refurbishment of Winchester Hall, elaborate stained-glass windows were added, reflecting a continued fascination with heraldry, chivalry, and legendary kings like Edward III, who led England through the Hundred Years' War, his son Edward, the Black Prince, and Henry V, the victor of Agincourt. These depictions, including Arthur's fictitious coat of arms and Edward IV's genealogy linking himself to the mythical king, highlight the enduring influence of Arthurian legend in shaping the lineage and identity of English royalty. (Snow, Lipscomb, and Lewis, 2024)

The phrase "King Arthur shall return when the nation calls upon him"—or at least when a generation longs for the return of the ideal king—evokes a mythic archetype that transcends literal history. Much like the prophecy tied to legendary figures in other cultures, it suggests Arthur's return is not bound by time but by need—when the land grows weary, leadership falters, and the people yearn not for mere authority but for a ruler who embodies justice, unity, and virtue. It is not so much a promise of resurrection as it is a call to remember—and to rekindle—a time when collective memory and moral yearning gave rise to the ideal of a true king, whether embodied in a person or reflected in principle.

Hta: The Classical Poetry of the Karen People

Like many ancient societies that relied on poetry to preserve knowledge, the Karen people have a rich oral tradition known as *Hta*. Across cultures, classical poetry serves as the foundation of a nation's memory, later studied and reinforced by new generations using modern tools and techniques to safeguard heritage. *Hta* embodies the literary soul of the Karen people—woven with stories, fables, proverbs, poetry, courtship songs, teachings, historical records, and divine essence.

The Practice of Poetry Before Modern Times

In the early part of the previous century, Western-educated Karen individuals remained closer to their roots, where the practices of ancient poetry were still alive. They had a deeper connection and understanding to their roots. Oral tradition—the cultural knowledge passed from one generation to the next through spoken word—was widely practiced. At the arrival of modern education, those traditions have dwindled. Regrettably, few contemporary Karen scholars have ventured to record or explore this legend in depth although some literature acknowledge this legend. If they mention it at all, they often reduce it to *a mythical romance*, dismissing it with a contemptuous tone.

Disservice to one's own people, such dismissiveness undermines the nation's memory, especially when such gestures are made without an understanding or genuine effort to appreciate the rationale, the longing, and the artistry of speech traditions.

The Decline of Oral Poetry

Two significant forces have accelerated the decline of Hta. First, those who receive formal education often lack the time and passion to dedicate themselves to the recitation of classical poems, which demand decades of mastery. Second, the rise of modern entertainment and digital media has hastened the erosion of this millennium-old generational practice.

Poetry as Intellectual Sport and Courtship

In traditional society, *Hta* was more than poetry; it was a dynamic part of life. Youths practiced and refined their verse, using poetry as a practical tool in courtship. Evening entertainment and education converged in poetry recitation, where clever rhymes and verbal agility were admired. For elders, mastery of *Hta* was a mark of intellectual strength.

Poetic duels were common. These exchanges began with an invitation: "La ah laa," called one master of verse, issuing a challenge.

"La ah laaa …," came the reply from another, signaling readiness to engage.

And so the poetic duel began—a test of memory, creativity, and wit, weaving words into an artful contest that delighted all who listened.

Has the Nation Deprived of National Imagination?

Much of human progress is founded on sheer imagination. Every institution and civilization ever created is a product of it. Imagination is what separates humans from the rest of the animal kingdom. Yet, among the Karen people, they are shy of bold imagination, particularly when it comes to embracing the richness of their own heritage after being influenced by the education of foreign. They are shy of themselves to accept the fact that nations are built on dreams, dreamers build the nation.

Unfamiliar with the oral tradition of Karen *Hta*, many intellectuals grow frustrated with ancient Karen history. Figures like Totmaeba are easily dismissed as mythical fabrications. But is Totmaeba truly irrelevant, or has the impoverishment of imagination stifled our inspiration and blinded us to the power of our own stories?

The Minority Mindset: Murderer of the Ageless Legend

Like a cancer, the minority mindset is spreading through the body of our nation, crippling its organs. Those infected with this mindset reject their ancient leaders while exalting foreign figures and imported ideas. They venerate distant thinkers and dismiss the wisdom of their own ancestors. Thinkers from distant lands sound smarter, their ideas more polished—so we hastily embrace them. Yet, these ideas, born of different contexts, are not always universal and may offer little benefit to our unique existence.

Why must the descendants of Totmaeba endure generations of hardship while other human societies enjoy technological progress and modern comfort? Is this suffering a coincidence, or is it the direct consequence of forsaking our own prophets and poets? Could it be that breaking ancient vows has left us vulnerable to tragedy?

The Generational Mandate

Our generation stands at a crossroads. We can break this spell. We can discard the toxic minority mindset that clouds our national thinking and erodes our self-esteem. Without a unified national spirit, our individual successes—no matter how stellar it is—will remain scattered and meaningless, failing to advance the collective progress of our people.

The "minority" label reduces us to a tragic race, a constant humanitarian crisis in the eyes of the world. When we resist and reclaim our land, we are branded separatists, destructive to the "state." When we work hard, our labor is not celebrated as a contribution to global progress but seen as a burden—a needy people trapped in a cycle of dependency.

It is time to reclaim our imagination and rewrite the narrative. The power to reshape our destiny lies within us, not in borrowed ideas but in the stories and strength of our own people.

Torrents of Abuse

No one ever knew whether Totmaeba truly entered the realm of immortality, but every generation awaited his return, yearning for him in songs and poems. Two centuries ago, outsiders seized upon this ancient hope, twisting the story to their advantage by replacing Totmaeba with a good-looking man from the distant Middle East.

A host of the Karen population fell prey to this deception. That fraudulent legacy persists. These invaders, disguised as saviors, subjugated the land, slashed our traditions, and demonized our native spiritual practices. Among the most trusting to foreign ideas, urban Karen elites began to scorn their rural kin, disparaging traditional practices and openly degrading them—even lamenting in song.

Educated urban dwellers grew embarrassed by their own roots, customs, and beliefs. What had once been a proud heritage became a mark of inferiority. Our esteem crumbled. We were reduced to untamed wild beasts in the eyes of the world, labeled as a "tribal minority," while the grounded legend of Totmaeba was dismissed as mere tribal fantasy.

How can a nation make progress by disparaging itself?

TOTMAEBA: THE NAMELESS AGELESS PATRIARCH

Never did we know the birth name of this ancient leader—only his alias, Tot-Mae-Ba. The practice of calling someone by a family name is still alive in rural Karen villages, where parents lose their personal names to their first child or eldest grandchild. A mother becomes "Mother of [child's name]," a grandmother becomes "Grandma of [grandchild's name]." Unlike most cultures where children's names derive from their parents, in Karen tradition, it is customary to address adults by the names of the eldest family member.

A juvenile in a Karen village would rarely know an elder's birth name since she never heard of it since growing up. Even if they did, using it would be considered far too direct. Proper etiquette requires addressing married adults by a family-based title. Thus, from his name Tot-Mae-Ba, we know this ancient leader as a patriarch.

Even though we refer to him as "he" in English the Karenic language does not distinguish gender in its pronouns. Younger generations call him Puu Tot-Mae-Ba, where *Puu* is an honorific prefix for elders, signifying respect. To address him without such a proper attribute would sound impolite and dismissive. He may not be elderly old.

An ancient Chinese sage, Lao Tsu, vanished into the realm of immortals after leaving behind one of the most enduring philosophies in human history—the *Tao Te Ching*, a text among the most translated in the world. According to legend, he wrote nothing himself but spoke his wisdom to a gatekeeper before disappearing into the west, remaining a semi-legendary figure whose thought shaped the soul of East Asian philosophy.

Totmaeba, too, is said to have entered that same mystical realm—a place beyond time, hidden in the vast stillness of western China, where those who lead through silence and guide without command may come together. Perhaps their paths crossed in that unseen domain, where wisdom flows, and the ages pause to listen. What would the two immortals exchange if their paths crossed?

THE CENTER OF NATION STUDIES

Our ancient leader left no surviving verbal message—no recorded dialogue or elder's counsel passed down through generations. Yet, the questions surrounding his life and leadership linger, demanding study and reflection:

Why did he organize the great migration in the first place?

What ancient threat compelled our ancestors to follow him?

How did he organize families and inspire such trust in his leadership?

Why did he allow such loose discipline during the long journey?

Did he promise to return if his people ever lost their way?

Why do we remember him as a leader, not a king or deity, unlike the ancient rulers of other civilizations?

Is this an indication that an anti-feudalistic spirit runs deep in the Karen psyche, even to this day?

What would he say if he saw our current plight?

Does his magical comb still possess its power to rejuvenate?

And when he returns, will he unify us once more?

Puu Totmaeba, will you return to mend this broken nation?

Awaken us from darkness and lead us into the light!

When the Karen people re-establish themselves as a nation, Totmaeba must be studied through an interdisciplinary lens at the center of our national studies—explored across fields such as history, philosophy, literature, archaeology, anthropology, linguistics, political science, climatology, Earth science, genome research, performing arts, and fine arts.

THE POWER OF MEMORY AND THE QUEST FOR UNITY

In an age of interconnected digital machinery, the pursuit of ancient mysteries may seem quaint and outdated. Yet we must have the power to decide. If we are willing, we can let this ancient figure live among us once more—just as he has lived for generations in poems and songs.

The search for ancient leaders does not rest solely on archaeological evidence. Hard evidence, no matter how durable, will turn to dust in time. But the stories passed down from generation to generation endure, retaining their freshness for millennia, giving birth to imagination to every generation.

Totmaeba has been immortalized in our oral traditions, but he will cease to live among us when we stop remembering him. He will vanish from our collective memory when his name is no longer uttered.

Without acknowledging our roots and this common leader, our quest for unity will remain elusive. Our identity will be hollow, and our existence fragile. But the return of Totmaeba—the restoration of his memory—will bring together the four main branches of the Karen people in a reunion of roundtable fellowship.

Unity is divine, as our forebears said. And when a nation's honor is restored, she no longer needs to be at war with others. She stands strong in peace, secure in her own dignity and destiny.

THE LEGEND WHO WALKS ON EARTH

Totmaeba is not merely an ancient legend or a pioneer of the past. As an ageless being, he must still be walking among us—unaware—studying pass midnight in libraries, teaching in classrooms, organizing communities, falling in love like any ordinary human being, composing poems, writing essays, cramming thesis papers in colleges, programing apps, testing robotic automation, carrying a rifle on her shoulder among freedom fighters, or commanding troops to drive out invading forces. They may be handsome, shy, or beautiful and quietly living, walking among us.

After all, we are his descendants. Totmaeba can relive through us again and again.

The spirit of Totmaeba in the Karen people is a national awakening. With a renewed spirit in our generation, we can end this ceaseless war and halt the senseless killings. We can rebuild this land and heal this nation.

THE REGENERATIVE SPIRIT OF TOTMAEBA

To labor for the progress of our nation, we must be creative, bold, and organized—acting not as isolated individuals but as a unified nation. A nation is the collective expression of its people, and individual character matters. Each of us must live with honor, dignity, and respect.

The spirit of Totmaeba is a regenerative spirit—a daring explorer's spirit, anti-stagnant, pioneering, and organizing leadership. It is a spirit with the power to lift up our people, to break the cycle of suffering, and to bring goodness not only to the Karen people but to our neighbors, their neighbors, and ultimately to all of humanity.

> Totmaeba's journey with his followers epitomizes the path of human civilization—ever moving, ever exploring. Societies that learn the unfamiliar and adapt with courage move forward. Those that cling to ignorance, status quo, and unexamined tradition, fearing new horizons, risk becoming lost—wandering in a jungle of confusion and disorientation.

Totmaeba's Spirit awakens. Arise, O nation—stand tall among the nations, and let your best shape a better world for all.

SawLab@Photography 2023

A Floating House by the River

Map of British Raj (India) – 1909

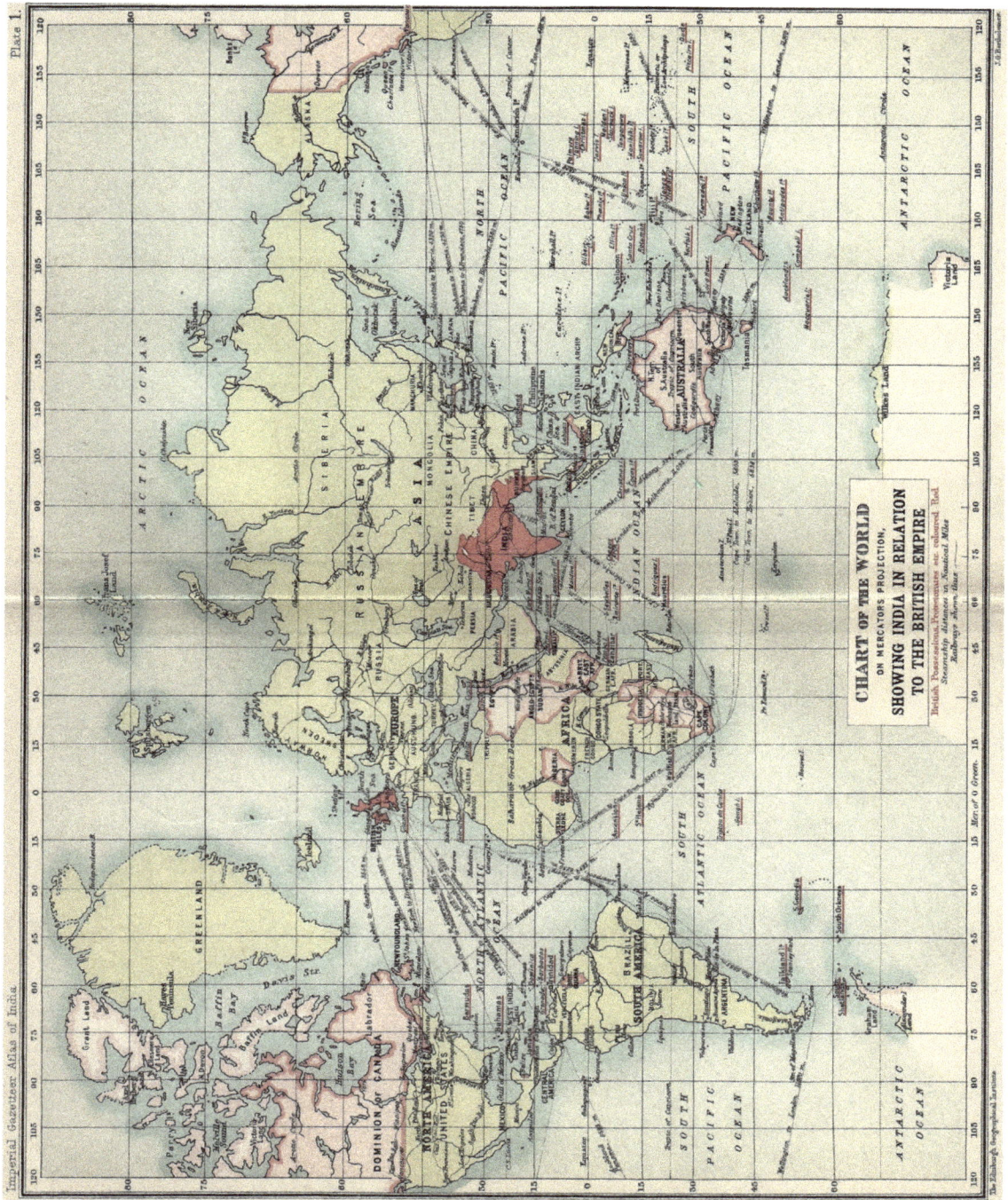

Source: J. Bartholomew, Edinburgh Geographical Institute (Public Domain)
https://en.wikipedia.org/wiki/British_Raj#/media/File:India-or-British-Raj-in-British-Empire-1909.jpg

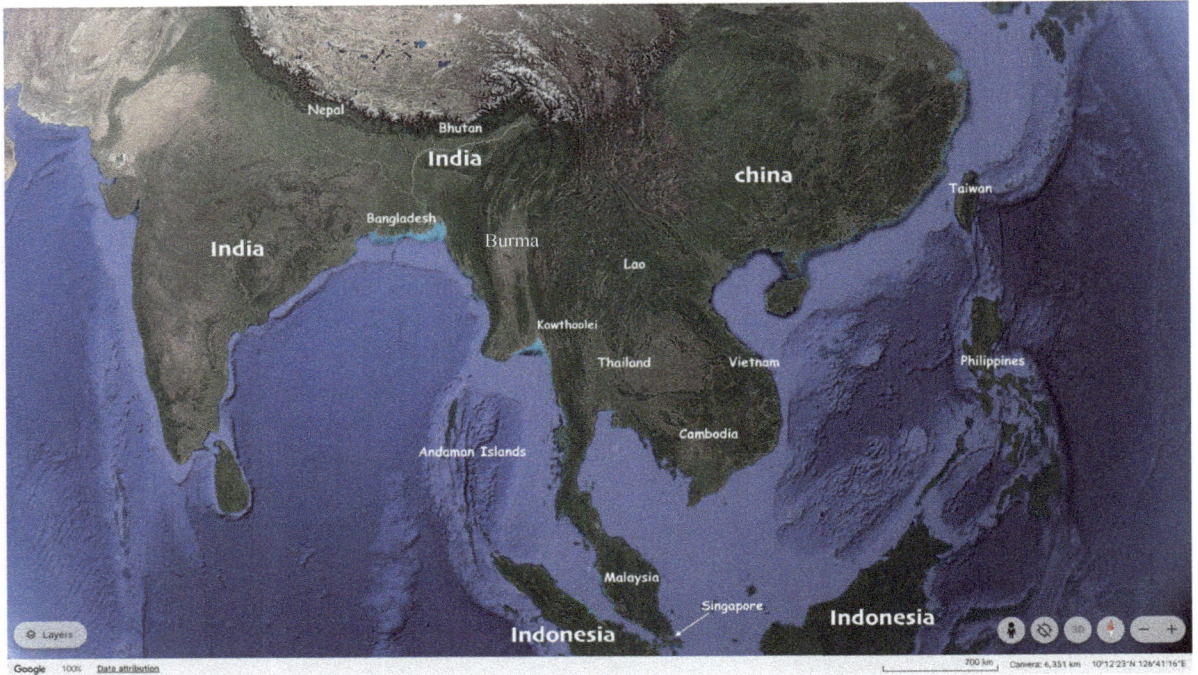

Map of South and East Asia

Google Map 2025

Kawthoolei Stamps

(1986, Marnerplaw Era)

source: digital.lib.washington.edu

NOTE ON THE USE OF BURMA VS. MYANMAR

The country known today as Myanmar remains understudied in contemporary academic circles. Decades of military rule, beginning in 1962, effectively sealed the nation off from international access, limiting research and reliable data. Even the name of the country reflects its complexity.

In popular journalism, the country is often referred to with parentheses—Myanmar (Burma)—while most international institutions use Myanmar as the formal name. This change was enacted by the ruling military junta in 1989, which declared *Myanmar* the official name to represent both the state and its diverse population, functioning as both *noun* and *adjective*. However, the United States government still officially refers to the country as Burma, reflecting the contested legitimacy of the military's renaming.

There are occasions when contemporary English literary circles refer to Burma as "Southeast India," a phrase rooted in colonial-era geography and literary memory. This usage is influenced in part by George Orwell, the renowned British author who spent a significant part of his early career in colonial Burma. Although geographically inaccurate today, the phrase reflects lingering historical and literary associations with an unfamiliar and often overlooked country. It speaks more to inherited perceptions than to any formal political recognition.

Notably, historian Thant Myint-U continues to use *Burma* in his book *The Hidden History of Burma*, where he elaborates on the historical roots of the term *"Myanma"*—a name that appears in inscriptions dating back centuries, used by people living along the Irrawaddy River valley.

In this book, I use *Burma* and *Myanmar* interchangeably, as they refer to the same geographical space. However, I make certain distinctions in usage:

- I use "Burma" specifically to refer to the same territory under British colonial rule (1858–1947), when it was administered as a province of British India.
- I use "Myanmar" to describe the contemporary state, particularly as it is recognized by younger generations as a multicultural society. Likewise, it is in international discourse. Yet outside of Southeast Asia, the name *Myanmar* still rings unfamiliar to many.
- I use "Burmese" in multiple senses: to denote the Burman ethnic majority, the Burmese language, and sometimes, the elite ruling class.
- I use "Burman" more narrowly, to refer to the indigenous ethnic group native to upper Burma who speak Burmese—a language that has now become the lingua franca across the country.

Explaining *Burma*, *Myanmar*, and *Burmese* is inherently complex—layered with competing historical narratives, political designations, and constructed meanings. In the spirit of self-determination, many non-Burmese-speaking ethnic communities do not refer to themselves as *Burmese*, as the term often implies submission to cultural or political dominance.

NOTES

CHAPTER ONE

ON THE CHARACTERISTICS OF THE KAREN PEOPLE

In the First Karen New Year Message of 1939, signed by prominent Karen national leaders—Dr. San C. Po, Shwe Ba, Hla Pe, Sydney Loo Nee, and Saw Pe Tha—the message affirmed

> *"Certain distinctive qualities that have been given us. These included simplicity, a love of music, honesty, steadiness, and a sense of God"*

In his seminal work *Burma and the Karens*, Dr. San C. Po further advocated for the recognition of the Karen nation and the right of its people to live free from domination, harassment, and persecution. His words reflect not only a historical moment of aspiration but also a timeless call for dignity, freedom, and self-determination.

ON SGAW LER TAW AND THE LEGACY OF LEADERSHIP

From 1950 to 1953, following the death of Saw Ba Oo Gyi—the first President of the Kawthoolei Government—Sgaw Ler Taw served as the Acting Head of the Kawthoolei Government. He was also the General Secretary of the Karen National Union (KNU) from 1949 to 1959. A committed statesman and voice of the Karen cause, he later authored *The Karens and Their Struggle for Freedom*, published by the Karen National Union in 1991.

In his writings, Sgaw Ler Taw offered not only a historical account, but a poetic affirmation of the Karen people's identity and relationship to their land:

> *"We were, according to most historians, the first settlers in this new land. The Karens named this land Kaw-Lah, meaning the Green Land. We began to peacefully clear and till our land free from all hindrances. Our labours were fruitful, and we were very happy with our lot. So, we changed the name of the land to Kawthoolei, a land free of all evils, famine, misery and strife: Kawthoolei, a pleasant, plentiful, and peaceful country. Here we lived characteristically simple, uneventful and peaceful lives, until the advent of the Burman."*

He also reflected on the character of the Karen people:

> *"By nature the Karens are simple, quiet, unassuming, and peace-living people, who uphold the high moral qualities of honesty, purity, brotherly love, co-operative living and loyalty, and are devout in their religious beliefs."*

Sgaw Ler Taw's legacy remains not only in his leadership during a pivotal era, but in his effort to record and affirm the moral and cultural foundation of the Karen nation.

ON THE VIRTUOUS CHARACTER AND IDEALISM OF THE KAREN PEOPLE

In *A Star in the East: An Account of American Baptist Missions to the Karens of Burma* (Fleming H. Revell Company, 1920), Rev. Edward Norman Harris, a missionary with the American Baptist Foreign Mission Society to the Shwegyin and Paku Karen missions, offered a compelling account of the Karen people's character. He described them as:

"Mild and peaceable, truthful and honest, affectionate and industrious."

Harris further remarked:

"The Karens were far and away the most moral and the most virtuous people of the East."

And added:

"As to the Karens in particular—if something aside from brute force is of value in the world, if virtue, idealism, and integrity are real assets and not mere liabilitie."

Such reflections—while written from the perspective of an early 20th-century missionary—nonetheless recognize the deep moral fabric, high idealism, and virtuous nature long embedded in the Karen worldview.

ON THE POETIC SPIRIT OF THE KAREN PEOPLE

1. In *The Rice Fairy: Karen Stories from Southeast Asia* (Simplicity Press, 1989), a collection of traditional Karen folktales, American Baptist missionary and anthropologist Rev. Edward Norman Harris recorded the rich oral traditions of the Karen people. Harris, who grew up in Shwegyin (Hsaw-Hteet) what is now the Kler-Lwee-Htu Administrative Area of the KNU, lived among the Karen community nearly a century ago.

   Reflecting on their character, Harris wrote: *"The Karens, a mountain tribe of Burma and northern Thailand, are unusual in several ways. They are poetic, musical, rigidly moral, and believe in one God."*

His work stands as one of the earliest efforts to document and honor the Karen worldview through its folklore—capturing the spiritual depth, moral clarity, and cultural richness of a people whose stories continue to carry meaning across generations.

2. In *The Loyal Karens of Burma* (1887, London), Donald Mackenzie Smeaton observed: *"The Karens all sing—they have an inborn love of music—and beautiful singers they are. The imagery used in many of their odes is rich and pleasing. The flowers, the birds, the great cliffs and crags, the rivers, the stars are all themes of song."*

3. The oral tradition of the Karen people—expressed through folklore, fables, and poems—offers deep insight into their moral values and way of life, often untouched by outside influences. Many of these stories, preserved on the KarenSAll YouTube channel, originate from elder mountain dwellers in Thailand who were never subjected to public education systems that promoted non-Karen values.

A central feature of this tradition is the **Hta** (pronounced *Taa*, with a strong "T"), a poetic form used to pass down knowledge, wisdom, historical events, teachings, and proverbs across generations. These tales reflect the Karen people's **social and moral worldview**, revealing how they relate to one another and how values are taught within the community.

ON EARLY VISIONS OF A MODERN KAREN NATION-STATE: KARENISTAN

Mary P. Callahan, in *Making Enemies: War and State Building in Burma* (Ithaca: Cornell University Press, 2003), documents early proposals for a sovereign Karen state following World War II. Among the suggested names were *United Frontier Karen States*, *Karenistan*, and *Autonomous Karenistan*—each reflecting evolving aspirations for self-determination during a turbulent phase in Burma's post-independence history.

ON SOCIAL, MORAL AND POLITICAL STABILITY

On Internal Decay and Bacterial Analogies

In *Earthly Order*, Ali draws a compelling analogy between bacterial destruction of a host and societal collapse driven by internal "thieves." Just as bacteria dismantle biological systems from within, these metaphorical thieves—be they corrupt individuals, exploitative institutions, or destructive ideologies—subvert and consume the foundational structures of a society.

On Consilience and Social Breakdown

The metaphor of societal decay through internal "thieves" resonates with Edward O. Wilson's concept of consilience as presented in *Consilience: The Unity of Knowledge* (1998). Wilson argues that knowledge across disciplines converges on shared principles—particularly the idea that cooperation sustains both biological and social systems. The collapse of this cooperation, whether through microbial disruption or social disintegration, reflects a common pattern: the breakdown of collective stability caused by self-serving forces operating within the system.

On Altruism and Societal Stability

In *Consilience: The Unity of Knowledge*, Edward O. Wilson explores the biological foundations of altruism as essential to social cohesion. He identifies two key evolutionary mechanisms: kin selection, which favors altruism toward genetic relatives, and group selection, which enables more cooperative groups to outcompete others. This balance between individual and collective interest forms a "genetic leash" that shapes social norms and ethics. Wilson contends that understanding the biological roots of altruism is critical for maintaining societal stability, linking evolutionary science with moral and political thought.

On *A World Without Thieves* and Moral Collapse

A World Without Thieves, directed by Feng Xiaogang (Media Asia Distribution Ltd., 2004), presents a moral allegory through the story of two reformed *thieves who wish to shield their child from a corrupt world*. This theme mirrors the situation in Burma, where the chronic misuse of political power has cultivated a culture of systemic theft—stealing not only material resources, but also the integrity of the nation and the future of its people.

CHAPTER TWO

On Constitutional Reviews

A wide range of national and regional constitutions were reviewed to explore the diverse legal, philosophical, and institutional foundations that shape different societies. These included the constitutions of the United States, Switzerland, Germany, Israel, South Korea, Taiwan, Thailand, Myanmar, Singapore, New Zealand, and the State of California. The systems studied span federal, unitary, and confederate arrangements—such as Switzerland's confederation with limited central authority and Taiwan's five-branch government. These documents reflect evolving understandings of governance and constitutional change over time.

CHAPTER SIX

On Tend Your Own Garden

Voltaire's *Candide* was first published in 1759. The famous quote about "tending one's own garden" is from the final chapter, where Candide, after experiencing many hardships, concludes that instead of chasing grand philosophical ideals, the best way to live is to focus on practical, everyday tasks such as tending to one's own garden. This idea reflects Voltaire's critique of optimistic philosophy and suggests a pragmatic approach to life.

On Self-Determination Theory (SDT)

In psychology, *Self-Determination Theory (SDT)*, developed by Edward Deci and Richard Ryan, describes self-determination as a fundamental human need. According to SDT, self-determination is essential for fostering motivation, particularly *intrinsic motivation*—the internal drive to engage in activities for their own sake, rather than for external rewards or pressures.

NOTES

A JAPANESE TRANSLATION ON THE NAME KAWTHOOLEI

In 1982, Japanese photojournalist Hiroshi Katoh published a book titled *Kawthoolei*, "A report on the un-charted states of Burma and the documents of the National Movement which seeks independence from Burma." In it, he captured many aspects of the Karen liberation struggle—from top leaders to soldiers setting explosives on the front lines. In the book's introduction, he noted that Kawthoolei means "the land of flowers."

ON THE NAME VARIATION OF SAW BA U GYI

In this book, both "Saw Ba U Gyi" and "Saw Ba Oo Gyi" are used interchangeably to refer to the same historical figure of the Karen people. He is the official martyr of the Karen Revolution. The variation arises from linguistic conventions in Burma. Historically, the Burmese language has used "U" to denote the long vowel sound "oo" as in "too" (IPA /uː/). This practice is evident in honorific male prefixes, such as "U Thant," the former UN Secretary-General, and "U Nu," the former Prime Minister of Burma. During the 19th century, Karen people living in the plains often had their names recorded in Burmese. For example, my great-great-grand father from the Sit-Ttaung Valley was known as "U Ba" while their generation and following rarely spoke Burmese. However, in modern usage, the spelling "Oo" has largely replaced the historical "U" to represent the long vowel sound. Contemporary references commonly use "Saw Ba Oo Gyi," while "Saw Ba U Gyi" remains a historical reference that reflects the original pronunciation.

BIBLIOGRAPHY

Ali, Saleem H. 2022. *Earthly Order: How Natural Laws Define Human Life*. Oxford University Press.

Anadolu Agency. "Putin Says Russian Armies Received Around 140,000 Drones in 2023." Accessed April 19, 2025. https://www.aa.com.tr/en/russia-ukraine-war/putin-says-russian-armies-received-around-140-000-drones-in-2023/3335132.

Animalia. "Green Pheasant." Accessed April 19, 2025. https://animalia.bio/green-pheasant.

Applied Energy Systems. "How Semiconductor Shortages Are Affecting the Auto Industry." Accessed April 19, 2025. https://www.appliedenergysystems.com/semiconductor-shortages-effect-on-auto-industry/.

Arirang News. 2024. "How Are Domestic Readers Reacting to Han Kang's Winning of the Nobel Prize in Literature?" Oct 11, 2024 https://www.youtube.com/watch?v=5pFv-FvXSzI.

Bansal, Arpit. 2021. "Asian Fairy-bluebird Irena Puella." November 22, 2021. https://macaulaylibrary.org/asset/503548841.

Bauer, P. T. *Equality, the Third World, and Economic Delusion*. Cambridge, MA: Harvard University Press, 1981.

BBC Ideas. "How Writing Changed the World." *YouTube*, May 4, 2021. https://www.youtube.com/watch?v=9wPZIWcA7Ec.

BBC News 2023b. "KIA သိမ်းလိုက်တဲ့ စစ်တပ်စခန်းများ၊ မြန်မာ့နိုင်ငံရေးနဲ့ ဒုဗိုလ်ချုပ်ကြီးဝွမ်မော် - BBC News မြန်မာ." https://www.youtube.com/watch?v=BLMkV3WHPpQ.

BBC News. "Denmark Helped U.S. Spy on Merkel." June 1, 2021. https://www.bbc.com/news/world-europe-57302806.

BBC News. "How a Community School Sparked a Global Movement." Accessed April 19, 2025. https://www.bbc.com/news/articles/c4g9wx2q09ko.

Bertrand, Jacques, Alexandre Pelletier, and Ardeth Maung Thawnghmung. 2022. *Winning by Process: The State and Neutralization of Ethnic Minorities in Myanmar*. Southeast Asia Program Publications.

Bi, Johnathan. "Meiji Japan." YouTube video. January 24, 2024. https://youtube.com/shorts/29a4yoXnxO8?si=6mEZ-yYvvJ0g59qv.

Bökset, Roar. 2006. Long Story of Short Forms: The Evolution of Simplified Chinese Characters.

Bosner, Leo, and I-wei Jennifer Chang. *Taiwan's Disaster Preparedness and Response: Strengths, Shortfalls, and Paths to Improvement*. Washington, DC: Global Taiwan Institute, October 2020. https://globaltaiwan.org/wp-content/uploads/2022/08/GTI-Taiwans-Disaster-Preparedness-and-Response-Oct-2020-final-1.pdf.

Bosner, Leo, and I-wei Jennifer Chang. *Taiwan's Disaster Preparedness and Response: Strengths, Shortfalls, and Paths to Improvement*. Washington, DC: Global Taiwan Institute, October 2020. https://globaltaiwan.org/wp-content/uploads/2022/08/GTI-Taiwans-Disaster-Preparedness-and-Response-Oct-2020-final-1.pdf.

Branding Forum. "Tech Meets Tradition: Drone Shows for Lunar New Year Celebrations." *World Branding Forum*, February 9, 2024. https://brandingforum.org/general/tech-meets-tradition-drone-shows-for-lunar-new-year-celebrations/.

Brown, Brené. "The Power of Vulnerability." *YouTube*, June 2010. https://www.youtube.com/watch?v=hG1O8Y6uH18.

Brownstein, Ronald. "Singapore's Caning Sentence Divides Americans, Poll Finds." *Los Angeles Times*, April 21, 1994. https://www.latimes.com/archives/la-xpm-1994-04-21-mn-48524-story.html.

Butler, Eamonn. 2015. *Classical Liberalism – a Primer*. London Publishing Partnership.

California Department of Water Resources. "State Water Project." *California Department of Water Resources*. Accessed April 19, 2025. https://water.ca.gov/programs/state-water-project.

California State Library. "California State Symbols." Accessed April 19, 2025. https://www.library.ca.gov/california-history/state-symbols/.

Callahan, M. P. (2003). Making Enemies: War and State Building in Burma. Cornell University Press.

Canadian Mathematical Society. "International Mathematical Olympiad (IMO)." Accessed April 19, 2025. https://cms.math.ca/competitions/imo/.

Carnegie Mellon University. "U.S. Finishes First in International Math Competition." July 22, 2019. https://www.cmu.edu/news/stories/archives/2019/july/us-first-in-math-competiton.html.

Center for Language Technology. "Indonesian." Accessed April 19, 2025. https://celt.indiana.edu/portal/Indonesian/index.html.

Centre for the Study of Existential Risk. "Yuval Noah Harari – Researcher Profile." Accessed April 19, 2025. https://www.cser.ac.uk/team/yuval-noah-harari/.

Chang, Ha-Joon. 2015. *Economics: The User's Guide*. Bloomsbury Publishing USA.

Chew, Valerie. "Michael Fay." *Singapore Infopedia*. National Library Board Singapore. Accessed April 19, 2025. https://www.nlb.gov.sg/main/article-detail?cmsuuid=61e0277e-fbeb-4ebc-88ea-8a9c58e13e05.

Chomsky, Noam, and Mitsou Ronat. 1998. *On Language : Chomsky's Classic Works, Language and Responsibility and Reflections on Language in One Volume. New Press eBooks.* http://ci.nii.ac.jp/ncid/BA39288589.

Clark, Wesley K. 2014. Don't Wait for the Next War: A Strategy for American Growth and Global Leadership. PublicAffairs.

Class Central. "Universities." Accessed November 25, 2024. https://www.classcentral.com/universities.

Clean & Green Singapore. "About Us." Accessed April 19, 2025. https://www.cgs.gov.sg/who-we-are/.

CNBC. "Google to Invest $1 Billion in Thailand Data Center and AI Push." September 30, 2024. https://www.cnbc.com/2024/09/30/google-to-invest-1-billion-in-thailand-data-center-and-ai-push.html.

CNBC. "Microsoft to Open Data Center in Thailand amid Southeast Asia Expansion." May 2, 2024. https://www.cnbc.com/2024/05/02/microsoft-to-open-data-center-in-thailand-amid-southeast-asia-expansion.html.

Commonwealth Club World Affairs (CCWA). 2024. "Sal Khan | How AI Will Revolutionize Education." https://www.youtube.com/watch?v=pHvEQ2quhiY.

Constitution Drafting Committee. The Constitution of the Federal Republic of the Union of Burma: Second Draft. Myanmar Peace Monitor. Accessed April 19, 2025. https://www.mmpeacemonitor.org/images/pdf/The-constitution-of-the-federal-republic-of-the-union-of-burma-second-draft.pdf.

Cooler, Richard M. 1995. *The Karen Bronze Drums of Burma: Types, Iconography, Manufacture, and Use.* BRILL.

CopRadar. "UTC Military Time Chart." Accessed April 19, 2025. https://copradar.com/utctime/.

Council on Foreign Relations. "How the Drone War in Ukraine Is Transforming Conflict." Accessed April 19, 2025. https://www.cfr.org/article/how-drone-war-ukraine-transforming-conflict.

Council on Foreign Relations. "The Humanitarian Crisis in Sudan." *Council on Foreign Relations*, July 18, 2024. https://www.cfr.org/event/humanitarian-crisis-sudan.

DeepMind. *AlphaGo – The Movie.* YouTube video, 1:30:27. March 13, 2020. https://www.youtube.com/watch?v=WXuK6gekU1Y.

DeFrancis, John. "The Language Revolution in Communist China." *The China Quarterly*, no. 31 (1967): 58–76. https://www.jstor.org/stable/3023892.

Demas, Alex. 2024. "Do Foreign Countries Have Military Bases in the United States?" *The Dispatch*, April 19, 2024. https://thedispatch.com/article/do-foreign-countries-have-military-bases-in-the-united-states/.

DW Business. "The Race to Invest in High-End AI Chips." *YouTube*, January 10, 2024. https://www.youtube.com/watch?v=pJcUNxOF0X4

Easterly, William. *The White Man's Burden: Why the West's Efforts to Aid the Rest Have Done So Much Ill and So Little Good.* New York: Penguin Press, 2006.

Economics Observatory. "Why Did Venezuela's Economy Collapse?" Accessed April 19, 2025. https://www.economicsobservatory.com/why-did-venezuelas-economy-collapse.

Edutopia. "Singapore's 21st-Century Teaching Strategies." YouTube video. Published March 14, 2012. Accessed April 19, 2025. https://www.youtube.com/watch?v=M_pIK7ghGw4.

Encyclopaedia Britannica. "Chulalongkorn." Accessed April 19, 2025. https://www.britannica.com/biography/Chulalongkorn.

Encyclopaedia Britannica. "Irrawaddy River." *Britannica.* Accessed April 19, 2025. https://www.britannica.com/place/Irrawaddy-River.

EO. 2023a. "How to Be a Creative Thinker | Carnegie Mellon University Po-Shen Loh." https://www.youtube.com/watch?v=JpYA7WXkHyI.

Essential Education. "The Evolution of Singapore's Education System: From 1965 to the Present." Accessed November 25, 2024. https://www.essentialeducation.com.sg/blog/the-evolution-of-singapores-education-system-from-1965-to-the-present.

Ethnic Nationalities Affairs Center (Union of Burma). 2016. "Key Principles and Characteristics for a Federal Union of Burma (Draft)." https://burmaenac.org/wp-content/uploads/2017/05/Federal-Key-Principles_eng_BH-final-.pdf.

Faculty of Asian and Middle Eastern Studies, University of Cambridge. "Introduction to Pinyin." Accessed April 19, 2025. https://www.ames.cam.ac.uk/undergraduates/undergraduate-resource/chinese-part-ia-information-incoming-students/introduction.

Feng, Xiaogang, dir. A World Without Thieves. China Film Group Corporation, 2004.

Ferragamo, Mariel, and Claire Klobucista. "Somaliland: The Horn of Africa's Breakaway State." *Council on Foreign Relations*, January 21, 2025. https://www.cfr.org/backgrounder/somaliland-horn-africas-breakaway-state.

Forbes Woman Georgia. "South Korea." Accessed April 19, 2025. https://www.forbeswoman.ge/en/post/southkorea#.

Freedom House. 2025. "Explore the Map." *Freedom House.* https://freedomhouse.org/explore-the-map?type=fiw&year=2024.

French, Howard W. "Thailand's Leader Wants to Switch Time Zones." New York Times, July 28, 2001. https://www.nytimes.com/2001/07/28/business/international-business-thailand-s-leader-wants-to-switch-time-zones.html.

G Teresa. 2021. "Tha Lay a Lah – Teresa, Marking Time with Celestial Bodies." https://www.youtube.com/watch?v=TmuahQpxbMI.

Gates, Bill, Nathan Myhrvold, and Peter Rinearson. 1996. The Road Ahead. Penguin U S A.

Global Times. "China Builds World's Biggest EV Charging Network, in Stark Contrast to US Failure." *Global Times*, June 19, 2024. https://www.globaltimes.cn/page/202406/1314382.shtml.

Graburn, Nelson H. H. "What is Tradition?" *Museum Anthropology* 24, no. 2/3 (2001): 6–11. https://www.researchgate.net/publication/230505685_What_is_Tradition.

Great Authors. "Neo-Classical and Romantic Literature – Voltaire, Candide." *YouTube*, uploaded by Great Authors, January 15, 2023. https://www.youtube.com/watch?v=sU3yB_mBSAo.

Harari, Yuval Noah. 2017. *Homo Deus: A Brief History of Tomorrow.* HarperCollins.

Harm Reduction International. *The Global State of Harm Reduction 2024: Global Overview.* March 2025. https://hri.global/wp-content/uploads/2025/03/hri-globaloverview-2024-final.pdf.

Harris, Edward Norman. 1920. A Star in the East: An Account of American Baptist Missions to the Karens of Burma. Gutenberg Australia, n.d. https://gutenberg.net.au/ebooks09/0900481h.html.

Harris, Edward Norman. n.d. The Rice Fairy: Kareń Stories From Southeast Asia. 1989.

Harvard Online. 2018. "Pros and Cons of Neoliberalism."
    https://www.youtube.com/watch?v=t41rFqVpB1I.

HebrewPod101. "Ask a Hebrew Teacher! Difference between Biblical and Modern Hebrew."
    YouTube, April 16, 2014. https://www.youtube.com/watch?v=xFNZ4aojgv8.

Hsia, T.-T. (1956). The language revolution in Communist China. *Far Eastern Survey, 25*(10), 145-154.
    Institute of Pacific Relations.

Huang, Chung-Ren, Jimmy Chen, Wen-Jen Chang, Tai-Shen Pan, Chen-Yuan Liao, and Chung-Yi
    Tsai. "Railway Underground Adjacent Construction and Design Issues in Soft Soil of Taipei
    Urban Area." In *Proceedings of the 2nd International Symposium on Asia Urban
    GeoEngineering*, edited by Renpeng Chen, Gang Zheng, and Changyu Ou, 258–272.
    Springer Series in Geomechanics and Geoengineering. Singapore: Springer, 2018.
    https://doi.org/10.1007/978-981-10-6632-0_20.

Hunter, Edward. "The Japanese Blade: Technology and Manufacture." *The Metropolitan Museum of
    Art*, October 1, 2003. https://www.metmuseum.org/essays/the-japanese-blade-
    technology-and-manufacture.

Indiana Historical Bureau. "Indiana State Bird." Accessed April 19, 2025.
    https://www.in.gov/history/about-indiana-history-and-trivia/emblems-and-
    symbols/indiana-state-bird/.

Indianaftali. "How A DEAD Language Came Back To Life! (Hebrew)." *YouTube*, June 17, 2021.
    https://www.youtube.com/watch?v=vrDnvnUZwGY.

International Criminal Court. "Situation in the State of Palestine: ICC Pre-Trial Chamber I Rejects
    State of Israel's Challenges." Accessed April 19, 2025. https://www.icc-
    cpi.int/news/situation-state-palestine-icc-pre-trial-chamber-i-rejects-state-israels-challenges.

International Criminal Court. *About the Court*. Accessed April 19, 2025. https://www.icc-
    cpi.int/about/the-court.

International Law MOOC. "A Foundational Moment." *YouTube*, August 2, 2016.
    https://www.youtube.com/watch?v=1SbdlteP9Qk.

Jin, Keyu. 2023. *The New China Playbook: Beyond Socialism and Capitalism*. Swift Press.

Kant, Immanuel, and Ted Humphrey. 2003. *To Perpetual Peace: A Philosophical Sketch*. Hackett
    Publishing Company Incorporated.

Karen National Union. The Karens and Their Struggle for Freedom. 2006 ed. Kawthoolei
    Education and Culture Department, April 2024. https://kecdktl.org/wp-
    content/uploads/2024/04/KNU-The-Karens-and-their-Struggle-for-Freedom-2006ed.pdf.

Karen Social and Ethnic Health Studies. *KSEHS Special Report: Education and Health in Conflict
    Areas*. Karen National Union, October 13, 2023.
    https://knuhq.org/admin/resources/publications/pdf/KSEHS_13Oct2023.pdf.

KarenS All. 2018. "No Se A To Pho Karen Story:นิทานกะเหรี่ยงเรื่อง หน่อเสอะโตพอ เจาะพอเจะ."
    http://www.youtube.com/watch?v=EQl-knbTf54. [Karen Fables and Moral Tales]

Kato, A. (2021). Typological profile of Karenic languages. *[Preprint]*. Retrieved from
    https://www.researchgate.net/publication/357448200

Katoh, H. Kawthoolei. Paperback. January 1, 1982.

Ker-Lindsay, James, and Mikulas Fabry. 2020. Secession and State Creation: What Everyone Needs
    to Know®. What Everyone Needs to Know(r).

Kim, Byung-Kook, and Ezra F. Vogel. 2013. The Park Chung Hee Era: The Transformation of
    South Korea. Harvard University Press.

KLEE BHO. 2018. "Klee Bho - Doo Lay Lay Al Lay TEDxChiangMai 2018."
    http://www.youtube.com/watch?v=Lqh--KQ-wx0.

Korea Legislation Research Institute. *Constitution of the Republic of Korea*. Accessed April 19, 2025.
    https://elaw.klri.re.kr/eng_service/ebook.do?hseq=1.

Kwok, Derek Tsang, dir. *Better Days*. China: Henan Film Group, 2019. Distributed by Well Go
    USA Entertainment. YouTube video, 2:15:31.
    https://www.youtube.com/watch?v=wUa2Ikn2eX4. Accessed April 19, 2025.

Levitsky, Steven, and Daniel Ziblatt. 2019. How Democracies Die. Crown.

Levitsky, Steven, and Daniel Ziblatt. 2023. Tyranny of the Minority: Why American Democracy Reached the Breaking Point. Crown.

Levy, and Michael. 2025. "United States Presidential Election of 1824 | Andrew Jackson, John Quincy Adams, Significance, Popular Vote, & Results." Encyclopedia Britannica. March 21, 2025. https://www.britannica.com/event/United-States-presidential-election-of-1824.

Linter, B. (1999). *Burma in revolt: Opium and insurgency since 1948*. Silkworm Books.

Lost Footsteps. "Founder of the Karen National Union Saw Ba U Gyi." *Lost Footsteps*. Accessed April 19, 2025. https://lostfootsteps.org/en/history/founder-of-the-karen-national-union-saw-ba-u-gyi.

Lu Xun, *Selected Works of Lu Xun*, Foreign Languages Press, 1980.

Mandela, N. (1994). *Long walk to freedom: The autobiography of Nelson Mandela*. Boston, MA: Little, Brown and Company.

Manson, K. (2009). Prolegomena to reconstructing Proto-Karen. *La Trobe Papers in Linguistics, 12*.

Manson, K. (2017). The characteristics of the Karen branch of Tibeto-Burman. In P. S. Ding & J. Pelkey (Eds.), *Sociohistorical linguistics in Southeast Asia: New horizons for Tibeto-Burman studies in honor of David Bradley* (pp. 149–168). Leiden: Brill.

Mao Zedong's Correspondence: *Mao Zedong's Letters: 1936-1950*, Harvard University Press, 1992.

Maren, Michael. *The Road to Hell: The Ravaging Effects of Foreign Aid and International Charity*. New York: Free Press, 1997.

Marshall, H. I. (1920). *The Karen people of Burma: A study in anthropology and ethnology*. Project Gutenberg of Australia. https://gutenberg.net.au/

Martin, Michael F. "What the BURMA Act Does and Doesn't Mean for U.S. Policy in Myanmar." *Center for Strategic and International Studies*, February 6, 2023. https://www.csis.org/analysis/what-burma-act-does-and-doesnt-mean-us-policy-myanmar.

Massachusetts Institute of Technology. "Singapore-MIT Alliance for Research and Technology." Accessed April 19, 2025. https://catalog.mit.edu/mit/research/singapore-mit-alliance-research-technology/.

Mearsheimer, John J. 2014. *The Tragedy of Great Power Politics*. W. W. Norton & Company.

Merriam-Webster. "200 New Words and Definitions Added to Merriam-Webster.com." *Merriam-Webster*, September 2023. https://www.merriam-webster.com/wordplay/new-words-in-the-dictionary.

Merriam-Webster. "We Added 690 New Words to the Dictionary for September 2023." *Merriam-Webster*, September 2023. https://www.merriam-webster.com/wordplay/new-words-in-the-dictionary-september-2023.

Ministry of Education Singapore. *Learn for Life: Preparing Our Students to Excel Beyond Exam Results*. September 28, 2018. https://www.moe.gov.sg/news/press-releases/20180928-learn-for-life-preparing-our-students-to-excel-beyond-exam-results.

Molaie, Sara. "How to Revive an Ancient Language, According to 19th-Century Hebrew and Persian Revivalists." *Stroum Center for Jewish Studies*, University of Washington, September 12, 2018. https://jewishstudies.washington.edu/israel-hebrew/reviving-hebrew-persian-ancient-languages-eliezer-ben-yehuda-manekji-limji-hataria/.

Moyo, Dambisa. *Dead Aid: Why Aid Is Not Working and How There Is a Better Way for Africa*. New York: Farrar, Straus and Giroux, 2009.

Muir, John. 2011. Wilderness Essays. Gibbs Smith.

Myanmar's Federal Democracy Charter: Analysis and Prospects. 2022. https://doi.org/10.31752/idea.2022.27.

Myint-U, Thant. 2019. *The Hidden History of Burma: Race, Capitalism, and the Crisis of Democracy in the 21st Century*. W. W. Norton & Company.

Mykhailyuk, O., and H. Pohlod. "The Languages We Speak Affect Our Perceptions of the World." *Journal of Vasyl Stefanyk Precarpathian National University* 2, no. 2–3 (2015): 36–41. https://doi.org/10.15330/jpnu.2.2-3.36-41.

National Center on Education and the Economy (NCEE). "Singapore: Education System Overview." Accessed November 25, 2024. https://ncee.org/country/singapore/.

National Planning Commission. *National Development Plan 2030: Our Future – Make It Work.* Government of South Africa, 2012. https://www.gov.za/sites/default/files/gcis_document/201409/ndp-2030-our-future-make-it-workr.pdf.

Naw, Angelene. 2023. *The History of the Karen People of Burma.*

NLCS Singapore. "International Baccalaureate (IB) Diploma Results – May 2024 Session." Accessed April 19, 2025. https://nlcssingapore.sg/news/international-baccalaureate-ib-diploma-results-may-2024-session/.

Nobel Prize. "The Nobel Prize in Literature 2024: Han Kang – Facts." *NobelPrize.org.* Accessed April 19, 2025. https://www.nobelprize.org/prizes/literature/2024/han/facts/.

Obama, Barack. "Remarks by the President at Arizona State University Commencement." *The White House Archives*, May 13, 2009. https://obamawhitehouse.archives.gov/the-press-office/remarks-president-arizona-state-university-commencement.

Off the Great Wall. "Why Chinese Characters Are So Complex." *YouTube*, August 21, 2014. https://www.youtube.com/watch?v=fojzNrwAAyI&t=322s.

Office of the Historian, U.S. Department of State. "The Opening to Japan, 1853." *Milestones in the History of U.S. Foreign Relations.* Accessed April 19, 2025. https://history.state.gov/milestones/1830-1860/opening-to-japan.

Office of the National Economic and Social Development Council (NESDC). *Thailand's National Strategy (2018–2037).* Accessed April 19, 2025. https://www.nesdc.go.th/article_attach/article_file_20230615134223.pdf.

Olympedia. "U Zaw Weik." *Olympedia.* Accessed April 19, 2025. https://www.olympedia.org/athletes/56028.

Olympics. "Paris 2024 Medals." *International Olympic Committee.* Accessed April 19, 2025. https://www.olympics.com/en/olympic-games/pari grantings-2024/medals.

Omniglot. "Evolution of Chinese Characters." *Omniglot: The Online Encyclopedia of Writing Systems & Languages.* Accessed April 19, 2025. https://www.omniglot.com/chinese/evolution.htm.

Omniglot. "Sgaw Karen Language and Alphabet." *Omniglot: The Online Encyclopedia of Writing Systems & Languages.* Accessed April 19, 2025. https://www.omniglot.com/writing/karen.htm.

Pathfinder Geospatial. "Indonesian Languages." *Pathfinder Geospatial*, August 15, 2022. https://www.pathfindergeospatial.ca/portfolio/indonesian-languages.

Paul, Andrew, Robin Roth, and Saw Moo. "Relational Ontology and More-than-Human Agency in Indigenous Karen Conservation Practice." *Pacific Conservation Biology* 27 (2021): 376–390. https://doi.org/10.1071/PC20016.

PBS. "Beauty Pageant Origins and Culture." *American Experience.* Accessed April 19, 2025. https://www.pbs.org/wgbh/americanexperience/features/missamerica-beauty-pageant-origins-and-culture/.

Perlroth, Nicole. "Fitness App Strava Reveals Military Bases Around the World." *New York Times*, January 29, 2018. https://www.nytimes.com/2018/01/29/world/middleeast/strava-heat-map.html.

Pinker, Steven. 2008. *The Stuff of Thought: Language as a Window Into Human Nature.* Penguin Group USA.

Prime Minister's Office Singapore. "Mr LEE Kuan Yew." *Prime Minister's Office Singapore.* Accessed April 19, 2025. https://www.pmo.gov.sg/Past-Prime-Ministers/Mr-LEE-Kuan-Yew.

Qian Xuantong, *Collected Works of Qian Xuantong*, Beijing University Press, 1997.

Rainbowendsfr. "Karen History." Accessed April 19, 2025. https://www.geocities.ws/rainbowendsfr/karen/history.htm.

Reuters. "Thailand Starts Aid Deliveries to Myanmar under Plan Aimed at Managing Conflict." *Reuters*, March 25, 2024. https://www.reuters.com/world/asia-pacific/thailand-starts-aid-deliveries-myanmar-under-plan-aimed-managing-conflict-2024-03-25/.

Reuters. "U.S. Security Agency Spied on Merkel, Other Top European Officials." May 30, 2021. https://www.reuters.com/world/europe/us-security-agency-spied-merkel-other-top-european-officials-through-danish-2021-05-30/.

Reuters. "U.S. State Dept. Approves Sale of 12 F-35 Jets to Singapore." *Reuters*, January 10, 2020. https://www.reuters.com/article/world/us-state-dept-approves-sale-of-12-f-35-jets-to-singapore-idUSKBN1Z90G8/.

Revolutions, Age Of. 2020. "What Makes a Language Policy Revolutionary?" Age of Revolutions. October 19, 2020. https://ageofrevolutions.com/2020/10/14/what-makes-a-language-policy-revolutionary/.

Roosevelt, T. (1900). *American ideals*. New York, NY: G. P. Putnam's Sons.

Sabharish Elamurugan. 2022. "1990 - You Cant Change Singapore Into A Christian State - Lee Kuan Yew Speech." https://www.youtube.com/watch?v=fwWyDl5nRXM.

Saha, Jonathan. 2022. "Racial Capitalism and Peasant Insurgency in Colonial Myanmar." *History Workshop Journal* 94 (August): 42–60. https://doi.org/10.1093/hwj/dbac023.

Saksornchai, Jintamas. "Thailand Sends Aid to War-Torn Myanmar, but Critics Say It Will Only Help Junta." *AP News*, March 25, 2024. https://apnews.com/article/thailand-myanmar-karen-state-aid-displaced-people-9836e1303203c0a9e6b23052bd14289d.

Sang-Hun, Choe. "Google's AlphaGo Defeats South Korean Master in Go Match." New York Times, March 16, 2016. https://www.nytimes.com/2016/03/16/world/asia/korea-alphago-vs-lee-sedol-go.html.

SBS Dateline. "Inside Singapore's World-Class Education System." YouTube video, 27:00. Published Oct 15, 2019. Accessed April 19, 2025. https://www.youtube.com/watch?v=_aB9Tg6SRA0.

Scheuring, Ann Foley. 2001. *Abundant Harvest: The History of the University of California, Davis*.

Scruton, Roger. 2019. *How to Be a Conservative*. Bloomsbury Continuum.

Shur, Natasha, Christina M. Lau, Cynthia J. M. Kane, and Monique A. Anderson. "Creating Safe and Welcoming Schools for Asian American and Pacific Islander (AAPI) Students." *NASN School Nurse* 38, no. 2 (2023): 105–110. https://www.ncbi.nlm.nih.gov/pmc/articles/PMC9987343/.

Slow, Oliver. "The Enduring Legacy of Karen Revolutionary Leader Saw Ba U Gyi." *Southeast Asia Globe*, August 17, 2020. https://southeastasiaglobe.com/the-legacy-of-karen-revolutionary-leader-saw-ba-u-gyi/.Southeast Asia Globe

Smeaton, Donald Mackenzie. 1887. *The Loyal Karens of Burma*.

Smil, Vaclav. "China's Great Famine: 40 Years Later." *BMJ* 319, no. 7225 (December 18, 1999): 1619–1621. https://www.ncbi.nlm.nih.gov/pmc/articles/PMC1127087/.

Smil, Vaclav. "China's Great Famine: 40 Years Later." *BMJ* 319, no. 7225 (December 18, 1999): 1619–1621. https://www.bmj.com/content/319/7225/1619.

Smith, M. (1993). *Burma: Insurgency and the politics of ethnicity*. White Lotus.

Smithsonian Center for Learning and Digital Access. *Understanding Chinese Characters*. Washington, DC: Smithsonian Institution, 2020. https://asia-archive.si.edu/wp-content/uploads/2020/06/LP11-Understanding-Chinese-Characters-FA2.pdf.

Snow, Dan, Suzannah Lipscomb, and Matt Lewis. 2024. "The Real History Behind the Legendary King Arthur | History Hit Originals | All Out History." YouTube video. Accessed April 19, 2025. https://www.youtube.com/watch?v=c8bVWF5sEPk

Sogge, David. *Give and Take: What's the Matter with Foreign Aid?* London: Zed Books, 2002.

Sowell Teachings, Thomas. "The Real Reasons Why Asians Outperform Westerners - Thomas Sowell." November 23, 2024. https://www.youtube.com/watch?v=LE2V6chLnwk.

Springfield College. "Gender Pronouns." *Springfield College Inclusion*. Accessed April 19, 2025. https://springfield.edu/inclusion/gender-pronouns.

Stanford Encyclopedia of Philosophy. "Locke's Political Philosophy." First published November 9, 2005; substantive revision October 6, 2020. https://plato.stanford.edu/entries/locke-political/.

Stolberg, Sheryl Gay, and Brian M. Rosenthal. "White Nationalists March in Charlottesville." New York Times, August 11, 2017. https://www.nytimes.com/2017/08/11/us/white-nationalists-rally-charlottesville-virginia.html.

Tandon, Yash. *Ending Aid Dependence*. Oxford: Fahamu Books, 2008.

Ted-Ed. "How the Chinese Writing System Works – ShaoLan." *YouTube*, January 4, 2016. https://youtu.be/SOkab7GyPtI?si=gfel0cB1GPDd717P.

Ted-Ed. "Why Chinese Is So Hard (And How to Fix It) – Moser." *YouTube*, May 3, 2021. https://youtu.be/ZPeIDPDk_-4?si=Jk7ExvC7lRgOgND9.

TED. 2018. "How Language Shapes the Way We Think | Lera Boroditsky | TED." https://www.youtube.com/watch?v=RKK7wGAYP6k.

Thai National Parks. "Siamese Fireback." Accessed April 19, 2025. https://www.thainationalparks.com/species/siamese-fireback.

Thako, Hayso, and Tony Waters. 2023. "Schooling, Identity, and Nationhood: Karen Mother-Tongue-Based Education in the Thai–Burmese Border Region." Social Sciences 12 (3): 163. https://doi.org/10.3390/socsci12030163.

Thananithichot, Stithorn. 2011. "Understanding Thai Nationalism and Ethnic Identity." *Journal of Asian and African Studies* 46 (3): 250–63. https://doi.org/10.1177/0021909611399735.

Thawnghmung, Ardeth Maung. 2008. The Karen Revolution in Burma: Diverse Voices, Uncertain Ends. Institute of Southeast Asian Studies.

The Associated Press. "$568 Billion in African Aid and Little to Show for It." 2007. NBC News. December 24, 2007. https://www.nbcnews.com/id/wbna22380441.

The May Fourth Movement and Language Reform: Zhou, H., "The Legacy of the May Fourth Movement," *Journal of Chinese Studies*, vol. 42, no. 3, 2010, pp. 98-123.

The Straits Times. "IB Results: Singapore Continues to Excel and Surpass Global Average." Accessed April 19, 2025. https://www.straitstimes.com/singapore/ib-results-singapore-continues-to-excel-and-surpass-global-average.

Thwe, Pascal Khoo. 2003. From the Land of Green Ghosts: A Burmese Odyssey. Harper Perennial.

Translators without Borders. "Language Data for Indonesia." *Translators without Borders*. Accessed April 19, 2025. https://translatorswithoutborders.org/language-data-for-indonesia.

U.S. Census Bureau. "Our History." *U.S. Census Bureau*. Accessed April 19, 2025. https://www.census.gov/about/history.html.

U.S. Department of Agriculture, Economic Research Service. "Global Rice Export Trends." Accessed April 19, 2025. https://www.ers.usda.gov/data-products/chart-gallery/gallery/chart-detail/?chartId=92983.

U.S. Department of State. "Thailand Background Notes." Accessed April 19, 2025. https://1997-2001.state.gov/background_notes/thailand_0010_bgn.html.

U.S. Department of State. Office of the Historian. "The Atlantic Conference & Charter, 1941." *Milestones in the History of U.S. Foreign Relations*. Accessed April 19, 2025. https://history.state.gov/milestones/1937-1945/atlantic-conf.

U.S. Intelligence Community. "Engineering and Physical Sciences Careers." Accessed April 19, 2025. https://www.intelligence.gov/careers/explore-careers/434-engineering-and-physical-sciences.

United Nations General Assembly. *Declaration on the Granting of Independence to Colonial Countries and Peoples*. OHCHR. Accessed April 19, 2025. https://www.ohchr.org/en/instruments-mechanisms/instruments/declaration-granting-independence-colonial-countries-and-peoples.

United Nations General Assembly. *Universal Declaration of Human Rights*. Resolution 217 A (III), December 10, 1948. https://www.un.org/en/about-us/universal-declaration-of-human-rights.

United Nations. n.d. "Specialized Agencies | United Nations." https://www.un.org/en/about-us/specialized-agencies.

University of California. "UC and the Nobel Prize." Accessed April 19, 2025. https://nobel.universityofcalifornia.edu/.

University of California. "UC Workforce Diversity." Accessed April 19, 2025. https://www.universityofcalifornia.edu/about-us/information-center/uc-workforce-diversity.

Victor Mochere. 2024. "Nvidia CEO Jensen Huang: People With Really High Expectations Have Very Low Resilience." https://www.youtube.com/watch?v=AoGmfcsoADI.

Wallace, Charles P. "Singapore Blasts Back at Clinton in Caning Case." *Los Angeles Times*, March 9, 1994. https://www.latimes.com/archives/la-xpm-1994-03-09-mn-31971-story.html.

Wan, Defu and Wuhan Unichem Chemicals Ltd. 2014. "The History of Language Planning and Reform in China: A Critical Perspective." *Working Papers in Educational Linguistics* 29–29 (WPEL Volume 29, Number 2): 65–79. https://wpel.gse.upenn.edu/sites/default/files/29.2Wan.pdf.

Washington, B. T. (1899). *The future of the American Negro*. Small, Maynard & Company.

Washington, B. T. (1901). *Up from slavery: An autobiography*. Doubleday, Page & Co.

Washington, Booker T. *Character Building: Being Addresses Delivered on Sunday Evenings to the Students of Tuskegee Institute*. New York: Doubleday, Page & Company, 1902. https://archive.org/details/characterbuildin00washuoft/page/12/mode/2up.

Watt, Paul. "Japanese Religions." *SPICE: Stanford Program on International and Cross-Cultural Education*, October 2003. https://spice.fsi.stanford.edu/docs/japanese_religions.

Williams, David R., Neighbors Priest, and Norman B. Anderson. "Understanding Associations among Race, Socioeconomic Status, and Health: Patterns and Prospects." *Health Psychology* 35, no. 4 (2016): 407–411. https://doi.org/10.1037/hea0000242.

Wilson, Edward O. 1999. *Consilience: The Unity of Knowledge*. Vintage.

Wilson, Edward O. 2006. The Creation: An Appeal to Save Life on Earth. W. W. Norton & Company.

Wilson, Edward O. 2015. *The Meaning of Human Existence*. National Geographic Books.

Winn, Patrick. "Lee Kuan Yew Is Dead. Here Are 7 of His Most Provocative Quotes." *The World from PRX*, July 30, 2016. https://theworld.org/stories/2016/07/30/lee-kuan-yew-dead-here-are-7-his-most-provocative-quotes.

World Atlas. "Indonesia Map / Geography of Indonesia / Map of Indonesia." *Worldatlas.com*. Archived April 7, 2017. Accessed April 19, 2025. https://web.archive.org/web/20171201024317mp_/http://www.worldatlas.com/webimage/countrys/asia/id.htm.

World Bank. "GDP (Current US$) – Myanmar, Indonesia, Thailand." *World Bank Open Data*. Accessed April 19, 2025. https://data.worldbank.org/indicator/NY.GDP.MKTP.CD?locations=MM-ID-TH.

World Wildlife Fund. "Kayah-Karen Montane Rain Forests (IM0119)." *World Wildlife Fund Ecoregions*. Accessed April 19, 2025. https://www.worldwildlife.org/ecoregions/im0119.

Worldometer. "GDP by Country." *Worldometer*, December 16, 2024. https://www.worldometers.info/gdp/gdp-by-country/.

Yale School of Management. "El Salvador Adopted Bitcoin as an Official Currency. Salvadorans Mostly Shrugged." Accessed April 19, 2025. https://insights.som.yale.edu/insights/el-salvador-adopted-bitcoin-as-an-official-currency-salvadorans-mostly-shrugged.

Yew, Lee Kuan. 2000. From Third World to First: The Singapore Story: 1965-2000. Harper Collins.

Zhang, Wei. "Simplification of Chinese Characters: A Historical Perspective," *Modern China Review*, vol. 36, no. 1, 2011, pp. 47-65.

KAREN LANGUAGE SOURCES

စီၤဘီဖိ, သရၣ်.၂၀၀၂. သီသံၣ်ပိုၤဂီၤယွၤစ့ဘီဒီး အရ့ဒိၣ်လံစၢဖှိၣ်သွဲၣ်. Saw Baw Poe. 2002. Nopburee Press, Chiangmai. Thailand. (Thaw Thi Bgraw Gaw Yaw Say Baw, A Rallying Call for Unity)

စီၤဘီဖိ. ၂၀၁၇. "အိၣ်ဖျဲၣ်ထိၣ်လၢ ကီၢ်သံၣ်ဘီ, အိၣ်ကဒုလၢ ကီၢ်ဘုမံၤဘီ." သလွၤလၢထိၣ်, ၂၇၅၆ကညီနံၣ်. ကီၢ်ကီၣ်တဲၣ်: Wanida Press ဝ့ၢ်က့ၢ်မဲ. ကဘၤပ ၂၄၁. (Born in Thibaw Kingdom and Took Refuge in Bumibaw Kingdom)

ဖုစကီၤလၢၢ်တီ. ၁၉၉၁. ကညီတၢ်ပၢၢ်ဆၢတၢ်စံၣ်စိၤတဲစိၤ. ဘၣ်တၢ်ကတဲာ်ကတီၤအီၤလၢ တၢ်စံၣ်စိၤတဲစိၤကမံးတံာ်-ကညီဒီက လုာ်စၢဖှိၣ်ကရၢ-လီၢ်ခၢၣ်သး [History of Karen Revolution by Pu Sgaw LerTaw, 1991. Published by Karen National Union]

ထိၣ်လွံၣ်ထူ. လံာ်ကစၢၢ်ဒိၣ်ဒီး ထံဆဲးမဲးယွၤအဂ့ၢ် အဘ့ၣ်(၁) [တၢ်ကွဲးဘၣ်ထွဲ ပှၤသူပှၤပိာ်အဂ့ၢ်] (An Account on the Invisible Virtuous Beings in Southern Kawthoole).

Thank

You

I am indebted to two retired professors—Alan Robson and David Williams (Kiwis)—who sowed in me the seed of intellectual discipline during my time in Chiang Mai, Thailand. They were my first encounter with true intellectual giants after stepping beyond the boundaries of Myanmar's education system. The wealth of knowledge they carried, their critical worldviews, and the technical and philosophical depth they shared laid a foundation that continues to support me. Those who taught and nurtured me during my primary and secondary school years in the conflict zones of Burma remain my earliest mentors.

To Saw Yotha Htoo, Saw Mue Pweh Thaw, Christabelle Naw, Dr. Saw Alwyn, Saw Albert Cho, Saw Jet, Sa Plone Aw, Lae Loe, and Saw Kaw Moo Takreh—your generous feedback and encouraging beta reviews gave me just enough light to keep moving forward.

To Mugar Naw Plaset—your honest advice and pointed questions kept me grounded. Your experiences across Kawthoolei, movement in the borderlands, Yangon life, and the international stage brought balanced gravity to this work. Your support for other Karen writers has also enriched the work here.

To Prezena Htoo—thank you for your generous help at every stage: reading drafts, offering thoughtful feedback, and connecting me with an editorial reader. To Thara Blaw Htoo—your contributions to indigenous knowledge and life sciences are also invaluable. To Saw Htoo—thank you for your steady moral support during our weekend fireside chats and for encouraging me to articulate the vision in writing, especially when I may be reserved.

Nancy—your extensive and discerning editorial assessment went far beyond review. Your veteran experience in the literary world gave me the compass I needed to be mindful of loaded terms when shaping ideas into a book.

To Teresa L, Ku Gay, and Manger Baw—your poems, tender and illuminating, brought warmth and light to these often somber topics. Your reflections on Kawthoolei through the eyes of a new generation should touch every heart.

To Kelly Han—your lived insight into China's social and political realities provided more than any book could. Your perspective brings the stories to a complete cycle and grounded my understanding.

To my big daughter, little Laurel—you walked beside me through seasons of silence and the ache of absence. In your innocence, you bore the weight of a father's divided heart. Your sincere, thoughtful comments on design and layout, your proofreading help, your constant offers of "can I help you," and fetching water unasked—acts well beyond your years—are forever cherished.

To my wife—thank you for your understanding during my absence from family life. Your steady presence, your patience, and your care for my well-being sustained me when my mind wandered far from home. Your strength, expressed through small acts, made this book possible.

ACKNOWLEDGEMENT

All your contributions were voluntary, but they are priceless. To all who read, questioned, challenged, or quietly believed—this book carries your fingerprints, even if not your names.

Above all, I thank God for the courage to begin, the strength to endure, and the grace of companions who made this work possible.

TO ALL WHO GAVE, BELIEVED, AND STOOD BY—THANK YOU.

SAW LAHKBAW

YEAR 2025

www.ingramcontent.com/pod-product-compliance
Lightning Source LLC
Chambersburg PA
CBHW041602260326
41914CB00011B/1350